Curriculum, Instruction, and Assessment

Intersecting New Needs and New Approaches

A Volume in The Handbook of Research in Middle Level Education

Series Editors

Steven B. Mertens
Illinois State University

Micki M. Caskey
Portland State University

Curriculum, Instruction, and Assessment

Intersecting New Needs and New Approaches

edited by

Sandra L. Stacki
Hofstra University

Micki M. Caskey
Portland State University

Steven B. Mertens
Illinois State University

MIDDLE LEVEL EDUCATION RESEARCH
SPECIAL INTEREST GROUP

INFORMATION AGE PUBLISHING, INC.
Charlotte, NC • www.infoagepub.com

MIDDLE LEVEL EDUCATION RESEARCH
SPECIAL INTEREST GROUP

The Handbook of Research in Middle Level Education is endorsed by the Middle Level Education Research Special Interest Group, an affiliate of the American Educational Research Association.

As stated in the organization's Constitution, the purpose of MLER is to improve, promote, and disseminate educational research reflecting early adolescence and middle-level education.

Library of Congress Cataloging-in-Publication Data

CIP record for this book is available from the Library of Congress
http://www.loc.gov

ISBNs: 978-1-64802-028-5 (Paperback)

978-1-64802-029-2 (Hardcover)

978-1-64802-030-8 (ebook)

Printed in the United States of America

We dedicate this volume to middle grades teachers who accept the challenge of working daily with young adolescents. We appreciate your courage, your humor, and your understanding of the academic and affective supports all middle level students need. As designers or co-designers of curriculum, you bring authentic, purposeful, and quality content to your students. Through your instructional practices, you engage young adolescents to make connections, construct meaning, and deepen understanding. You also know your students well and intentionally invite them into assessment processes—knowing that their self-assessment is critical to their learning and self-efficacy. What you do matters significantly and makes a difference in the lives of young adolescent learners.

CONTENTS

SECTION II: EXPLORING CURRICULUM, INSTRUCTION, AND ASSESSMENT THROUGH TEACHERS' DISPOSITIONS AND PERSPECTIVES

SECTION III: EXAMINING LEARNING THROUGH BROADER LENSES

FOREWORD

Years as an observer of child and adolescent behavior have led me to a simple theorem that would be wise for educators to reflect upon: *learning is innate*. Anyone who observes infants and preschoolers realizes that learning is a constant need and desire—essential for survival. Educators do not need to encourage, persuade, or cajole students to learn—it is as natural and autonomous as breathing. Students at every level are learning, most often *without* teacher guidance. Teachers must ask, "Is that same natural desire occurring during my class?"

I recall the excitement of my daughters' capabilities to "use their words" as they stumbled through their toddler years; however, I could not have predicted the onslaught of questions that accompanied their command of words. The very essence of learning is defined by asking questions. I inquired of my daughters when they arrived home each day, "Did you ask good questions at school?" They would share some of their queries, with pride, through those first 6 years of schooling.

The motivation associated with curiosity and questioning suddenly disappeared as my daughters entered middle school. I have no idea how many of their teachers discouraged their curiosity and the questions that accompanied it—but I noticed the end of their excitement for most schooling. How is it that at a time when cognitive growth is exponentially increasing from the ages of 10–15, students lose their curiosity and motivation for learning while at school?

Curriculum, Instruction, and Assessment:
Intersecting New Needs and New Approaches, pp. xi–xii
Copyright © 2020 by Information Age Publishing

When 13-year-olds have questions such as "Why are people treated differently if their skin is darker?" "Why doesn't everyone receive free health care?" "How can we use cloning to better the world?" "Why are some people destroying the Earth even though they know better?" teachers should respond to these concerns as an integral part of their curricula.

An entire generation—iGen'ers—are constantly watching the "Me Too" movement, the Brexit dilemma, severe climate change, debates about immigrants' rights, and weekly gun violence. Will teachers hand students a list of content standards and say, "We don't have time to discuss and learn about social justice, immigrants' rights, or whether you're safe at school?"

If teachers reflect on this learning-need reality as they imagine what they will be doing each day, for many, their classrooms will be entirely different from the traditional top-down, teacher-driven, standardized, curricular delivery system that many have relied upon for too long. I say to those who insist upon a list of items to teach and a perfect lesson plan to deliver that content—step into this 21st century reality. This new world is not *your* learning experience of 30, 20, or even 10 years ago. Young adolescents have unfettered access to world events and an emotional social milieu. They need to "manipulate" this constant barrage of tragedies, social miscues, changing demographics, environmental change, and funny cat videos to which they are exposed. Students learn when they discuss, research, write about, and present to others their reflections on these daily events as they attempt to digest these constant stimuli.

Middle level educators can tap into the natural and advanced curiosity of young adolescents, but only through explicitly planned *listening*. Purposeful, responsive listening has value when teachers elicit students' questions, concerns, and ideas to transform their classrooms into learning meccas. Through their research, this handbook's authors explore and provide several phrases associated with evidence of genuine student learning: "personalized learning," "student-centered approaches," "connections to the real world," "student voice," "self-directed learning," "active participants," and "place-based education." These authors provide evidence that learning is occurring in the classrooms they visited, but these models must become the new "standard" of middle level classrooms rather than the exception. I encourage you to read these studies, and through this action, step into today's young adolescent lives and 21st century learning.

Dave F. Brown, EdD
Educational Researcher, Professor Emeritus
College of Education and Social Work
West Chester University

ACKNOWLEDGMENTS

We offer our thanks to the authors for conducting and sharing their research about curriculum, instruction, and assessment at the middle level. By disseminating the results of your research in this handbook, you contribute to the evolving and expanding middle grades knowledge base. We also thank the students, teachers, and principals who agree to participate and the schools and districts that open their doors to educational researchers.

Curriculum, Instruction, and Assessment:
Intersecting New Needs and New Approaches, pp. xiii–xiii
Copyright © 2020 by Information Age Publishing
All rights of reproduction in any form reserved.

INTRODUCTION

CHAPTER 1

STUDENT-CENTERED LEARNING

Evolving Curriculum, Instruction, and Assessment—Intersecting New Needs

Sandra L. Stacki
Hofstra University

Micki M. Caskey
Portland State University

Steven B. Mertens
Illinois State University

The lives of middle school students are dynamic; their needs and desires are always evolving, especially as they experience perhaps the most developmentally challenging few years of their lives. Young adolescents experience more complicated lives as influences of the broader society including technology, popular and social media (Martin, Wang, Petty, Wang, & Wilkins, 2018), immigration and cultural diversity, amplified

Curriculum, Instruction, and Assessment:
Intersecting New Needs and New Approaches, pp. 3–27
Copyright © 2020 by Information Age Publishing

political divisiveness, bullying (Hicks, Jennings, Jennings, Berry, & Green, 2018), and violence effect their daily lives both in and out of school. Some students live in poverty (Li, Allen, & Casillas, 2017), experience homelessness (Moulton, 2019), or have little parental presence or support. Students endure health problems, may be medicated in school, and have special needs (Graham, Wenzel, Linder, & Rice, 2018). Furthermore, the rates of middle school students' suicidal thoughts or behaviors have increased (Salle, Wang, Parris, & Brown, 2017). In fact, according to the Centers for Disease Control (2015), "Suicide is the third leading cause of death among persons aged 10–14" (p. 2). Certainly, these complicated experiences and changes can weigh heavily on the students themselves and the middle school culture; they affect the ways students interact with school settings and remind educators that the real world of middle school students is complex, demanding, and constantly in flux.

Educators designed the middle school to balance social-emotional needs through structures and programs such as teaming, advisories, and extracurricular activities; however, the complexities of the young adolescent years have grown, leading middle schools to increase support for students with additional social workers and school psychologists. While these students need extra supports, they also need more comprehensive, intersectional, and interactional approaches to curriculum, instruction, and assessment (CIA) that address their complex day-to-day realities. Through CIA, teachers must take a critical approach to ensure student engagement with authentic, real world issues. In class and out of class, schooling activities must include a variety of social-emotional supports and inquiry-oriented academic approaches, and importantly address the desire of students and teachers alike to make choices—to find and express their voices. Since the publication of the *Middle School Curriculum, Instruction, and Assessment* (Anfara & Stacki, 2002), the ideas, approaches, and practices of middle school educators and researchers have been evolving and changing in many ways to meet these changing realities and the needs of students, teachers, schools, and communities.

In this current volume, the authors have explored numerous areas that intersect with traditional academic subjects. These areas reflect broader frameworks within which to envision CIA such as historical thinking, social justice, critical and culturally relevant pedagogies, a commitment to self-directed and student-centered approaches, the challenge-skill imbalance of "flow" theory, use of technology and digital tools, after school and placed-based learning, year-round schooling, and so on. Social-emotional learning intersects in many chapters as do more individualized or personalized approaches for learners, differentiation for diverse or special need learners, and prioritizing authentic and formative assessments. These varied and engaging research chapters on CIA include ideas and practices of both students and teachers. Preservice and in-service teachers and all middle level personnel will gain new perspectives on supporting, teaching, and improving student understanding of not only academic disciplines, but also themselves and their larger local and global community.

In this introductory chapter, we provide a brief overview of the foundations of middle level CIA including concepts, priorities, and practice. Then, we discuss some notable newer approaches and opportunities for young adolescents in schools. In the final section, we summarize the volume contents. Organized in three sections, we highlight first the perspectives of students, then of practicing teachers, and finally a broader focus on topics through views of both students and teachers. We know these chapters will provoke new thoughts and challenge current practices to support our middle school students' needs.

Building on Foundations: CIA Concepts, Priorities, and Practices

The growth of the middle school model in the late 1900s and early 2000s fostered trends in school organizational structures and approaches to curriculum, instruction, and assessment (CIA). While CIA concepts are inseparable in practice, it may be useful to describe the foundations that undergird each. In the following paragraphs, we provide a brief overview of curriculum, instruction, and assessment in the middle schools.

Curriculum. Organizational changes in the middle school such as interdisciplinary teaching teams prompted the design of more collaborative, learner-centered curricula. The developmental characteristics of the young adolescent learner became the focal point of the middle school curricular models. For example, Alexander, Williams, Compton, Hines, and Prescott (1968) proposed a model with learning opportunities for young adolescents centered on (a) personal development, (b) skills for continued leaning, and (c) organized knowledge (i.e., English, math, science, social studies). Similarly, Eichhorn (1972) advanced a curriculum model for young adolescents with three broad goals: (a) value goal, (b) learning goal, and (c) personal development goal. Along the same trajectory, Lounsbury and Vars (1978) recommended a "core" curriculum for addressing young adolescents' personal characteristics and social concerns, while Toepfer (1997) suggested supporting young adolescents by designing curriculum at the local level. All of the aforementioned models included an intentional focus on the developmental characteristics of middle level learners.

Core curriculum, curriculum that organized students' educational experiences around social-personal issues and problems (Gross, 2002; Wraga, 1996), also took root in middle schools. In particular, Vars (1969, 1993) as well as Lounsbury and Vars (1978) were staunch advocates for core curriculum in the middle school. Lounsbury and Vars defined the core as "a form of curriculum organization, usually operating within an extended block of time in the daily schedule, in which learning experiences are focused directly on problems of significance to students" (p. 56). They delineated two forms of core curriculum, structured and unstructured. In a structured core curriculum, the teachers determine the broad issues and experiences for students to explore; in an unstructured core curriculum, the teachers and students work together to identify the worthwhile issues or sets of experiences for exploration (Lounsbury & Vars, 1978; Vars, 1969, 1993). Using such interdisciplinary, problem-centered curricula to address the personal and social concerns of young adolescents was a departure from the traditional subject-centered curriculum; however, the nationwide "back to basics" and "excellence" movements of the 1970s and 1980s compelled the return to subject-centered curriculum in middle schools (Caskey, 2006).

In the late 1980s, the call for middle grades curriculum reform resurfaced. Two significant reports—*Caught in the Middle* (California State Department of Education, 1987) and *Turning Points: Preparing America's Youth for the 21st Century* (Carnegie Council on Adolescent Development [CCAD], 1989)—challenged educators to focus their attention on a core academic curriculum. The CCAD (1989), in particular, called for an academic program "for all students that integrates English, fine arts, foreign languages, history, literature and grammar, mathematics, science, and social studies" (p. 42). Subsequently, Beane (1990) articulated his view of curriculum in *Middle School Curriculum: From Rhetoric to Reality*. He argued for the conceptualization of general education curriculum at the intersection of young adolescents' personal concerns and social issues. Beane's innovative ideas (1990, 1993, 1997) along with those of other middle grades scholars (e.g., Drake, 1998; Stevenson & Carr, 1993; Vars, 1993, 1996, 1997) led to renewed interest in curriculum for the middle school. During the 1990s, numerous academics and practitioners (e.g., Brazee & Capelluti, 1995; Five & Dionisio, 1996; Pate, Homestead, & McGinnis, 1997; Springer, 1994) contributed to the knowledge base with their thoughts, designs, and exemplars of integrated curriculum. During this time, Lipka et al. (1998) produced a thoughtful review of the Eight-Year Study—"the most comprehensive, long-range, experimental education research study conducted in school settings" (p. 1)—one focused on developing and implementing curriculum to meet the needs of adolescent (i.e., high school) learners. The lessons learned from this study held implications for studying integrated curriculum in the middle school. Importantly, middle school researchers conducted studies about integrated curriculum and substantiated its effectiveness related to student achievement (see Davies, 1992; Drake, 1998) as well as student motivation, higher order thinking, and stronger interpersonal skills (see Vars, 1997). Based on their systematic review of research, Vars and Beane (2000) reported that young adolescents engaged in integrated curriculum do as well, and often better, than those in traditional separate subject curriculum. In sum, a strong conceptual and research base supported the use of integrated curriculum in middle school.

In the early 2000s, an intense focus on standards and standards-based accountability (see No Child Left Behind, 2002) swept the United States, prompting another directional change in curriculum design for many middle schools—a narrowing of the curriculum and a return to subject-centered curricula (Caskey, 2002l Chaille & Caskey, 2001; Hargreaves, Earl, Moore, & Manning, 2001). As Caskey (2006) asserted, the ongoing pressure for disciplinary content coverage as well as "the deeply ingrained separate-subject approach to curriculum impedes the hard work of many middle grades teachers to provide a coherent integrative curriculum" (p. 52). While middle school teachers questioned whether curriculum integration could exist within the standards-based movement, scholars suggested that teachers could use the standards to reveal connections across disciplines (Jackson & Davis, 2000; Pate, 2001). Further, researchers continued to identify research highlighting the effectiveness of "relevant, challenging, integrative, and exploratory" (Anfara et al., 2003, p. 14; Caskey et al., 2010, p. 22) middle school curriculum. Despite the efforts of middle grades teachers, scholars, and researchers, the standards-based movement took root in most middle schools.

Given that curriculum is a comprehensive plan for learning, it describes all the learning experiences, instructional processes, and assessments to take place in middle school (Caskey, 1996). In the next section, we explore the learning experience and instructional practices to engage young adolescent learners.

Instruction. Interdisciplinary teaching teams provided the forum for teachers to collaborate on instructional practices that meet the needs of middle school learners. Analogous with middle school curriculum, the developmental characteristics of young adolescents became pivotal to their teachers' pedagogical practice. Numerous publications appeared and garnered national attention given the importance of instruction programs for middle school learners. For example, Lipsitz (1984) explored successful schools for young adolescents, the National Middle School Association (NMSA, 1982) promoted 10 essential elements of a "true" middle school including "varied instructional strategies" (p. 17), and the National Association of Secondary School Principals (1985) noted features of quality instruction for excellence at the middle level (e.g., provides variety of instructional approaches, attends to the needs of young adolescents, fosters cooperative learning). In 1989, the CCAD asserted in *Turning Points* that "all young adolescents should have the opportunity to succeed in every aspect of the middle grade program" (p. 49) and offered specific recommendations such as (a) grouping students for learning (i.e., cooperative learning, not tracking), (b) providing flexible scheduling for students and teachers, and (c) offering expanded opportunities for learning. All of these early works ignited widespread interest among middle grades educators that carried into the next decade.

During the 1990s, scholars and researchers alike purported that young adolescents deserve a dynamic, challenging, and balanced instructional program—one that incorporates concept-based teaching, cooperative learning experiences, and learner-centered knowledge construction (Caskey, 1996; Lounsbury, 1992; Tomlinson, 1998). Scholars described and explained essential ideas about student engagement—"student's psychological investment in and effort directed toward learning, understanding, or mastering the knowledge, skills, or crafts that academic work is intended to promote" (Newmann, Wehlage, & Lamborn, 1992, p. 12). They also articulated standards for authentic instruction (i.e., higher-order thinking, depth of knowledge, connectedness to the world, substantive conversation, social support) that advance student learning and success (Newmann & Wehlage, 1993). Another major instructional focus was differentiation or differentiated instruction to respond to students' diverse learning needs. In response to the heterogeneous classroom (i.e., mixed ability), Tomlinson (1995, 1999) recommended using a differentiated instruction—instruction based on students' level of readiness, interests, and learning profiles. Certainly, many of the aforementioned essential ideas were apropos for middle school teaching and learning. Correspondingly, the NMSA (1995) called for "varied learning and teaching approaches" (pp. 24–26)—ones highlighting student engagement and interaction, appropriate levels of challenge, and developmentally responsive instruction—in their position statement, *This We Believe: Developmentally Responsive Middle Schools*. Similarly, Vars (1993) and Pate et al. (1997) not only articulated the reasons for teaching an integrated curriculum, but they also described methods (e.g., student involvement) and instructional strategies (e.g., storytelling, jigsaw, simulation) for making it work in middle grades classrooms. In addition, Vars (1996, 1997) explicated the positive effects on students' educational experiences when using instruction methods to teach integrated curriculum. Moreover, to build an empirical knowledge base about what works in middle schools, including practices to ensure that all students meet with academic success (see CCAD, 1989), research teams developed tools (e.g., Middle Grades Self-Study) and conducted systematic studies to measure the outcomes of middle grades reform efforts (Lipsitz, Jackson, & Austin, 1997).

During the 1990s and early 2000s, researchers from the Center for Prevention Research and Development (CPRD) at the University of Illinois in partnership with state, regional, and national middle school reform initiatives conducted large-scale studies using their School Improvement Self-Study tool (Flowers, Mertens, & Mulhall, 2000). For example, when Flowers, Mertens, and Mulhall (2000) examined the effects of interdisciplinary teaching teams, they reported, "Interdisciplinary teams with regular common planning time, staffed by teachers prepared to teach young adolescents, tend to engage in classroom practices that result in better student behavior and higher achievement" (p. 55). Continuing this line of inquiry, Mertens and Flowers (2003) found seven classroom practices associated with interdisciplinary teaching including "(a) small group, active instruction; (b) integration and interdisciplinary practices; (c) authentic instruction and assessment; (d) critical thinking practices; (e) mathematical skill practices; (f) reading skill practices; and (g) writing skill practices" (pp. 35–36).

During this era, Joan Lipsitz cofounded The National Forum to Accelerate Middle Grades Reform (2003)—a coalition of educators, researchers, and professional associations—to serve as a think tank for middle grades education. In addition to defining high-performing middle schools as *academically excellent, developmentally responsive,* and *socially equitable,* The Forum also initiated the Schools to Watch (STW) program to identify and recognize *high-performing middle-grades schools.* Using the STW tools and criteria, schools engage in a self-appraisal process for consideration of selection as a STW.

During the early 2000s, instructional practices appeared to be mostly student-centered and inquiry-driven (e.g., problem-based learning, project-based learning) with more emphasis on relevant, meaningful, and collaborative experiences for young adolescents. Scholars including Jackson and Davis (2000), Manning (2001), and Stevenson (2002) advocated for developmentally appropriate educational experiences for middle school learners—ones that were active and provide opportunities for student choice. Stevenson also encouraged teachers to use shadowing and inquiry techniques to observe and learn from and about young adolescents. Drawing on the ideas of Gay (2000), Brown (2002) described the importance of culturally responsive instructional practices for middle school youth. He underscored the value of using collaborative learning, inductive teaching, contextual experiences, and discussion to tap the voices of students from disparate cultural, social, and economic backgrounds.

During this decade, scholars, researchers, and policy makers remained curious about teachers' instructional practice in middle grades classrooms. Scholars reiterated that academic excellence required teachers to "use instructional strategies that include a variety of challenging and engaging activities that are clearly related to the concepts and skills being taught" (Lipsitz & West, 2006, p. 58). In light of the No Child Left Behind (2002) mandates, researchers conducted studies to examine the changing instructional practices of middle school teachers (Faulkner & Cook, 2006; Greene et al., 2008). Faulkner and Cook (2006) reported that many teachers relied on instructional strategies that supported the tested curriculum. Similarly, Greene et al. (2008) noted teachers' reluctant movement away from developmentally appropriate instructional practice, in spite of their implicit and explicit support for these approaches. Nevertheless, other scholars promoted instructional strategies to retain a focus on integrative curriculum (e.g., Virtue, Wilson, & Ingram, 2009) and developmentally responsive pedagogical practice for young adolescents (e.g., Mee, 2006). In the next section, we consider the role of assessment in middle grades education during the foundational years.

Assessment. Assessment is the third dynamic component of the curriculum, instruction, and assessment triangle (Gross, 2002). Not only does it help educators (e.g., teachers, principals, parents) and students to discern what students have learned, but teachers can also use assessment to inform future instructional practice and improve student performance (Black & Wiliam, 1998; Wiggins, 1998). A balanced assessment system includes both formative and summative assessments. Briefly, formative assessment is assessment *for* learning, while summative assessment is assessments *of* learning (Stiggins & Chappuis, 2006). More specifically, formative assessment occurs during learning and informs both the teachers and students about students' understanding (e.g., questioning, setting goals and criteria for meeting goals, teacher feedback, self- and peer-assessment); whereas, summative assessment occurs after learning and attempts to measure what students know at a specific time after learning (e.g., chapter tests, semester exams, state assessments, standardized tests). When used "in concert, they [formative and summative assessments] offer local and global evidence that teaching and learning are progressing" (Capraro et al., 2011, para. 13).

Naturally, scholars and researchers have long studied the importance and effect of assessment in the middle grades. The CCAD (1989) advanced eight essential principles to transform learning for young adolescents. One of these principles—"middle grades schools transmit a core of common knowledge to all students" (p. 36)—specified that schools can improve curriculum and instruction by "teaching students to learn as well as to test successfully" (p. 48). In other words, in the United States the assessment of student academic performance can have a tremendous influence on both curriculum and instructional practice (CCAD, 1989). Additionally, two overarching questions captured the attention of middle grades practitioners as eloquently posed by Lounsbury (1989) in his column in the *Middle School Journal*. " 'What should every early adolescent know?' And the related question 'How should we organize middle level schools to provide these educational experiences?' " (p. 39). Lounsbury's questions continue to be relevant today.

During the 1990s, the focus on authentic curriculum and authentic instruction also extended to assessment. For example, Darling-Hammond, Ancess, and Falk (1995) conducted research studies to examine authentic assessment in school settings. They reported that authentic assessment occurred in numerous formats, yet the common feature across all formats was real world applicability. With regard to middle schools specifically, NMSA (1995) called for assessment and evaluation to promote student learning. In particular, their position statement highlighted the importance of problem-solving, hands-on learning, and authentic assessment. During this decade, scholars and associations agreed that assessment for middle school students must not be limited to simple recall of isolated facts measured by tests (teacher-made or standardized tests); instead, assessment requires complex displays of students' ability to communicate, process, apply, and construct knowledge in meaningful ways (Caskey, 1996).

In the 2000s, scholars and researchers continued to emphasize the value of assessment to inform instructional practice and advance student learning. For instance, Jackson and Davis (2000) recommended the use of a variety of assessment methods "ranging from informal to formal" that include (a) informal checks for understanding, (b) traditional quizzes and tests, (c) interviews, questionnaires, and conferences, and (d) performance tasks and projects (p. 55). Not surprisingly, they also advocated for the use of authentic assessments (e.g., exhibitions, projects, portfolios, simulations) that allow students "to apply and transfer knowledge and skills in different contexts" (p. 56). Similarly, Gross (2002) underscored that assessment in the middle grades should focus on learners' understanding using projects, journals, demonstrations, and other forms of authentic assessment. Based on their work in schools, Black, Harrison, Lee, Marshall, and Wiliam (2004) identified formative assessments that appeared to work well for students: questioning, feedback, peer assessment, and self-assessment. They concluded that formative assessment holds the potential to play an active, positive, and vital role in students' learning.

During this decade, the intended and unintended consequences of the No Child Left Behind (2002) legislation became evident. Educators across the nation faced demands for increased rigor and began preparing students for annual, high-stakes standardized tests. Scholars and researchers posed questions and investigated the effects of high-stakes testing. For example, Gross (2002) wondered, "Will there be enough time for in-depth units and hands-on learning? Will teachers be able to attend to both the developmental needs of learners and represent the state testing system?" (p. xxv). Researchers gathered evidence about the effects of high-stakes testing. Based on their investigation of 18 states with high-stakes tests, Amrein and Berliner (2002) reported that student learning remained "at the same level it was before the policy was implemented, or actually goes down when high-stakes testing policies are instituted" (p. 2). They also identified some of the unintended consequences of high-stakes tests such as higher school dropout rates, cheating on exams at the teacher and school level, and increases in teacher attrition. Middle grades researchers also conducted studies about the effects of No Child Left Behind. As noted, middle school teachers described shifting their instructional practices to address the tested curriculum (Faulkner & Cook, 2006; Greene et al., 2008). With regard to assessment, Faulkner and Cook (2006) noted, "Some expressed the desire to use research-supported authentic assessments but did not because these techniques were not used on the state assessment" (p. 8). Likewise, Greene et al. (2008) reported:

> The majority of respondents (70%) agreed that state and national policies are changing how they view the nature of their work, and 72% agreed that they are changing their instructional strategies to focus on preparing students to succeed on state exams and grade level benchmarks. (p. 52)

In other words, middle school teachers felt *caught in the middle* again (Greene et al., 2008). Nevertheless, assessment and assessment practices (e.g., formative, summative, authentic) remain an indispensable priority for middle school teachers and their students.

Evolving Directions and Approaches for Schooling Young Adolescents

As of 2010, CIA research topics and practices evidence the foundations of earlier areas of interest; yet, they also expand discussion and provide nuanced findings, thus evolving as new needs and opportunities arise and providing new directions. Topics are sometimes problematized or overlapping in new ways. These "intersections" help to conceptualize and to recognize within our research and practices both the multiple and often overlapping emphases of topics and findings and the indivisible subjectivities within groups and within individuals. Middle school education demands authentic and integrated CIA and considerations of multiple types of intersections are evident in this review of recent middle school CIA research. While discussion in this section does not include all topics researched in the past decade, some salient, evolving, and intersecting ones include the policy and standards environment, global curriculum foundations including the International Baccalaureate Middle Years

Programme, and growth in personalized curriculum, diversity—especially LGBTQ (lesbian, gay, bisexual, transgender, and questioning/queer) needs, social emotional learning (SEL), technological uses, and authentic and informative assessments.

Current reality in schools includes Common Core State Standards and standardized tests as dominant intersecting pieces of the educational culture, especially as standardized testing has been part of sixth, seventh, and eighth grade assessment since the implementation of the No Child Left Behind (2002) federal education policy. Citing Smith and McEwin's (2011) study, Schaefer, Malu, and Yoon (2016) reported the two practices that were "particularly harmful to the movement: Attempts to standardize the curriculum, and the imposition of standardized tests to measure achievement" (p. 14). Opting out of standardized testing has been the reality for some parents and children as they challenge the philosophies and understandings of the value of standardized testing. The Every Student Succeeds Act (ESSA) (2015), the current federal bill guiding K-12 education, has continued middle school standardized testing but has allowed for more authentic assessment as states are responsible for "selecting more inclusive school quality and student success indicators for accountability systems" (Penuel, Meyer, & Valladares, 2016, p. 1).

Schaefer et al. (2016) highlighted studies on common planning time, advisors, and student voices as notable influences in their overview of the middle school movement from 2010 to 2015. Building on international themes also became evident (Mertens, Anfara, & Roney, 2009; Stacki, 2012). Schaefer et al. (2016) identified growing trends in research describing education abroad, international influences on U.S. middle schools, valuing international students' knowledge in expanding curricular experiences, comparing issues and teacher perspectives across countries, and preparing children for the global economy. In some schools, the International Baccalaureate Middle Years Programme (MYP) has realized a broader focus on understanding of global and diversity issues, problem-solving skills, and self-assessment. Used around the world, the MYP framework adapts the International Baccalaureate (IB) learner profile used in high schools to the middle school level. In 2010, a broad review of MYP resulted in significant change with respect to the program's curriculum framework, structure, implementation, and assessment. The honed curriculum framework focused on "the specification of concept-driven education; the elevation of global contexts; an expanded notion of learning skills; and a more theoretically-robust and practical understanding of what it means to be interdisciplinary" (Harrison, 2015, p. 45). The *Approaches to Learning* (ATL) framework emphasized overarching concepts and engages students in inquiry and risk taking; challenging, higher-level critical thinking; and real-world application. This curricular framework and assessment tools intended to "create a better and more peaceful world through intercultural understanding and respect" (International Baccalaureate Organization, 2013).

The number of schools following the MYP increased 56% between 2005 and 2009 alone (Bunnell, 2011), and 2012 marked the 20th anniversary of MYP as an IB program. Within the United States, the number of schools offering IB programs at all levels has grown exponentially from 88 in 1997 to 1,470 in 2013 (International Baccalaureate Organization, 2013). Public schools offer 90 % of these programs. In studying four MYP programs, Quaynor (2015) recommended that the global education framework be more connected and relevant to the experiences and perspectives of diverse youth, especially for immigrant and refugee youth who are in a particular MYP school. Implemented with intersecting subjectivities of all students in mind, the MYP can aid schools and teachers in bringing the world to middle school students and sharing the worldly experiences of the rising number of diverse students in U.S. schools.

In reinforcing integrated curriculum and literacy across the disciplines, Taylor (2004) advised that instruction in the early 2000s be individualized and personalized. Moving beyond individualized education plans for special education students, in the last decade, educators have more clearly articulated personalized learning approaches. Personalized learning definitions vary but have shared the goal to create an instructional environment that meets each student's needs, skills, and interests. Fostering student learning through this student-centered approach helped students to make choices and share their voices. The active role of students in helping to design the curriculum was what distinguished personalized learning from differentiated or individualized curriculum (Bray & McClaskey, 2015). Promoted in many states and in some teacher education institutions, teacher educators have worked with preservice teachers to understand personalized needs and how to teach to these needs (Bishop et al., 2018). In *This We Believe: Keys to Educating Young Adolescents* (NMSA, 2010), middle grades leaders advocated for curriculum that goes beyond recognizing student interest and wonder to advancing engagement and exploration. Recently, numerous initiatives to personalize education have become more pervasive such as in Iowa, Oregon, and New England states—while Vermont legislated that all students have personalized learning plans by 2018 (Center for Digital Education, 2013). New standards, connected with more personalized learning plans, have been under development in the Next Generation Standards in New York State. The New York Board of Regents adopted revised English Language Arts and Mathematics Learning Standards on September 11, 2017. The New York State Education Department (2019) expected to have full implementation by September 2020, following its phase in schedule, with new Grade 3–8 testing to measure these new standards in spring 2021.

Intersecting with a personalized approach or personalized learning plans is an emphasis on self-regulated learning (SRL) frameworks for learning environments. When teachers facilitate SRL principles that equip students to be self-directed, independent problem solvers, students will develop strategic approaches for engaging in academic tasks (Denis & Neitsel, 2011), including the ability to evaluate and monitor their performance toward academic goals and to adjust their strategic activity when goals are not being met. SRL complements an integrated CIA approach, as assessment is not separate from instruction. Many middle school studies within the last five years emphasize self-regulated learning including connecting with social interactions (Alvi & Gillies, 2015), math (Cleary & Kitsantas, 2017), science (Johnson, 2019), and technology with writing studies (Hughes, Regan, & Evmenova, 2019).

Understanding LGBTQ student issues, gender identity, and coming out in middle school (Denizet-Lewis, 2009) has become a more prevalent part of the curriculum. Educators must transform their thinking to understand the intersecting and complex concepts related to gender identity, sexual orientation, and race (Horowitz & Itzkowitz, 2011; Mayo, 2014) as they attempt to make all students more welcome in their schools. Lewis and Sembiante (2019) discussed professional development for teachers, especially around transgender issues, and teachers' potential to be educational change agents to spur deeper understanding of and advocacy for students' gender inclusivity. Wickens and Wedwick (2011) found a very limited number of novels with LGBTQ characters or relevant themes, thus calling for an increased discussion around and inclusion of content in middle grades classrooms. Schools are doing more to make school environments safe for LGBTQ students. Mayo (2014) contended that teachers should see these students in a balanced way that acknowledges their problems, yet understand that they have agency and resiliency.

Increasing middle school students' understanding of sexual identity issues is part of the expanding SEL emphasis in schools. Clarity on the cognitive aspects of young adolescent development through neuroscience (Caskey & Ruben, 2007) helps educators to understand middle school students' risky behavior and lack of ability to discern long-term consequences. Thus, educators need to understand the pervasive need for SEL in the curriculum to help students make good decisions. An increase of mindfulness activities in schools also brings together social-emotional well-being and clarity of thinking for academic success. Community service learning (Main, 2018), providing both academic and SEL benefits, is also a prominent feature of some middle schools, especially in eighth grade, and in schools with community and global minded learning goals, such as schools with MYP frameworks (Harrison, 2015).

A search of journal databases reveals numerous research studies of SEL middle school programs and interventions in the last decade. In their study, Espelage, Rose, and Polanin (2016) evaluated the effectiveness of the Second Step–Student Success Through Prevention (SS-SSTP) social emotional learning program over three years. In this study, middle school students completed self-report measures of school belonging, empathy, caring, and willingness to intervene in bullying situations. Notably, students with disabilities in the program increased their willingness to intervene in bullying incidents in comparison with students with disabilities in control schools. Espelage et al. concluded that their study demonstrated the promise of social-emotional learning programming for students with disabilities.

McBride, Chung, and Robertson (2016) studied an experiential SEL program with goals of reducing school disciplinary incidents. In their study, seventh grade students in social studies curricula experienced the school-based SEL service-learning program. The results indicated that the program might reduce disciplinary incidents; however, changing some attitudes and skills needed further intervention. A 2018 multilevel analysis determined that setting did matter when implementing an SEL program. Coelho and Sousa (2018) found that those middle school students experiencing the program within school gained more self-esteem, self-control, and social awareness than did those students taking the program after school. While SEL has been part of middle school learning for decades, the prioritizing and balancing of social-emotional activities and creation of new programs demonstrated the evolving need at the middle school level with differing students and diverse communities.

An explosion of technology studies focused on intersections of student use, teacher preparedness, and effects on student-centered school climate have continued to engage readers of middle school research. Researchers acknowledged the central role of technology in instructional delivery to advance the multifaceted abilities and skills that student success requires (Powell et al., 2015). For example, Smith and Santori (2015) reported on a phenomenological qualitative research project that observed iPad-based teaching and learning in six public-school middle-grades. They shared teachers and students' perspectives and ways to realize the most effective results. In another study, Varier et al. (2017) found that teachers and students experienced a shift toward student-centered learning and instruction. While they noted limitations of test taking with devices, middle school use with tablets and Chromebooks supported "self-directed learning, increased peer-peer and student-teacher communication, collaboration, and immersive use of technology tools to produce, organize, and share academic work" (p. 987). Other studies focused on multimedia and digital arts and literacy preparedness are essential for teachers to learn. Falk-Ross and Linder (2018) noted that teacher educators must model use of technology repeatedly for preservice students so that they can use it with clear purpose in their own classrooms.

Researchers have explored standards connection to achievement and expanded the breadth of ideas and practice of authentic assessment, including a more prominent use of formative or informal assessments. Authentic assessment complements the developmental characteristics and needs of middle school students by promoting critical thinking, inquiry, and discovery such as in multidimensional projects and exhibitions. With expanding cognitive abilities, especially for abstract thinking, students wanted real world knowledge and contexts that nourish their growing interests in the larger community and their own self-identity within it. Authentic assessment encouraged students to self-express, create in many directions, and exhibit various abilities and multiple intelligences (Stacki, 2016).

One formative assessment study examined assessment conversations or dialogic interactions in the classroom. Ruiz-Primo (2011) argued, "Assessment conversations make students' thinking explicit in an unobtrusive manner, and when students' thinking is explicit, it can be examined, questioned, and shaped as an active object of constructive learning" (p. 15). In their study of a comprehensive standards-based assessment program, Abrams, Varier, and Jackson (2016) examined teachers' data use for instruction and alignment with established content standards and assessment. Teachers had goals of improving student performance and determined that every day informal assessments were essential to shaping instruction. Periodic formal assessments also helped teachers to monitor student progress and remediation efforts.

Informal formative assessments (IFAs) blended in everyday instruction can be used to collect evidence of learning each time students are participating (Sezen-Barriea & Kelly, 2017). Findings from an analysis of the classroom discourse in four middle schools revealed that teachers sometimes have difficulty implementing different types of IFA. However, in this study, "teachers came to see IFA as a process of ongoing assessment and readjustment (metaphorically, a video of everyday life), rather than as a measure of achievement at a given time (a still shot photograph)" (Sezen-Barriea & Kelly, 2017, p. 208). This finding signified a conceptual change in thinking about how to understand and respond to students. Sezen-Barriea and Kelly (2017) concluded that IFAs should be part of a robust, interactive classroom assessment portfolio.

Clinchot et al. (2017) suggested ways to implement responsive approaches to formative assessment in the science classroom. They concluded that responsive formative assessment could elicit students' ways of thinking and make sense of how students solve problems. They noted the use of Robertson, Scherr, and Hammer's (2016) ideas to reveal and highlight student ideas, recognize disciplinary connections, and take actions to scaffold student learning productively. They asked about the intention of the task to reveal students' thinking and to consider what captures students' attention. These questions helped Robertson et al. to identify teaching strategies that promote responsive modes of formative assessment.

Throughout the studies in this volume, many of these salient ideas are intersecting in ways that highlight specific research sites, participants, and goals. These studies demonstrate the dynamic, evolving nature of our middle schools and our education field.

Overview of Chapters: Intersecting Realms and Converging Ideas

We organized this volume in three sections, (a) focusing on the possibilities of curriculum, instruction, and assessment with students, (b) teachers' perspectives on curriculum, instruction, and assessment, and (c) examining learning through broader lenses. The first section includes four chapters that describe research studies with middle level students involving varying aspects of curriculum, instruction, and assessment. In Chapter 2, Claravall and Irey describe their mixed methods, action research study where seventh grade students in special education classes were taught to "think like historians" by critically examining primary and secondary sources for credibility and corroboration of evidence. In Chapter 3, Ardito discusses a case study with eighth grade biology students participating in a self-directed, autonomy-supportive learning environment. He describes how his students worked through the units of a science course at their own pace, pursuing content, selecting learning strategies, and determining when they reached levels of proficiency. In Chapter 4, McGinnis and Garcia examine an after-school writing program as a space where Black middle school students learned about and developed their 21st century literacy skills through a digital writing workshop. Their research study considers the role of literacy and digital practices in these young adolescents' negotiation of racial, ethnic, and cultural identity. In the last chapter in this section (Chapter 5), Akhavan addresses middle school students' strategies to comprehend complex texts and information. In this mixed methods study, she focuses on student identification and the benefit of specific reading comprehension strategies. She also reports the need, as reported by students, for teachers who care about their students and their learning.

The four chapters in Section 2 focus on teachers' dispositions and perspectives concerning curriculum, instruction, and assessment. In Chapter 6, Shockley, Ivy, and Peters, examine culturally relevant pedagogy and assessment of diverse learners in a STEM classroom. Their study includes several vignettes from teachers in middle schools describing interactions with students, concepts for lessons, and strategies for instruction and assessment. They also discuss implications for classroom culture, making connections, disciplinary literacy skills, and digital learning. In Chapter 7, Radice describes her ethnographic case study exploring pedagogical responses to technology in the classroom. Using data collected from three teachers in a diverse school district, this study focuses on a one-to-one Chromebook initiative and how it influences the instructional methods that supported the development of digital literacy practices of middle level students. Jackson and Delaney (Chapter 8) investigate teachers' beliefs about society, their students, learning, and themselves as well as how these beliefs influence their instructional practices. In their qualitative study, they examine the beliefs that a White, sixth grade mathematics teacher has about Black students, how those beliefs are reflected in classroom instruction, and how reflecting on instructional practices begins to foster productive beliefs about Black students in the mathematics classroom. In the last chapter in this section (Chapter 9), Brinthaupt, Haupt, Lipka, and Robinson examine the challenges, barriers, and successes of middle level teachers' use of educational technology. They present the results of a comprehensive quantitative survey of middle level educators from New York and Tennessee designed to examine middle level teachers' experiences with educational technology across various stakeholders they are likely to encounter.

The four chapters in Section 3 include studies that examined curriculum, instruction, and assessment through a broader lens. In their chapter, Grodoski and colleagues (Chapter 10) describe their collaborative, action research project designed to identify instructional strategies that supported middle level students in personalizing their own learning. Using a mixed methods approach, including pre/post surveys and text-based qualitative data, they examine the experiences of students in arts and electives classes through "flow" theory. Fitzpatrick and van Hover investigate the use of authentic assessment, including a "tapestry" in a history classroom in Chapter 11. Using a case study research design, they explore how a middle school history teacher integrated his instruction and assessment practices and how the students described their learning experiences from the classroom. Meyer (Chapter 12) discusses how middle level students and their teachers experienced writing and the teaching of writing in an out of school, summer setting. Using a mixed methods approach including data from surveys, interviews, and observations, he describes how teachers and their students appreciated selectively exploring topics of interest in an outdoor setting with opportunities to be alone and think. Lastly, in Chapter 13, Mallory and Davis examine how schools can blend best practices and next (highly innovative) practices. In their qualitative case study, they explore how one year-round, Title I middle school worked to operationalize best and next practices in school organization, instructional practices, uses of technology, and student engagement.

In this volume, the authors of the chapters highlight and describe a variety of intersecting new needs and new approaches for middle level curriculum, instruction, and assessment. We hope the research studies described in these chapters serve to inform teachers, administrators, district office personnel, and higher education faculty about new and innovative approaches to middle level curriculum, instruction, and assessment practices.

REFERENCES

Abrams, L., Varier, D., & Jackson, L. (2016). Unpacking instructional alignment: The influence of teachers' use of assessment data on instruction. *Perspectives in Education, 34*(4), 15–28.

Alexander, W. M., Williams, E. L., Compton, M., Hines, V. A., & Prescott, D. (1968). *The emergent middle school.* New York, NY: Holt, Rinehart and Winston.

Alvi, E., & Gillies, R. M. (2015). Social interactions that support students' self-regulated learning: A case study of one teachers' experiences. *International Journal of Educational Research, 72*, 14–25. doi.org/10.1016/j.ijer.2015.04.008

Amrein, A. L., & Berliner, D. C. (2002). High-stakes testing, uncertainty, and student learning. *Educational Policy Analysis Archives, 10*(8). Retrieved from https://epaa.asu.edu/ojs/article/viewFile/297/423

Anfara, V. A., Jr., Andrews, P. G., Hough, D. L., Mertens, S. B., Mizelle, N. B., & White, G. P. (2003). *Research and resources in support of* This We Believe. Westerville, OH: National Middle School Association.

Anfara, V. A., Jr., & Stacki, S. L. (Eds.). (2002). *Middle school curriculum, instruction, and assessment.* Greenwich, CT: Information Age.

Beane. J. A (1990). *Middle school curriculum: From rhetoric to reality.* Columbus, OH: National Middle School Association.

Beane, J. A. (1993). *The middle school curriculum: From rhetoric to reality* (2nd ed.) Columbus, OH: National Middle School Association.

Beane, J. A. (1997). *Curriculum integration: Designing the core of democratic education.* New York, NY: Teachers College Press.

Black, P., Harrison, C., Lee, C., Marshall, B., & Wiliam, D. (2004). Working inside the black box: Assessment for learning in the classroom. *Phi Delta Kappan, 86*, 9–21.

Black, P., & Wiliam, D. (1998). Assessment and classroom learning. *Assessment in Education, 5*(1), 7–74.

Bishop, P. B., Downes, J., Netcoh, S., DeMink-Carthew, J., Farber, K., LeGros, L., & Stokes, T. (2018). Middle grades teachers' dispositions in personalized learning environments. In P. B. Howell, S. A. Faulkner, J. P. Jones, & J. Carpenter (Eds.), *Preparing middle level educators for 21st century schools: Enduring beliefs, changing times, evolving practices* (pp. 229–254). Charlotte, NC: Information Age.

Brazee, E. N., & Capelluti, J. (1995). *Dissolving boundaries: Toward an integrative curriculum.* Columbus, OH: National Middle School Association.

Bray, B., & McClaskey, K. (2015). *Make learning personal: The what, who, wow, where, and why.* Thousand Oaks, CA: Corwin Press.

Brown, D. F. (2002). Culturally responsive instructional practices. In V. A. Anfara, Jr., & S. L. Stacki (Eds.), *Middle school curriculum, instruction, and assessment* (pp. 57–73). Greenwich, CT: Information Age.

Bunnell, T. (2011). The International Baccalaureate Middle Years Programme after 30 years: A critical inquiry. *Journal of Research in International Education, 10*(3), 261–274.

California State Department of Education. (1987). *Caught in the middle.* Sacramento, CA: Author.

Carnegie Council on Adolescent Development. (1989). *Turning points: Preparing American youth for the 21st century.* New York, NY: Carnegie Corporation.

Capraro, R. M., Roe, M. F., Caskey, M. M., Strahan, D., Bishop, P.A., Weiss, C. C., & Swanson, K. W. (2011). *Research summary: Assessment.* Westerville, OH: Association for Middle Level Education. Retrieved from https://pdxscholar.library. pdx.edu/cgi/viewcontent.cgi?article=1006&context=ci_fac

Caskey, M. M. (with Johnston, J. H.) (1996). Hard work ahead: Authentic curriculum under construction. *Schools in the Middle, 6*(2), 11–18.

Caskey, M. M. (2002). Authentic curriculum: Strengthening middle level education. In V. A. Anfara, Jr., & S. L. Stacki (Eds.), *Middle school curriculum, instruction, and assessment* (pp. 103–117). Greenwich, CT: Information Age.

Caskey, M. M. (2006). The evidence for the core curriculum—Past and present. *Middle School Journal, 37*(3), 48–54.

Caskey, M. M., Andrews, P. G., Bishop, P. A., Capraro, R. M., Roe, M., & Weiss, C. (2010). *Research and resources in support of* This We Believe (2nd ed.). Westerville, OH: National Middle School Association.

Caskey, M. M., & Ruben, B. (2007). Under construction: The young adolescent brain. In S. B. Mertens, V. A. Anfara, Jr., & M. M. Caskey (Eds.), *The young adolescent and the middle school* (pp. 47–72). Charlotte, NC: Information Age.

Centers for Disease Control. (2015). *Suicide: Facts at a glance 2015.* Retrieved from https://www.cdc.gov/violenceprevention/pdf/suicide-datasheet-a.pdf

Center for Digital Education. (2013). *Pathway to personalized learning: Tapping the potential, realizing the benefits.* Retrieved from http://www.centerdigitaled.com/paper/2013-Q3-Special-Report-Pathways-to-Personalized-Learning.html

Chaille, C., & Caskey, M. M. (2001). A lingering question for middle school. What is the fate of integrated curriculum? *Childhood Education, 78*(2), 97–99.

Cleary, T. J., & Kitsantas, A. (2017). Motivation and self-regulated learning influences on middle school mathematics achievement. *School Psychology Review, 46*(1), 88–107. doi.org/10.17105/SPR46-1.88-107

Clinchot, M., Ngai, C., Huie, R., Talanquer, V., Lambertz, J., Banks, G., … Sevian, H. (2017). Better formative assessment: Making formative assessment more responsive to student needs. *The Science Teacher, 84*(3) 69–75.

Coelho, V. A., & Sousa, V. (2018). Differential effectiveness of a middle school social and emotional learning program: Does setting matter? *Journal of Youth and Adolescence, 47*, 1978–1991. doi.org/10.1007/s10964-018-0897-3

Darling-Hammond, L., Ancess, J., & Falk, B. (1995). *Authentic assessment in action: Studies of schools and students at work.* New York, NY: Teachers College Press.

Davies, M. A. (1992). Are interdisciplinary units worthwhile? Ask students. In J. H. Lounsbury (Ed.), *Connecting the curriculum through interdisciplinary instruction* (pp. 37–41). Columbus, OH: National Middle School Association.

Denis, D., & Neitsel, C. (2011). A self-regulated learning perspective on middle grades classroom assessment. *Journal of Educational Research, 104*(3), 202–215.

Denizet-Lewis, B. (2009, September 29). Coming out in middle school. [The school issue: Junior high.] *The New York Times, 27*, 36–55.

Drake, S. M. (1998). *Creating integrated curriculum: Proven ways to increase student learning.* Thousand Oaks, CA: Corwin Press.

Eichhorn, D. H. (1972). A successful curriculum change. *Middle School Journal, 3*(3), 27–32. doi.org/10.1080/00940771.1972.11495803

Espelage, D. L., Rose, C. A., & Polanin, J. R. (2016). Social-emotional learning program to promote prosocial and academic skills among middle school students with disabilities, *Remedial and Special Education, 37*(6), 323–332.

Every Student Succeeds Act (ESSA) of 2015, Pub. L. No. 114-95 § 114 Stat. 1177 (2015-2016).

Falk-Ross, F., & Linder, R. (2018). Advocating for increased use of digital literacies for future middle school teachers for literacy instruction. In P. B. Howell, S. A. Faulkner, J. P. Jones, & J. Carpenter (Eds.), *Preparing middle level educators for 21st century schools: Enduring beliefs, changing times, evolving practices* (pp. 203–226). Charlotte, NC: Information Age.

Faulkner, S. A., & C. M. Cook. (2006). Testing vs. teaching: The perceived impact of assessment demands on middle grades instructional practices. *Research in Middle Level Education Online, 29*(7), 1–13. doi.org/10.1080/19404476.2006.11462030

Five, C. L., & Dionisio, M. (1996). *Bridging the gap: Integrating curriculum in upper elementary and middle schools.* Portsmouth, NH: Heinemann.

Flowers, N., Mertens, S. B., & Mulhall, P. F. (2000). How teaming influences classroom practices. *Middle School Journal, 32*(2), 52–59.

Gay, G. (2000). *Culturally responsive teaching: Theory, research, and practice.* New York, NY: Teachers College Press.

Graham, T. J., Wenzel, A., Linder, R., & Rice, M. F. (2018). Special populations in middle level classrooms. In S. B. Mertens & M. M. Caskey (Eds.), *Literature reviews in support of the middle level education research agenda* (pp. 53–77). Charlotte, NC: Information Age.

Greene, W. L., Caskey, M. M., Musser, P. M., Samek, L. L., Casbon, J., & Olson, M. (2008). Caught in the middle again; Accountability and the changing practice of middle school teachers. *Middle Grades Research Journal, 1*(4), 41–72.

Gross, S. J. (2002). Introduction: Middle-level curriculum, instruction, and assessment. Evolution or an innovation at risk. In V. A. Anfara, Jr., & S. L. Stacki (Eds.), *Middle school curriculum, instruction, and assessment* (pp. ix–xxxii). Greenwich, CT: Information Age.

Hargreaves, A., Earl, L., Moore, S., & Manning, S. (2001). *Learning to change: Teaching beyond subjects and standards.* San Francisco, CA: Jossey-Bass.

Harrison, R. (2015). Evolving the IB Middle Years Programme: Curriculum. *The International Schools Journal, 34*(2), 45–58.

Hicks, J., Jennings, L., Jennings, S., Berry, S., & Green, D. (2018). Middle school bullying: Student reported perceptions and prevalence, *Journal of Child and Adolescent Counseling, 4*(3), 195–208. doi.org/:10.1080/23727810.2017.1422 645

Horowitz, A., & Itzkowitz, M. (2011). LGBTQ youth in American schools: Moving to the middle. *Middle School Journal, 42*(5), 32–38. doi.org/10.1080/0094077 1.2011.11461780

Hughes, M. D., Regan, K. S., & Evmenova, A. (2019). A computer-based graphic organizer with embedded self-regulated learning strategies to support student writing. *Intervention in School* & Clinic, *55*(1), 13–22. doi.org/10.1177/1053451219833026

International Baccalaureate Organization. (2013). *International baccalaureate.* Retrieved from http://www.ibo.org

Jackson, A. W., & Davis, G. A. (2000). *Turning points 2000: Educating adolescents in the 21st century.* New York, NY: Teachers College Press.

Johnson, E. K. (2019). Waves: Scaffolding self-regulated learning to teach science in a whole-body educational game, *Journal of Science Education & Technology, 28*(2), 133–151. doi.org/10.1007/s10956-018-9753-1

Lewis, R. K., & Sembiante, S. F. (2019). Research and practice in transition: Improving support and advocacy of transgender middle school students. *Middle Grades Review, 5*(1), Article 2. Retrieved from https://scholarworks. uvm.edu/mgreview/vol5/iss1/2

Li, Y., Allen, J., & Casillas, A. (2017). Relating psychological and social factors to academic performance: A longitudinal investigation of high-poverty middle school students. *Journal of Adolescence, 56*, 179–189.

Lipka, R. P., Lounsbury, J. H., Toepfer, C. F., Vars, G. F., Alessi, S. P., & Kridel, C. (1998). *The eight-year study revisited: Lessons from the past for the present.* Columbus, OH: National Middle School Association.

Lipsitz, J. (1984). *Successful schools for young adolescents.* New Brunswick, NJ: Transaction.

Lipsitz, J., Jackson, A. W., & Austin, L. M. (1997). What works in middle-grades school reform. *Phi Delta Kappan, 78*, 517–519.

Lipsitz, J., & West, T. (2006). What makes a good school? Identifying excellent middle schools. *Phi Delta Kappan, 88*, 57–66. doi.org/10.1177/003172170608800110

Lounsbury, J. H. (1989). As I see it: Just what should every early adolescent know? *Middle School Journal, 20*(3), 39. doi.org/10.1080/00940771.1989.11495015

Lounsbury, J. H. (1992). Interdisciplinary instruction: A mandate for the nineties. In J. H. Lounsbury (Ed.), *Connecting the curriculum through interdisciplinary instruction* (pp. 1–2). Columbus, OH: National Middle School Association.

Lounsbury, J. H., & Vars, G. F. (1978). *A curriculum for the middle school years*. New York, NY: Harper & Row.

Main, K. (2018). Community-based service learning: Building preservice teachers' confidence to work in the middle years. In P. B. Howell, S. A. Faulkner, J. P. Jones & J. Carpenter (Eds.). *Preparing middle level educators for 21st century schools: Enduring beliefs, changing times, evolving practices* (pp. 255–270). Charlotte, NC: Information Age.

Manning, M. L. (2002). *Developmentally appropriate middle level schools* (2nd ed.). Olney, MD: Association for Childhood Education International.

Martin, F., Wang, C., Petty, T., Wang, W., & Wilkins, P. (2018). Middle school students' social media use. *Educational Technology & Society, 21*, 213–224.

Mayo, C. (2014). *LGBTQ youth and education: Policies and practices*. New York, NY: Teachers College Press.

Mee, M. M. (2006). Socratic seminar and young adolescent motivation: A developmentally appropriate practice. In S. B. Mertens, V. A. Anfara, Jr., & M. M. Caskey (Eds.), *The young adolescent and the middle school* (pp. 141–161). Charlotte, NC: Information Age.

Mertens, S. B., Anfara, V A., & Roney, K. (Eds.). (2009). *An international look at educating young adolescents*. Charlotte, NC: Information Age.

Mertens, S. B., & Flowers, N. (2003). Middle school practices improve student achievement in high poverty school. *Middle School Journal, 35*(1), 33–43.

McBride, A. M., Chung, S., & Robertson, A. (2016). Preventing academic disengagement through a middle school–based social and emotional learning program. *Journal of Experiential Education, 39*, 370–385.

Moulton, M. J. (2019). The (un)muted voices of middle grades youth experiencing homelessness. In K. Brinegar, L. Harrison, & E. Hurd (Eds.), *Equity and cultural responsiveness in the middle grades* (pp. 69–91). Charlotte, NC: Information Age.

National Association of Secondary School Principals. (1985). *An agenda for excellence at the middle level*. Reston, VA: Author.

National Forum to Accelerate Middle-Grades Reform. (2003). *Vision statement*. Newton, MA: Education Development Center.

National Middle School Association. (1982). *This we believe*. Columbus, OH: Author. Columbus, OH: Author.

National Middle School Association. (1995). *This we believe: Developmentally responsive middle level schools*. Columbus, OH: Author.

National Middle School Association. (2010). *This we believe: Keys to educating young adolescents*. Westerville, OH: Author.

Newmann, F. M., & Wehlage, G. G. (1993). Five standards for authentic instruction. *Educational Leadership, 50*(7), 8–12.

Newmann, F. M., G. G. Wehlage, &. Lamborn, S. D (1992). The significance and sources of student engagement. In F. M. Newmann (Ed.), *Student engagement and achievement in American secondary schools* (pp. 11–30). New York, NY: Teachers College Press.

New York State Education Department. (2015-2019). *Next Generation Learning Standards Roadmap and Implementation Timeline*. Retrieved from http://www.nysed.gov/curriculum-instruction/next-generation-learning-standards-and-assessment-implementation-timeline

No Child Left Behind (NCLB) Act of 2001, Pub. L. No. 107-110, § 115, Stat. 1425 (2002).

Pate, P. E. (2001). Standards, students, and exploration: Creating a curriculum intersection of excellence. In T. S. Dickinson (Ed.), *Reinventing the middle school* (pp. 79–95). New York, NY: RoutledgeFalmer.

Pate, P. E., Homestead, E. R., & McGinnis, K. L. (1997). *Making integrated curriculum work: Teachers, students, and the quest for coherent curriculum*. New York, NY: Teachers College Press.

Penuel, W., Meyer, E., & Valladares, M. R. (2016). *Making the most of the Every Student Succeeds Act (ESSA): Helping states focus on school equity, quality, and climate*. Retrieved from ERIC database. (ED578780)

Powell, A., Watson, J., Staley, P., Patrick, S., Horn, M., Fetzer, L., … Verma, S. (2015). *Blended learning: The evolution of online and face-to-face education from 2008-2015. Promising practices in blended and online learning series*. Retrieved from ERIC database. (ED560788)

Quaynor, L. (2015). Connections and contradictions in teacher practices for preparing globally minded citizens in two IB public schools. *Teachers College Record, 117*(9), 1–38.

Robertson, A. D., Scherr, R. E., & Hammer, D. (Eds.). (2016). *Responsive teaching in science and mathematics*. New York, NY: Routledge.

Ruiz-Primo, M. A. (2011). Informal formative assessment: The role of instructional dialogues in assessing students' learning. *Studies in Educational Evaluation, 37*(1), 15–24. doi.org/10.1016/j.stueduc.2011.04.003

Salle, T., Wang, C., Parris, L., & Brown, J. (2017). Associations between school climate, suicidal thoughts, and behaviors and ethnicity among middle school students. *Psychology in the Schools, 54*, 1294–1301.

Schaefer, M. B., Malu, K. F., & Yoon, B. (2016). An historical overview of the middle school movement, 1963–2015. *Research in Middle Level Education Online, 39*(5), 1–27.

Sezen-Barrie, A., & Kelly, G. J. (2017) From the teacher's eyes: Facilitating teachers noticings on informal formative assessments and exploring the challenges to effective implementation. *International Journal of Science Education, 39*(2), 181–212. doi.org/10.1080/09500693.2016.1274921

Smith, C. A., & Santori, D. (2015). An exploration of iPad-Based teaching and learning: How middle-grades teachers and students are realizing the potential. *Journal of Research on Technology in Education, 47*(3), 173–185. doi.org/10.1080/15391523.2015.1047700

Smith, T., & McEwin, C. K. (Eds.). (2011). *The legacy of middle school leaders: In their own words*. Charlotte, NC: Information Age.

Springer, M. (1994). *Watershed: A successful voyage into integrative learning*. Columbus, OH: National Middle School Association.

Stacki, S. L. (2012). Internationalizing the field of middle level education. *Middle School Journal, 44*(1), 6–7.

Stacki, S. L. (2016). Authentic assessment. In S. B. Mertens, M. M. Caskey, & N. Flowers (Eds.), *The encyclopedia of middle grades education* (2nd ed, pp. 61–64). Charlotte, NC: Information Age.

Stevenson, C. (2002). *Teaching ten to fourteen year olds* (3rd ed.). Boston, MA: Allyn & Bacon.

Stevenson, C., & Carr, J. F. (1993). *Integrated studies in the middle grades: Dancing through walls.* New York, NY: Teachers College Press.

Stiggins, R., & Chappuis, J. (2006). What a difference a word makes: Assessment "for" learning rather than assessment "of" learning helps students succeed. *Journal of Staff Development, 27*(1), 10–14.

Taylor, R. T. (2004). Using literacy leadership to improve the achievement of struggling students. *Middle School Journal, 36*(1), 26–31.

Toepfer, C. (1997). Middle level curriculum's serendipitous history. In J. E. Irvin. (Ed.), *What current research says to the middle level practitioner* (pp. 163–177). Columbus, OH: National Middle School Association.

Tomlinson, C. (1995). *How to differentiate instruction in mixed-ability classrooms.* Alexandria, VA: Association for Supervision and Curriculum Development.

Tomlinson, C. (1998). For integration and differentiation choose concepts over topics. *Middle School Journal, 30*(2), 3–8.

Tomlinson, C. (1999). *The differentiated classroom: Responding to the needs of all learners.* Alexandria, VA: Association for Supervision and Curriculum Development.

Varier, D., Dumke, E. K., Abrams, L. M., Conklin, S. B., Barnes, J. S., & Hoover, N. R. (2017). Potential of one-to-one technologies in the classroom: teachers and students weigh in. *Education Tech Research Development, 65*, 967–992. doi.org/10.1007/s11423-9509-2

Vars, G. F. (1969). A contemporary view of the core curriculum. In G. F. Vars (Ed.), *Common learnings: Core and interdisciplinary team approaches* (pp. 5–18). Scranton, PA: International Textbook.

Vars, G. F. (1993). *Interdisciplinary teaching: Why and how.* Columbus, OH: National Middle School Association.

Vars, G. F. (1996). Effects of interdisciplinary curriculum and instruction. In P. S. Hlebowitsh & W. G. Wragra (Eds.), *Annual review of research for school leaders* (pp. 147–164). Jefferson City, MO: Scholastic.

Vars, G. F. (1997). Effects of integrative curriculum and instruction. In J. E. Irvin. (Ed.), *What current research says to the middle level practitioner* (pp. 179–186). Columbus, OH: National Middle School Association.

Vars, G. F., & Beane. J. A. (2000). *Integrative curriculum in a standards-based world.* Retrieved from ERIC database. (ED441618)

Virtue, D. C., Wilson, J. L., & Ingram, N. (2009). In overcoming obstacles to curriculum integration. L.E.S.S. can be more! *Middle School Journal, 40*(3), 4–11.

Wickens, C. M., & Wedwick, L. (2011). Looking forward: Increased attention to LGBTQ students and families in middle grades classrooms. *Voices from the Middle, 18*(4), 43–51.

Wiggins, G. (1998). *Educative assessment: Designing assessments to inform and improve student performance*. San Francisco, CA: Jossey-Bass.

Wraga, W. G. (1996). A century of interdisciplinary curricula in American schools. In P. S. Hlebowitsh & W. G. Wragra (Eds.), *Annual review of research for school leaders* (pp. 117–145). Jefferson City, MO: Scholastic.

SECTION I

SEEING THE POSSIBILITIES WITH STUDENTS

CHAPTER 2

HISTORICAL THINKING IN THE MIDDLE SCHOOL CLASSROOM

Integration of Authentic Curriculum, Instruction, and Assessment

Eric B. Claravall
California State University, Sacramento

Robin Irey
University of California, Berkeley

ABSTRACT

When teachers align their curriculum goals with authentic teaching of history, their instruction moves beyond the use of textbooks. In this chapter, the authors lay out how historical thinking constitutes an authentic social studies curriculum. Historical thinking requires the use of critical analysis skills while constructing a deep understanding of the past. The authors present the findings from a mixed methods action research study they conducted in which seventh grade students in self-contained special education classes were taught to "think like historians." Like historians, students interrogate primary and

Curriculum, Instruction, and Assessment:
Intersecting New Needs and New Approaches, pp. 31–53
Copyright © 2020 by Information Age Publishing

secondary sources' believability and look for corroboration of evidence before making a narrative interpretation of the past. The authors embedded formative assessment as an instructional approach to the teaching of historical thinking. Furthermore, the authors measured the mastery of skills using an on-demand writing task that served as an authentic assessment.

Middle school represents a unique developmental stage for learners that is under-researched and remains less understood than other developmental periods. Of utmost importance to researchers and educators of this population is how to best facilitate learning in the middle grades. This time represents a transition from learning how to learn to the application of that learning. Thus, it requires thoughtful adoption of appropriate and effective curriculum, instruction, and assessment (CIA) to meet these learners' needs. Gross (2002) defined curriculum as the learning agenda, instruction as the means to communicate the learning agenda, and assessment as the way in which learners demonstrate understanding of the agenda. We adopt this framework to explore how these elements blend well in an authentic way in a middle school history classroom and review the benefits of doing so for middle school students with special needs.

Research in disciplinary literacy has suggests a need to transform the teaching of history beyond the use of textbooks (Shanahan & Shanahan, 2008). To accomplish this, teachers need to align their curriculum goals with the authentic teaching of history using primary and secondary sources (Nokes, 2013; Reisman, 2012a). Using historical sources provides students an authentic way of understanding how historians think and grapple with historical evidence. In addition, this document-based instruction fosters critical thinking and a deeper understanding of historical narratives (De La Paz & Felton, 2010; Ferretti, MacArthur, & Okolo, 2001; Reisman, 2012b). In spite of this positive development in disciplinary literacy research, the use of historical documents to develop historical thinking remains used in teaching of history and, based on our review of extant literature, is nonexistent in special education classrooms.

Not only have curriculum and instruction not kept pace with current research, assessment remains an area that needs revamping in many history classrooms. In typical middle school history classrooms, teachers gauge students' knowledge of historical events based on first-order thinking—who, what, where, when, why, and how questions—using a multiple-choice answer test format. This type of assessment privileges rote memorization and focuses more on summative historical knowledge, rather than creating a corroborative interpretation of past events based on multiple sources. Testing students' ability to recall or recognize a variety of historical concepts, names, dates, and events undermines students' ability to demonstrate their knowledge of historical understanding using "the full range of crucial forms of knowledge" (VanSledright, 2014, p. 8). These forms of knowledge, according to VanSledright (2014), are germane to how historians interrogate sources and find corroborative historical evidence.

The goal of this chapter is to present authentic CIA as it applies to the middle school history classroom. First, we lay out how historical thinking frames and constitutes an authentic social studies curriculum. Then, we explain how document-based lessons represent authentic instruction, and we discuss the integration of formative assessment within this pedagogical framework. Finally, we review the role and importance of authentic assessment in the classroom. Subsequently, we present the findings from a mixed methods action research study we conducted in which seventh grade students in self-contained special education classes were taught to "think like historians" within the framework of authentic curriculum and instruction using both formative and authentic assessment. As an exemplary lesson, we focus on a unit on the expansion of the early Islamic Empire. We used qualitative and quantitative data sources to understand the process of teaching and learning historical thinking. We conclude the chapter by exploring the implications of this study to research and practice.

HISTORICAL THINKING

Historical thinking requires the use of critical analysis skills while constructing a deep understanding of the past (Wineburg, 2001). Historians read primary and secondary documents with an eye for potential biases while seeking to understand the author's perspective (Nokes, 2013). They interrogate the source's believability and look for corroboration of facts before making a narrative interpretation of the past. They eschew an interpretation based on present ethos; instead, they contextualize historical events based on people's sociopolitical mores, cultural values, and behavioral norms at that time. Historical thinking, as a disciplinary literacy, aims to develop higher order thinking and depth of historical knowledge beyond the use of textbook and memorization of facts (Reisman, 2012a). Historical thinking connects students' classroom learning to the real work of historians. Historical thinking prepares students to become critical consumers of information and informed citizens in a democratic society (Claravall & Irey, 2018).

Authentic Curriculum

We ground our conceptualization of authentic curriculum using Caskey's (2002) argument that a curriculum engages students to think critically through fluid and dynamic real-world learning. Authentic curriculum integrates a disciplinary perspective of learning and connects classroom experiences to life outside school, making it more relevant and meaningful as students participate in a democratic way of life (Caskey, 2002). Historical thinking represents an authentic curriculum in social studies. As a curricular goal, it reflects Caskey's three essential elements of authentic curriculum—integrative, coherent, and democratic in nature.

The heart of historical thinking lies in how students understand sourcing. Reading textbooks represents an inauthentic instructional practice because it strips away the opportunity for students to engage in collecting evidence from primary and secondary sources. Historians identify and read the source of a document 98% of the time before reading the actual document (Wineburg, 1991). When reading a historical document, the skilled historian decodes the author's perspective and biases, which is vital to the overall understanding and interpretation of the historical events. Wineburg (1991) used the courtroom metaphor to describe how historians conduct their inquiry and look for evidence by interrogating different sources and the authors' conscious and unconscious motives. Historians look for discrepancies and corroboration of evidence from different sources before they create a narrative interpretation of the past (Barton, 2005). Teaching the sourcing heuristic encourages students to construct multiple historical views and promotes critical thinking. This authentic historical inquiry provides meaningful, rigorous, and challenging ways of thinking in social history classes.

Authentic Instruction

Authentic instruction involves real world tasks that allow students to engage actively in the learning process (Donovan, Bransford, & Pellegrino, 1999). As opposed to standard history instruction that features teacher-centered instruction and often leads to passive student learning, authentic instruction requires students to use higher-order critical thinking skills and be active participants in their own learning (Mims, 2003). Additionally, using authentic instruction guides students' understanding of learning through exploration and inquiry. Applied to the teaching of history, the students demonstrate understanding of historical events in varied perspectives and support it with evidence pulled from multiple sources.

History instruction, more than any other content area, has traditionally relied primarily on textbooks as the vehicle for content delivery; relying on textbooks can limit student-learning capacity. In contrast, document-based instruction provides an alternative to this type of instruction and allows for analysis of historical narratives rather than taking their veracity for granted (De La Paz & Felton, 2010; Ferretti et al., 2001; Reisman,

2012b). It requires that students be critical readers of documents, a skill that they can apply broadly. Document-based instruction teaches students to use corroborated and contextualized evidence from provided primary and secondary historical documents to construct a historical narrative of the past (Reisman, 2012b). This constitutes real-world learning in history by requiring that students analyze, synthesize, and question the documents just as historians would (Wineburg & Martin, 2009). Students enact the principles of historical thinking (e.g., sourcing, contextualization, corroboration) when analyzing and interpreting these documents.

Embedding formative assessment in instruction. Formative assessment is a process wherein teachers provide students feedback throughout an instructional sequence to gain information about students' developing understanding with the goal of improving learning outcomes (Furtak & Ruiz-Primo, 2008). Teacher feedback and the learning progression are two intricately entwined components of formative assessment that play a pivotal role in the development of student learning. Within the context of teaching, teachers provide feedback to correct faulty interpretation, provide corrective information, present alternative strategies, clarify concepts and procedures, and evaluate ideas (Hattie & Timperley, 2007). These kinds of feedback have the potential to support students' learning experiences, allowing a new level of understanding and a higher level of skill development. Through successive administration of teacher feedback, students' knowledge develops, and learning becomes progressive (Heritage, 2008). Students revise their prior understanding of the concept and accommodate teacher input to create more sophisticated ways of thinking.

In the context of teaching historical thinking, formative assessment suits well within document-based history instruction. Providing scaffolded explicit instruction and multiple opportunities to practice critical thinking and higher-order processing skills is inherently part of a formative assessment process (Pryor & Crossouard, 2008). Included in this scaffolded explicit instruction is the multiple feedback the teacher gives to the students to develop historical thinking skills. Providing multiple opportunities to practice these skills results in students' progressive learning of contextualization, sourcing, and corroboration. The multiple opportunities for feedback embedded in the learning progression lay the groundwork for students' writing performance as a culminating activity, demonstrating learning and constituting an authentic assessment.

Authentic Assessment

Assessment is a necessary part of any classroom, and yet, it is the least important aspect when compared to curriculum and instruction (Brenner & Pearson, 1998). Of course, the goal of instruction is student learning;

assessment is secondary to learning. However, good quality assessment provides feedback about what learning has occurred and thereby serves as a means by which to measure the appropriateness of the curriculum and the effectiveness of the instruction of that curriculum, making it a key part of the learning process. Nevertheless, not all assessments are equally created and many poorly designed assessments waste valuable learning time and fail to inform the learning process. It is critical, then, to use an assessment that is both effective and informative.

As it pertains to history classrooms, typical assessments have been multiple choice, content-oriented measures (VanSledright, 2014). This type of assessment aligns with the curriculum and instructional goals focused on rote memorization of dates and events in history. However, as previously reviewed, current research suggests this may not be the most efficacious way to teach students to be critical consumers of history, and thus may not be the best measure of learning. Authentic assessment, as an alternative means of assessment, seeks to assess students' ability to complete a task that mimics what an expert in the field would engage in. To make assessment meaningful and authentic in the context of a history classroom, it needs to engage students to use domain specific strategies such as evaluating the believability of the sources, making sense of the author's perspective, and deciding what constitutes historical evidence (VanSledright, 2014). In addition, assessment of historical knowledge should also include how students contextualize the significance of historical events using their background knowledge about people's way of thinking and behavior in that period (Wineburg, 2001). These are all skills a historian may engage in when conducting research. An assessment of this type is an effective measure of a student's knowledge and ability because it allows the student to demonstrate "deep understanding, higher-order thinking, and complex problem solving through the performance of exemplary tasks" (Koh, 2017, p. 1). Indeed, an authentic assessment fosters the relationship between assessment and learning and serves to inform the process, rather than being an activity that is separate and detracts from learning (Valencia, McGinley, & Pearson, 1990).

HISTORICAL THINKING IN AN INCLUSIVE CONTEXT

Historical thinking has been studied extensively in secondary classrooms (De La Paz & Felton, 2010; De La Paz, Ferretti, Wissinger, Yee, & MacArthur, 2012; De La Paz & Wissinger, 2017; Nokes, Dole, & Hacker, 2007; Reisman, 2012a; Wissinger & De La Paz, 2016). Although some of this research included middle school students with disabilities in general education classes (e.g., De La Paz et al., 2016; De La Paz, Morales, & Winston

2007; De La Paz & Wissinger, 2017; Wissinger & De La Paz, 2016), based on our extant review of literature and on our personal communication with De La Paz, studies with students with disabilities in self-contained special education classrooms are nonexistent. However, the results for students with individual education plans (IEPs) in general education classrooms showed evidence of the development of historical thinking in their argumentative writing. Students demonstrated an ability to contextualize an event, provide evidence from different sources, and recognize the author's perspective (De La Paz et al., 2016).

Adolescents with disabilities continue to face academic challenges in middle school due to the cognitive and literacy demands in social studies and history (Bulgren, Graner, & Deshler, 2013). Understanding historical documents requires higher order processing and problem-solving skills (Bulgren et al., 2013). These skills are necessary for students to process and organize information, make inferences, understand relationships, and distinguish main ideas from specific details, but they are underdeveloped for many students with disabilities (DiCecco & Gleason, 2002). Explicit scaffolded instruction and multiple opportunities to apply disciplinary literacy skills to tasks requiring sourcing, corroboration, and contextualization may lead to better understanding of historical documents in self-contained special education classrooms (Claravall & Irey, 2018).

HISTORICAL THINKING: REACHING ALL LEARNERS THROUGH AUTHENTIC CURRICULUM, INSTRUCTION, AND ASSESSMENT

This study was part of a 3-year design-based research project focusing on historical thinking instruction in middle school for students receiving special education services. The overall goal of this project was to develop students' understanding of the medieval world and early modern period using historical thinking as a curricular framework and document-based instruction as the pedagogical framework. We explored the integration of authentic instruction of history and formative assessment when analyzing historical documents and the use of authentic assessment to measure learning.

We adopted the excerpted primary and secondary documents created and published by the Stanford History Education Group's (SHEG) "Reading Like a Historian." Teachers and researchers can access these documents free on SHEG website (www.sheg.stanford.edu/rlh). Included in this curriculum are 42 lessons on world history representing different time periods from the development of Egyptian civilization to 19th century China. Each lesson contains PowerPoint slides, 3–5 documents, and a lesson plan. We selected 12 lessons that correspond to the scope of the California seventh grade content area of Medieval Age and Early Modern Period. We used excerpted documents, PowerPoint slides, and modified lesson plans to fit the needs of the students included in this research. In this chapter, we present a unit on the expansion of the early Islamic Empire. We chose this unit because of its relevance to the current international geopolitical issues.

Informed by our previous research (Claravall & Irey, 2018), we created a conceptual framework that reflects the integration of formative assessment in the implementation of document-based history instruction and conceives of it as an instructional approach. In Figure 2.1, we present a model that integrates multiple opportunities for teacher feedback as the learning progression unfolds. This learning progression shows students' development of historical thinking as evidenced by their engagement in and completion of the formative assessment tasks and culminates in their performance on the written response. Students receive feedback at three different points during the learning progression. As they assimilate this feedback into their own learning, they continue to learn to read multiple sources with a critical eye and gain deeper understanding of specific historical events.

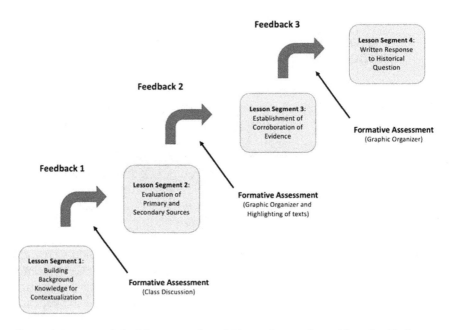

Figure 2.1.   A model of document-based history instruction with embedded formative assessment.

The instructional sequence consists of four distinct parts: (a) building background knowledge to develop contextualization of historical events, (b) evaluation of primary and secondary sources, (c) establishment of corroboration of evidence from different historical documents, and (d) written response to a historical question. In the first segment of the lesson, the teacher presents the SHEG PowerPoint slides to students, and then students read two different texts—one is from a commercially available history shorts and the other is an online platform for curated nonfiction articles available in varying levels of complexity using a Lexile score. The slide presentation and the reading of the two texts provide background knowledge that students can use to contextualize the historical event. The second segment of the lesson involves the evaluation of the primary and secondary sources. The teacher introduces students to at least three historical documents and provides explicit scaffolded instruction about how to evaluate the author's perspective, purpose in producing the document, and the overall reliability of the source. In the third segment of the lesson, students have the opportunity to read the documents three times. The first time is guided reading during which the teacher reads the text aloud, and the students follow along. The second time students engage in close reading, and the teacher provides explicit instruction about highlighting important ideas and writing annotations. Finally, the students read the text independently and look for corroborative evidence as they compare and contrast different documents and identify agreements and disparities between documents. The last segment of the lesson is the writing of an expository/argumentative essay responding to a historical question posted in the first segment of the lesson.

After each lesson segment, the teacher administered a formative assessment. The whole class discussion about the reading materials and the information presented in the slides is the first formative assessment. Shavelson et al. (2008) argued that assessment for learning falls along a continuum—from informal to formal. Classroom discussion is an example of informal assessment during which the teacher "elicits or notices student thinking, makes inferences, and then takes instructional action" (Furtak, 2012, p. 1184) and is used in this context to monitor and develop knowledge for contextualization of the historical event and documents. The second formative assessment occurs when the teacher provides feedback on students' graphic organizers and the highlighting they did on the texts. The teacher pays attention to whether a student highlighted the part of the text that reflects information about the author's background and how the students answered the question relevant to sourcing on the graphic organizer. The feedback given to students at this stage helps them further undergird their knowledge that historical sources are "pieces of evidence that must be interrogated and corroborated" (Reisman, 2012b,

p. 88) and prepares them for the next level of historical thinking. The teacher administers the final formative assessment after teaching explicit instruction on corroboration of evidence. The teacher then gives feedback on how the students interpreted the historical event based on presentation of corroborative evidence. These feedback opportunities support students' progression of learning toward being able to read critically historical documents and write a narrative interpretation of a historical event.

METHODOLOGY

This study is part of a multiyear design-based research project exploring the implementation of a historical thinking curriculum incorporating formative assessment and authentic assessment within document-based history instruction. The first author was the teacher of record during the time of the study. The second author, on the other hand, added rigor and validity to the study and tempered inherent biases associated with studying your own classroom.

We aimed to answer the following research questions:

1. How can formative assessment be embedded in document-based history instruction?
2. How can authentic assessment be used in a middle school special education history classroom to measure learning of the curricular goal?

Research Design

We present the results of the third phase of the study using a mixed-methods action research design—mixing qualitative and quantitative research methods into action research (Ivankova & Wingo, 2018). According to Ivankova (2015), incorporating mixed methods procedures into the action research produces rigorous and contextually relevant data necessary for effective intervention. For this mixed methods research, we collected, analyzed, and integrated both quantitative and qualitative data within an action research design. The pre- and posttest within subject data served as both a quantitative and qualitative data source, and the data collected during the selected exemplar historical thinking unit lesson on Islamic Empire was qualitative in nature. This study exemplifies action research because we link theory and practice while exploring the development of historical thinking for a group of special education students over the course of the academic school year (2017–18).

From a philosophical stance, conducting mixed-methods action research affords us the ability to combine the emic and the etic perspective. While we do not intend to generalize the findings of this study, we want to show evidence that students in special education have the capacity to access challenging curriculum and improve their learning through authentic instruction with embedded formative assessment. We argue that to affect change in students' historical thinking capacity, the teacher should have a deep understanding of historical thinking and content knowledge of history. Furthermore, the teacher needs to have the ability to integrate formative assessment effectively within history instruction.

Participants and Setting

Twelve seventh grade demographically diverse middle school students in two intact classrooms in a suburban area of Northern California participated in this study. Table 2.1 shows the demographic details of the students. We used fictional names to maintain anonymity of the students and confidentiality of the information presented. These students attended classes for specialized academic instruction in language arts and history. All students had an IEP, with specific academic goals for reading and writing. These students had the eligibility classification of learning disability, autism spectrum disorder, or other health impairment (a proxy term for students with attention deficit hyperactivity disorder in California). Based on students' performance in the Gate-MacGinitie Reading Comprehension Test, their average stanine score was 2.33 with an average Lexile reading level of 660. Using data from the same test, students' reading comprehension grade level ranged from Grades 2.0 to 12.5, with a median grade level performance of 3.8. Except for Laura, all students performed below their expected grade level in reading comprehension.

Data Sources

We collected both qualitative and quantitative data throughout the academic school year. For qualitative data, we collected artifacts students produced throughout the learning process for the Early Islamic Empire Unit. These include graphic organizers, a set of three excerpted documents from each student, highlighted reading materials from each student, and their written response to a historical question. We also included the first author's field notes and a selected audio recording of the lesson. The second author conducted an in-class observation two times and nine times via Skype.

Table 2.1.
Student Demographics

Student	Gender	Race	Disability
Adel	Female	White	Learning Disability
Arlyn	Female	Latina	Learning Disability
Benito	Male	Latino	Learning Disability
Danilo	Male	Latino	Other Health Impairment
David	Male	White	Learning Disability/Other Health Impairment
Emily	Female	White	Autism Spectrum Disorder
Juanito	Male	Latino	Learning Disability
Laura	Female	White	Learning Disability
Maria	Female	Latina	Learning Disability
Nora	Female	White	Learning Disability
Rachelle	Female	White	Learning Disability
Veronica	Female	Latino	Learning Disability

We also collected quantitative prior to and after implementing the entire historical thinking curriculum to assess individual growth in historical thinking. We administered a writing performance test measuring historical thinking as a pretest in August 2017 and the same test again in May 2018. Although there was potential for a practice effect, we used the same documents at pretest and posttest because using the same assessment mitigated the potential influence of topical knowledge affecting performance. Additionally, the testing periods were separated by a substantial time period, 9 months, and practice effect has been shown to be minimal for students with disabilities (Cirino et al., 2002), especially after a time period of that length. As observed, students did not mention seeing the assessment previously and did not appear to remember the documents or task.

To assess historical thinking, we administered a pre- and posttest. The students took an entire class period (60 minutes) to read a set of three excerpted documents about the spread of Christianity in the Roman world. While students were familiar with this topic as part of their sixth-grade world history curriculum, personal communication with the sixth-grade special education teacher who taught the same group of students the year previously, indicated they had not previously read historical documents for this time period and had not engaged in historical thinking practices, as defined within this study. We provided each student a highlighter and a pencil so he or she could highlight information and/or write annotations on the margins of each text. Students received no further instructions regarding highlighting of information and writing annotations. The next day, we administered an on-demand expository writing task based on the documents. The question students responded to was: *Why did the Roman Empire persecute Christians?* The students took a full 60-minute class period to complete this task. We allowed students to refer to the documents read the previous day while answering the prompt. All students completed this task in the allotted time.

Data Analysis

We developed a researcher-created rubric based on a historical reading strategies chart (Reisman, 2012b) to evaluate and score the writing task as an artifact of historical thinking. As such, the rubric reflected each of the key components of historical thinking: sourcing, contextualization, and corroboration (Wineburg, 2001). Students received a score that ranged from 0 (absence of the skill) to 4 (explicit demonstration of the skill) for each of the three components. All pretests and posttests were scored by both authors. If disagreement occurred, both researchers discussed the rationale for their original score, reevaluated the essay, and reached a final agreement rate of 100% for all scores.

RESULTS AND DISCUSSION

This section presents evidence of effective integration of authentic curriculum, instruction, and assessment in a middle school special education classroom. We argue that document-based history instruction serves as the vehicle to attain the larger curricular goal of developing historical thinking. Using qualitative data, we provide an example of how to embed formative assessment effectively, as an instructional approach, in the teaching of this skill. Furthermore, by integrating quantitative and qualitative data, we demonstrate the use of authentic assessment in a middle school special education history classroom to measure learning progress toward the curricular goal and mastery of the skills introduced during instruction.

Embedding Formative Assessment in Document-Based History Instruction

Reflecting on Furtak's (2012) study, we argue that learning progression and teacher feedback are important in the development of students' understanding of historical thinking when reading primary/secondary sources and writing an essay in response to a historical question. In the first segment of the lesson, the students' discussion on the expansion of the early caliphates (based on the PowerPoint slides) and Muhammad's influence of the Islamic Empire (based on the 398-word passage students read) built students' background knowledge about the beginning of the Islamic Empire. The teacher posed questions to stir the conversation and facilitated the interpretation of a political map of the Arabian Peninsula, which reflected the instructional dialogue (Duschl, 2003) that took place during the first formative assessment. The teacher listened and responded to students' thinking that led to the refinement of their understanding of the Islamic empire expansion. For example, when the first author asked the students about what kind of hypothesis they could make based on the medieval map presented in one of the slides, the students agreed that this was like the crusades. Then Rachelle, one of the students, suggested that the spread of the Islamic Empire started from where Muhammad was born. This was the beginning of the students' learning progression. They used background knowledge to understand the context for the formation of Islam.

The learning progression continued when students evaluated the trustworthiness of the three sources. Document A was written by a local Muslim historian; Document B was an excerpt from the Treaty of Tudmir; and Document C was written by a contemporary historian. The students had already learned the importance of evaluating sources from earlier units. In this case, the teacher's only role was to scaffold the reading of the three documents. Initially, the teacher read each document aloud consistently across the units, while the students followed along, to take the cognitive load off the students—thereby channeling their mental energy into the meaning making process of reading. The students had a second opportunity to read the documents independently while they highlighted important information on the texts. It is interesting to note that all the students highlighted the footnoted source in each document. Likewise, all students highlighted important information that aided them to evaluate the source's credibility. Table 2.2 shows four randomly selected students and their highlighted information from the documents. As students worked on their graphic organizer for sourcing, the teacher gave feedback to the group on using the highlighted information to anchor their responses in the graphic organizer. We selected three focal students to show how they responded to the questions related to sourcing and corroboration. These focal students belong to high, middle, and low performing students. We based our criterion for classifying high, middle, and low on students' performance in the posttest. Laura was high, Nora was middle, and David was low. Table 2.3 shows their respective answers to the sourcing questions. The students' responses indicate clearly that they understood the value of the author's credibility and the genre (i.e., type of document) for them to judge the trustworthiness of the source. However, it was not clear from the responses of focal students whether they understood how the author's purpose for writing the document could affect the trustworthiness of the source.

Table 2.2.
Information Students Highlighted on the Texts

Student	Highlighted Information From the Documents
Arlyn	*Muslim forces took control of Syria in 636 c.e. (current era) when they fought the Eastern Roman Empire; Muslim historian Ahmad al-Biladuri in 800s; signed in 713; Abd al-'Aziz; the Muslim forces invading Spain; Theodemir; Fred Donner is a historian at the University of Chicago; specializes in early Islam and Islamic expansion.*
Danilo	*Written by Muslim historian Ahmad al-Biladuri in the 800s c.e.; signed in 713 c.e. between 'Abd al-Aziz; Fred Donner is a historian at the University of Chicago who specializes in early Islam.*
Maria	*Written by Muslim historian Ahmad al-Biladuri; signed in 713 c.e.; between Abd al'-Aziz; Theodemir; historian at the University of Chicago; he challenges some of the common knowledge about early Islamic conquests.*
Nora	*Written by Muslim historian Ahmad al-Biladuri; signed in 713 c.e.; 'Abd al-Aziz; Theodemir; is a historian at the University of Chicago who specializes in early Islam; challenges some of the common knowledge about early Islamic conquests.*

Table 2.3.
Focal Students' Responses to Sourcing Questions

Document A: Who is al-Biladuri? Why do you think he wrote this document?

Do you think this document is a reliable source for determining how the caliphates expanded in the seventh and eighth centuries? Why or Why not?

Laura: (1) al-Biladuri was a Muslim historian. I think he wrote the document to tell the people about the war against the Muslims and Greeks. (2) Yes, this document is reliable because it was written by a Muslim historian, though on the other hand, it could be unreliable because it was written 164 years after the event happened.

Nora: (1) He is a Muslim historian, he wrote this document so that people know what had happened and how it was the bloodiest battle. (2) Yes this could be reliable because the document was made by a Muslim historian Ahmad al-Biladuri. On the other hand, the historian wrote in a different time zone. The story happened in 636 c.e. but he wrote it in 800s c.e.

David: (1) He was a historian live in the 800s c.e. to give information to his ancestor and kids. (2) Yes this document is a reliable source because it was written by a muslim historian and published 150 years later. So he got his information from maybe their elders. On the other hand, this document is not reliable because he was not at the event and it was published 164 years after the event.

(Table continues on next page)

Table 2.3.
Focal Students' Responses to Sourcing Questions (Continued)

Document B: What type of document is this? What is its purpose? Do you think this document is a reliable source for determining how the caliphates expanded in the seventh and eighth centuries? Why or Why not?	***Laura:*** (1) This document is a primary source and a treaty between Muslims and Southern Spain. The purpose of this treaty is to create peace between Muslims and Christians. (2) Yes, this document is reliable for determining how the caliphates expanded because this is a primary source and they would expand by creating peace treaties and having their allies fight with them to expand their territory. ***Nora:*** (1) Primary and a treaty. (2) Yes, it is a reliable source because it is exactly what happened and how it was written by an historian. ***David:*** (1) This document is a primary source and it is a treaty between Muslims and Christians southern Spain. The purpose of this treaty is to create peace between Muslims and Christians. (2) Yes this document is reliable source because, it was done in 713 c.e. and it is a primary source.
Document C: What type of document is this? What is its purpose? Do you think this document is a reliable source for determining how the caliphates expanded in the seventh and eighth centuries? Why or Why not?	***Laura:*** (1) This document is a secondary source. The purpose of this document is about how you get paid to embrace Islam. (2) I think this document is a reliable source for determining how the caliphates expanded in the seventh and eighty centuries because Fred Donner was a historian who specializes in early Islam and the Islamic expansion. ***Nora:*** (1) This document is a secondary document and its purpose is to tell the readers the rules in the Islamic Empire or what they would do. (2) Yes, because it shows how they would pay, and how the rules are so it was easier and many people came. The source is reliable too because it was written by an historian. ***David:*** (1) This document is a secondary source because it was published a long time after the event. The purpose of this document is to tell us how the Islamic empire expanded. (2) Yes I think this document is reliable because it cooperates with other document and it was written by a historian. The caliphates expand by having a ruler. Also they had to hide and they were forced to pay one dinner [dinar] every year or half if you were a slave.

Lesson segment three shows the spiraling up of ideas where previously learned concepts build on each other to understand historical thinking. Shavelson (2009) called this a cognition and instruction type of learning progression. In this lesson, students look for corroborative evidence from across the three documents for them to create a plausible hypothesis. They need to recognize the similarities and discrepancies between accounts when answering the question *"How is the account of Muslim expansion in Document C different from the accounts in Documents A and B?"* This is the most challenging element of historical thinking. Students need to see the subtext of the document as they reread it and unravel the author's perspective on the event (Wineburg, 1991). In spite of the teacher's scaffolded instruction on corroboration, all students exhibited difficulty responding to the question found on their graphic organizer. The students' responses were more descriptive than analytical. Table 2.4 shows the focal students' response to the corroboration question. Interestingly, these responses are representative of the answer from the rest of the students in this study.

Table 2.4.
Response to Corroboration Question

Corroboration Question	Focal Students' Response
How is the account of Muslim expansion in Document C different from the accounts in Documents A & B?	*Laura:* This account on the Muslim expansion was better in some ways because it had more of a perk to it then the other ways.
	Nora: Document C is just about payment, but Document A is about the war and how it was the bloodiest and most fiercest, and Document B is about the treaty upon the Greeks because the Muslim won. So Document C is different because it expanded differently by the payments.
	David: In this document it states that they gave gift and they had a social class and an easy/peaceful environment. In Document A it states that there was lot of war and many were slaughtered in the fighting. Finally in Document B they had prisoners and made harsh laws for the Muslims.

The final phase of the formative assessment involved the writing of the response to the historical question: *"How did the early Islamic Empire expand?"* To answer this question, one has to provide contextualization of the event (Lesson Segment 1), synthesize the information from different sources (Lesson Segment 2), and establish corroborative evidence from the sources (Lesson Segment 3). The linking of this learning progression and the teacher feedback students received in the different segments of the lesson constitute the enactment of formative assessment (Furtak, 2012). The students used their graphic organizers, the outline they created, and the three documents to complete this writing task. All the students, except one, in this study wrote a five-paragraph essay with a thesis statement in the first paragraph and a concluding paragraph. This was the fourth time that these students wrote an expository essay responding to a historical question. Previously, the teacher heavily scaffolded students' writing; the teacher provided input about how to write an essay of this nature. The gradual release of responsibility was applied since then, so students gradually increased their level of responsibility. This unit on the Islamic Empire was the first time the students wrote an essay with less support from the teacher.

Authentic Assessment of Historical Thinking

The writing assessment administered as a pretest/posttest in this study served as an authentic assessment aligned with both the curricular and instructional goals of this unit. The curricular goal was historical thinking, thus, this assessment measured that skill as opposed to simply surveying content knowledge of historical events. The method used to achieve this curricular goal was document-based instruction; the assessment was an application of this skill, which had been honed and scaffolded during the learning units. Additionally, this assessment constituted an authentic assessment because of the task itself and the scoring method. First, it was not a multiple-choice assessment focused on knowledge regurgitation and constrained by inherent limitation of that format but instead a writing task that allowed students to demonstrate historical thinking in a more open-ended manner that was student-directed. The scoring of the writing task focused on the skills associated with historical thinking rather than writing conventions and/or content knowledge. Thus, both the alignment of the assessment with the curriculum and instruction as well as the format and scoring make this an authentic measure of learning.

Students improved both quantitatively and qualitatively with regard to historical thinking as measured by the on-demand writing task. Focusing on the quantitative improvement, the difference between pretest (M = 0.92, SD = 0.52) and posttest (M = 3.67, SD = 1.67) composite scores using the rubric was statistically significant ($t(11)$ = 6.70, p < .001) and yielded a large effect size (Cohen's d = 2.22). Students' scores on the pretest ranged from 0–2, suggesting that students demonstrated minimal historical thinking prior to explicit instruction, and there was a lack of score diversity. However, this range increased to 1–7 on the posttest, demonstrating a wide developmental spectrum of students' historical thinking, as expected when learning a new skill.

Qualitatively, students also demonstrated improved historical thinking through their writing. It is helpful to break down historical thinking into the three skills assessed by the rubric: sourcing, contextualization, and corroboration when considering students' development. Sourcing, the recognition of the source of the document as well as the evaluation of that source, was not present in students' writing at pretest. However, all but two students mentioned sourcing at posttest. On her posttest Laura wrote, "I do not believe this document is trustworthy because Tacitus wrote this in 116 CE but the event of the great rome fire happened in 64 CE." Benito also improved from pretest to posttest and wrote, "Tacitus would have to over 50 years old (at the time of writing this document), and your memory is not the most reliable after that amount of time." Both of these responses demonstrate not only awareness of the source, but also an appraisal of that source, which represents critical thinking.

Contextualization, recognizing that documents are products of a particular point in time, is an important component of historical thinking. All but three students improved in this area from pretest to posttest and all students demonstrated at least a beginning awareness of contextualization on the posttest. On his pretest Benito implicitly explained the context of one of the documents, "Christians were often persecuted at the local level" but on his posttest he explicitly discussed the context of the document, "A roman historian named Tacitus who was born in 56 AD wrote this document during a time period when Christians were persecuted in large numbers," demonstrating a higher level of understanding of the role of context. On her pretest Rachelle wrote, "Romans killed and arrested many Christians because of their abominations," which provides a description of the context of the document but does not explicitly contextualize the document itself. However, she did do this on her posttest, "According to Document B, written by Tacitus in 116 CE, is an excerpt, a great fire destroyed Rome in 64 CE during the reign of the unpopular emperor Nero." This shows her awareness that a document is an artifact of a particular time, which may be different from the event itself, which is a higher-level analytical skill.

Corroboration, the ability to compare and contrast different accounts of the same event, was the final skill that the rubric assessed. Like sourcing, this skill was not present at pretest; four students did not demonstrate this skill at posttest, and no student scored at the highest level for this ability, suggesting it may be the most challenging skill assessed or the slowest to develop. Regardless, several students did exhibit growth in this ability. Emily demonstrated that she was thinking across the documents as opposed to considering them each singularly by writing, "In documents a, b, and c, they all talked about the how the Roman Empire had suffered the spreading of the Christians." As did Nora who wrote, "I think all of these documents can say why the Romans persecuted the Christians." Looking for consistencies and inconsistencies across documents is an aspect of historical thinking that informs the interpretation of a document's accuracy, so it is essential that students recognize that they can and should use documents to verify the accounts of other documents.

CONCLUSION

We reviewed the application of authentic curriculum, instruction, and assessment to a special education history classroom. Using the CIA model proposed by Gross (2002), we conceived of the curriculum, the learning agenda, as historical thinking. This represents a shift from the typical content/event-focused inauthentic curricular goals traditionally employed in history classrooms. We adopted this goal based on current research suggesting that history, as a content area, requires disciplinary literacy and as such, curricular goals should represent cognitive tasks that can be broadly applied for critical consumership of historical documents. To achieve this goal, we employed document-based instruction, which requires that students actively engage in critical appraisal of primary and secondary sources using historical thinking skills: sourcing, contextualization, and corroboration—rather than passively reading a textbook. Embedding formative assessment in historical thinking instruction served not only as a learning check, but also served simultaneously as an opportunity for tailored teaching response and clarification. Finally, we assessed learning of the curricular goal via mastery of the skills instructed upon via an on-demand writing task. This served as an authentic assessment because it aligned with the curricular goal and instruction; it required students to think critically and allowed them to demonstrate this ability in an open-ended manner.

The middle school time period continues to be a context that is less well researched than other developmental stages. However, the middle school years represent a distinctive developmental period, and educators must understand the unique needs of this population and incorporate this understanding in the classroom. In this chapter, we presented one way to address the needs of young adolescents: the thoughtful adoption of authentic CIA (see Figure 2.2). We demonstrated that authentic CIA is appropriate for *all* students, those served in a general education setting as well as those with special needs. Teachers can adopt authentic CIA across content areas, as we highlighted its application to history. Our hope is that educators and researchers alike will consider use of this model to meet the needs of middle school learners.

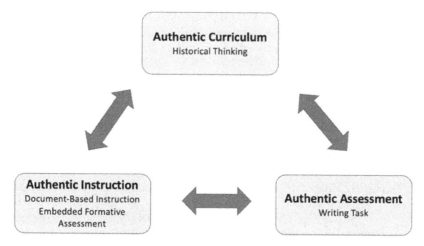

Figure 2.2.   Application of authentic CIA to a middle school history unit.

REFERENCES

Barton, K. C. (2005). Primary sources in history: Breaking through myths. *Phi Delta Kappan, 86*, 745–753.

Brenner, D., & Pearson, P. D. (1998). Authentic reading assessment in middle school classrooms. In K. Beers & B. Samuels (Eds.), *Into focus: Understanding and creating middle school readers* (pp. 281–312). Norwood, MA: Christopher-Gordon.

Bulgren, J. A., Graner, P. S., & Deshler, D. D. (2013). Literacy challenges and opportunities for students with learning disabilities in social studies and history. *Learning Disabilities Research and Practice, 28*, 17–27.

Caskey, M. M. (2002). Authentic curriculum: Strengthening middle level education. In V. A. Anfara, Jr., & S. L. Stacki (Eds.), *Middle school curriculum, instruction, and assessment* (pp. 103–117). Greenwich, CT: Information Age.

Cirino, P. T., Rashid, F. L., Sevcik, R. A., Lovett, M. W., Frijters, J. C., Wolf, M., & Morris, R. D. (2002). Psychometric stability of nationally normed and experimental decoding and related measures in children with reading disability. *Journal of Learning Disabilities, 35*, 526–539.

Claravall, E., & Irey, R. (2018, April). *Developing historical thinking in special education: A mixed methods study.* Paper presented at the annual meeting of the American Educational Research Association, New York City, NY.

De La Paz, S., & Felton, M. K. (2010). Reading and writing from multiple source document in history: Effects of strategy instruction with low to average high school writers. *Contemporary Educational Psychology, 35*, 174–192.

De La Paz, S., Ferretti, R., Wissinger, D., Yee, L., & MacArthur, C. (2012). Adolescents' disciplinary use of evidence, argumentative strategies, and organizational structure in writing about historical controversies. *Written Communication, 29*, 412–454.

De La Paz, S., Monte-Sano, C., Felton, M., Croninger, R., Jackson, C., & Piantedosi, K. W. (2016). A historical writing apprenticeship for adolescents: Integrating disciplinary learning with cognitive strategies. *Reading Research Quarterly, 52,* 31–52.

De La Paz, S., Morales, P., & Winston, P. M. (2007). Source interpretation: Teaching students with and without LD to read and write historically. *Journal of Learning Disabilities, 40,* 134–144.

De La Paz, S., & Wissinger, D. R. (2017). Improving the historical knowledge and writing of students with or at risk for LD. *Journal of Learning Disabilities, 50,* 658–671.

DiCecco, V., & Gleason, M. (2002). Using graphic organizers to attain relational knowledge from expository text. *Journal of Learning Disabilities, 35,* 306–331.

Donovan, M. S., Bransford, J. D., & Pellegrino, J. W. (Eds.). (1999). *How people learn: Bridging research and practice.* Washington, DC: National Academy Press.

Duschl, R. (2003). Assessment of inquiry. In J. M. Atkin & J. Coffey (Eds.), *Everyday assessment in the science classroom* (pp. 41–59). Arlington, VA: NSTA Press.

Ferretti, R., MacArthur, C., & Okolo, C. (2001). Teaching for historical understanding in inclusive classrooms. *Learning Disability Quarterly, 24,* 59–71.

Furtak, E. M. (2012). Linking a learning progression for natural selection to teachers' enactment of formative assessment. *Journal of Research in Science Teaching, 49,* 1181–1210.

Furtak, E. M., & Ruiz-Primo, M. A. (2008). Making students' thinking explicit in writing and discussion: An analysis of formative assessment prompts. *Science Education, 92,* 799–824.

Gross, S. J. (2002). Introduction: Middle-level curriculum, instruction, and assessment: Evolution or an innovation at risk? In V. A. Anfara, Jr. & S. L. Stacki (Eds.), *Middle school curriculum, instruction, and assessment* (pp. ix–xxxii). Greenwich, CT: Information Age.

Hattie, J., & Timperley, H. (2007). The power of feedback. *Review of Educational Research, 77,* 81–112.

Heritage, M. (2008). *Learning progressions: Supporting instruction and formative assessment.* Washington, DC: Council of Chief State School Officers.

Ivankova, N. V. (2015). *Mixed methods applications in action research: From methods to community action.* Thousand Oaks, CA: SAGE.

Ivankova, N., & Wingo, N. (2018). Applying mixed methods in action research: Methodological potentials and advantages. *American Behavioral Scientist, 62,* 978–997.

Koh, K. H. (2017). Authentic assessment. *Oxford research encyclopedia of education.* Retrieved from https://oxfordre.com/education/view/10.1093/acrefore/9780190264093.001.0001/acrefore-9780190264093-e-22 doi:10.1093/acrefore/9780190264093.013.22

Mims, C. (2003). Authentic learning: A practical introduction & guide for implementation. *Meridian: A Middle School Computer Technologies Journal, 6*(1), 1–3.

Nokes, J. D. (2013). *Building students' historical literacies: Learning to read and reason with historical texts and evidence.* New York, NY: Routledge.

Nokes, J. D., Dole, J. A., & Hacker, D. J. (2007). Teaching high school students to use heuristics while reading historical texts. *Journal of Educational Psychology, 99*, 492–504.

Pryor, J., & Crossouard, B. (2008). A socio-cultural theorisation of formative assessment. *Oxford Review of Education, 34*, 1–20.

Reisman, A. (2012a). 'The document-based lesson': Bringing disciplinary inquiry into high school history classrooms with adolescent struggling readers. *Journal of Curriculum Studies, 44*, 233–264.

Reisman, A. (2012b). Reading like a historian: A document-based history curriculum intervention in urban high schools. *Cognition and Instruction, 30*, 86–112.

Shanahan, T., & Shanahan C. (2008). Teaching disciplinary literacy to adolescents: Rethinking content-area literacy. *Harvard Educational Review, 78*, 40–59.

Shavelson, R. J. (2009). *Reflections on learning progressions.* Proceedings of the Learning Progressions in Science Conference. Iowa City, IA. Retrieved from http://education.msu.edu/projects/leaps/proceedings/Default.html

Shavelson, R. J., Young, D. B., Ayala, C. C., Brandon, P. R., Furtak, E. M., Ruiz-Primo, M., & Yin, Y. (2008). On the impact of curriculum-embedded formative assessment on learning: A collaboration between curriculum and assessment developers. *Applied Measurement in Education, 21*, 295–314.

Valencia, S. W., McGinley, W., & Pearson, P. D. (1990). *Assessing reading and writing: Building a more complete picture for middle school assessment* (Technical Report No. 500). Champaign, IL: Center for the Study of Reading, University of Illinois at Urbana-Champaign. Retrieved from https://www.ideals.illinois.edu/bitstream/handle/2142/18056/ctrstreadtechrepv01990i00500_opt.pdf?sequence

VanSledright, B. A. (2014). *Assessing historical thinking & understanding: Innovative designs.* New York, NY: Routledge.

Wineburg, S. (1991). On the reading of historical texts: Notes on the breach between school and academy. *American Educational Research Journal, 28*, 495–519.

Wineburg, S. (2001). *Historical thinking and other unnatural acts: Charting the future of teaching the past.* Philadelphia, PA: Temple University Press.

Wineburg, S., & Martin, D. (2009). Tampering with history: Adapting primary sources for struggling readers. *Social Education, 73*, 212–216.

Wissinger, D. R., & De La Paz, S. (2016). Effects of critical discussions on middle school students' written historical arguments. *Journal of Educational Psychology, 108*, 43–59.

CHAPTER 3

SCIENCE AT MY OWN PACE

The Impact of a Self -Directed Learning Environment on Eighth Grade Life Science Students

Gerald Ardito
Pace University

ABSTRACT

In this chapter, I describe a case study in which eighth grade biology students participated in a fully self-directed, autonomy-supportive learning environment. Despite research showing that these types of learning environments have demonstrated a positive relationship with academic performance and the development of self-regulatory skills in learners, they are rare in K–12 educational settings. In this science class, 19 eighth grade students were able to work through the course's units at their own pace, pursuing the content in ways that made sense to them, working with others as they chose, and determining when they were proficient in the course content. The findings demonstrated an increase in student academic performance and in the development and expression of self-regulatory behaviors, suggesting that this type of autonomy-supportive learning environment is productive and possible

Curriculum, Instruction, and Assessment:
Intersecting New Needs and New Approaches, pp. 55–77
Copyright © 2020 by Information Age Publishing

with young adolescent students. The chapter ends with a discussion of the implications for middle school level teaching and learning practices and some suggestions for further research.

I taught science in a middle school to seventh and eighth grade students for eight years. During that time, my teaching evolved from a primarily instructivist paradigm, in which teaching follows a top-down transmission model (Dron & Ostashewski, 2015). At first, I organized class time around lectures, students completed homework centered on textbook readings, and assessments of student learning were primarily traditional types of quizzes and tests. Within my first year or so of teaching, I came to understand that this structure focused primarily on the transmission of information as opposed to student engagement. I worked diligently and quickly to adopt more student-centered, social constructivist learning practices, especially inquiry-based learning and project-based learning (Rosen & Salomon, 2007; Smith, Sheppard, Johnson, & Johnson, 2005). I found my students to be both more engaged participating in this type of learning environment, along with demonstrating much more ownership over their learning (Clayton & Ardito, 2009).

Observing these types of student outcomes, I became curious about what seemed to be a logical extension of this type of student-centered pedagogy, namely, a fully self-directed learning environment. I spent the last two years in this eighth grade classroom designing and implementing such a learning environment. In this chapter, I describe this case study through the experiences of a cohort of eighth grade middle school students taking a high school level biology class, by asking the following research questions:

1.   How do eighth grade science students perform in a self-directed learning environment?
2.   In what ways does a self-directed learning environment shape the self-regulatory and collaborative behavior of eighth grade science students?

THEORETICAL FRAMEWORK

In this chapter, I describe the case study that investigated the impact of an autonomy-supportive, student-centered learning environment on the collaborative behavior and academic achievement of a group of eighth grade science students. Figure 3.1 depicts the theoretical framework for this chapter.

I ground the theoretical framework in the work of self-determination theory (SDT) and the relatively new learning theory of connectivism. SDT

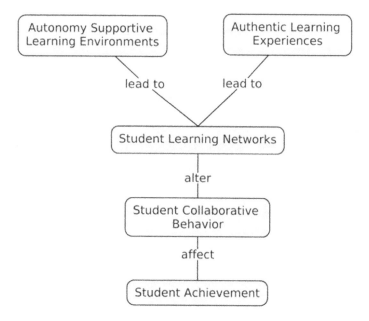

Figure 3.1.   Theoretical framework for study.

posits that humans have three fundamental human needs: (a) autonomy, a need to regulate one's experiences and actions; (b) competence, a need to feel effectiveness and mastery; and (c) relatedness, a need to feel being socially connected (Ryan & Deci, 2017). An extensive body of research demonstrates that when these needs are met, people at all ages in a variety of activities—working, maintaining their health, and participating in physical activity and sports, for example—experience fulfillment and are authentically, intrinsically motivated (Gagné & Deci, 2005; Ng et al., 2012; Ryan & Deci, 2007; Schewe, 2016).

Siemens (2005) and Downes (2007) developed connectivism, a learning theory, as a response to a perceived need to address the uniqueness of online learning environments. Siemens described connectivism as learning theory characterized as the "amplification of learning, knowledge and understanding through the extension of a personal network" (Siemens, 2005, p. 8).

Central to the theory of connectivism is the phenomenon of networks. Downes (2012) made a distinction between groups and networks as they pertain to learning environments and flows of information and knowledge. In his model, groups have the characteristics of unified (i.e., they have a narrow purpose), coordinated (i.e., they are organized), closed (i.e., boundaries exist between members and nonmembers), and distributed (i.e., knowledge flows from a central source to group members). In contrast, networks have the characteristics of diversity (i.e., they have multiple purposes), autonomy (i.e., members are considered autonomous), *openness* (i.e., all members are free to contribute), and connectivity (i.e., the flow of knowledge moves freely between participants).

This study explored the relationship between the experience of an autonomy-supportive and student-centered learning environment and the collaborative behavior of students. The fundamental premise was that this type of learning environment promotes the development of student collaboration, and that this increased student collaboration leads to a positive impact on student achievement.

LITERATURE REVIEW

Educational research into secondary science, technology, engineering, and mathematics (STEM) classrooms has focused on pedagogical practices and strategies that increase student engagement, motivation, and authentic experiences within the STEM content areas. This literature review discusses several related areas of research, including social constructivist pedagogical practices in secondary STEM classrooms, self-determination theory and learner motivation, and groups versus networks.

Social Constructivist Pedagogical Practices in Middle School STEM Classrooms

Much research has investigated the benefits of social constructivist pedagogies, such as project-based, problem-based, and inquiry-based learning, especially in STEM learning settings (Hay & Barab, 2001). Project-based learning has students engaged in learning activities that seek to deepen and apply key concepts for a particular content area or areas. Problem-based learning has students, typically working collaboratively, attempting to solve a real-world problem through the application of core content area skills. Inquiry-based learning is a set of strategies that provides opportunities for learners to explore key concepts and skills powerfully for themselves. Research into these pedagogies and strategies has demonstrated an increase in understanding, retention, engagement, and the development of critical thinking skills in middle school aged students as well as other adolescents (Hmelo-Silver, 2004; Krajcik et al., 1998; Rhodes, 2016; Smith et al., 2005).

Typically, these gains/benefits arise from increased engagement and motivation, increases in student self-regulation, and higher levels of authenticity in terms of the students' experiences of the STEM content areas (Albanese, 1993; Egberink, Gijlers, & Saab, 2015; Ge, Law, & Huang, 2016; Loftin, 2015). These findings are all consistent with Zimmerman's (1990) definition of self-regulatory strategies:

> Self-regulated learning strategies refer to actions and processes directed at acquisition of information or skills that involve agency, purpose, and instrumentality perceptions by learners. Undoubtedly, all learners use regulatory processes to some degree, but self-regulated learners are distinguished by (a) their awareness of strategic relations between regulatory processes or responses and learning outcomes and (b) their use of these strategies to achieve their academic goals. (p. 5)

Notably, much of this research on student-centered pedagogical strategies has focused on student collaboration. This work has demonstrated that students derived several real benefits by working in collaborative groups. These benefits include increased understanding of content knowledge (Rhodes, 2016; Shope & McComas, 2015), enhanced critical thinking and problem-solving skills (Duran & Dökme, 2016; Raes, Schellens, De Wever, & Benoit, 2016), and improved collaboration skills (Ardito, Mosley, & Scollins, 2014).

Self Determination Theory and Learner Motivation

Self-determination theory (SDT) research has found that students in autonomy-supportive learning environments benefited greatly from project-based learning (Liu, Wang, Tan, Koh, & Ee, 2009). Research into social constructivist practices in STEM classrooms identified learner motivation as a function of engagement. This research has interpreted student performance and retention in STEM areas as a function of an increase in engagement and therefore motivation in these types of learning environments. SDT understands the motivation of learners as something other than a function of engagement. As such, it provides another lens through which we can investigate these reported gains in student behavior and performance in social constructivist learning environments.

Several researchers have applied SDT to educational settings. SDT research into learning has described a positive relationship between high levels of autonomy and competence support in the learning environment and student engagement and learning (Black & Deci, 2000; Niemiec & Ryan, 2009; Reeve, 2012). These findings have also been demonstrated in a variety of content areas and for students at all levels of abilities and disabilities (Lee, Soojung, & Park, 2016; Rizzo & Taylor, 2016).

SDT, then, allows us to see the implementation of social constructive pedagogical strategies, such as problem-based, project-based, and inquiry-based learning, which researchers have studied extensively in secondary STEM classrooms, as cases of the positive effects of learning settings with high degrees of autonomy support. Learner motivation, engagement, and student performance become natural and organic responses to an autonomy-supportive learning environment.

Connectivism: Groups Versus Networks

The research into social-constructivist pedagogical practices and strategies discussed above has focused on collaborative work with students engaged in middle school and other secondary STEM classrooms. For this chapter, distinguishing between groups and networks in learning environments is important. The learning theory of connectivism makes this distinction.

Research into connectivism has focused primarily on the development and evolution of these learning networks within online settings, especially with massive open online courses (MOOCs), the first iterations of which Siemens (2005) and Downes (2007) pioneered, and their impact on higher education and professional development in workplaces (Bell, Mackness, & Funes, 2016; Conole, Galley, & Culver, 2010; Strong & Hutchins, 2009). While some research has been conducted that applied the concepts of connectivism to face-to-face and blended learning settings, little work has been done to apply them to K–12 classrooms (Drexler, 2010; Rahimi, van den Berg, & Veen, 2015; Roche-Smith, 2004; Smidt, Thornton, & Abhari, 2017).

Central to the unique features of connectivism as a learning theory is the nature of networks of different types. In the 1960s, Baran (1964) developed a typology of network architectures to determine which types of communication networks might best provide the most reliability in terms of the reliable and uninterrupted flow of information. Baran described three kinds of networks: centralized, decentralized, and distributed. Figure 3.2 depicts these networks. Baran characterized both the centralized and decentralized networks as vulnerable due to the ease with which damage to their central nodes would cause the breakdown of the entire network. On the other hand, Baran considered distributed networks to be the most robust. Their redundant, peer-to-peer structure acted as a powerful safeguard against the disruption of any one node.

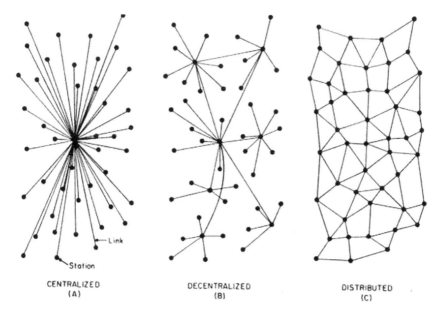

Source: Baran (1964).

Figure 3.2.   Baran network structures

One can read Baran's (1964) network diagrams as models of classroom practice. The *centralized network model* easily describes a teacher-centered or instructivist classroom, where the teacher is the primary source of knowledge and learning. Information in this type of learning environment moves in one direction from teacher to student. In this type of network, the removal of the central node (the teacher) would have a lasting negative impact on the network itself. The flow of knowledge and information would literally disappear. The *decentralized model* correlates to the normal structures in social constructivist classrooms, where students work in collaborative groups. In this scenario, the knowledge and information flow from the teacher to student groups, who then exhibit some further distribution of learning. This network, too, is highly dependent upon the central node (the teacher) and is clearly vulnerable to disruption. Much of the research into collaborative work in secondary STEM learning environments has focused on this type of group and network structures.

In this chapter, I am primarily concerned with the emergence, development, and evolution of Baran's (1964) *distributed network structure* within middle school STEM learning environments and its effects on student collaboration and self-regulation. Some prior research has studied the emergence of these types of distributed, peer-to-peer networks in middle school classrooms (Ardito, 2010). Additionally, other research has used the tools of social network analysis (SNA) to document student-to-student peer networks (Dafoulas & Shokri, 2016; Grunspan, Wiggins, & Goodreau, 2014). However, a formal and focused investigation into the emergence and evolution of student learning networks in autonomy supportive middle school STEM classrooms is an area ripe for research. As such, this chapter explores these rich areas.

METHODOLOGY

This study necessitated an active and responsive redesign of a course, its readings, assignments, projects, and assessments. Additionally, I served as both teacher and researcher. Therefore, I considered an action research design to be both appropriate and necessary. Action research is useful in cases where research seeks to improve the processes of teaching and learning (Berg, Lune, & Lune, 2004; Caskey, 2005). Given the context and circumstances of this study, a true experimental design was neither practical nor possible. Therefore, I used an *ex post facto* design, in which "the researcher identifies events that have already occurred or conditions that are already present and then collects data to investigate a possible relationship between these factors and subsequent characteristics or behaviors" (Leedy & Ormrod, 2005, p. 232).

Context and Participants

This study took place in an eighth grade classroom in a small suburban school district about 45 minutes north of a major U.S. city. According to the 2010 Census, the population of this community is 8,000 with a median annual income of $131,000.00 (U.S. Census Bureau, 2010). The district has three school buildings: one elementary school, one middle school, and one high school, with a combined enrollment of approximately 1,600 students in Grades K–12. The participants in this study were 19 eighth grade students enrolled in a life science course I taught. Although typically taught to high school students, the district required this life science course for all students. At the end of the course, students completed a state-mandated final exam. Successful completion of the exam resulted in students earning a high school science credit.

This life science class had 10 girls and 9 boys. Three students had special needs. One girl had an IEP that indicated processing delays. One boy had Down syndrome, who mainstreamed into this class with the support of a teacher's assistant. He was high functioning but needed support with course content, organization, and social skills. Another boy read and spoke

English at a third grade level. He received special education services and the same teacher's assistant supported him.

All 19 students were enrolled in this section of the life science course as a result of their mathematics class placement for the year. The middle school offered two options for mathematics courses for eighth grade students. One was comprised of a high school algebra curriculum. The second was a pre-algebra class. The school's administrators and mathematics instructors considered several factors in determining student math placements: student grade point average, scores on a placement exam, and teacher evaluation of the student's degree of organization and self-regulation. The 19 students in this study were in the pre-algebra course.

Importantly, this school district including the middle school building has a track record of encouraging and supporting student-centered learning practices. While these students had no prior experience in managing their own work and learning over the course of an entire school year, they had engaged frequently in inquiry-based and project-based learning throughout their academic careers.

Curricular (Re)design for Self-Directed Learning

This study involved redesigning a typical secondary level biology course into an entirely self-directed learning environment. The application of the *Understanding by Design* framework (Wiggins, McTighe, Kiernan, & Frost, 1998) resulted in the development of learning priorities through the development of essential questions and enduring understandings. The state-supplied curriculum was reviewed through these learning priorities and the course was divided into five units of study: (a) homeostasis, which included human body systems, cell biology, biochemistry, and feedback mechanisms; (b) evolution, which included natural selection, patterns of evolution, and population dynamics; (c) reproduction, which included asexual reproduction, sexual reproduction, male and female reproductive systems, and embryonic development; (d) genetics, which included inheritance, Mendelian genetics, molecular genetics, and bioengineering; and (e) ecology, which included food webs and chains, the flow of energy through a system, biomes, and human impact on the environment. Additionally, I employed practices and principles that supported the development of self-regulation, such as peer-, instructor-, and self-assessment (Gomes, 2014). Fundamentally, this curricular redesign sought to maximize the amount of autonomy students were able to experience by providing them with choices over pace (i.e., they could determine the right length of time with which to engage in each unit), place (i.e., they could choose from a variety of seating options [see Figure 3.3]), access (i.e., they could access course materials from school laptops or their own connected devices), and assessments (i.e., they could determine when they were ready to be assessed on their learning).

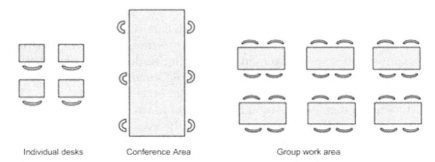

Individual desks   Conference Area   Group work area

Figure 3.3.   Physical arrangement of the classroom depicting types of seating choices.

A Technology-Enhanced Learning Environment

To support student access to the learning materials in the various units of study, I incorporated two technology tools into the course redesign. Moodle, a web-based learning management system, became the digital container for the learning pathways for each unit of study. Each of these units of study had the same structure: (a) an overview, which made explicit the big ideas and essential questions for the unit and provided resources and materials for the students, such as a study guide; (b) content chunks, which organized the various content, readings, activities, projects, and assessments in meaningful chunks (depending on the unit, these content chunks may or may not have been followed sequentially); and (c) a self-assessment, which allowed the students to determine whether they were ready to take the culminating test for the unit. Edmodo became the online communication tool that facilitated interactions between teachers and students and between students. For each unit, student Edmodo groups discussed and organized questions around specific content areas.

Classroom structures and supports. Throughout the school year, the course met six times per week for approximately 40-minute periods. During these sessions, I provided small group and individual instruction as needed or if students requested it as well as coaching and instruction on productivity and time management. Frequent and consistent feedback has been a key component of student-centered, self-directed learning environments (Schelfhout, Dochy, & Janssens, 2004; van Dinther, Dochy, Segers, & Braeken, 2014). The course redesign included several structures to operationalize this feedback. To support student learning, I established several processes and structures, including regular conferencing with students in small group and one-to-one settings as well as written and oral feedback on weekly student progress reports. The goal of these processes and structures was to maximize the opportunities to customize appropriate support for each student.

Data Collection and Analysis

In this study, I collected data on both academic achievement and student collaborative behavior. In this section, I describe the data collected and the methods I used for analyzing them.

Student academic achievement. I defined student academic achievement as a function of the difference in scores between a pretest, designed to predict success on the state-mandated final exam, and the actual student performance on the final exam.

The design of the pretest was consistent with the design of the actual final exam. The pretest used typical questions from previous final exams. The pretest and the final exam had a similar distribution of question types (multiple choice, short answer, and constructed response questions) as well as the distribution of content area topics. I analyzed student scores on both the pretest and final exam in terms of both raw scores and scoring bands. The state reported student data as a function of five scoring bands: (a) 95–100, (b) 85–94, (c) 75–84, (d) 65–74, and (e) less than 65. The state considered a score of 65 or above on the final exam to be passing. I used descriptive statistics to analyze these data and paired t-tests to determine the statistical significance of any differences.

Student collaborative behavior. For the purpose of this study, collaborative behavior refers to the ways that these students worked with other students to accomplish the work of the course. While some of the students in this class were friends or had other social relationships with one another, I focused specifically on collaborative behavior that directly related to academic tasks. I collected a rich set of data to document these collaborative relationships, including: (a) teacher field notes which documented student collaborative behaviors and changes to group structures over time; (b) user data from the digital systems (Moodle and Edmodo), which documented student communications with one another as well as individual and collective progress through the units of study; and (c) fieldnotes kept on the frequent and informal discussions with students regarding their participation in this autonomy and competence supportive learning environment.

I used the data from the field notes and user systems to document the shapes and direction of the student collaborative behavior. This study made use of social network analysis (SNA) to model and visualize these student learning relationships. SNA is a tool that allows researchers to visualize connections between people, and researchers have implemented its strategies in a variety of settings (Borgatti, Mehra, Brass, & Labianca, 2009; Granovetter, 1983). SNA has been primarily used in online learning environments and has only rarely been used in face-to-face and K–12 educational settings (Grunspan et al., 2014). For this study, the SNA tool SocNetV was used to generate social graphs (Kalamaras, n.d.). Given these findings, as well as the focus on the influence students had on the learning of one another, I used a Fruchterman and Reingold (1991) forced-directed placement analysis.

Limitations

The research described in this chapter certainly allowed me to collect very rich, longitudinal data through working with these students on a daily basis for an entire school year. However, the relatively small sample of students and the quasi-experimental methodology that I employed provide limitations in being able to generalize the findings of this study. Further research is ongoing that seeks to extend and refine the findings from this study.

FINDINGS

This study was interested in the impact of an autonomy and competence supportive learning environment on the academic achievement and the collaborative behavior of eighth grade life science students. This section outlines the findings of the study.

Student Achievement

The major indicator of student achievement in this study was the difference between predicted versus actual scores on the state-mandated final exam. Three students of the 19 students enrolled in the class did not take the final exam. The first was a boy with Down syndrome. While he made great progress throughout the school year, he did not meet the eligibility requirements for the final exam. The second was a boy reading at a third grade level. He also failed to meet the eligibility requirements for the final exam. The third was a girl who transferred to this middle school from another district with content and literacy gaps that prevented her from being eligible for the final exam. Figure 3.4 displays these differences for the 16 students who did meet the eligibility requirements for the state-mandated final exam.

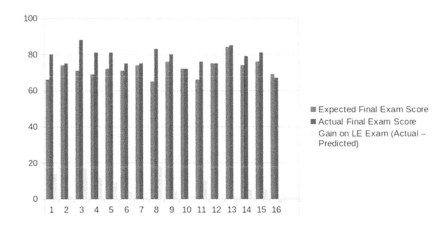

Figure 3.4.   Differences between predicted and actual final exam scores.

These data demonstrate that for the 16 students who took the final exam, 88% (*n* = 14) achieved gains on the final exam score over their predicted score. I conducted a paired-samples *t*-test to compare the predicted final exam score and the actual final exam score. There was a significant difference in the scores for level 1 (*M* = 72.13, *SD* = 4.75 and level 2 (*M* = 78.31, *SD* = 5.20) conditions; *t*(15) = -3.88, *p* = .001. The average score gain was 6.1 points, while the range of scores was between -2 and 17. These gains also reflected gender differences. The girls (students 1–9 in Figure 4) showed an average gain of 8.9 points, while the boys (students 10–16 in Figure 4) showed an average gain of 2.7 points.

I also investigated these differences by comparing differences between the predicted versus actual performance on the final exam in terms of scoring bands. As discussed earlier, the state segregates student scores into five possible scoring bands: (a) 95–100, (b) 85–94, (c) 75–84, (d) 65–74, and (e) < 65. Table 3.1 depicts these differences in terms of changes to the predicted versus actual scoring band levels.

The analysis found that 56% of students (*n* = 9) achieved a gain of at least one scoring band ("+" or "++" types of change), while the remaining 44% of students (*n* = 7) showed neither a gain nor a loss between predicted and actual final exam scoring bands ("="). These results also reflected gender differences. Sixty-seven percent of the girls (*n* = 6) had gains in at least one scoring band, as compared to only 43% of the boys (*n* = 3).

Table 3.1.
Differences Between Predicted and Actual Final Exam Performance Depicted as Scoring Bands

Type of Change	# of Students	% of Students
++	1	6%
+	8	55%
=	7	44%
–	0	0%
—	0	0%
Total	16	100%

Self-Regulatory Behaviors and Collaborative Behavior

Perhaps the most surprising finding in this study was that each of the students in this course completed all the readings, laboratory activities, projects, and related assessments for each of the five units comprising the course. It is noteworthy that they did so without any prior experience in managing their work and learning for an entire school year, as this learning environment required of them. These students were able to navigate and manage the learning paths outlined in Moodle, as well as organize their time, work, and collaborative activities in ways that exceeded previous levels of self-regulation.

I also noted important changes in the ways that students organized themselves to work and collaborate. I made extensive field notes of student collaborative behavior. These observations showed the students transitioning from being passive participants in the course to active drivers of their own work and learning. The types of questions the students posed typified this transition. In the beginning of the school year, students required significant reassurances about assignments, projects, schedules, and so on. By the third quarter, they were asking more pointed questions in order to create schedules and plans for themselves. As the course developed, these students were far more autonomous and productive in their work than they were in the beginning of the school year.

I combined the data from field notes of student collaboration with user data from Moodle and Edmodo to document the types and evolution of student collaborative behaviors throughout the course. Social network analysis enabled me to create sociograms that served to visualize student collaboration. Figure 3.5 depicts this behavior from the first three weeks of the course. As can be observed, students organized themselves into the dyads and triads typically supported by teachers during group work of various kinds, along with one student working alone by choice. Note that the figure includes students who took the course but were not eligible to take the final exam as discussed earlier.

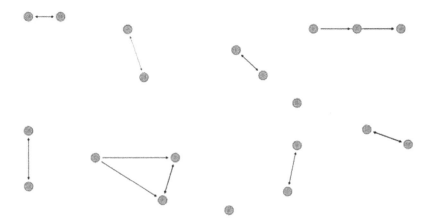

Figure 3.5.   Student groupings at week 3 of the course.

Figure 3.6 depicts student collaborative behaviors in the 35th week of the course. The dyads and triads initially depicted in Figure 3.5 have evolved into more elaborate, networked relationships. In their initial groupings, students essentially worked in parallel, with each group member doing the same work as their partner(s) at the same time, and with little observable synergistic effect. These groupings likely helped provide confidence to their members, but little else. However, in these later networks, the various nodes (students) in a network exhibited interconnected behaviors, such as the ability to serve as a vehicle for distributing a contagion. For example, late in the school year (about six weeks before the final exam) students from one group realized that they could work on multiple units simultaneously, instead of strictly completing them in sequence. This behavior became "contagious" and "infected" other groups, until 12 students (60%) ended up also working on units simultaneously about 12 weeks before the end of the school year. This type of behavior suggests the development of a distributed network from what had been a group (or set of groups). I observed no gender differences in the emergence and development of these student-learning networks.

Portraits of Student Networks

Additionally, certain students (nodes in the network) had larger influence than others did, as is often seen in social network analysis (Borgatti, Mehra,

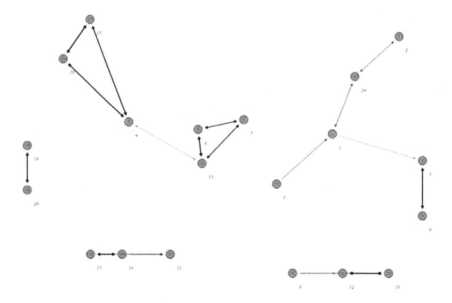

Figure 3.6. Student groupings at week 35 of the course.

Brass, & Labianca, 2009). Figure 3.7 isolates two clusters of students (nodes) from Figure 3.6. The cluster on the left was comprised of all girls; the cluster on the right was comprised of all boys.

The cluster on the left represents two sets of three girls. Within each of these triads, the members worked together; only rarely, did the larger group of six collaborate. However, two students (#4 and #13) talked often and their connection, in which they provided additional academic support to one another, ended up linking their groups in ways that demonstrated networking behavior, as discussed earlier. The cluster on the right represents six boys who worked together in a much looser configuration. At times, they operated as two sets (one of four boys, the other of two), and at other times, they reconfigured themselves as needed. As with the girls, these various configurations provided academic support for these students, and their ability to form and reform their working patterns was indicative of the high level of autonomy support available in this learning environment.

Figure 3.8 represents another cluster of two students from Figure 3.5. This figure represents two boys who worked together throughout the course. Frank (pseudonyms used throughout), a boy with Down syndrome, was high functioning enough to be able to spend most of his school day mainstreamed into eighth grade courses with the help of a teaching assistant. This learning environment permitted the development of a curriculum just

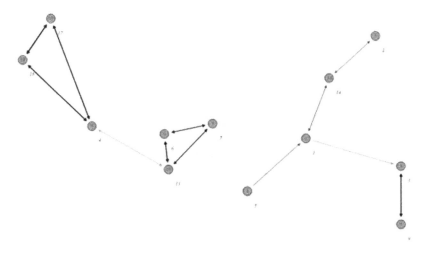

Figure 3.7.   Two clusters of students from week 35 of the course.

for Frank, in which he would focus on two of the course units—*homeostasis* and *ecology*. The course structure allowed him to both move at his own pace and receive individualized instruction from me. Frank's partner, Otto, a native Spanish speaker, was an English language learner and was only able to read at a second or third grade level in both Spanish and English. Otto followed the same curriculum as Frank; he was also able to move at his own pace and received individualized instruction. Otto and Frank shared a teaching assistant.

Figure 3.8.   Pair of students from week 35 of the course.

Despite their academic, linguistic, and intellectual limitations, their collaboration behavior went beyond a pairing based on organizational need. In fact, as was seen in other groupings in this course, Frank exhibited influence in this pairing. The high degree of autonomy support allowed Frank to be successful in a setting where he might not have been, which allowed him to assume a leadership role with Otto, frequently nudging and cajoling Otto to do his work, to try new things, to work harder.

DISCUSSION AND CONCLUSION

Research has raised concerns about the developmental appropriateness of self-directed learning environments for adolescents (Porter, McMaken, Hwang, & Yang, 2011). Nevertheless, the middle school students in this study were able to be successful in this type of self-directed learning environment. Most of them had prior experience with project-based work, but their teachers had closely managed that work. This was the first time that any of these students were required to manage their own time, work, and work products for an entire school year. Each of these students was able to complete the required work successfully in the time allotted. Each was able to demonstrate successfully their proficiency in the core concepts of each unit of instruction. Each was able to collaborate effectively with others in realizing learning and behavioral objectives. These results all support the hypothesis that this type of autonomy and competence supportive learning environment can be effective at increasing the development of self-regulatory skills and academic performance in eighth grade students. These findings are consistent with earlier research on middle school classroom climate (Duchesne, Ratelle, & Roy, 2012); however, the emergence and evolution of student learning networks is unique.

Additionally, this study found gender differences in student performance on the state-mandated final exam. The girls demonstrated a larger effect in terms of both a gain of points between their predicted and actual scores on this exam. They also showed a greater effect on the increase between these two scores in terms of grading bands. I believe that these gains are associated with the girls' ability to form larger and more robust learning networks than their male peers. These findings are consistent with other research into gender differences between middle school students in terms of collaboration strategies (Barton, Tan, & Rivet, 2008; Barton et al., 2013). Importantly, these prior studies have not highlighted these gender differences in the emergence and evolution of student learning networks. Given the size of the study sample, such conclusions are limited and require further research.

This study also provides evidence that this type of self-directed learning environment can be particularly effective for struggling students. As mentioned above, the eighth graders were in this class based on their placement in a pre-algebra mathematics class. A key component of the placement criteria for that class was their low degree of organization and self-regulation. This criterion serves as a baseline for their development of the various skills required for them to succeed in this self-directed life science class. Despite these recognized deficits, in this learning environment these middle school students were successful academically, passing a state-mandated final exam and achieving gains over their predicted scores on that exam. Additionally, these students were successful at forming productive collaborative relationships with their peers.

Perhaps the most interesting finding is the emergence and evolution of what I term student-learning networks. Student groups, in general, evolved from the dyads and triads typically seen in classroom group work into larger and more robust student networks. For this case study, I consider the presence of these networks (see Figure 3.6), the contagion-like behavior exhibited in terms of sharing knowledge about lab activities, and the simultaneous engagement in multiple units to be evidence of the emergence of distributed networks, as opposed to the workings of groups (Downes, 2012). These outcomes have promise in terms of investigating the implications of connectivist learning theory on student performance and self-regulation in K–12 students, as well as suggesting innovations in teacher practice. While much research has addressed the factors shaping academic achievement and student collaboration, these findings have broad implications for the development of middle school teachers in terms of designing autonomy and competence supportive learning environments. Some of this work is currently underway.

REFERENCES

Albanese, M. A. (1993). Problem-based learning: A review of literature on its outcomes and implementation issues. *Academic Medicine, 68*(1), 52–81.

Ardito, G. P. (2010). *The shape of disruption: XO laptops in the fifth grade classroom* [Unpublished doctoral dissertation]. Pace University, New York, NY.

Ardito, G., Mosley, P., & Scollins, L. (2014). We, robot: Using robotics to promote collaborative and mathematics learning in a middle school classroom. *Middle Grades Research Journal, 9*(3), 73–88.

Baran, P. (1964). On distributed communications networks. *IEEE Transactions on Communications Systems, 12*(1), 1–9.

Barton, A. C., Tan, E., & Rivet, A. (2008). Creating hybrid spaces for engaging school science among urban middle school girls. *American Educational Research Journal, 45*(1), 68–103. doi.org/10.3102/0002831207308641

Barton, A. C., Kang, H., Tan, E., O'Neill, T. B., Bautista-Guerra, J., & Brecklin, C. (2013). Crafting a future in science: Tracing middle school girls' identity work over time and space. *American Educational Research Journal, 50*(1), 37–75. doi.org/10.3102/0002831212458142

Bell, F., Mackness, J., & Funes, M. (2016). Participant association and emergent curriculum in a MOOC: Can the community be the curriculum? *Research in Learning Technology, 24*, 1–19. doi.org/10.3402/rlt.v24.29927

Berg, B. L., Lune, H., & Lune, H. (2004). *Qualitative research methods for the social sciences* (5th ed.). Boston, MA: Pearson.

Black, A. E., & Deci, E. L. (2000). The effects of instructors' autonomy support and students' autonomous motivation on learning organic chemistry: A self-determination theory perspective. *Science Education, 84*, 740–756.

Borgatti, S. P., Mehra, A., Brass, D. J., & Labianca, G. (2009). Network analysis in the social sciences. *Science, 323*, 892–895.

Caskey, M. M. (Ed.). (2005). *Making a difference: Action research in middle level education.* Greenwich, CT: Information Age.

Clayton, C. D., & Ardito, G. (2009). Teaching for ownership in the middle school science classroom: Towards practical inquiry in an age of accountability. *Middle Grades Research Journal, 4*(4), 53–79.

Conole, G., Galley, R., & Culver, J. (2010). Frameworks for understanding the nature of interactions, networking, and community in a social networking site for academic practice. *The International Review of Research in Open and Distributed Learning, 12*(3), 119–138.

Dafoulas, G., & Shokri, A. (2016). Investigating the educational value of social learning networks: a quantitative analysis. *Interactive Technology and Smart Education, 13*, 305–322.

Downes, S. (2007, February 3). *What connectivism is* [Blog post]. Retrieved from http://halfanhour.blogspot.com/2007/02/what-connectivism-is.html

Downes, S. (2012). *Connectivism and connective knowledge: Essays on meaning and learning networks.* Retrieved from https://www.downes.ca/cgi-bin/page.cgi?post=58207

Duchesne, S., Ratelle, C. F., & Roy, A. (2012). Worries about middle school transition and subsequent adjustment: The moderating role of classroom goal structure. *The Journal of Early Adolescence, 32*(5), 681–710. doi.org/10.1177/0272431611419506

Drexler, W. (2010). The networked student model for construction of personal learning environments: Balancing teacher control and student autonomy. *Australasian Journal of Educational Technology, 26*, 369–385.

Dron, J., & Ostashewski, N. (2015). Seeking connectivist freedom and instructivist safety in a MOOC. *Educación XXI, 18*(2), 51–76.

Duran, M., & Dökme, İ. (2016). The effect of the inquiry-based learning approach on student's critical-thinking skills. *Eurasia Journal of Mathematics, Science & Technology Education, 12*, 2887–2908.

Egberink, A., Gijlers, H., & Saab, N. (2015, June). *The effect of task and collaboration support on learning processes and learning results in a CSCL environment.* Paper presented at the 11ᵗʰ International Conference on Computer-Supported Collaborative Learning, Gothenburg, Sweden.

Fruchterman, T. M. J., & Reingold, E. M. (1991). Graph drawing by force-directed placement. *Software: Practice and Experience, 21*, 1129–1164.

Gagné, M., & Deci, E. L. (2005). Self-determination theory and work motivation. *Journal of Organizational Behavior, 26*, 331–362.

Ge, X., Law, V., & Huang, K. (2016). Detangling the interrelationships between self-regulation and ill-structured problem solving in problem-based learning. *Interdisciplinary Journal of Problem-Based Learning, 10*(2). doi.org/10.7771/1541-5015.1622

Gomes, G. (2014). *Blended learning, student self-efficacy and faculty an interpretative phenomenological analysis* (Unpublished doctoral dissertation). Northeastern University, Boston, MA.

Granovetter, M. (1983). The strength of weak ties: A network theory revisited. *Sociological Theory, 1*(1983), 201–233.

Grunspan, D. Z., Wiggins, B. L., & Goodreau, S. M. (2014). Understanding classrooms through social network analysis: A primer for social network analysis in education research. *CBE-Life Sciences Education, 13*(2), 167–178.

Hay, K. E., & Barab, S. A. (2001). Constructivism in practice: A comparison and contrast of apprenticeship and constructionist learning environments. *Journal of the Learning Sciences, 10*, 281–322.

Hmelo-Silver, C. E. (2004). Problem-based learning: What and how do students learn? *Educational Psychology Review, 16*(3), 235–266.

Kalamaras, D. (n.d.). *Social network visualizer* (SocNetV). Retrieved from http://socnetv.sourceforge.net

Krajcik, J., Blumenfeld, P. C., Marx, R. W., Bass, K. M., Fredricks, J., & Soloway, E. (1998). Inquiry in project-based science classrooms: Initial attempts by middle school students. *Journal of the Learning Sciences, 7*, 313–350.

Lee, O., Soojung, C., & Park, E.-Y. (2016). Meta-analysis of the effects of self-determination for individuals with disabilities. *Transylvanian Review, 24*(10). Retrieved from http://transylvanianreviewjournal.org/index.php/TR/article/view/117

Leedy, P. D., & Ormrod, J. E. (2005). *Practical research* (8th ed.). New York, NY: Pearson.

Liu, W. C., Wang, C. K. J., Tan, O. S., Koh, C., & Ee, J. (2009). A self-determination approach to understanding students' motivation in project work. *Learning and Individual Differences, 19*(1), 139–145.

Loftin, C. (2015). *Evaluating self-efficacy after a team-based learning activity.* Retrieved from http://gradworks.umi.com/37/02/3702681.html

Ng, J. Y. Y., Ntoumanis, N., Thøgersen-Ntoumani, C., Deci, E. L., Ryan, R. M., Duda, J. L., & Williams, G. C. (2012). Self-determination theory applied to health contexts: A meta-analysis. *Perspectives on Psychological Science, 7*, 325–340.

Niemiec, C. P., & Ryan, R. M. (2009). Autonomy, competence, and relatedness in the classroom. *School Field, 7*(2), 133–144.

Porter, A., McMaken, J., Hwang, J., & Yang, R. (2011). Assessing the common core standards: Opportunities for improving measures of instruction. *Educational Researcher, 40*(4), 186–188.

Raes, A., Schellens, T., De Wever, B., & Benoit, D. F. (2016). Promoting metacognitive regulation through collaborative problem solving on the web: When scripting does not work. *Computers in Human Behavior, 58*, 325–342.

Rahimi, E., van den Berg, J., & Veen, W. (2015). Facilitating student-driven constructing of learning environments using Web 2.0 personal learning environments. *Computers & Education, 81*, 235–246.

Reeve, J. (2012). A self-determination theory perspective on student engagement. In S. L. Christenson, A. L. Reschly, & C. Wylie (Eds.), *Handbook of research on student engagement* (pp. 149–172). New York, NY: Springer.

Rhodes, A. (2016). *Effects of constructivist approach in science* [Master's thesis]. California State University, Northridge, CA.

Rizzo, K. L., & Taylor, J. C. (2016). Effects of inquiry-based instruction on science achievement for students with disabilities: An analysis of the literature. *Journal of Science Education for Students with Disabilities, 19*(1), 1–16.

Roche-Smith, J. R. (2004). *Multiple literacies, new pedagogy: Emerging notions of oneself and others in a digital storytelling after-school program for middle school students* [Doctoral dissertation]. (Order No. 3165541). Available from ProQuest Dissertations & Theses Global. (305212727).

Rosen, Y., & Salomon, G. (2007). The differential learning achievements of constructivist technology-intensive learning environments as compared with traditional ones: A meta-analysis. *Journal of Educational Computing Research, 36*(1), 1–14.

Ryan, R. M., & Deci, E. L. (2007). Active human nature: Self-determination theory and the promotion and maintenance of sport, exercise, and health. In M. S. Hagger & N. L. D. Chatzisarantis (Eds.), *Intrinsic motivation and self-determination in exercise and sport* (pp. 1–19). Champaign, IL: Human Kinetics.

Ryan, R. M., & Deci, E. L. (2017). *Self-determination theory: Basic psychological needs in motivation, development, and wellness.* New York, NY: Guilford Press.

Schelfhout, W., Dochy, F., & Janssens, S. (2004). The use of self, peer and teacher assessment as a feedback system in a learning environment aimed at fostering skills of cooperation in an entrepreneurial context. *Assessment & Evaluation in Higher Education, 29*(2), 177–201.

Schewe, A. (2016). *Making student engagement visible: Using self-determination theory to examine how two social studies teachers support students' needs for autonomy, competence, and relatedness*(Doctoral dissertation). Georgia State University, Atlanta, GA.

Shope, R. E., & McComas, W. F. (2015). Modeling scientific inquiry to guide students in the practices of science: The ED3U teaching model of conceptual change in action. In P. Blessinger & J. M. Carfora (Eds.), *Inquiry-based learning for science, technology, engineering, and math (stem) programs: A conceptual and practical resource for educators* (Vol. 4, pp. 12–217). Bingley, England: Emerald.

Siemens, G. (2005). Connectivism: A learning theory for the digital age. *International Journal of Instructional Technology and Distance Learning, 2*(1), 3–10.

Smidt, H., Thornton, M., & Abhari, K. (2017). The future of social learning: A novel approach to connectivism. In *Proceedings of the 50th Hawaii International Conference on System Sciences* (pp. 2116–2125). Waikoloa Village, HI.

Smith, K. A., Sheppard, S. D., Johnson, D. W., & Johnson, R. T. (2005). Pedagogies of engagement: Classroom based practices. *Journal of Engineering Education, 94*(1), 87–101.

Strong, K., & Hutchins, H. M. (2009). Connectivism: A theory for learning in a world of growing complexity. *Impact: Journal of Applied Research in Workplace E-Learning, 1*(1), 53–67.

U.S. Census Bureau. (2010). *QuickFacts: Croton-on-Hudson village, New York.* Retrieved from https://www.census.gov/quickfacts/crotononhudsonvillagenewyork

van Dinther, M., Dochy, F., Segers, M., & Braeken, J. (2014). Student perceptions of assessment and student self-efficacy in competence-based education. *Educational Studies, 40*(3), 1–22.

Wiggins, G. P., McTighe, J., Kiernan, L. J., & Frost, F. (1998). *Understanding by design.* Alexandria, VA: Association for Supervision and Curriculum Development.

Zimmerman, B. J. (1990). Self-regulated learning and academic achievement: An overview. *Educational Psychologist, 25*(1), 3–17.

CHAPTER 4

"THE ROUGH WRITERZ"

Young Adolescent Boys Exploring, Constructing, and Recreating Racial Identities in an After School Program

Theresa McGinnis
Hofstra University

Andrea Garcia
Literacy Consultant

ABSTRACT

The literacy performances of adolescent males of color have been a central theme of current educational debates. Much of these debates centered on perceived deficits in reading comprehension, leaving out discussions of the youths' literacy strengths and writing practices. This chapter describes a young men's after school writing program, as a space where middle school Black students were supported in their development of 21st century literacies through a digital writing workshop. In this chapter, we consider the role of literacy and digital practices in the young men's negotiations of racial, ethnic, and cultural identity constructions and explorations. This research

Curriculum, Instruction, and Assessment:
Intersecting New Needs and New Approaches, pp. 79–98
Copyright © 2020 by Information Age Publishing

contributes to how middle level educational contexts can support youth in discovering the power of writing.

Miking, a young African American boy, wrote, "As my teacher wrote on the board, I stared the clock down." His digital story, "A Baller's Dream," about a boy bored in school and waiting for the bell to ring so he could go outside and play basketball, was his project for the Young Men's Writing Project. Renamed by the youth participants as the "The Rough Writerz," the project was an out-of-school-time program that ran from 5:00 p.m. to 7:00 p.m. for local middle school young adolescent males. Interestingly, while he wrote a story about a boy wanting the school day to end, he said to us, "I wish we could stay here till eight." Miking was deeply engaged in his project and wanted to continue searching for the right images and revising each line of his story to make it clearer. He was determined to create a multimodal text that expressed his emotions and perspectives on his daily life.

The literacy performance of young adolescent males of color has been a central theme of current educational debates. Much of these debates focused on perceived deficits or high incidences of under achievement, particularly in reading comprehension (Messner, 1990; Tatum, 2012). Tuck (2009) considered these debates as damage centered, because they support stereotypes of Black males as not literate. Kirkland (2013) added to this debate arguing that "perspectives on the literacy of Black males that are validated only by "achievement" tests also rely on a single story that fault Black males for not performing well in mainstream literacy settings" (p. 136). Tuck (2009), Kirkland (2013), and Kinloch, Burkhard, and Penn (2017) called for the re-imagination of how to view the literacy practices of young adolescent males of color, and to consider their own creative literacy uses in ways that allow for exploration of identity, race, ethnicity, and power structures. Kirkland also raised questions about what it means for Black adolescent youth to have entry into 21st century literacies.

In addition, with a focus on improving reading comprehension in schools, writing instruction has been neglected constraining opportunities for youth to discover the power of writing in their own lives (National Commission on Writing in America's Schools and Colleges, 2003; Tatum, 2012). More recently, standards-based writing instruction in middle schools has focused on formulaic writing models that take away students' voices and tend to limit the expression of their own diversity, knowledge, and the values they bring with them to school (Davis, 2018).

Out-of-school-time learning programs, such as the Young Men's Writing Program discussed in this chapter, are spaces for youth to engage in transformative literacy practices and identity work, because they have the ability to complement the curriculum of schools with alternative pathways to learning (Smith & Van Egeren, 2008). This chapter describes a young men's writing program, "The Rough Writerz," established by the authors of this chapter. The program, an after-school writing workshop, was an out-of-school space that supported culturally and linguistically diverse young men: young men from Caribbean American, African American, and Latino backgrounds who attended middle schools in the community of this northeastern university. While a suburban community of New York City, NY State Department of Education labeled these schools as "high needs" and the experiences of the students in school and their educational outcomes mimic that of their urban counterparts (Ascher & Branch-Smith, 2005). Our university-based program, therefore, was designed to support the young men's development of 21st century literacies through participation in a digital writing workshop, where they were introduced to multimodal composition and new technologies.

Two interrelated questions about the role of writing and digital composition in the lives of young adolescent males of color are addressed. Particularly for the purposes of this chapter, we highlight the ways the digital compositions of two of the young adolescent men, Miking and Jonathan, became sites for identity positioning and construction. First, we examine the complex multiple identifications for the youth as Caribbean American and African American young adolescent males, and the ways they expressed their voice and multiple loyalties through the layered meanings of their digital texts, including narratives of masculinity and cultural practices. Then, we explore how providing the youth composing opportunities through multimodal and multimedia platforms, allowed them to engage in the critical work of countering the positioning of others, positions which are often linked to power and ascribed through social structures such as race, class, and gender.

SOCIOCULTURAL PERSPECTIVES OF LITERACY AND IDENTITY

Thirty years ago, a movement occurred within the field of literacy studies. Scholars such as Heath (1983), Scribner and Cole (1981), and Street (1984) challenged previous autonomous models of literacy by suggesting that literacy is not merely the decontextualized ability to read and write, but also the ability to construct meaning socially. The researchers revealed that literacy is an ideological act and cannot be separated from social factors, culture, and a group's political and economic conditions. Street (1995) argued, "We need to move beyond teaching children technical features of language 'functions' and help them instead towards awareness of the socially and ideologically constructed nature of the specific forms we inhabit and use at given times" (p. 6). The sociocultural perspective of the New Literacy Studies (NLS) (Barton, 1994; Gee, 1996; Street, 1995) provided a framework for considering the relational aspects of youth's literacies and identities. Work within the NLS examined the ways literacy practices are situated in social, cultural, and political contexts, and the ways these practices and contexts play a role in identity construction (Mahiri & Sablo, 1996; McCarthey & Moje, 2002; Street, 2003).

Though initially NLS research privileged print-based texts, newer theories of visual and digital literacies recognize that there are new means for representation, expression, and communication (Carrington, 2005; Kress, 2003; Lankshear & Knobel, 2003). Within these new forms of literacies, the written word is not by any means the sole method of communication (Gee, 2003; Kress, 2003). Multimodality, the integration of words with visual images, sound, streamed video, and/or paralinguistic symbols, is an important aspect of 21st century literacies (Carrington, 2005; Hull & Nelson, 2005; Lankshear & Knobel, 2003). Drawing on the sociocultural perspectives of the NLS, we examine the intersections of the youth's literacies, identities, and cultures. In investigating the writing of the young men, we consider how the writing act is situated within social systems, shaped by social interactions, and tied to social identities (Schultz & Fecho, 2000). Digital literacies are also viewed not as isolated textual practices but linked with the local community, global social structures, and identities in which they are embedded and which they help to shape.

In addition, views of identity recognize that youth construct themselves in terms of multiple identities related to histories, culture, and social relations (Gee, 1996; Hall, 1997; Holland, Lachiccotte, Skinner, & Cain, 1998). According to The New London Group (2000), "People are simultaneously members of multiple lifeworlds, so their identities have multiple layers that are in complex relation to each other" (p. 17). These multiple identities include the negotiation of class, race, religion, ethnicity, and gender which can at times present contradictions and challenges for the youth. Twenty-first century literacies afford youth the spaces where multifaceted identities can be constructed, experienced, explored, and performed (Luke, 2003). Therefore, we draw from Hall's (1997) notion of multiple social identities in exploring how each of these youth "narrate the self" within their writing and digital compositions. People or youth use artifacts to develop figured aspects of their identities to create spaces of authoring (Holland et al., 1998). Therefore, their work on identity informs our discussion of how the youth in our research used images, symbols, music, and narratives to critically consider social positionings, their own and those of others, and which positionings have been historically linked to power and ascribed through social structures such as race, class, and gender.

LITERACY, WRITING, AND INSTRUCTION FOR
BLACK MIDDLE SCHOOL MALES

Young adolescents face higher demands on their literacy skills than they did as elementary school students. While it is difficult to separate reading from writing, as stated earlier, writing instruction has been constrained due to a focus on reading comprehension. The National Council of Teachers of English (NCTE) (2016) made clear that writing is indeed an important aspect of literacy learning for the 21st century. NCTE (2014) argued for writing process pedagogies where "students develop strategies to help them come to understand how their language and ideas can be used to communicate, influence, reflect, explain, participate, and create" (para. 1). Davis (2018) elaborated on this statement, explaining, "We need to give students opportunities to do all sorts of writing, benefit from good models, have choice in what they write, understand that writing is a process, use their own voices, and develop habits of mind about writing" (p. 1).

Nancie Atwell's (1987) seminal work, *In the Middle,* has been one of the most influential texts on writing instruction for middle school classrooms. In the text, she described her practice as a middle school teacher and her use of a reading/writing workshop. Central to her writing workshop approach was allowing students time to write, providing them with choice of topics and genres, seeking for their voices to be represented, and conferencing with the teacher for instruction and for publication. More recently, Atwell (1998) has stressed a more fluid, subtle balance of her as the teacher, one that continues to allow students' choices, but who also provides more instruction of what they need to do with their writing. She considered her approach as having greater interrelation of writer, teacher, and larger rhetorical context. She wrote:

> I have come on like gangbusters in terms of teaching and expecting a lot in writing and reading workshop. And instead of diminishing or silencing their voices, I think that raising my voice, in the company of students in the workshop, has had the effect of strengthening theirs. (p. 48)

Overall, her approach is to allow opportunities for all kinds of writing and to honor the students' ideas and voices.

Also important to writing instruction in schools is the recognition of how the changing technological landscape has produced new uses of writing and communication (Gee, 2003; Lankshear & Knobel, 2003). Lankshear and Knobel (2007) argued that using technology for conventional literacies such as looking up information on the internet, or writing essays using Microsoft Word rather than a pen and paper, is not the same as participating in the creation of new texts, distributing knowledge, and communicating through a wide range of modes. In their extensive review of the shifts in writing composition due to new technologies, Andrews and Smith (2011) found that composition of texts is more fluid allowing for the combination of modes and genres. Therefore, they argued, "The abilities of interpreting and designing visual and multimodal texts are critical as we move into an age where it is not only prevalent, but possible and expected for the layman to create such pieces" (p. 124).

Unfortunately, however, too often in schools, students' writing is measured through timed tasks for standardized exams. This process of high stakes testing leads to formulaic writing or writing assignments where youth are expected to demonstrate knowledge of the conventions of writing for school. These assignments are void of choice or student voice (Behizadeh, 2015; Brown, 2018; Haddix, 2018). For many Black youths in school, power is given to particular types of writing and other literacies that are school sanctioned and assessed (Haddix, 2018). For example, in their research with young adolescent Black youth, Mahiri and Sablo (1996) found that youth expressed discontent and frustration with writing in school or with the unauthentic nature of academic writing. Behizadeh (2015) explained that for Black youth formulaic writing suggests that school writing does not connect to their lives outside of school or to their interests. Similarly, Kirkland's (2013) work documenting the literate lives of Black youths showed a disconnect between their literacy practices outside of school and inside of school. This disconnect led to teachers' misunderstanding and often the youth themselves were faulted for not performing well in the mainstream literacy setting. Yet outside of school, the youth were engaged in producing cultural artifacts to make sense of life and to react against racism and social isolation (Kirkland, 2013). According to Yaffe (2012), it is simply that many schools "fail to engage Black boys, offering curriculum that is dull, insufficiently rigorous or irrelevant to their lives" (p. 2).

Researchers argued instead that writing instruction for adolescent Black youth should affirm their literacy practices in humanizing ways (Brown, 2018; Kirkland, 2013; Perry, 2018). More specifically, in her micro-ethnographic study of her seventh grade classroom, Brown (2018) noted that academic writing should not be valued more than artistic expression but be held in tandem with various forms of expression. Behizadeh (2015) argued for authentic writing forms that allow for expression, choice of topic, and writing for impact. She emphasized, however, that the definition of what is authentic resides in the student, that "students are the only ones who can determine the authenticity of writing" (p. 290). In her research with middle school Black youth, Haddix (2018) found that writing can be considered one way for students to give voice to their experiences and to teach them to think critically about how their personal perspectives are part of a broader dialogue on issues that matter to them.

In 2012, as documented by Yaffe (2012), Tyrone Howard of the Graduate School of Education and Information Studies at the University of California, Los Angeles, said "At the end of the day, authentic, caring, competent, highly qualified teachers, no matter the gender, no matter the race, have a profound impact on the outcomes of Black males. What works for Black males is not significantly different from what works with other groups of students" (p. 10).

DIGITAL STORYTELLING: VOICE AS A MULTIMODAL EXPRESSIVE ACT

Digital storytelling is considered the modern art of oral storytelling blending narrative with multimodal composing or the juxtaposition of images, spoken word, and music to tell a story. As part of a writing curriculum, digital storytelling supports the learning and refining of traditional writing forms of narrative, memoir, poetry, nonfiction, and biography (McGinnis, 2013). These are genres and modes of writing that school highly values. Digital storytelling also supports the writing process pedagogies of schools. These include "mulling an idea, developing the seed of an idea, trying various 'voices' or styles, gathering evidence via research, allowing a gestation period for the rhythm of a piece to identify itself " (Andrews & Smith, 2011, p. 10). Youth need to take the time to draft and revise the scripts for their digital stories in order to get to the deep thinking essential to telling the best stories. Digital storytelling is also a multimedia hybrid narrative form, argued to be a means through which people or youth make sense of their world, construct a sense-of-self, and/or narrate the self (Davis, 2009; Hull & Katz, 2006). The affordances of digital storytelling are also noted for including the youth's ability to develop an "authorial stance" or the "practice of taking on literate-identities and claiming a presence as an author and narrator of ones' own experiences" (Vasudevan, Schultz, & Bateman, 2010, p. 461). Hull and Katz (2006) extended this idea in their discussion of the potential for authorial agency or the ways their case study participants "borrowed and repurposed texts, images, photographs, and music in their multimodal compositions" (p. 52).

Therefore, the narrative power of digital storytelling is in its ability to afford youth a space to mediate their experiences of the world or to shape their interpretations of life in relation to broader sociopolitical contexts (Davis, 2009; Hull & Nelson, 2005). Thus, there can be a political aspect to digital storytelling where the producer can position himself in order to shape and tell his story (Davis, 2009). For marginalized youth, therefore, digital storytelling can become a space for counterhegemonic construction (Pleasants, 2008) or for counternarratives (McGinnis & Garcia, 2012).

Kinloch et al. (2017) suggested for "teachers and researchers to think deeply about how, what, when, and why Black youth participate in literacy" (p. 53). Our work, informed by prior research, explores how our out-of-school time program became a space that nurtured and supported the literacies of male Black youth, and also how creating digital compositions afforded the Black youth possibilities to mediate their own experiences, share their ideas, and become critical thinkers as part of larger dialogues among identity construction, positioning and representation.

METHODOLOGY

The research presented in this chapter is part of a larger project conducted in an out-of-school-time writing workshop that met in a university-based literacy clinic in a suburban community of New York City. The overarching goals for the project, codirected by the authors of this chapter, included developing a writing workshop for youth, specifically male middle school students. The project focused on supporting culturally and linguistically diverse youth in their development of 21st century literacies through participation in a digital storytelling workshop, where the young men were introduced to multimodal composition and multimedia platforms. Because we viewed multimodal literacy practices as situated within social and cultural contexts, we adopted the ethnographic approaches of the NLS to investigate the intersection of the young adolescent Black males' identities with their multimodal literacy practices.

Participants and Context of the Study

The participating youth were enrolled in four local middle schools from three different school districts and their guidance counselors recommended them to the project. Participation in the writing workshop, Young Men's Writing Project, was voluntary and a total of 20 African American, Caribbean American, and Latino young men accepted the invitation to attend the program during the spring and summers of 2009, 2010, and 2011. The program has served 20 young men who produced two to three digital stories each, have used other digital presentation programs, and have returned over the years to participate in the program a second or third time. In the program, they used technology and writing for self-expression, as spaces to explore identities, and as ways to consider issues they faced as young adolescent males of color.

The youth in this project lived in communities with a long history of changing demographics due to shifts in local immigration patterns, thus resulting in communities with rich cultural and linguistic diversity. In this chapter, we present data stemming from 15 students who were primarily from Caribbean American and African American backgrounds, highlighting two of the students in detail. Miking (all student names are pseudonyms) is an African American boy who attended the program for two years. Miking lived with his mother, sister, and grandmother. The other participant, Jonathan, was from Trinidad. His background is Afro-Trinidadian; however, within his school district he fell under the label Black. Jonathan lived with his father, mother, and younger brother and sister. Jonathan also attended the program two years in a row. Both young men claimed they liked the "creativity of the program." They attended a middle school that reported the following demographic composition during the 2010–11 academic year: 39% of the population identified themselves as Hispanic or Latino and 61% as African American or Black. Other socioeconomic indicators of the community revealed that 80% of the students qualified for free lunch, while 12% were eligible for reduced-price lunch. In terms of language, 13% of the students in their school were English language learners who the school identified as limited English proficient students.

Research Design

Data for this chapter are part of an ethnographic case study exploring the intersection of identity, literacy, and digital practices of the Young Men's Writing Project. We adopt the ethnographic approaches of the NLS that examine literacy and language as embedded with sociocultural practices (Street, 1995). Adding to these ethnographic approaches, digital stories as a research epistemology privileges the oral narrative of personal experience as a source of knowledge (Delgado Bernal, Buriciaga, & Flores Carmona, 2012), reclaiming the youth's authority to narrate their own stories.

In our role as participant observers, we collaborated with the program teacher, an African-American male, who had graduated with his New York State literacy certification from our university program. We developed curriculum based on work we had conducted with other youth in the community and based on Atwell's (1998) interrelation approach where the student writer and the teacher work within a rhetorical context. To get an in-depth picture and documentation of the nuances of the youth's experiences within the program we utilized several data collection methods over the course of the 3-year program offerings. We wrote ethnographic field notes of each of the 10 two-hour class sessions (total of 30 class sessions over 3 years) documenting instruction, student engagement with making a digital story, and student interactions with the instructor and with each other. As we engaged in the work of supporting students with technical support and ideas for stories, we recorded our personal communications with the students within the sessions where we worked with the 20 young men, as they needed help with ideas, writing, or technology. Within these personal conversations, we were able to learn the youths' process of creating and their thinking about the types of images they were hoping to use, the narration they preferred, and the type of music they hoped to find. We conducted formal taped interviews with each of the students during the middle of each summer program, and each of the young men who had time during their last session completed a questionnaire. We collected a total of 40 completed surveys where the young men indicated what they liked or did not like about the program, their process of creating a digital story, and any other points they wanted to note. We collected all written student narratives and completed digital stories for 60 stories over the 3 years the program was in place.

Fundamental to our analysis of field notes, interview transcripts, and digital story productions was an iterative, open, and focused coding of the data, from which we drew out patterns, developed themes, and wrote analytic memos (Merriam, 2009). Sociocultural literacy theory (Street, 1995) enabled the authors to identify themes from the data that included larger sociopolitical forces that shape the youths' experiences and identities. Social semiotic theory informed our analysis of the nonlinguistic modes with focus placed on intersemiotic relations (Kress & van Leeuwen, 1996; Mills, 2016). More specifically, we combed through the narratives for common themes and repeated topics; then, we analyzed the digital stories based on the youth's representational practices or how their choices and compositions signify their life experiences as young adolescent males of color. By focusing our analysis on the role of racial, ethnic, and culture specific negotiations, our goal in the sections that follow is to describe the youth's productions as a space of humanizing practices and for a reimagining of their identities.

Limitations

The data for this chapter come from the years of 2009, 2010, and 2011. We acknowledge the passage of time since we collected the data. However, we feel, and the literature in our review demonstrates, that the writing curriculum in schools has not developed in a way to include the literacies of Black males, and in fact, the curriculum may have become narrower due to testing policies in schools since that time. In addition, we recognize that digital platforms and youths' digital literacies have developed since we conducted this study; however, a digital divide still exists based on economics and school availability to digital tools and to digital pedagogies. Therefore, the participatory nature of our out-of-school-time digital writing workshop can lend insight to improving the writing and digital literacy practices in classrooms.

In addition, as an ethnographic case study, we share in detail two snapshots of the digital productions from the program. We can report that each year 20 students completed a project to share with their families and communities, so our review of the data includes approximately 60 digital stories.

"THE ROUGH WRITERZ": DIGITAL STORY PRODUCTIONS

Central to the meaning conveyed within the youth's overall digital text productions became the process of transmediation or the translation of semiotic content across modes (Mills, 2016; Suhor, 1984). Transmediation is a generative process grounded in the idea that alternative sign systems (e.g., linguistic, image, music) are available for making sense of the human experience. This research explores this idea of semiosis—how the students use one sign system to mediate another (Siegel, 1996).

Before creating their digital compositions, the young men wrote several different narratives. Michael, the program teacher, provided many discussions about his own life as a Black man and led the youth into critical reflection about their own lives. He connected with the youth through popular culture interests, such as rap and sports. We shared powerful models with the youth of examples of digital stories, narrative writing pieces, and poetry performances. However, we feel that if the teacher had been different, their stories might represent different topics.

The youth felt free in their choices of topics and genres and felt comfortable writing about ideas that mattered to them, whether about a favorite athlete, parkour, or racial stereotypes. They developed a narrative of their choice onto a storyboard, where they made decisions about what visual image might represent their words. They also noted songs that would reflect the mood or emotion they wanted to convey. To translate the storyboards into digital texts, they had to navigate the digital interface they were provided. In this case, the program was MS Photo Story software, a software program that could run on the computers that were available. The program allowed for transitional movements of frames, image insertion, oral narration, and music choices. In their navigation of this process, we found overwhelmingly that the youth's search for and selection of images was purposeful, finding images or symbolic representations of their experience and repurposing the images as expressions of their lives and their stories. Music or songs were another source of expression that the youth sought out in meaningful ways. Our observations were confirmed by the student interviews, where they noted, second to the pizza we served, their favorite part of the process was selecting images and music. In addition, they felt most proud of learning how to search for and import images and music into their digital stories.

The following discussion will focus on the digital productions of two youths, Jonathan and Miking, whose narratives reflect the larger themes that cut across the group's digital stories, such as racism, stereotypes, narratives of masculinity, making a difference in the world, and ideas of possible futures. Jonathan, a young man of Afro-Trinidadian heritage created his digital story, *Remember Me*, to share his feelings on the theme of difference. Miking, an African American youth created his second story, *Look into my Eyes*, as a poetry performance that expressed aspects of his life and being misunderstood. Miking's first story, *A Baller's Dream*, was briefly discussed in the introductory paragraph of this chapter. Both Jonathan and Miking were entering eighth graders the summer they created these digital stories, and each was 13 years old.

Jonathan's Digital Story

Remember Me

Lovelace is one of a kind.
A name that is not often heard
It's real easy to make fun of
I've basically been all over the country,
And not once have I heard the name
Lovelace.
Sometimes it can feel as though
My father, and also my Grandfather,
And of course Me,
That each one of us have been
Singled out from the whole world.
I think a lot as being cursed.
When you're cursed people call you the most
Hateful and cruel word which is
Difference. Things that are uncalled for like
Death, stereotypes, most of all Racism.
Then again if you think about it
Difference isn't always a bad thing.
If everybody was the same everyone the whole world would be bored
Difference can be a good thing
Make a difference in the world. When people make a
Difference in the world they are also remembered

And, I want to make a difference too.
This way Lovelace is not just another name you can make fun of, but another name
That will be remembered forever.

Jonathan's digital story, *Remember Me*, was an approximately two-minute story. Jonathan combined narration, autobiography, Google images, family photographs, popular culture, and music with social critique. Jonathan created his story in the summer of 2010; however, his theme fits the shifting and changeable nature of difference reflected in current social and political climates. His story raised questions of how differences can be seen, made, marked, removed, maintained, and altered. That is, Jonathan expressed how being marked as different can be a curse situated in stereotypes or racism. Yet, he also recognized that difference "can be a good thing," especially when people like Martin Luther King, Jr. make a difference in the world, an insight he communicated through his careful selection of images for the composition of his digital story. Through his orchestration of multimodal components and as told through his narration, Jonathan altered his position of difference as "cursed" to his possible future of being remembered or leaving a legacy as someone who makes a difference in the world.

Jonathan began his digital story with a discussion of his family name, Lovelace, which he stated is "a name that is not often heard but easy to make fun of." The image he used is the character, Lovelace, from the movie *Happy Feet*. When asked about his choice of the Happy Feet character, Jonathan explained he was the only personified character with his name (personal communication, June 22, 2010). Then, he moved to his father, grandfather, and himself, highlighting three generations of Lovelace males sharing photographs of each while exposing through spoken narration how each "has been singled out" for being different. The next photo of himself he digitally altered to reflect the idea of his word choice—cursed. The frame transitioned to a simple black background displaying the word Difference, emphasizing the word with his oration of it as hateful and cruel. Jonathan then shared troubling aspects of his life and his world—stereotyping and racism. Again, his choice to have a frame where he only stated orally one word emphasized the nature of these words. The background music, however, added another layer to this story, the lyrics stating, "I'm more than just an option. Refuse to be forgotten."

As he transitioned into his repositioning of Difference as a "good thing," Jonathan changed the music to Travis McCoy and Bruno Mars' "Billionaire" where they stated, "I want to be on the cover of *Forbes* magazine smiling next to Oprah and the Queen." He began to note that difference is a good thing or as he says, "Another way to think about this is when people make a difference in the world they are always remembered." At this moment, he inserted a photograph of Martin Luther King, Jr. realizing that he does not need to state his name. He then reflected on this idea by saying that "I want to make a difference too. Then the name Lovelace won't simply be a name that is made fun of, but of someone who has made a difference in the world." As the digital story ends, we viewed a photomontage of Jonathan as a young child. He explained how he will tell his whole life story from childbirth to now and be remembered forever. Then the narration ended, and only music and photographs of himself and his father are displayed. Jonathan specifically chose treasured family photos that he asked us to scan for him, because it was important to him to end his digital story with the photographs of himself and his father (personal communication, June 17, 2010). Throughout his digital story, Jonathan moved from the personal to the global, and providing a commentary on the sociopolitical nature of his world.

Jonathan revealed his knowledge of multimodal composition through his complementary use of images, photographs, music, and spoken word. He engaged in critical analysis and selection of images and music that would not only communicate his message but would extend the meanings of his words. His appropriation or repurposing of borrowed images and music, a "process that involves both analysis and commentary" (Jenkins, Clinton, Purushotma, Robinson, & Weigel, 2006, p. 33) signified Jonathan's authorial agency, his self-identification with his name, and his self-positioning, or repositioning, of his possible future as someone who will make a difference in the world. Overall, Jonathan's employment of multimodal design for responding to social positioning expressed critical identity work.

Miking's Digital Story

Look Into My Eyes

Look into my eyes and tell me what you see.
You don't see anything because you can't relate to me
Even if you have the same color eyes as me
You could still never ever see what I see
When I look at people, I see pain and sorrow, So we talk
But my trust is just something you cannot borrow
Stress is something that I witness
But at the end of the day, music is my forgiveness
We are blinded by our differences
My life makes no sense to you
Are you the crazy one?
It just might be true
Walk into these halls, might be my concern

But they know nothing about me until which they turn
Even still they don't know what problems come my way
When I see all those problems, I just say hey
To all those people who doubted me I shall bow
But later on in life, I'll say look at me now

Miking's digital story, *Look into my Eyes*, is also an approximately two-minute story. Miking, who usually sat alone in the back of the room, wrote a poem as his narrative on his phone. Then, he transferred it over to the Microsoft Photo Story software program. His digital poem included some personal reflections, Google images, symbolic representations, music, and a photograph of himself. His poem also raised the theme of difference and marked it through an idea that others do not understand him and might position him in certain ways. Through his orchestration of multimodal components, Miking also projected a future self that will speak back to the people who have misunderstood him as a young African American male.

Miking began his digital poem with a literal representation of an image of brown eyes in juxtaposition with his narration, "look into my eyes." Within his next line, he used a literal representation, "even if you have the same color eyes as me, you will not see what I see." When he talked about pain and sorrow, we saw an image of a Black male with tears running down his face depicting sadness. The digital poem transitioned to slides with words, *trust* and *stress*, emphasizing Miking's points. In this way and throughout his digital production, Miking made the focal point of his digital composition his words. Similar to a poetry performance, his words were his art. One slide depicted an image with all White people sitting along a wall. This image was set to the words "walk into these halls, might be my concern," followed by the line, "but they know nothing about me." While, Miking did not explicitly state it, there were themes of stereotyping and of racism in his production. Like Jonathan's, Miking's production ended with his idea of his possible future, his hope for his future to be someone who people will look at and say, "wow."

Miking also had a knowledge of multimodal composition that he revealed through his use of images, music, and spoken word. He played one song throughout the composition, a fast tempo, modern classical piece, which sets a rhythm for his narration. While his words were his focal point of the production, he extended their meanings through the images he selected to accompany them. He also restated throughout his production his feelings of difference and of not being understood by others—how they know nothing about him. He wrote in his final survey, "I am most proud of my final production," referencing the amount of time he spent trying to convey his overall message. His digital poem became a commentary on the social and cultural contexts in which Black youth negotiate daily, and on the assumptions that people make about others without knowing anything about them.

DISCUSSION: THE COMMUNITY OF ROUGH WRITERZ

It has been noted that once a digital story is complete, "its' telling" does not require the participation of the storyteller; it stands as a work of art, a representation apart from the teller, an "object" for reflection and critique. While we accept this as true, and assert that Jonathan's and Miking's digital stories can stand alone as artful narratives on difference and that each of the other youths' digital stories can also stand alone, we argue that viewing of the youths' stories together forms a greater whole, exposing the identities of the "Rough Writerz" as a community of young adolescent males of color. That is when the thematic threads of racism, stereotypes, narratives of masculinity, making a difference in the world, and ideas of possible futures run through a viewing of 20 digital stories, creating power in their collectivity. Each year, we held a celebration of their stories inviting family and community members to an evening viewing. As such, the stories became an education to the audience on the ways young men of color experience the world.

We live in a world where there are standards for what counts as masculine, and where certain versions of masculinity dominate in the media and in current educational debates of males of color. However, we saw through the digital stories produced by the "Rough Writerz," through their borrowing, repurposing, and appropriation of images, including images of violence and pain, of athletes, and through narrations of possible futures, articulations of their values and beliefs. These beliefs are reflected in the following excerpts of the other youths' stories (all names are pseudonyms):

- "A man is not a man if he cannot ask for help" (Sharod);
- "A person's courage is not measured by how many crazy actions one does, but rather the way they carry out the actions and handle certain situations" (Kaelin); and
- "Everybody will stumble upon many obstacles in their life. It is the weak ones that go around the obstacles, the strong ones go through the obstacles in life" (Tyler).

We argue that the young men also educated us about the expectations placed on them as young adolescent males of color. In addition, we begin to see how through their digital stories and critical identity work, the young men counter these standards and debates which construct boys as one homogeneous group. They demonstrate how narratives of masculinity can vary over time and across cultures. In fact, the youth used symbolic and figured elements of identity to construct and reposition themselves through their stories as respectful, compassionate, and as agents of change.

Overall, the experiences of the youth in this out-of-school-time writing workshop contributed to supporting educators in organizing social experiences and interactions within classrooms and out-of-school-time settings that are meaningful and engaging to middle school aged youth. As authors and narrators of their own digital productions, the young men expanded their writing of multiple genres and incorporated a wider range of text types (Mills, 2016). In their digital productions, they drew on their own life histories with authority and power to disclose and disseminate knowledge, becoming designers of critical texts (Avila & Zacher-Pandya, 2013). The integration of multimodalities and digital text design created a participatory culture within the out-of-school-time space, where the young men became participants in the creation of knowledge and became more literate in the powerful way they can use new digital tools to express themselves. This work echoes the call from Everett (2018) to create more humanizing pedagogies that "affirms the lives and minds of Black youth" (p. 37).

CONCLUSION

Tatum and Gue (2012) argued that honoring the voices of young adolescent males of color is overlooked in many classrooms. This exclusion is due to many rigid, formulaic writing programs required in schools that do not accommodate students' writing needs or 21st century literacies (Brown, 2018; Haddix, 2018). These researchers, therefore, argued for schools to carve out spaces that affirm the lives and voices of young Black males and for the words of the youth to "go out into the world" (Tatum & Gue, 2012, p. 141).

Using a sociocultural perspective to our investigation of the multimodal compositions of young Black adolescents, we echo these points. We find that *place* and *space* can make a difference in terms of how young Black adolescents feel agency in expressing, experiencing, and enacting their voices and masculine identities. We argue that middle level educational contexts must find ways to provide space to allow youth to write about ideas and issues that matter to them and that allow them to produce multimodal compositions which allow for representation and distribution of their ideas. Overall, middle level education needs to recognize that young adolescent Black youth have powerful stories to share and through the sharing of their stories they are able to develop as writers and as youth who can make a difference in the world.

REFERENCES

Andrews, R., & Smith, A. (2011). *Developing writers: Teaching and learning in the digital age*. Berkshire, England: Open University Press.

Ascher, C., & Branch-Smith, E. (2005). Precarious space: Majority Black suburbs and their public schools. *Teachers College Record, 107*(9), 1956–1973.

Atwell, N. (1987). *In the middle: Reading and learning with adolescents*. Portsmouth, NH: Heinemann.

Atwell, N. (1998). *In the middle: New understandings about writing, reading, and learning* (2nd ed.). Portsmouth, NH: Heinemann.

Avila, J., & Zacher-Pandya, J. (2013). "Traveling textuality, and transformation: An introduction to critical digital literacies. In J. Avila & J. Zacher-Pandya (Eds.), *Critical digital literacies as social practice: Intersections and challenges* (pp. 1–15). New York, NY: Peter Lang.

Barton, D. (1994). *Literacy: An introduction to the ecology of written language*. Oxford, England: Blackwell.

Behizadeh, N. (2015). Xavier's take on authentic writing: Structuring choice for expression and impact. *Journal of Adolescent and Adult Literacy, 58*, 289–298.

Brown, A. (2018). "Beautiful, also, are the souls of my people": Literacies within and without. *Voices from the Middle, 25*(3), 16–21.

Carrington, V. (2005). The uncanny, digital texts and literacy. *Language and Education, 19*, 467–482.

Davis, A. (2009). Co-authoring identity: Digital storytelling in an urban middle school. *THEN: Technology, Humanities, Education & Narrative, 1*(1). Retrieved from http://thenjournal.org/index.php/then/article/view/32/31

Davis, M. (2018). *Real students, real writing*. Urbana, IL: National Council of Teachers of English. Retrieved from http://www2.ncte.org/blog/2018/08/real-students-read-writing/

Delgado Bernal, D., Buriciaga, R., & Flores Carmona, J. (2012). Chicana/Latina testimonios: Mapping the methodological pedagogical, and political. *Equity and Excellence in Education, 45*, 363–372.

Everett, S. (2018). "Untold stories:" Cultivating consequential writing with a Black male student through a critical approach to metaphor. *Research in the Teaching of English, 53*(1), 34–54.

Gee, J. (1996). *Social linguistics and literacies: Ideology in discourses* (2nd ed.). London, England: Falmer Press.

Gee, J. (2003). *What video games have to teach us about learning and literacy*. New York, NY: Palgrave.

Haddix, M. (2018). What's radical about youth writing? Seeing and honoring youth writers and their literacies. *Voices from the Middle, 25*(3), 8–12.

Hall, S. (1997). Old and new identities, old and new ethnicities. In A. King (Ed.), *Culture, globalization and the world system: Contemporary conditions for the representation of identity* (pp. 41–69). Minneapolis, MN: University of Minnesota Press.

Heath, S. B. (1983). *Ways with words: Language, life and work in communities and classrooms*. Cambridge, England: Cambridge University Press.

Holland, D., Lachicotte, W., Skinner, D., & Cain (1998). *Identity and agency in cultural worlds*. Cambridge, MA: Harvard University Press.

Hull, G., & Katz, L. (2006). Crafting an agentive self. *Research in the Teaching of English*, *41*, 44–81.

Hull, G., & Nelson, E. (2005). Locating the semiotic power of multimodality. *Written Communication*, *22*(3), 224–259.

Jenkins, H., Clinton, K., Purushotma, R., Robinson, A., & Weigel, M. (2006). *Confronting the challenges of participatory culture: Media education for the 21st century*. Chicago, IL: The McArthur Foundation. Retrieved from https://www.macfound.org/media/article_pdfs/JENKINS_WHITE_PAPER.PDF

Kinloch, V., Burkland, T., & Penn, C. (2017). When school is not enough: Understanding the lives and literacies of Black youth. *Research in the Teaching of English*, *52*(1), 34–54.

Kirkland, D. E. (2013). *A search past silence: The literacy of young Black men*. New York, NY: Teachers College Press.

Kress, G. (2003). *Literacy in the new media age*. London, England: Routledge.

Kress, G., & van Leeuwen, T. (1996). *Reading images: The grammar of visual design*. London, England: Routledge.

Lankshear, C., & Knobel, M. (2003). *New literacies: Changing knowledge and classroom learning*. Philadelphia, PA: Open University Press.

Lankshear, C., & Knobel, M. (2007). Sampling "the new" in new literacies. In M. Knobel & C. Lankshear (Eds.), *A new literacies sampler* (pp. 1–24). New York, NY: Peter Lang.

Luke, C. (2003). Pedagogy, connectivity, multimodality, and interdisciplinarity. *Reading Research Quarterly*, *38*, 397–403.

Mahiri, J., & Sablo, S. (1996). Writing for their lives: The non-school literacy of California's urban African American youth. *The Journal of Negro Education*, *65*(2), 164–180.

McCarthey, S., & Moje, E. B. (2002). Identity matters. *Reading Research Quarterly*, *38*, 403–407.

McGinnis, T. (2013). Creating a balanced literacy curriculum in the 21st century: Authentic integration of literacy 1.0 with literacy 2.0. In J. Whittingham, S. Huffman, W. Rickman & C. Wiedmaier (Eds.), *Technological tools for the literacy classroom* (pp. 64–80). Hershey, PA: IGI Global.

McGinnis, T., & Garcia, A. (2012). "The road to freedom:" How one Salvadoran youth takes an agentive stance to narrate the self across time and space. *Association of Mexican American Educators Journal*, *6*(3), 30–36.

Merriam, S. B. (2009). *Qualitative research: A guide to design and implementation* (3rd ed.). New York, NY: Jossey-Bass.

Messner, M. A. (1990). Boyhood, organized sports, and the construction of masculinities. *Journal of Contemporary Ethnography*, *18*, 416–444.

Mills, K. A. (2016). *Literacy theories for the digital age: Social, critical, multimodal, spatial, material and sensory lenses*. Toronto, Canada: Multilingual Matters.

National Commission on Writing in America's Schools and Colleges. (2003). *The neglected R": The need for a writing revolution*. New York, NY: The College Board. Retrieved from https://www.nwp.org/cs/public/download/nwp_file/21478/the-neglected-r-college-board-nwp-report.pdf?x-r=pcfile_d

National Council of Teachers of English. (2014). *Position statement: NCTE beliefs about the students' right to write*. Retrieved from http://www2.ncte.org/statement/students-right-to-write/

National Council of Teachers of English. (2016). *Professional knowledge for the teaching of writing*. Retrieved from http://www2.ncte.org/statement/teaching-writing/

New London Group. (2000). A pedagogy of multiliteracies: Designing social futures. In B. Cope & M. Kalantzis (Eds.), *Multiliteracies: Literacy learning and design of social futures* (pp. 9–37). New York, NY: Routledge.

Perry, T. (2018). Using texts to nurture reading, writing, and intellectual development: A conversation with Alfred Tatum. *Voices from the Middle, 25*(3), 13–15.

Pleasants, H. (2008). Negotiating identity projects: Exploring the digital storytelling experiences of three African American girls. In M. Hill & L. Vasudevan (Eds.), *Media learning, and sites of possibility* (pp. 205–234). New York, NY: Peter Lang.

Schultz, K., & Fecho, B. (2000). Society's child: Social context and writing development. *Educational Psychologist, 35*(1), 51–62.

Scribner, S., & Cole, M. (1981). *The psychology of literacy*. Cambridge, MA: Harvard University Press.

Siegel, M. (1996). More than words: The generative power of transmediation for learning. *Canadian Journal of Education, 20*, 455–475.

Suhor, C. (1984). Towards a semiotics-based curriculum. *Journal of Curriculum Studies, 16*, 247–257.

Smith, C., & Van Egeren, L. (2008). Bringing in the community: Partnerships and quality assurance in 21st century community learning centers. *Afterschool Matters: Occasional Paper Series, 9*, 15–30.

Street, B. (1984). *Literacy in theory and practice*. Cambridge, England: Cambridge University Press.

Street, B. (1995). *Social literacies*. London, England: Longman.

Street, B. (2003). What's "new" in new literacy studies? Critical approaches to literacy in theory and practice. *Current Issues in Comparative Education, 18*, 258–282.

Tatum, A. W. (2012). *Literacy practices for African-American male adolescents*. The Students at the Center Series. Washington, DC: Jobs for the Future. Retrieved from https://jfforg-prod-prime.s3.amazonaws.com/media/documents/Literacy_Practices.pdf

Tatum, A. W., & Gue, V. (2012). The sociocultural benefits of writing for African American adolescent males. *Reading & Writing Quarterly, 28*(2), 123–142.

Tuck, E. (2009). Suspending damage: A letter to communities. *Harvard Educational Review, 79*, 409–427.

Vasudevan, L., Schultz, K., & Bateman, J. (2010). Rethinking composing in a digital age: Authoring literate identities through multimodal storytelling. *Written Communication, 27*, 442–468.

Yaffe, D. (2012). Middle school matters: Improving the life course of Black boys. *ETS Policy Notes, 20*(4), 1–11. Retrieved from https://www.ets.org/Media/Research/pdf/PICPNV20n4.pdf

CHAPTER 5

IN STUDENTS' VOICES

How Middle School Students Perceive Their Need for Effective Reading Comprehension Strategies

Nancy Akhavan
Fresno State University

ABSTRACT

Middle school students need strategies to comprehend complex texts and information; however, they also need to make personal connections to the teacher. In this chapter, I share the results of a mixed methods study conducted with 690 middle school students regarding student identification and use of reading comprehension strategies with text. Sixth through eighth grade students participated in the study; they came from five different schools. The findings of the study revealed that students learn a narrow repertoire of reading comprehension strategies, yet other strategies may benefit them, and students need to learn comprehension strategies. Students reported the need for a teacher who cares about them and their learning needs; this was more important to the students than having strategies for reading comprehension. Students also reported how what they read becomes more interesting if they

Curriculum, Instruction, and Assessment:
Intersecting New Needs and New Approaches, pp. 99–123
Copyright © 2020 by Information Age Publishing
99

are involved in discussion and sharing of ideas about the meaning of texts. This study is significant as it provides middle school teachers with information about what reading comprehension strategies students should use and which strategies teachers should teach.

Having successful literacy experiences in school will help students be successful with the increasingly complex literacy abilities needed to be a productive adult (Stahl & Yaden, 2004). Students face increasingly complex texts and real-world reasons to read and understand the texts that they encounter; however, they cannot always understand what they read. Middle school students are in classes that focus on content, not strategies, and comprehension instruction is not often taught or taught well. This lack of instruction occurs even though research supports comprehension instruction for middle school students (Pressley & Wharton-McDonald, 1997). The fact that comprehension instruction is not taught, or taught well, impacts middle school students as they often struggle to learn from the text they are reading and teachers expect them to know how to learn from the text they are reading (National Center for Education Statistics, 2011; Vaughn et al., 2011). Seventy percent of middle school students who struggle to read the complex texts need assistance with reading comprehension (Biancarosa & Snow, 2006; Ness, 2009). Understanding the perceptions of middle school students regarding their use of reading comprehension strategies when reading nonfiction or content area texts can help teachers know how to teach adolescents to read to learn.

PURPOSE AND RESEARCH QUESTIONS

By understanding how teachers help students sustain attention and comprehension while reading texts and applying skills and comprehension strategies to multiple literacies, more teachers can learn effective instructional techniques to increase middle school students' reading comprehension in all content areas (Ness, 2009). Additionally, by bringing all forms of text into classrooms and giving students the cognitive tools to understand, access, and manipulate the information in texts, teachers can make necessary adjustments to ensure learning occurs.

In this study, I examined the information that students shared when they voiced their experiences of learned reading strategies by sharing perceptions about strategy use and use of texts. The information gathered from students can guide future instruction in ways that examine past instruction cannot. Two main purposes guided this study: (a) to understand the reading comprehension strategies middle school students use, and (b) to understand the instructional strategies teachers use in class to help students comprehend content area text that they read on their own.

Research questions included:

- What strategies do middle school students use most often when reading texts in class?
- What actions do middle school students take as readers when reading texts in, or for, a class?
- What strategies do middle school students who like to read use compared to students who do not like to read?
- How do students compare in their ability to understand text if they like to read or do not like to read?
- In what ways do students want the teacher to help them based on the students' grade levels?

THEORETICAL FRAMEWORK

The foundation for this research is the belief that reading comprehension instruction is important to middle school students. Reading comprehension instruction is a way for students to read, learn, and retain domain specific information in content area classes. Also reflected in this research is the idea that students thrive when they are determining their own outcomes for their learning (Brooks & Young, 2011). If students know how to comprehend domain specific text, they can exercise self-determination in content area classes.

Motivation is a significant factor of students' desire to engage with reading strategies. Atkinson (1964) noted that motivation to achieve is a function of expectancy and value. In other words, the person's perception of his or her ability to achieve the goal affects his motivation to pursue the goal, and the value the person places on the goal (Wigfield & Asher, 1984). Weiner et al. (1971) posited four factors to explain achievement motivation, including ability, effort, task difficulty, and luck (Weiner et al., 1971). Wigfield and Asher (1984) classified the four attributes into two dimensions: stability and locus of control. Stability refers to whether the cause of achievement motivation is changeable or not, and locus of control refers to whether it is considered to be internal (i.e., personal), or external (i.e., environmental) (Wigfield & Asher, 1984). Both stability and locus of control are important factors in understanding student motivation for use of reading strategies.

Pragmatic theory grounds the study. The pragmatic approach works well for studies looking at a problem of practice that occurs in the real world (Mackensie & Knipe, 2006). Pragmatic theory defines truth in terms of utility and the action people are taking that makes the findings of the study true. With pragmatism, I can consider the findings of surveys in the framework of what makes sense given the real-world context of the study (Morgan, 2007). When asking students directly about their thoughts and ideas regarding what they have experienced in school, I need to consider the context of the students' schooling experiences and how their experiences affect their perceptions. I also need to consider what teachers are teaching, and what they might teach that would benefit students.

LITERATURE REVIEW

Research on middle school students' use of reading strategies often focuses on understanding what reading comprehension strategies students need to learn (Pressley, 2000). Comprehension instruction can include the direct instruction of strategies as well as the scaffolding of strategies while students are reading (Boardman, Boelé, & Klingner, 2017; Houge, Geier, & Peyton, 2008). This literature review discusses what strategy instruction is, the ways educators teach comprehension instruction, and the need for comprehension instruction in content areas.

Strategy Instruction

Strategy instruction focuses on developing students' procedural and conditional knowledge to comprehend texts (Dole, Brown, & Trathen, 1996). Strategy instruction has been a focus of instruction to improve student reading ability, but not always taught in middle school (Block & Pressley, 2002). These strategies include before-reading and during-reading strategies. Before-reading strategies may include predicting what a text will be about and activating prior knowledge by skimming a text before reading (Vaughn et al., 2011). Teachers looking for a response from students initiate most of these strategies, rather than the students initiating a strategy. These strategies include (a) focusing attention of the reader, (b) using advance organizers, and (c) building background knowledge from the discussion of context and content before reading, and (d) preteaching vocabulary (Tierney & Cunningham, 1984). During-reading strategies include visualization, questioning, and self-questioning to monitor comprehension. After-reading strategies can include post questions, thinking about reading to add to prior knowledge, and summarizing (Tierney & Cunningham, 1984). Overtime with instruction middle school students can acquire the ability to use reading comprehension strategies with more complex texts (Boardman et al., 2017).

A large body of knowledge on strategy instruction relates to good and poor readers. Educators and researchers have described reading strategy instruction in practice and theory through a variety of articles and print sources since 1971 (Gaffney & Anderson, 2000). The basic and applied research in reading during the first 20 years of reading strategy research resulted in new understandings of how students read (the process) and what we should teach in response to how they learn to read (Dole, Duffy, Roehler, & Pearson, 1991). Reading strategy research has recently had a narrower focus that has led to classroom instruction working from a short list of strategies including predicting, summarizing, questioning, visualizing, and inferencing (Palinscar & Schultz, 2011). This narrowed list may have occurred based on the National Reading Panel's (2000) recommendations. In its report, the National Reading Panel highlighted strategy instruction and focused on certain strategies as important to teach. This list included comprehension monitoring, cooperative learning, graphic and semantic organizers, story structure, question answering, question generation, summarization, and multiple strategy instruction (Ness, 2009).

Reading instruction in the content areas is also important, as content areas such as math, social studies, and science require different comprehension skills (Afflerbach & VanSledright, 2001; Barton, Heidema, & Jordan, 2002). Learning in these content areas often revolves around reading; but content area texts have a different organization than the texts in English language arts. However, content area teachers do not always share the goal of teaching reading as they see students for short amounts of time and focus on teaching content information (Fang & Coatam, 2013). Middle school students need coherence in reading comprehension strategies between classes as they see a variety of teachers during the day. It can be confusing if their teachers use different strategies and helpful if their teachers work together to decide on specific reading comprehension strategies to focus on (see Boardman et al., 2017).

Literacy Instruction Foundations

Students often receive effective literacy instruction early in their schooling because primary grade reading ability connects to future success in school (Allington & Cunningham, 2002). Contrarily, students do not often receive focused literacy instruction in middle school, as content area teachers perceive this to be the English teacher's job.

Nonschool factors influence student reading ability. These factors decrease influence over time as school-related factors, like instruction differentiated based on student needs, become leading predictors of student achievement (Aikens & Barbarin, 2008; Kainz & Vernon-Feagans, 2007). However, many students enter middle school still not being able to read content texts; instruction in comprehension strategies could make a difference.

Having successful literacy experiences in school will help students navigate the increasingly complex literacy abilities needed in middle school and beyond (Stahl & Yaden, 2004). Students practice these increasingly difficult skills as they advance through middle and high school (Boardman et al., 2017). They need extensive practice with supportive adults to help them become successful readers and writers (Stahl & Yaden, 2004).

Comprehension Instruction

The Common Core State Standards promise to raise student achievement and develop students prepared for careers and jobs needed for the 21st century (Swanson & Wanzek, 2013). The Common Core State Standards expect students to read widely and deeply from a wide range of challenging literary and informational texts to prepare students for college and career (Swanson & Wanzek, 2013). As schools continue to transition from current standards to the Common Core Standards or implement challenging state standards, more rigorous standards will become the basis for literacy instruction in content areas and expectations for student reading ability will be elevated.

Comprehension instruction, though highly supported by research, is often not taught or taught well (Pressley & Wharton-McDonald, 1997). Comprehension instruction begins with teacher explanation of strategies (Pearson, Roehler, Dole, & Duffy, 1984). After modeling, students practice the strategies on their own with real reading (Pressley, 2000). This two-step process is much more complex than it appears. What is occurring is the gradual release of responsibility from teacher to student as the student begins to own the learning (Fisher & Frey, 2013). Duke and Pearson (2002) expanded the process into five steps including explicit description, teacher modeling, collaborative use of the strategy, guided practice with the strategy, and independent use of the strategy. Teachers need access to practical teaching strategies to bring this process alive in their classrooms.

Comprehension and Scaffolding

Often students who need instruction to support their comprehension do not receive it (Brown & Broemmel, 2011; Means & Knapp, 1991). Middle school students receive little help to read textbooks and other texts in their content area classes. Students who struggle with reading need supports to enhance their comprehension of texts. Instruction should support their needs (Pitcher, Martinez, Dicembre, Fewster, & McCormick, 2010). These students benefit from direct and explicit instruction to support their learning (Houge et al., 2008).

Improving core literacy instruction focused on informational text is essential (Dymock, 2005; Faggela-Luby, Ware, & Capozzoli, 2009). This includes teaching essential vocabulary, frontloading content, teaching higher level thinking skills, and improving student engagement with texts (Faggela-Luby et al., 2009). Students need scaffolding to support their learning as they read more complex texts in the content areas. Scaffolding occurs when the teacher provides meaningful support that meets students' needs prior to and during reading (Brown & Broemmel, 2011). This type of support involves in-depth schema building and critical understanding of text (Brown & Broemmel, 2011). Schema building and critical understanding are two important factors in students being able to understand increasingly complex text.

METHODOLOGY

In this study, I used a mixed methods approach. Students from middle school took surveys regarding their reading interest and use of reading strategies. Students also participated in focus group interviews to develop a deeper understanding of students' reading needs in the classroom.

Context and Participants

The participants were 690 sixth, seventh, and eighth grade students between the ages of 11 and 14 years. The sample for the survey was comprised of 25% sixth graders ($n = 176$), 26% seventh graders ($n = 183$), and 49% eighth graders ($n = 341$). Originally, fifth-grade teachers who were part of the middle school were invited to participate, but only one fifth-grade teacher elected to participate; therefore, the fifth-grade scores were not included as the fifth-grade sample size was too small. The sample for the focus group was comprised of 25 students including 19% sixth graders ($n = 5$), 37% seventh graders ($n = 9$), and 44% eighth graders ($n = 11$). Nine boys and 16 girls were included in the focus group interviews. The students attended schools receiving Title I funds and that were diverse, both culturally and linguistically. The majority race/ethnicities from all schools were White, Latino, and Asian (Ed-Data, 2019). Five schools in the area participated in the study. The population of School One was 836 students; School Two was 591 students; School Three was 859 students;

School Four was 434 students, and School Five was 723 students (Ed-Data, 2019). All schools were from four school districts and located in the central valley of California. The region ranks in the top five of the poorest metropolitan areas in the state and the nation.

Principals recruited the students in May, 4 weeks before the end of the school year. Parents provided informed consent for the children to participate. The students participated voluntarily and received a special pencil and eraser for participating. Principals of each school asked teachers if they were interested in having their classrooms participate in the study. Once teachers volunteered their classrooms to participate, which meant they were willing to give up class time for the students to take the survey in their class, teachers gave the consent forms to the students to take home. Those students who returned the consent forms with a parent signature participated in the study. Students who were in self-contained classrooms receiving services for special education were not included in the participant sample as these students were on individualized educational plans and did not receive the comprehension instruction that the students not in self-contained classrooms received. Students who had an individualized educational plan and received services in the mainstream classroom were included in the study; however, due to privacy concerns, these students did not state if they were receiving special education services. Students designated as English learners did participate in the study; however, these students did not state if they self-identified as English learners. Each school had a percentage of students who were English learners.

All the students were in the last month of their school year and were preparing to transition. Sixth and seventh graders were preparing to transition to the next grade level at their school, and the eighth graders were preparing for transition to high schools in the same school district in which they were already attending. For the focus group interviews, all the students were fluent English speakers. Teachers chose the students to participate by considering whether they thought their parents would consent to their child participating in the study.

Context of the Study

The five school districts who had students involved in the study were located in the Central Valley of California. The Central Valley is a high-poverty area with low educational attainment. The area has school districts in urban, suburban, and rural areas. The five schools represented in the sample came from one urban district, one suburban, and two rural districts. Of the approximately 591 students in the school, 76.3% were Latino, 6.6% were Black, 9.3% were White, 4.2% were Asian, and 3.6% were

Native American. School Two was located in the same urban district. Of the approximately 859 students in the school, 51.2% were Latino, 12.3% were Black, 26.5% were White, 4.8% were Asian, 3.2% identified as two or more races, and 2.0% declined to answer. School Three was located in a suburban district. Of the approximately 735 students in the school, 90.2% were Latino, 3.8% were Black, 4.8% were White, and 0.4% were Asian. School Four was located in a rural district. Of the approximately 861 students in the school, 81.8% were Latino, 0.3% were Black, 10.1% were White, 4.4% were Asian, and 3.4% declined to answer. School Five was located in a rural district. Of the approximately 491 students in the school, 97.4% were Latino, 0.2% were Black, and 1.4% were White (Ed-Data, 2016).

Procedure

The teachers who had volunteered to participate in the study administered the survey to the students at the school. More than one teacher from each school volunteered, and the teachers gave the surveys in their classrooms during English, science, or social studies courses. The students in all grade levels took the survey once. Students spent between 10–15 minutes to take the survey. I distributed the surveys to the teachers within a two-week window. The response rate of the surveys for the identified English, science, or social studies classes was 100%.

After administering the survey to students in the classrooms, teachers identified students for the focus group interviews. There were five focus groups, one from each of the five participating schools. Purposive sampling was the method used to identify the focus group participants. The classroom teacher chose the possible focus group participants, and teachers determined who should participate by evaluating the students' ability to talk in a small group. I combined all student names provided by the teachers into a list for each school, and I randomly selected 12 names from each list. Each focus group had at least six students on the day that the interview was to occur. The principals of each school did not tell me the teachers' names or what grade the students were from to protect the students' anonymity. I conducted the focus group interviews during school hours, with all the schools on different schedules. The teachers contacted the parents and asked the parents of all students a second time for consent, and students completed a second assent prior to the interviews.

The office clerk or the office manager pulled the students from class for the focus group interviews at a time that the principal had arranged at each school. Students spent approximately 30 minutes in the focus group interview. I conducted the focus group interviews within 1 week of the completion of the data collection by survey. I read the questions and audiotaped the focus group interview. Prior to data collection, I piloted all instruments with five participants to examine the questions and language demands of the questions for students who might speak English as a second language.

Instruments

I used the survey to determine students' use of strategies previously taught by teachers. Jeff Wilhelm at Boise State University developed the survey to assess readers' engagement with texts (J. Wilhelm, personal communication, January 29, 2013). Wilhelm had used the survey numerous times in his own research but did not provide the reliability or validity of the instrument. The survey has 44 items and includes Likert scale items ranging from (1) *never,* (2) *rarely,* (3) *occasionally,* (4) *frequently,* and (5) *almost always/always.* The survey has six sections. Section 1 collects demographic data and has four items. Section 2 asks about students' like or dislike for reading and has six items. Section 3 asks students about how often they participated in specific study activities in class and has nine items. Section 4 asks students about the strategies they use to help them read and this section has 10 items. Section 5 asks students about the activities that students like to engage in to read better; this section has three items. Section 6 asks students about types of texts read in class and has 12 items. I changed three of the sections on the scale from the original survey so that the item would not measure engagement in reading, but measure student use of a reading strategy (see Appendix A).

In addition to the questions regarding preferred and teacher-led reading strategies, I added additional demographic questions, including gender, grade level, and class section to the survey. The survey included questions for each of the reading comprehension strategies assessed. Questions asked about students' perceived use of reading comprehension strategies, types of texts read in content courses, and grouping models for learning. One section included 13 questions regarding types of texts read and in which courses students read the texts; an additional section had 13 questions about reading comprehension strategies. Sample items included, "When you read in the class you are in now, do you understand what you are reading?" and "For the class you are in now, please read the list of activities below and mark on the scale the word that describes how often you are doing these activities in class."

The focus group interviews used an interview protocol (see Appendix B). I developed the interview protocol using questions designed to understand students' interest in reading. I based the items on questions from the *Elementary Reading Attitude Survey* (McKenna & Kear, 1990) to focus on understanding students' use of reading comprehension strategies and their perceptions about support they receive in class to read. I developed the reading comprehension questions based on the processes mature readers use regularly when reading (Pressley, 2000). I asked the students 19 questions addressing three topic areas: students' habits as readers, the comprehension strategies they use when reading, and supports they use or desire when reading in class. I asked students questions including, "Do you like to read? Why or why not?" and "Tell me how you help yourself read and understand." There were also questions that asked students about their most favorite and least favorite teacher and asked what their favorite teacher did to help them read better. I piloted the interview protocol with a group of middle school students not involved in the study. The pilot included reviewing questions with the students to ensure the questions were understandable. I made changes to the protocol based on students' answers in the pilot. If students stated a question was unclear, I revised the question and presented it again to students for review.

Limitations

This study has a number of limitations. The first limitation is that the schools involved, while diverse, did not represent ethnic diversity overall. The schools heavily represented Latino students and did not represent all ethnic groups in an equal distribution of the population of the country. Therefore, the study is not generalizable to all populations. Another limitation was the number of students surveyed. While 690 is a large sample size, it was not equally distributed between the three grades (6, 7, 8) that a middle school typically serves. Therefore, the data highly represented one group's perception (eighth graders) over the other grade levels. The third limitation was that I conducted the interviews in focus groups, and the larger focus groups of seven to eight students limited the ability of all students' voices to be heard. These phenomena can skew the data that resulted as the transcripts very likely represent the voices of students who are more likely to speak out. Survey sample bias also existed, as some students did not return the positive parent permission slips; and therefore, they did not take the survey. Another limitation was focus group sampling bias. As teachers selected the students they thought would likely obtain parents' consent for the interview, some students who could have been interviewed were not considered for the sample.

Data Analysis

I analyzed the data by students' like or dislike of reading and by grade level. When examining the data on whether students like to read or not and because a categorical independent variable existed, an independent *t*-test was used to compare to the variables of whether students like to read or not based on grade level. I used a one-way MANOVA to analyze the data for determining the relationship between students' grade level with types of reading strategies used by the students. There were 3 independent variables and 10 continuous variables. The independent variables were grade levels (6, 7, 8); this was measured with a nominal scale. The dependent variables were types of reading materials. The 12 dependent variables were also nominal. These variables were textbooks, anthologies, supplements, magazines, short books, online texts, websites, copies, novels, chapter books, newspapers, and picture books.

RESULTS

In this section, I report the quantitative results from the student survey and the qualitative results from the focus group interviews.

Quantitative Analysis

Table 5.1 shows the mean differences between the grade levels and the materials used for reading in school. A lower mean value indicates that the type of reading material appeared less often in the middle school classrooms. A one-way MANOVA determined the association between how reading materials (textbooks, anthologies, supplements, magazines, short books, online texts, websites, copies, novels, chapter books, newspapers and picture books) as dependent variables are being used in middle school classrooms based on grade level (6, 7, 8) as the independent variable. I chose a one-way MANOVA as the statistical test because of the multiple dependent variables. There was a significant difference in how different types of texts were used in class based on the students' grade level $F = 3.58$, $p < .000$; Wilk's λ .870 partial η^2 .931.

Students' penchant for reading. An independent samples *t*-test determined the relationship between students' desire to read and their understanding of what they read. The *t*-test results indicated a statistically significant difference between students' desire to read (whether they like it or not) and if they understand what they read, $t(683)=4.83$, $p < .001$,

Table 5.1.
Means and Standard Deviations for Text Types

Item	Mean (St. Dev.)
Textbooks	3.41 (1.14)
Anthologies	2.36 (1.34)
Supplements	2.32 (1.47)
Magazines	1.99 (1.16)
Short Books	2.38 (1.32)
Online Texts	2.76 (1.21)
Websites	2.98 (1.41)
Copies	2.61 (1.31)
Novels	2.61 (1.31)
Chapter Books	2.61 (2.65)
Newspapers	2.06 (2.07)
Picture Books	1.98 (1.24)

Response metric: (1) never, (2) rarely, (3) occasionally, (4) frequently, (5) almost always/always.

$d = .36$. This means that students who do not like to read differ in understanding of what they read compared to students who like to read.

An independent samples t-test determined the relationship between students' desire to read and what comprehension strategies they use when reading. The reading comprehension strategies measured included summarizing, identifying main ideas, identifying key details, identifying vocabulary, inferring, synthesizing, visualizing, asking questions of text, making connections, and monitoring reading. Of these strategies, six were significant. For the strategy, making connections, the data indicate a statistically significant difference in the use of the strategy between students who like to read and students who do not like to read, $t(578) = 3.708, p <. 000$, $d = .31$. For the strategy, identifying key details, the data indicate a statistically significant difference in the use of the strategy between students who like to read and students who do not like to read, $t(585) = 3.054, p < .002$, $d = .25$. For the strategy, identifying vocabulary, the data indicate a statistically significant difference in the use of the strategy between students who like to read and students who do not like to read, $t(589) = 2.724, p < .007$, $d = .23$. For the strategy, asking questions of text, the data indicate a statistically significant difference in the use of the strategy between students who like to read and students who do not like to read, $t(585) = 2.607, p = .009$, $d = .22$. For the strategy, monitoring for understanding, the data indicate a statistically significant difference in the use of the strategy between students who like to read and students who do not like to read, $t(533) = 4.571\ p <$ .0005, $d = .39$. For the strategy, visualizing, the data indicate a statistically significant difference in the use of the strategy between students who like to read and students who do not like to read, $t(584) = 4.650\ p < .000, d = .39$.

Teachers helping during reading instruction. A Chi-square test was run on the data regarding students' grade level and the type of reading help students wanted from teachers (e.g., go over reading step by step, teach vocabulary, visualize during reading, ask questions of the text, help to find main idea, help to find details, help to synthesize, help to make inferences, show how to make connections, and teach summarizing). I chose a Chi-square test as there were two categorical measures identified for each student (grade level and type of reading help desired). Three of these variables were statistically significant as demonstrated by the frequencies cross tabulated; there is a significant relationship between the students' preference for step-by-step help and grade level, X^2 (2, $N = 690) = 8.67$, $p < .05$. Additionally, there is a significant relationship between the students' preference for teachers to help with visualization and grade level, X^2 (2, $N = 690) = 6.12, p < .05$. There is also a significant relationship between the students' preference for teachers to help students ask questions during reading and grade level, X^2 (2, $N = 690) = 6.35, p < .05$.

Qualitative Analysis

I conducted the focus group interviews, recorded the interviews, and kept field notes during the interviews. The transcribed interviews resulted in 49 pages of data that were verbatim from the recording. I made corrections to the transcript as necessary for coherence. I identified themes from the analysis of the data. Once I identified a trend in the data, I noted and coded patterns, and then, derived subcodes. I compared my field notes to the codes and added narrative reflections to develop understanding of possible themes. I identified three themes from the analysis of the transcripts: (a) Increases in student learning occur when teachers work with students in reading; (b) Students prefer activities more than reading and have exposure to limited text types; and (c) Teachers can demonstrate they believe in students through reading instruction.

Researcher's subjectivities. For the qualitative portion of this study, my position as the researcher, asking questions, recording answers, and taking notes, did not change throughout the process of the interviews. However, my attitudes did change as my subjectivities as a White female, former teacher, principal and English language arts staff developer provided a lens through which I listened to and interpreted the data. My research with the diverse student population stemmed from my personal and professional interests in closing achievement gaps in reading between races, ethnicities, classes, and gender. I realized that the students' identities, including their racial, ethnic, class, and gender identities affected their responses.

While analyzing the data, I discussed my findings and thoughts with two critical friends who could provide a perspective different from my own (Miles & Huberman, 1994). The critical friends identified assumptions that I was bringing to the data and helped me to alter my analysis when I shared my perspectives with them. I met with two colleagues and discussed the trends that I saw in the data. My colleagues made suggestions based on what I stated and explained regarding what I saw as trends. They suggested that I eliminate one trend that I had identified, as it appeared that perhaps my knowledge about the reading instruction in the classrooms was affecting my judgment. These discussions with critical friends happened during the identification of the themes while coding the data and after identification of all the themes.

Increases in student reading with teachers' help. Students' ability to read often changed due to direct intervention from the teacher. Students shared that when teachers connected reading to the real world, they enjoyed reading and read more. They also shared that they wanted the teacher to help them with reading, and to do something that made a difference, not simply to repeat what the teacher had said. Students gave examples about what they enjoyed reading in class and how they wished their teachers would work with them in reading. One student shared:

> Once in a while we have to go to the book. We do big projects on the unit to understand it instead of just sitting there reading the books and taking notes. We would be interacting with each other. Usually we read primary source instead of the textbook, or like we read both and then compare them to see how they match up.

Students also described teachers who they thought were good teachers and how those teachers helped with reading. One student said that good teachers know when the class needs help, "She just reads it over with us and summarizes it with us and helps us understand it at the same time because I know that more than half the class does not understand it." Another student described a teacher who helps students read in this way, "Sometimes they go around and help when they get upset with us, but it's better to tell us what we're doing [wrong, in reading] instead of just giving it to us and starting to teach it." Another student described an exact strategy, "They say to mark the text, to annotate it, do whatever makes us comfortable with the reading [of] the text and make you understand it. Go over it and summarize."

Students think reading is hard, but persist. Students did not report that they liked to read. Twenty-five students from six focus groups reported that they did not like to read. Students gave several reasons why they do not like to read. They stated, "It's boring." "I am not that patient to read." "I don't like to read because it kinda takes time. I am better at just listening." "Reading is hard … our teacher, he gives us pages in a book and we have to find the answers and it is on a certain topic." "They make us read it on our own and it is hard." "I find it boring to read; when I read my head hurts."

Even though students reported overwhelmingly that they did not like to read, they discussed in depth what they did enjoy during reading. Mostly the students reported on specific genres they read like horror or mystery or science. Some reported that their teachers have them read in class and then do something with the information. One student described, "They make us think about that and then our class in tech; we are doing this one thing where we have to solve real problems, like in the community." Students enjoyed working on real problems and reading to solve them. "We search information on websites and look for books that have stuff on it."

Students also kept at their reading if the reading involved activities like searching on the internet or reading a script and doing Readers' Theater. Students who discussed how they persisted at reading gave specific ideas about what helped them keep trying to read even though they did not like to read. Students shared ideas about reading in groups or pairs and sharing the reading, having teachers give definitions of words, and taking stories and rewriting the endings, or writing about a poem that they had read in class. Students persisted at reading even when they found reading difficult. About one-half the students reported that they do not read at home.

Belief in students through reading instruction. Teachers can show that they believe in their students by providing support or scaffolding during the reading of text in the classroom. The students described support in a variety of ways from rereading a passage, helping a student sound out a word and telling how to pronounce a word, or giving the meaning of a word. The message about how teachers believed in their students came through in how students described how their teachers made them feel during reading. One student when describing how it felt not to get help in reading said, "[It's] Frustrating because you feel like you're arguing and it's useless." Another student said, "[You feel like] you're the dumbest one in the class." Students shared their thinking when discussing how a teacher can show he or she cares about how well the student was reading. One said, "If the teacher believed in you, they would actually care."

Students also discussed that help in reading shows that a teacher cares. One student described the teacher's caring, "That she would give us examples of it [the reading]." A second student added, "They would actually work with you." Another student added to the idea by stating a specific action; she said, "Like, if it's a harder level reading then they will go through it with us and annotate it and explain what it means and how it relates to other things." Students were also specific about what helped them read. One student shared a story from his background, "When I was in first grade, my teacher would give me random books, and I would have to read the book for about 30 minutes. That helped me a lot."

DISCUSSION

The results of this study revealed information about what comprehension strategies students' use, and the ways they wish their teacher would help them when reading. The results also indicated that teachers could make a difference for middle school students, showing them that they believe in them by focusing on reading instruction.

Given the findings regarding the use of comprehension strategies and the significant difference between students' comprehension of text they liked to read, it is possible that increased instruction of reading comprehension skills in middle school could impact students' desire to read and provide breadth to the types of strategies they use, as stronger readers use a variety of reading comprehension strategies (Boardman et al., 2017). For example, if students in middle school classrooms learned to visualize while reading or synthesize ideas in texts, in addition to summarizing and finding the main idea, students may be able to understand increasingly difficult text with greater ease. As Brown and Broemmel (2011) discussed, students who need comprehension instruction do not often receive what they need to increase their learning. The findings of this study indicate that teachers teach only some comprehension strategies.

This study also looked at students' thoughts and experiences in the classroom, specifically considering what students want their teachers to do to help them during reading. There were 10 items listed on the survey describing how teachers might help during reading and students picked their top three. The data indicated a significant relationship between students' grade level and the ways they wish their teacher would help. Given these findings, if teachers show students how to read step by step, help students visualize during reading, and teach students to ask questions of the text, students in middle grades might have more success in comprehending what they are reading. The qualitative and quantitative findings support the need to teach reading comprehension skills that are different from summarizing and finding the main idea. Students spoke about how they felt teachers did not believe in them if they did not help them understand what they are reading, and this supports the data findings regarding the teaching of comprehension strategies.

Teachers need to show students they believe in them by keeping the expectations at a level that is not so rigorous that it is out of reach for students, but rather, at a level that communicates, "You can do this." Students need a teacher who cares. Teachers can demonstrate this care through engaging work that respects students' intelligence and gives them real world problems to work through in reading and research. When teachers support students through care and focus, they are scaffolding instruction for students to ensure their success. Students need authentic instruction and practice completing real-world reading tasks; using real-world tasks to engage students is one way teachers scaffold student success (Akhavan, 2018).

The findings from this study indicate a statistically significant difference in understanding what students read based on whether they like to read or do not like to read. As in Gaffney and Anderson's (2000) study, the data confirm that students who do not like to read often do not understand what they are reading. These findings also indicate that success in understanding text is somewhat connected to the desire to read. At a broad level, these findings reinforce the idea that teachers need to teach broader reading comprehension skills at the middle school level. At a more granular level, the findings indicate that students want their teachers to teach them reading comprehension strategies, and based on frequency of what the teachers teach, it would be helpful for teachers to broaden students' repertoire of strategies by teaching visualization and asking questions of text, in addition to lesser-used strategies like synthesizing and identifying vocabulary. Teachers who help their students read by teaching comprehension strategies indicate to students that they really care; they develop relationships and increase the students' overall positive feelings about reading.

Based on what the students said about reading in middle school, it appeared that they desire a relationship with their teacher—a relationship that shows that their teacher cares enough to help them in ways beyond repetition or giving worksheets. Students indicated that they feel teachers care when giving them interesting reading materials in class and help by breaking the reading down. Students said that they do better with their reading when teachers care.

REFERENCES

Afflerbach, P., & VanSledright, B. (2001). Hath! Doth! What? Middle graders reading innovative history text. *Journal of Adolescent & Adult Literacy, 44*, 696–707.

Aikens, N. L., & Barbarin, O. A. (2008). Socioeconomic differences in reading trajectories: The contribution of family, neighborhood, and school contexts. *Journal of Educational Psychology, 100*, 235–251.

Akhavan, N. (2018). *The big book of literacy tasks, grades K–8: Balanced literacy activities students do, (not you!).* Thousand Oaks, CA: Corwin.

Allington, R. L., & Cunningham, P. M. (2002). *Schools that work: Where all children learn to read and write* (2nd ed.). Boston, MA: Allyn & Bacon.

Atkinson, J. W. (1964). *An introduction to motivation.* Princeton, NJ: Van Nostrand.

Barton, M. L., Heidema, C., & Jordan, D. (2002). Teaching reading in mathematics and science. *Educational Leadership, 60*(3), 24–28.

Biancarosa, G., & Snow, C. (2006). *Reading next: A vision for action and research in middle and high school literacy. A report to Carnegie Corporation of New York* (2nd ed.). Washington, DC: Alliance for Excellent Education. Retrieved from https://www.carnegie.org/media/filer_public/b7/5f/b75fba81-16cb-422d-ab59-373a6a07eb74/ccny_report_2004_reading.pdf

Block, C. C., & Pressley, M. E. (2002). *Comprehension instruction: Research-based best practices, solving problems in the teaching of literacy.* New York, NY: Guilford Press.

Boardman, A. G., Boelé, A. L., & Klingner, J. L. (2017). Strategy instruction shifts teacher and student discussions during text-based discussions. *Reading Research Quarterly, 53,* 175–195.

Brooks, C. F., & Young, S. L. (2011). Are choice-making opportunities needed in the classroom? Using self-determination theory to consider student motivation and learner empowerment. *International Journal of Teaching and Learning in Higher Education 23,* 48–59.

Brown, C. L., & Broemmel, A. D. (2011). Deep scaffolding: Enhancing reading experiences of English language learners. *The New England Reading Association Journal, 46*(2), 34–39.

Dole, J. A., Brown, K. J., & Trathen, W. (1996). The effects of strategy instruction on the comprehension performance of at-risk students. *Reading Research Quarterly, 31,* 62–88.

Dole, J. A., Duffy, G. G., Roehler, L. R., & Pearson, P. D. (1991). Moving from the old to the new: Research on reading comprehension instruction. *Review of Educational Research, 1,* 239–264.

Duke, N. K., & Pearson, P. D. (2002). Effective practices for developing reading comprehension. In A. E. Farstrup & S. J. Samuels (Eds.), *What research has to say about reading instruction* (3rd ed., pp. 205–242). Newark, DE: International Reading Association.

Dymock, S. (2005). Teaching expository text structure awareness. *The Reading Teacher, 59,* 177–181.

Ed-Data, Education Data Partnership. (2019). *School summary data.* Retrieved from http://www.ed-data.org/

Faggela-Luby, M. N., Ware, S. M., & Capozzoli, A. (2009). Adolescent literacy—Reviewing adolescent literacy reports: Key components and critical questions. *Journal of Literacy Research, 41,* 453–475.

Fang, Z., & Coatam, S. (2013). Disciplinary literacy: What you need to know about it. *Journal of Adolescent & Adult Literacy, 56,* 627–632.

Fisher, D., & Frey, N. (2013). *Better learning through structured teaching.* Alexandria, VA: Association for Supervision and Curriculum Development.

Kainz, K., & Vernon-Feagans, L. (2007). The ecology of early reading development for children in poverty. *The Elementary School Journal, 107*, 407–427.

Gaffney, J. S., & Anderson, R. C. (2000). Trends in reading research in the United States: Changing intellectual currents over three decades. In M. L. Kamil, P. B. Mosenthal, P. D. Pearson, & R. Barr (Eds.), *Handbook of reading research* (Vol. III, pp. 53–74). New York, NY: Erlbaum.

Houge, T. T., Geier, C., & Peyton, D. (2008). Targeting adolescents' literacy skills using one-to-one instruction with research-based practices. *Journal of Adolescent & Adult Literacy, 51*, 640–650.

Mackensie, N., & Knipe, S. (2006). Research dilemmas: Paradigms, methods and methodology. *Issues in Educational Research, 16*, 193–205.

Means, B., & Knapp, M. S. (1991). Cognitive approaches to teaching advanced skills to educationally disadvantaged students. *The Phi Delta Kappan, 73*, 282–289.

Miles, M. B., & Huberman, A. M. (1994). *Qualitative data analysis: An expanded sourcebook.* Thousand Oaks, CA: SAGE.

McKenna, M. C. & Kear, D. (1990). Measuring attitude toward reading: A new tool for teachers. *The Reading Teacher, 43*, 626–639.

Morgan, D. L. (2007). Paradigms lost and pragmatism regained: Methodological implications of combining qualitative and quantitative methods. *Journal of Mixed Methods Research, 1*, 48–76.

National Center for Education Statistics. (2011). *The Nation's Report Card: Reading 2011* (NCES 2012–457). Washington, DC: National Center for Education Statistics, Institute of Education Sciences, U.S. Department of Education. Retrieved from https://nces.ed.gov/nationsreportcard/pdf/main2011/2012457.pdf

National Reading Panel. (2000). *Teaching children to read. An evidence-based assessment of the scientific research literature on reading and its implications for reading instruction. Reports of the subgroups.* Washington, DC: U.S. Department of Health and Human Services, Public Health Service, National Institutes of Health, NIH Publication No. 00-4769. Retrieved from https://www.nichd.nih.gov/sites/default/files/publications/pubs/nrp/Documents/report.pdf

Ness, M. (2009). Reading comprehension strategies in secondary content area classrooms: Teacher use of and attitudes toward reading comprehension instruction. *Reading Horizons, 49*(2), 143–166.

Palinscar, A. S., & Schutz, K. (2011). Reconnecting strategy instruction with its theoretical roots. *Theory Into Practice, 50*, 85–92.

Pearson, P. D., Roehler, L. R., Dole, J. A., & Duffy, G. G. (1984). *Developing expertise in reading comprehension: What should be taught? How should it be taught?* Champaign, IL: Center for the Study of Reading, University of Illinois at Urbana-Champaign.

Pitcher, S. M., Martinez, G. Dicembre, E. A., Fewster, D., & McCormick, M. K. (2010). The literacy needs of adolescents in their own words. *Journal of Adolescent and Adult Literacy, 53*, 636–645.

Pressley, M. (2000). What should comprehension instruction be the instruction of? In M. L. Kamil, P. Mosenthal, P. D. Pearson, & R. Barr (Eds.), *Handbook of reading research* (Vol. III, pp. 545–562). New York, NY: Longman.

Pressley, M., & Wharton-McDonald, R. (1997). Skilled comprehension and its development through instruction. *School Psychology Review, 26*, 448–466.

Stahl, S. A., & Yaden, D. B. (2004). The development of literacy in preschool and primary grades: Work by the center for the improvement of early reading achievement. *Elementary School Journal, 105*, 141–165.

Swanson, E., & Wanzek, J. (2013). Applying research in reading comprehension to social studies instruction for middle and high school students. *Intervention in School and Clinic, 49*, 142–147.

Tierney, R. J., & Cunningham, J. W. (1984). Research on teaching reading comprehension. In P. D. Pearson, R. Barr, M. L. Kamil, & P. Mosenthal (Eds.), *Handbook of reading research* (Vol. 1, pp. 609–656). New York, NY: Longman.

Vaughn, S., Klingner, J. K., Swanson, E. A., Boardman, A. G., Roberts, G., Mohammed, S. S., & Stillman-Speak, S. J. (2011). Efficacy of collaborative strategic reading with middle school students. *American Educational Research Journal, 48*, 938–964.

Wigfield, A. & Asher, S. R. (1984). Social and motivational influences on reading. In P. D. Pearson (Ed.), *Handbook of reading research* (pp. 423–452). Mahwah, NJ: Erlbaum.

Weiner, B., Frieze, I., Kulka, A., Reed, L., Rest, S., & Rosenbaum, R. M. (1971). Perceiving the causes of success and failure. In E. E. Jones, D. E. Kanouse, H. H. Kelley, R. E. Nisbett, S. Valins, & B. Weiner (Eds.), *Attribution: Perceiving the causes of behavior* (pp. 95–120). Morristown, NJ: General Learning Press.

APPENDIX A

Student Survey

1. What is your gender?   Boy   Girl   Decline to state
2. What grade are you in school?   6   7   8
3. In what class are you taking this   English   Social Studies   Science
    survey?
4. Do you like to read?   Yes   No
5. Do you read when you are not in   Never   Sometimes   Always
    school?

Please use the scale to answer the following questions. You will choose one answer on the scale, for example,
never, rarely, occasionally, frequently, or almost always/always.

6. Do you read in the class you are   Never   Rarely   Occasionally   Frequently   Almost
    in   always/always
    now?

7. When you read in the class you   Never   Rarely   Occasionally   Frequently   Almost
    are in now, do you understand   always/always
    what you are reading?

8. For the class you are in now,
    mark the word on the scale that
    best describes how often your
    teacher involves you:

    (a) Whole class: teacher talking,   Never   Rarely   Occasionally   Frequently   Almost
        you listening   always/always

    (b) Small group: teacher teaching,   Never   Rarely   Occasionally   Frequently   Almost
        you listening   always/always

    (c) Small group: teacher and   Never   Rarely   Occasionally   Frequently   Almost
        students talking together   always/always

    (d) Whole class: teacher and   Never   Rarely   Occasionally   Frequently   Almost
        students talking together   always/always

    (e) Teacher reteaches something   Never   Rarely   Occasionally   Frequently   Almost
        the whole class didn't   always/always
        understand

    (f) Teacher teaches you   Never   Rarely   Occasionally   Frequently   Almost
        something you didn't   always/always
        understand by yourself

9. For the class you are in now,
    please read the list of activities
    below and mark on the scale
    the word that describes how
    often you are doing these   Almost
    activities in class.   always/always

    (a) Taking notes   Never   Rarely   Occasionally   Frequently   Almost
                                                                                                  always/always
    (b) Comparing or sharing notes   Never   Rarely   Occasionally   Frequently
        with other students   Almost
                                                                                                  always/always
    (c) Giving a presentation   Never   Rarely   Occasionally   Frequently   Almost
                                                                                                  always/always
    (d) Role playing   Never   Rarely   Occasionally   Frequently   Almost
                                                                                                  always/always
    (e) Writing short assignments/   Almost
        writing answers   always/always
                                         Never   Rarely   Occasionally   Frequently

(Appendix A continues on next page)

APPENDIX A (CONTINUED}

Student Survey

(f) Writing long assignments/writing papers	Never	Rarely	Occasionally	Frequently	Almost always/always
(g) Playing games with reading content	Never	Rarely	Occasionally	Frequently	Almost always/always
(h) Solving a problem	Never	Rarely	Occasionally	Frequently	Almost always/always
(i) Asking a question or researching an answer	Never	Rarely	Occasionally	Frequently	Almost always/always

10. For the class you are in now, please read the list of activities below and mark on the scale the word that describes how often you are using these strategies to help you read.

(a) Summarizing	Never	Rarely	Occasionally	Frequently	Almost always/always
(b) Identifying main ideas	Never	Rarely	Occasionally	Frequently	Almost always/always
(c) Identifying key details	Never	Rarely	Occasionally	Frequently	Almost always/always
(d) Inferring	Never	Rarely	Occasionally	Frequently	Almost always/always
(e) Synthesizing	Never	Rarely	Occasionally	Frequently	Almost always/always
(f) Visualizing	Never	Rarely	Occasionally	Frequently	Almost always/always
(g) Asking questions of text	Never	Rarely	Occasionally	Frequently	Almost always/always
(h) Making connections	Never	Rarely	Occasionally	Frequently	Almost always/always
(i) Monitoring your reading to make sure you understand	Never	Rarely	Occasionally	Frequently	Almost always/always

11. For the class you are in now, please choose the three activities you like best that help you read better.

It helps me when my teacher:

_____ Shows me how to read by going over the reading step-by-step
_____ Teaches me vocabulary for the reading.
_____ Helps me visualize what I am reading.
_____ Helps me ask question of the text or author.
_____ Teaches me to find the main idea.
_____ Teaches me to find the details.
_____ Helps me synthesize information I am learning.
_____ Helps me make inferences about the topic I am reading.
_____ Shows me how to make connections to my reading.
_____ Teaches me to summarize.

(Appendix A continues on next page)

APPENDIX A (CONTINUED}

Student Survey

12. How often does your teacher have
    you read these texts in class?

(a) Textbooks	Never	Rarely	Occasionally	Frequently	Almost always/always
(b) Literature anthologies	Never	Rarely	Occasionally	Frequently	Almost always/always
(c) Supplementary books	Never	Rarely	Occasionally	Frequently	Almost always/always
(d) Magazine articles	Never	Rarely	Occasionally	Frequently	Almost always/always
(e) Short, interesting books	Never	Rarely	Occasionally	Frequently	Almost always/always
(f) Online texts/articles	Never	Rarely	Occasionally	Frequently	Almost always/always
(g) Websites	Never	Rarely	Occasionally	Frequently	Almost always/always
(h) Copies of short stories/texts	Never	Rarely	Occasionally	Frequently	Almost always/always
(i) Novels	Never	Rarely	Occasionally	Frequently	Almost always/always
(j) Chapter books	Never	Rarely	Occasionally	Frequently	Almost always/always
(k) Newspaper articles	Never	Rarely	Occasionally	Frequently	Almost always/always
(l) Picture books	Never	Rarely	Occasionally	Frequently	Almost always/always

APPENDIX B

Student Interview Questions From
the Focus Group Interview Protocol

1. Do you like to read? Why, or why not?
2. What types of material do you like to read?
3. Do you have to do any reading in English, science or social studies class?
4. (If yes) What kinds of reading do you do in those classes?
5. Does your teacher help you to read those texts (articles) on your own?
6. When you read in those classes on your own, do you understand what you are reading?
7. What makes understanding those texts (articles) easier?
8. How do you share your "reading" or what you learn from your reading of those texts?
9. How do you "use" or apply your reading or what you learn from your reading, to your thinking, your life, or other tasks you do inside or outside of school?
10. Do your teachers in English, science or social studies help you learn to read better?
11. (If yes) Tell me how, what does your teacher do exactly that helps you read in that class better.
12. (If no) Tell me what you wish your teacher would do to help you read in that class better.
13. Tell me about your most, and least, favorite teacher that taught you to read better.
14. What did you learn from your favorite teacher in order to read better?
15. Did that teacher ever talk about reading comprehension, or reading strategies? If yes, explain.
16. (If yes) Do you think these strategies would help you read in English, science or social studies? (If no, explain)
17. (If student is positive overall) Tell me how you help yourself read and understand.
18. (If student seems to struggle as a reader) Tell me what you wish your teachers would do to help you read in those classes.
19. Is there anything else you would like to share with me that could help your read better in school?

SECTION II

EXPLORING CURRICULUM, INSTRUCTION, AND ASSESSMENT THROUGH TEACHERS' DISPOSITIONS AND PERSPECTIVES

CHAPTER 6

CULTURALLY RELEVANT PEDAGOGY AND CONNECTIVISM

Disciplinary Literacy Challenges in Linguistically Diverse STEM Classrooms in the Middle Grades

Ebony Terrell Shockley and Kelly K. Ivy
University of Maryland College Park

Maria Peters
University of the District of Columbia

ABSTRACT

Possibilities for practices that support culturally and linguistically diverse students appear widely in the context of elementary and secondary literature but are not as prevalent in the young adolescent or middle grades literature. Using a culturally relevant pedagogy lens, in this study we reveal considerations for the teaching and assessment of diverse learners. The vignettes of

Curriculum, Instruction, and Assessment:
Intersecting New Needs and New Approaches, pp. 127–153
Copyright © 2020 by Information Age Publishing
All rights of reproduction in any form reserved.

a purposive sample of teachers in high performing middle schools show how they enact a culturally relevant pedagogy in STEM (science, technology, engineering, and mathematics) classrooms. In this chapter, we present teacher narratives that describe interactions with students, concepts for lessons, and strategies for instruction and assessment. We also discuss implications for classroom culture, making connections, disciplinary literacy skills, and digital learning.

Over time, teachers in the United States have had an increased chance of interacting with students who are culturally and linguistically diverse (CLD) (Carter & Darling-Hammond, 2016; National Center for Education Statistics, 2015; Zhang, 2017). These teacher-student interactions include students of color, students who speak other dialects of English (Baugh, 2003; Gibson & Terrell Shockley, 2018; Solano-Flores, 2006; Wolfram & Schilling-Estes, 1998), and students in English for Speakers of Other Languages (ESOL) programs (Bailey & Carroll, 2015). In some states, learners in ESOL programs represent more than a quarter of the K–12 population (i.e., California, Texas), and in other states, they represent more than one-fifth of the K–12 population (i.e., Arizona, Florida, Nevada, New Jersey, New Mexico, New York, Rhode Island) (National Center for Education Statistics, 2015). Teachers need to be prepared to meet the needs of the growing population of CLD learners (Carter & Darling-Hammond, 2016).

STATEMENT OF THE PROBLEM

According to the U.S. Census Bureau (2015), more than 350 languages exist in the United States. With many languages also having multiple dialects (Solano-Flores, 2006), teachers in classrooms with students who are culturally and linguistically different from their students need effective instructional and assessment practices and appropriate communication strategies (Abedi, 2006; Bailey & Carroll, 2015). Some studies that investigate effective practices for culturally and linguistically diverse learners highlight the importance of teachers' content knowledge and expertise (Liu, 2013) as well as their content proficiency (Zhang, 2017). Other studies highlight the need for teachers to integrate culturally appropriate resources (e.g., cultural scaffolding) (Gay, 2002) and instructional strategies that align with students' language or literacy proficiency (de Schonewise & Klingner, 2012). The strategies in the literature for supporting CLD learners are often fragmented, and researchers are only beginning to understand the effective practices for CLD learners (Carter & Darling-Hammond, 2016; Faltis & Valdés, 2016; International Literacy Association, 2015).

Compacting the issue with identifying effective practices, particularly for CLD learners, is the disciplinary knowledge required for each content area, especially in science, technology, engineering, and mathematics (STEM) (Faltis & Valdés, 2016; Graham, Kerkhoff, & Spires, 2017). Each content area brings a discipline-specific culture, its own language, and distinct vocabulary (Faltis & Valdés, 2016; Graham et al., 2017; Short, Vogt, & Echevarría, 2011). "Disciplinary literacy has been slow to be recognized by middle school researchers, perhaps because on the surface, disciplinary literacy seems counter to the interdisciplinary nature of middle school curriculum" (Graham et al., 2017, p. 64). The literacy practices to teach the specialized vocabulary are presented by content area, in isolation (Casey, 2013), and students do not receive opportunities to make global connections (Carter & Darling-Hammond, 2016) or text connections to apply the terms to other contexts as the CLD literature suggests (Carter & Darling-Hammond, 2016; Faltis & Valdés, 2016). CLD learners who bring different languages or different forms of English are attempting to make connections and acquire their school English (Gibson & Terrell Shockley, 2018), as well as their content vocabulary (Bailey & Carroll, 2015; Crandall, 1993; Short et al., 2011; Wolfram & Schilling-Estes, 1998). At the middle grades, this is particularly challenging given the stages of adolescence during which learners' dispositions may be in flux (Cook, Faulkner, & Howell, 2016; Kaywell, 2009), and they may bring different skills for which their teachers are not prepared (Carter & Darling-Hammond, 2016; Faulkner et al., 2017; Short et al., 2011).

PURPOSE STATEMENT

In this chapter, we examined data from middle school STEM teachers who enact a culturally relevant pedagogy (CRP) (Ladson-Billings, 1995) to appeal to culturally and linguistically diverse students. We considered other culturally significant concepts and decided that CRP as an established framework captures the inclusive lens of the study. As Howard and Rodriguez-Scheel (2017) explained:

> CRP provided an important landmark in research, theory, and practice because it promoted the idea that students of color possess a rich, complex, and robust set of cultural practices, experiences, and knowledge that are essential for learning and understanding. Furthermore, the call for cultural relevance in pedagogy was made to recognize that the rich cultural fabric that students possess was valuable. (p. 5)

The aim is to highlight the strategies that middle school educators of CLD students identified as effective practices. From these teacher narratives, we share practices that highlight discipline-specific strategies in STEM that appeal to diverse learners.

THEORETICAL FRAMEWORK

Culturally relevant pedagogy (CRP) exists within the teaching practices of the carefully selected educators in this study. CRP is an integral component of teaching CLD students. To have CRP, an educator should consider their relationships with students and the ways in which they can bridge the cultural differences between home and school.

Teachers must contend that all students are capable of success and maintain the following goals:

- Students must experience academic success;
- Students must develop and/or maintain cultural competence; and
- Students must develop a critical consciousness through which they challenge the status quo (Ladson-Billings, 1995, p. 160).

Documenting strategies and describing the contexts and habits of mind of teachers using CRP will add to the literature and to the pedagogical knowledge of teachers working with CLD learners in middle-level classrooms. Ladson-Billings (1994) described CRP as "a pedagogy that empowers students intellectually, socially, emotionally, and politically by using cultural referents to impart knowledge, skills, and attitudes" (p. 382). Teachers enacting this pedagogy have a positive disposition toward students and their culture. Integrating culture that is relatable to students is an opportunity to build knowledge, rather than to view students and their intersectional culture with a deficit lens. Teachers need to move beyond a general sense of relevance when incorporating CRP. The goal is to help students become critically conscious (Ladson-Billings, 1995) and move CRP from theory to practice by integrating CRP into problem-solving that is inclusive of issues that impact students and topics that are of interest to students (Brown, Boda, Lemmi, & Monroe, 2019). In an examination of 20 years of CRP, Howard and Rodriguez-Scheel (2017) described Ladson-Billings work as a call to action for practitioners and researchers to collaborate on the "marriage of culture and pedagogy" (p. 5). This call to action continues in this study, positioned with a similar aim, to deploy practices and research-based experiences that result in educational outcomes and experiences that are equitable for CLD learners.

While CRP frames our study, connectivism (Siemens, 2005) is a secondary lens for this work. Connectivism extends from a combination of objectivism (similar to behaviorism), interpretivism (similar to constructivism), and pragmatism (similar to cognitivism). Connectivists recognize knowledge as a network and define knowledge as inclusive of Vygotsky's (1978) zone of proximal development. They centralize technology as a resource and network of knowledge. Siemens (2005) also described nodes, or pieces of information, that learners can experience or critique as part of the learning process. Nodes include emotions and interactions and combined with other points of information, these nodes create a network (Jacobsen, 2019). "A node grows in importance with the number of connections it has" (Jacobsen, 2019, p. 4). Increasing nodes increases knowledge and learners acquire knowledge by actions and experience. For example, they organize information and apply information using personal resources. Given the role that networks play in acquiring knowledge in STEM with the middle grades' learner, connectivism is appropriate to use as a secondary lens for our work.

Connectivism is a theory for teaching in a connected world (Siemens, 2005); it builds on other learning theories while acknowledging new knowledge in a digital age (Siemens, 2005). The principles of connectivism are that (a) learning is a connected process, (b) learning requires a critical lens, and (c) learning requires the sustaining and nurturing of connections. The principles of connectivism also state that learning and knowledge require diverse opinions. Considering the social nature of middle school STEM contexts, we use the principles of connectivism to study the CLD learner.

LITERATURE REVIEW

The review of literature documents the role of connectivism for CLD learners who are skillful with digital resources and shows how technology and information (i.e., nodes) link to networks, future careers, and prior knowledge. In addition, this section proffers the literature on preparing CLD learners in the middle grades in STEM and literacy contexts. Literacy and language are essential content areas needed to acquire many of the STEM concepts. As part of investigating effective strategies for middle school learners in STEM classrooms, this section also explicitly extends these disciplines (i.e., STEM, literacy, and language) to teacher education for CLD learners.

Connectivism and the Technology Proficient CLD Learner

Connectivism is beneficial when examining how learning and communication happen when technology is a classroom resource. As future careers depend on learners who are skillful in their communication (e.g., reading, writing, speaking, listening, viewing), the current digital age classroom needs to include technology proficiency (Andrei, 2016; Tierney, 2009; Wang & Vásquez, 2012), the "T" in STEM. The combination of different forms of communication integrated with technology increases language use and content proficiency (Tierney, 2009; Wang & Vásquez, 2012). With this in mind, teachers can use technology to build upon existing communication skills for CLD students (Terrell Shockley, Orellana, & Chicas, 2018) and provide opportunities for students to use their home language and their school language to acquire content in the classroom (González, Moll, & Amanti, 2005).

Opinions differ on whether building upon one particular communication skill or language domain at a time (e.g., reading, writing, speaking, listening) (Chen, Zhang, & Lui, 2014) is more effective than teaching a combination of communication skills simultaneously (Garrett, 2009; Hartley, 2007; Levy, 2009; Tan, Spinks, Eden, Perfetti, & Siok, 2005). If teachers in the middle grades teach language domains separately, they could build dexterity in one domain. The challenge is when students receive instruction or guidance in one domain without building proficiency in another, it is possible in this case, that teachers are supporting or creating semiliteracy. Semiliteracy occurs when students develop or reach grade-level proficiency in one domain of language but not others (Kaywell, 2009). An example of semiliteracy is teachers spending instructional time teaching reading without an accompanying writing task. The student becomes a skilled reader but not a skilled writer. Research literature addresses whether or not language domain instruction should happen simultaneously or in isolation, the findings vary on which is the best strategy. What is consistent in the literature is the inclusion of technology as part of the development of language proficiency in each domain (Garrett, 2009; Hartley, 2007; Levy, 2009; Tan et al., 2005).

Preparing the Middle Grades CLD Learner in Science and Mathematics

In science and mathematics classrooms, learners must acquire ways to gain language proficiency with reading, writing, speaking, and listening, along with the content vocabulary within the discipline. Unlike the research occurring in the field of linguistics on isolated versus interrelated domains, the disciplinary literacy research at the middle grades assumes that these communication skills are different (Graham et al., 2017). More than 40 states have adopted requirements for secondary teachers (including middle school teachers) to complete coursework on content area reading instruction (Farrell & Cirrincione, 1984; International Literacy Association, 2015). It is critical to note that disciplinary literacy is not the same as content area reading or content area literacy. Disciplinary literacy "involves unique or highly specialized skills not likely to be developed in the English language arts" (International Literacy Association, 2015, p. 2). Disciplinary literacy is different from content area literacy because it is designed for the comprehension or thinking for students to be emics and experts in the specific discipline. Students are to read, write, speak, and question in the ways articulated by the discipline (Graham et al., 2017). This is more complicated for a CLD learner, one who is possibly navigating a different language, dialect, and culture compared to other learners (Baugh, 2003; Gibson & Terrell Shockley, 2018; Wolfram & Schilling-Estes, 1998). Digital resources and technology may provide possibilities to assist CLD learners in navigating language differences in both isolated and inter-related content and literacy domains.

Lara-Alecio et al. (2012) studied 166 CLD middle school students as part of a quasi-experimental design measuring the effectiveness of a literacy-integrated science intervention on middle grades English learners' science and reading literacy achievement on accountability-based state assessments, with 80 students in the comparison group. The intervention group's instruction consisted of literacy-embedded instruction in science, inquiry-based instruction, and technology. The results of student performance on district-wide science and reading tests, as well as standardized tests of oral reading, were significant with a positive intervention effect. Specifically, the researchers used the 5Es' instruction cycle (i.e., engage, explore, explain, elaborate, evaluate) in the lessons. Developed by Bybee (1996), science teachers widely use the 5E cycle that "has a growing base of research to support its effectiveness," according to a report prepared for the Office of Science Education National Institutes of Health (Bybee et al., 2006, p. 41). The treatment group received daily 85-minute lessons that began with oral and written opportunities to use and apply science language, including direct instruction based on discipline-specific literacy (i.e., reading and writing) strategies, modeled by teachers, and a technology component. The technology component included science software that explained the science terminology using animation and simulation. Each classroom in the treatment group received computers, document cameras, digital cameras, an interactive whiteboard, and web-based resources.

Woodrich and Fan (2017) used Google Docs with CLD students through online, face-to-face, and anonymous writing activity. The use of this technology as a resource encouraged participation in literacy. The collaborative nature of the technology and the digital features assisted students in building their language and literacy skills. Given the increasing popularity of using digital resources, such as smartphones, allows for the app version of digital tools in the classroom (e.g., Google Docs) (Thorne, 2016). CLD learners can continue their engagement in discipline-specific literacy practices that include technology.

The increase of CLD learners in many U.S. classrooms, as well as the increase of technology in the middle grades, provides a greater opportunity to work with CLD students and enhance their discipline knowledge, technology skills, and communication (Bailey & Carroll, 2015; Lara-Alecio et al., 2012; Taylor & Dorsey-Gaines, 1988; Thorne, 2016). The previously described outcomes show increased participation and gains. Hwang, Shih, Ma, Shadiev, and Chen (2016) examined the influence of a mobile game system on CLD students' speaking and listening skills. Compared with control-group students who received the traditional method, students who engaged in game-based learning activities scored higher on the verbal test provided to all participants in the study.

The Language of Science and Mathematics

Matching assessments to instruction using the same objective aligns the pedagogical practices enacted by content teachers. The literature suggests that effective pedagogical practices for content teachers' CLD learners require proficiency in both English language instruction and content area instruction (Short et al., 2011). As students acquire English, teachers create opportunities for learning content (Brooks, 2016) such as mathematics and science. Learners need to acquire the language of science or mathematics while also learning English (Short et al., 2011). The language of science includes the concepts and word knowledge that help students articulate their thinking and demonstrate their conceptions of science phenomena (Carey, 1986; Short et al., 2011; Zwiers, 2008). According to Lee, Quinn, and Valdés (2013):

> Engagement in any of the science and engineering practices involves both scientific sense-making and language use. The practices intertwine with one another in the sense-making process, which is a key endeavor that helps students to transition from their naïve conceptions of the world to more scientifically based conceptions. Engagement in these practices is also language intensive. (p. 224)

With regard to mathematics, Zwiers et al. (2017) described the language of math as:

> the very doing of math, students have naturally occurring opportuni- ties to learn and notice mathematical ways of making sense and talking about ideas and the world. It is our responsibility as educators to structure,

highlight, and bolster these opportunities ... help students develop their own command of the "mathematical register" is therefore not an additional burden on teachers, but already embedded in a commitment to supporting students to become powerful mathematical thinkers and "do-ers." (p. 4)

For STEM teachers of CLD learners, in addition to teaching content vocabulary, they need to help students build upon their prior knowledge as novices in exploring science phenomena and mathematical register. They also need to help students make sense of the terminology in the content. To this end, STEM teachers must embody skills necessary for navigating students' cultural and linguistic differences so that the students can adequately engage in discipline-specific practices.

Culturally Relevant Pedagogy and Teaching Diverse Audiences

The pedagogical practices of teachers of CLD students vary and may depend on student characteristics (Carter & Darling-Hammond, 2016; Terrell Shockley, 2017). The variation ranges from the use of different resources (e.g., technology), classroom contexts (e.g., whole group or cooperative groups), and their rationale for teaching diverse audiences (Carter & Darling-Hammond, 2016; Faltis & Valdés, 2016; Gay, 2002). Determining the rationale for teaching, along with the barriers for teaching, is helpful in planning to reach and meet the instructional needs of the students. Teachers may have their own goals but also work to meet the goals of their school, school district, or even the parents. To meet these goals, teachers are encouraged to build a rapport with parents and students to identify learners' strengths both in school and outside of school (González et al., 2005; Terrell Shockley et al., 2018).

The literature refers to considering students' out of school knowledge and the culture that they value at home as funds of knowledge (González et al., 2005). Advocates of funds of knowledge maintain that bringing students' home experiences into the classroom provides a rich opportunity for in-school cultural validation. A culturally relevant pedagogy aligns with a funds of knowledge classroom culture, in that, CRP is an approach that teachers use to connect with their students and engage them, by capitalizing on their culture and differences in their ethnicity, race, gender, age, language, or socioeconomic status (Howard & Rodriguez-Scheel, 2017; Ladson-Billings, 1995). In the middle grades, considering CRP as a resource to reach students is helpful, as some students are disengaged and disinterested in course topics given the challenges of adolescence (Cook et al., 2016; Kaywell, 2009; Taliaferro & Parris, 2009). Cultivating a culturally relevant classroom culture can aid teachers with classroom engagement and uninvolved students (Blanchard et al., 2015; Howard & Rodriguez-Scheel, 2017).

A lack of involvement and engagement are contributing factors that lead to the academic failure of adolescent CLD learners (Kaywell, 2009; Taliaferro & Parris, 2009; Taylor & Dorsey-Gaines, 1988). For instance, students may feel that they are less smart, experience fewer opportunities to participate, or conclude that they do not belong when their peers or teachers are unsupportive when they read, write, or speak differently than they do (Fisher, Frey, & Rothenberg, 2008; Gibson & Terrell Shockley, 2018; Taylor & Dorsey-Gaines, 1989). This includes speakers of various forms of English such as African American English (Gibson & Terrell Shockley, 2018). Studies show gains when linguistically diverse learners receive a teacher, a school community, and a curriculum that values and incorporates their culture (Blanchard et al., 2015; Carter & Darling-Hammond, 2016; Gay, 2002; Taylor & Dorsey-Gaines, 1988).

Culturally Relevant Pedagogy and Building Relationships

As teacher-student relationships are an essential part of CRP, educators must foster relationships with CLD students that recognizes and validates their culture (González et al., 2005). Bonner (2014) suggested that academic achievement influences students' negative mathematics identity development. However, teachers can strengthen students' mathematics identities through building positive teacher-student relationships. Cholewa, Amatea, West-Olatunji, and Wright (2012) also noted that engaging interactions between teachers and students are meaningful in building relationships that facilitate learning. In their case study, they examined the practices of a highly effective mathematics teacher in a CLD elementary school. Bonner's work highlighted teachers who focus on building teacher-student relationships by gaining knowledge about students' culture. This cultural knowledge is what teachers use to communicate with students more effectively and provide them with access to mathematics content (Bonner, 2014). Students were able to relate to the content through examples that were meaningful to them because of the cultural connection.

Meaningful mathematics instruction centered on students' culture is critical to student engagement and involvement (Taylor, 2013; Ukpokodu, 2011). For example, middle grades Common Core Mathematics Standards include Ratios and Proportions. If students have shared that they attend church, for example, teachers may be able to use tithing as a culturally relevant mathematics practice to engage students with the familiar and build upon background knowledge, as tithing is the concept of 1/10 of a particular amount (Taylor, 2013). Battey (2013) noted that in diverse classroom contexts, cultural knowledge is necessary. Battey also stated that the lack thereof is unfortunate because children in CLD schooling contexts are often students who would benefit from teachers with strong content and cultural knowledge. Ukpokodu (2011) observed that culturally responsive teachers infuse content and cultural knowledge into their classrooms by "using word problems that are culturally familiar; integrating social issues relevant to the students' community; and evaluating instructional materials and resources for hidden curriculum and bias" (p. 51). Recognizing students' cultural forms of knowledge provides educators an opportunity to leverage relationships with students' families (González et al., 2005).

METHODOLOGY

To study the inherent complexity of CRP in adolescent middle school STEM classrooms with large percentages of CLD learners, the research design for this study was qualitative. A qualitative approach allowed examination of the teachers' pedagogy and the way instruction occurred from their perspective. We employed qualitative methods to capture the in-depth experiences that the teachers provided (Marshall & Rossman, 1995). We drew upon interviews and reflections to understand how teachers engage their CLD students and how they provide culturally relevant instruction and assessment. We aimed to build on existing literature and provide insight into instructional strategies missing from the literature on CLD learners in middle school STEM classrooms. We guided our work by the following, broad research questions.

Research Questions

- What are the perspectives and recurring practices among teachers of CLD learners in STEM middle school classrooms?
- What are the instructional resources including technology that teachers with CRP use to ensure that CLD middle school students receive effective instruction in STEM classrooms?
- What instructional practices are used to build CLD students' discipline-specific literacy skills in the STEM middle school classroom?

Context and Participants

A purposeful sampling of 12 teachers participated in the study. The participants taught in the Mid-Atlantic region of the United States in middle school science, mathematics, or STEM classrooms in high performing schools. The three districts in which the teachers provide instruction were either predominantly African-American, contained a large ESOL population, or both. Teachers in the study received an invitation to participate in the project based on their statements regarding their commitment to values, habits of mind, and practices consistent with CRP during a local STEM conference. The teachers' ages ranged from 25–53 and included three Caucasian, two Latinx, one Asian American, and six African American teachers. The sample included four individuals who identify as male and eight who identify as female. The teachers reported no other race/ethnicity or gender categories. All teachers held an undergraduate degree (BS or BA) in mathematics or science. The participating teachers also held a Master of Education or a Master of Art in Teaching degree. They graduated from teacher education master's programs at public universities requiring a minimum of six graduate semester hours of diversity coursework introducing CRP.

Data Collection

Participants joined the project after completing a two-year resident teacher/alternative certification program or a one-year master's certification program at colleges in the Mid-Atlantic. We interviewed participants in summer 2017 and asked them to reflect on what they consider best practices for teaching CLD students during the 2017–18 school year. In the sample for this study, we included only teachers with at least three years of teaching experience by the summer of 2017. We collected reflections in the fall and spring semesters over a one-year period. These multiple sources served as artifacts and a means of data triangulation.

Interviews. Each teacher participated in one interview that lasted 60-90 minutes. Teachers replied to inquiries about resources that they used for literacy instruction in their STEM classrooms as well as their credentials for teaching STEM, specifically their coursework and certification that they felt most relevant to their preparation for CLD learners. (Note: The teachers are in states requiring a content-area reading course at both preservice and in-service levels for teacher certification.) The interview served as an introduction to the project, and as an initial data point for participants to share verbally parts of what they would later respond to in writing in their fall and spring reflections. Using both artifacts confirms ongoing practices, as the research questions articulate.

Although semistructured, the interview protocol included a written prepared sequence of questions to ensure that each participant received the same questions. The interviews began with thanking teachers for their participation and reviewing the consent for participation again. The interview questions centered on the research questions to gain a deeper understanding of the gaps in the literature on CLD learners in middle school STEM classrooms. The questions and information we aimed to understand included:

- The goals and perspectives of teachers who employ CRP in a STEM classroom with CLD learners.
- The barriers to the STEM learning experience for CLD learners in middle school classrooms.
- The instructional and assessment strategies in the STEM classroom of a teacher with a CRP lens and how they are tailored to the middle school CLD learner.
- The strategies participants are employing that align with the disciplinary literacy research.
- How technology is used as an instructional resource in the middle school STEM classroom for CLD learners.

Following the approved IRB process, one of us recorded, and others transcribed the interviews for data analysis (see Appendix A: Interview Protocol).

Reflections. During the fall and spring semesters, participants submitted a reflection about effective practices for CLD learners in STEM classrooms that probed:

> *In your classes, you have employed a culturally relevant pedagogy. What is your purpose for CRP in your classroom? In what ways is your pedagogy intended to help your culturally and linguistically diverse students access course content and engage with you and their peers in your STEM class(es)? Describe how you organize your instruction for the adolescent learner. Explain any instructional resources (e.g., technology, literacy, content-specific resources) that you use explicitly to connect with your CLD learners. Write how your students respond when you enact what you see are your **best** practices and any evidence from your CLD learners that you can identify or that you have observed to support your response. Identify any barriers that students face to accessing STEM content or to demonstrating their understanding of STEM content. Expand upon any solutions that worked to assist with or eliminate these barriers.*

We examined the responses from the teachers for common strategies to serve as resources for other STEM teachers of CLD students in middle schools. Participants submitted reflections stored in a data-sharing site that ranged in length from 1–2 pages and included pedagogical strategies, technology resources, literacy strategies, communication strategies, STEM lesson feedback, routines and norms, grouping strategies, reflections from lessons, and inexpensive ideas for manipulatives. Together, the research team analyzed the reflection responses along with the interview data to determine common practices among the teachers in the study.

Data Analysis

We examined the content of the interviews and the reflections to look for recurring CRP practices, disciplinary literacy instruction, and technology resources. As mentioned previously, we documented practices that were common across each participant and identified how teachers conceptualized effective practices for CLD learners in STEM classrooms. We studied each teacher to document their experiences as middle school STEM teachers of CLD students who integrated CRP in their classrooms. We employed a content analysis (Marshall & Rossman, 1995) to understand how the teachers serving as participants in the study collectively utilized and described instructional strategies, with respect to CRP, disciplinary literacy, and technology. In content analysis, examinations of text addressed the research questions. Our qualitative content analysis confirmed similar practices across reflections and the interview (Marshall & Rossman, 1995). We analyzed the content of the data and took several passes across the data sources (Merriam, 1998). The analyses included pre-coding through the documentation and identification of the excerpts relevant to this study from the interview transcripts and the analysis from each participant. Qualitative content analysis, "best thought of as an overall approach, a method, and an analytic strategy, content analysis entails the systematic examination of forms of communication to document patterns objectively" and is "a more objectivist approach than any other qualitative methods (Marshall & Rossman, 1995, p. 85). It "facilitates discovery of nuances of culture" (Marshall & Rossman, 1995, p. 100). After an iterative process of inductive coding, analysis of the reflections, and transcribed interviews, we organized what the data showed based on the research questions and agreed on the findings as the common practices.

FINDINGS

Concerning the research and the research questions, we sought to understand common practices among the participants. Based on the information gathered for the methodology used in this study, we report the consistent practices as our findings from the middle school STEM teachers enacting CRP. We organize these findings by the research questions in a discussion format and highlight the categories using narratives from the teachers in the study. Some findings parallel the literature, and those instances include citations accordingly, while the other results are not prevalent in the research literature.

Recurring Practices of Middle School STEM Teachers

In this section, we include the practices that occurred most frequently among the teachers. Teachers described the importance of both academic and personal connections between themselves and their students. Providing culturally relevant models that are authentic and specific became a common thread for teachers of CLD learners.

Student-teacher relationships. Most participants reported that transience is popular in classes with large numbers of CLD students, which means that getting to know the learners to build relationships is challenging as enrollments shift. One common practice among the teachers was systematically collecting information about students' interests and skills to build teacher-student relationships (Bonner, 2014; Wright, 2012) once students arrived in their classes. Using the collected information to connect to the students not only gave teachers an opportunity to tap into students' funds of knowledge and to develop their CRP, but it also added context for the teacher by including the students' community and culture (González et al., 2005).

While matching and identifying student interest is Vygotskian (1978) in nature, the practice of considering interest and skill was an important part of preparation for students to begin to feel prepared to read, write, speak, and listen across culturally and linguistically different contexts. Socialization across the context is a principle of connectivism (Siemens, 2005). Teachers reported that the student-teacher connection is the most critical component of a CRP classroom, creating a space where students feel safe and appreciated. In the interview, we asked teachers how they managed differences between themselves and their students as a follow up to the narrative, which asks teachers to explain why they employ CRP. A collective response across the data showed that teachers maintained that having the same cultural experiences, the same race/ethnicity or speaking the same native language or dialect was helpful when there are similarities; however, those similarities did not matter as much as having a pedagogy of caring and respect for students, their experiences, their communities, and their families.

Making content connections relevant. Teachers also shared that they tried to compensate for teachers who seemed less interested in making connections to the content. A middle school math educator teaching in a public charter school with a diverse population of African American, Hispanic, Caribbean, and African students shared:

> Math is the one content that they feel "smart" in because I allow them to lead the classroom discussion and answers their questions. Students reported that I show them why it's important to know math. Some students have expressed their lack of interest in science because of the teacher and their inability to help students make connections with the material.

Making connections was critical to a CRP, a framework with a goal for students to gain success in classrooms (Ladson-Billings, 1995). The goal understood how to integrate CRP in a classroom to empower students (Howard & Rodriguez-Scheel, 2017; Ladson-Billings, 1995) and engage them with the material. Making connections to the material builds interest among CLD learners (González et al., 2005).

Cultural validation, culturally relevant resources, and STEM identity. Consistent with both the CRP and the funds of knowledge research (González et al., 2005; Ladson-Billings, 1995), building student's confidence in STEM courses is a consistent narrative among the participants. Teachers reported that most students did not see themselves with a future career in a STEM field. Many of the responses to the perspectives and rationale for CRP for CLD classrooms consisted of commentary to make sure that students could see themselves in a future STEM career. Participants explained that they were committed to helping students succeed and chose to highlight students' cultures in the classroom for representation and validation. As described throughout the chapter, integrating and adopting CRP comes from incorporating the culture of students and their families (González et al., 2005) and merging these cultural concepts (Gay, 2002) with the curriculum. Reported culturally relevant topics included using real-world events (e.g., elections) and data to engage students with content (e.g., statistics and probability). Teachers also incorporated local and global issues as topics for students to discuss and propose individual and group solutions directly related to content objectives (e.g., water supply). With respect to pop culture, teachers incorporated film including movie trailers from popular movies among their students and their families (e.g., *Black Panther*, *Crazy Rich Asians*). Teachers selected issues, scenes, and segments from movies that used various languages and dialects. They referenced the stories of films based on real characters to reinforce and discuss STEM identities (e.g., *Hidden Figures*).

Instructional Resources and Technology for CLD Learners

The resources that teachers of CLD learners described as best practices included platforms that supported communication and demonstration of STEM concepts in multiple forms. Teachers shared tools that helped their learners build language proficiency in their content area. These instructional resources are free and available, and most are digital and accessible.

Technology and communication. Teachers reported the use of Web 2.0 tools, which are online resources that they use on computers and devices such as tablets (Wang & Vásquez, 2012). The use of technology helped teachers make connections with the students and allowed students to connect with one another. The social aspect of Web 2.0 and the ways students are able to communicate using multiple domains of language, which most teachers reported that they teach simultaneously and not in isolation (Garrett, 2009; Hartley, 2007; Levy, 2009; Tan et al., 2005) served as a resource for teachers to build students communication skills in the classroom. The most widely used among the teachers were Padlet, Class Dojo, Google Classroom, and Seesaw. Understanding that technology use varies based on availability, Web 2.0 tools as a free resource, also allowed teachers to remain in touch with families.

Seesaw, for example, is a free app that works like a Google classroom, a learning management system. Once the teacher creates an account, a code generates for students to join the class. Once students have joined, they can take pictures, upload video, compose drawings, upload other file formats, write notes in their home and target language, or insert links from other sites. Students can also take tests formally or informally in their home language or the target language, which in U.S. classrooms is usually English. A middle grades STEM teacher explained:

> In my native speakers' classroom, I have used the video feature of Seesaw; students can record up to five minutes of conversation in any language. This app can also link to students' email accounts. I like this app because students are able to complete simulated dialogues; it also serves as a practice to complete the county exams related to interpersonal skills, because they are part of the formal assessments that were started this year; they are replacing semester exams.... With this app, I am able to replay the videos, and I am able to give feedback to students.

Teachers suggested that a culturally relevant classroom ensures that the digital learning environment makes students comfortable in taking risks, participating in discussions, and possibly making errors, particularly as some students are learning a new language, a new dialect, and new customs.

Cultural competence, assessment, and technology use for English learners. The teachers revealed barriers to progress that without asking the students, they may not have considered. Many students had technology in middle schools with iPads and Chrome books for each student; however, newcomers to the school and to the United States, like ESOL students, struggled to use them without an orientation to the keyboard. One of the teachers shared how his experiences as a former ESOL student helped shape his cultural competence:

> There are many ways teachers can be culturally competent, but to do so one must acknowledge that students come into our classroom with linguistic and cultural differences, and educational experiences that might be different from their teachers'... I was given the freedom to create the curriculum for the ESOL class. The first thing that came to my mind was that in order for students to be able to compete and adapt to the U.S. education system, they must be able to engage and know how to navigate certain tools and technologies that are used all the time across subjects. I used Mavis Beacon to help students understand the English and Spanish keyboard.

Mavis Beacon is a computer-based program that allows students to practice the proper way of typing in the target language. Mavis Beacon comes with pre-installed lessons, or users can customize their own lessons. Some students in the class did not have the experience of typing on a Spanish keyboard, and other students in the ESOL class did not have experience typing on an English keyboard, a barrier to their success. Teachers shared challenges regarding the Partnership for Assessment of Readiness of Colleges and Careers (PARCC) assessments. PARCC assessments are online and are annual required tests in the districts researched in the study. Teachers with international students or ESOL students may consider the disadvantage for students who are using a different keyboarding system when assigning instructional tasks and taking PARCC assessments. As described, CRP is more than becoming familiar with a language; it is also learning the experiences of a student.

Disciplinary Literacy Skills

Teachers shared the discipline specific skills that are critical to success in their classrooms and the formats that they used to teach these skills. Teachers discussed the inclusion of the CLD learner in the instruction and planning process. Students acquired disciplinary literacy skills as a result of inquiry, individual work, group work, and interest-based tasks.

The Five E Lesson Plan. Teachers shared their use of the 5 E lesson plan (Bybee, 1996), because reportedly that is what they are required to use and that is what they were prepared to use in their teacher preparation programs. Teachers found that the 5 E format allowed for discipline specific skills, such as procedural fluency, argument, reasoning, replication, exploration, synthesis, and analysis. Teachers used the 5 E—engage, explore, explain, elaborate, and evaluate—consistently, except there was inconsistency on whether a best practice is to use "explain" as a teacher directed component for CLD learners, or as a student-directed space for CLD learners to explain concepts. In other words, some teachers used this section for students to demonstrate their understanding of discipline specific skills; other teachers used this section to model and explain discipline-specific skills to the students. Both groups reported this "explain" section of the 5 E plan as one of their best practices.

Problem solving with peers, by design, choice, and reciprocal teaching. Most teachers found that peer teaching at the middle grades, particularly with linguistically diverse students, proved successful in STEM classrooms. They measured this success by assignments completed, participation (verbal and written), and the number of questions asked. Teachers matched ESOL students with a more English proficient peer or placed students homogenously in small groups based on same language use (de Schonewise & Klingner, 2012). Teachers explained that allowing students to share strategies from their families for problem solving (González et al., 2005; Taylor, 2013) as well as words and experiences from their home culture helped to (a) break power structures between them and the students, (b) unpack concerns with differences that exist in classrooms, and (c) give students an opportunity to be the expert or source of knowledge. A seventh grade instructor shared a class project with various groups in a CLD STEM classroom composing their version of a stadium-cell analogy. For one group, she explained:

> Right now, they are interpreting a story about a cell analogy, and they can choose what they want to compare the cell to in order to show that they understand the form and function of a cell. One group of students used a drawing app on their iPads to create a soccer stadium, while others used recycled products for their stadium. I explained to the group that I did not understand soccer well, so the project emerged into a reciprocal relationship where I learned from them, and they learned from me. The stadium became the cell wall, because they built a plant cell. The students labeled the vacuole as the location where the water is stored in the stadium (and the sports drinks). Students made sure to include energy bars, which served as the mitochondria. The students explained that the team captain was the nucleus. The students eventually led this project and said, "we are teaching you something!"

This example of reciprocal teaching, where students become the teacher, and the teacher becomes the student, allows for the power sharing of knowledge.

Teachers reported mostly project-based, co-constructed examples as evidence of disciplinary literacy (Fisher & Frey, 2004). In these examples, teachers consistently showed mechanisms of a design-based methodology for creative problem solving, and the student-centered examples like reciprocal teaching. Teachers were integrating content literacy and disciplinary literacy in their classes by supporting student ideas to create, a helpful skill in the STEM fields that builds disciplinary and communication knowledge. In addition, teachers reported the importance of curricular choice where possible. These choices included but are not limited to a choice of (a) resources (e.g., in the example above some students used technology and others used recycled products), (b) methods (e.g., teachers reported that students could choose a design of interest), and (c) public issue (e.g., students selected a public issue and composed a public service announcement to communicate the issue).

IMPLICATIONS AND CONCLUSIONS

Enacting a culturally relevant pedagogy creates an environment for multiple perspectives and prepares both teachers and students to engage actively in building knowledge. The participants reported strategies in digital literacy and STEM instruction that aligns with cultural competence and critical consciousness (Ladson-Billings, 1995). Results aligned with the literature include, building relationships, making connections to content, the use of 5 E lesson plans (Bybee, 1996), and interest-based teaching (González et al., 2005. As these are explicitly CRP positioned concepts, these are not surprising responses for middle school teachers of CLD learners. What is surprising and not prevalent in the literature is the consideration of students' varying digital knowledge. The implications for teachers assuming that students have dexterity managing a keyboard have long-term impacts for written assignments and online assessment and instruction. Teachers aiming to use technology to increase content knowledge and disciplinary literacy skills should consider supporting students' digital language skills, like their keyboards. This is essential to consider, given the shifts to online assessments that are formal and high-stakes in the middle grades (e.g. PARCC), impacting placements in classes and programs. Other critical results that add to the literature are the practical examples from teachers that are incorporating CRP to teach digital and disciplinary literacy in middle school STEM classrooms

Teachers need more than content knowledge and literacy knowledge (both disciplinary and digital) to teach CLD learners in STEM classrooms effectively. Based on the results of this study, teachers should make sure that their pedagogical knowledge and their technological knowledge is inclusive and reflexive, considering their students and the students' families experience as what counts as knowledge. These nodes (Siemens, 2005) or funds of knowledge (González et al., 2005) encourage middle school student participation in classroom instruction. Providing students an opportunity to demonstrate their intellect takes courage for some middle school students, including their home knowledge, which may vary from their school knowledge. Also important is building confidence and capitalizing on cultural models to build STEM identity for CLD learners. Providing representation or mirrors of CLD learners in STEM careers from popular culture or other resources offers students a chance to see themselves in a STEM context to feel that they are capable of success in a STEM field, as described in the identity development literature (Bonner, 2014).

STEM educators can capitalize on the uniqueness of culturally and linguistically diverse classrooms that foster a pollination of ideas that may be different from classrooms that are more homogeneous. Students can collaborate on issues and collectively solve problems relevant STEM challenges that are both local and global. Navigating the various interactions and experiences between and within regions and cultures may catalyze new perspectives to add to the classroom context. Providing students a choice to demonstrate their understanding and to co-construct flexible components of the curriculum proved beneficial.

Using connectivism as a lens to examine CLD learners and their interactions across their classroom networks provides an opportunity for research to bring CLD learners into frameworks that are atypical for the subject, but relevant. Language is a critical component for the CLD learners and finding ways to connect them to their network, that is, their teachers and their peers aids their participation and therefore, their performance in school. Implications for future research include increasing the sample size to study CLD STEM teachers in the middle grades to make the study more generalizable and expanding the sample to include teachers beyond the Mid-Atlantic region of the United States.

Teachers did not report any challenges with language differences or dialect differences in their classrooms; rather they relied on student data to drive their planning and their instruction. Teachers design CRP to empower students, so teachers are encouraged to use CRP to engage learners. Future questions to study the context of CLD middle school STEM classrooms warrant consideration. Does having a CRP mean that teachers permit students to speak languages or dialects other than school English in STEM classes without reprimand? How do CLD students with teachers enacting CRP perform on standardized tests compared to CLD students who do not? Are graduates from teacher education programs with diversity courses that teach CRP more effective teachers? Teachers in this sample used the 5 E Lesson template not only because it was appropriate, but also because it was required and they learned it in their teacher preparation program. Will teachers enact some of the instructional goals and practices of CRP and funds of knowledge in lesson plans for required use?

While teachers in this study did not indicate whether they focused on one communication or literacy skill in isolation, technology, including free technology (e.g., Web 2.0 skills), does provide a route to disciplinary literacy. Technology gives students an opportunity to demonstrate their understanding and navigate their smartness and their language proficiency (i.e., reading, writing, speaking, and viewing) across content areas. We encourage both researchers and practitioners to continue to use technology as a resource and to examine practices in STEM classrooms of CLD learners at the middle grades. Because the CLD learner brings a unique set of skills, teachers should continually seek strategies. We conclude that the recurring practices of STEM educators of CLD learners in high performing middle schools should continue to be a line of inquiry to identify additional strategies for teachers.

REFERENCES

Abedi, J. (2006). Psychometric issues in the ELL assessment and special education eligibility. *Teachers College Record, 108*, 2282–2303.

Andrei, E. (2016). Technology in teaching English language learners: The case of three middle school teachers. *TESOL Journal, 8*, 409–431. doi.org/10.1002/tesj.280

Bailey, A., & Carroll, P. (2015). Assessment of English language learners in the era of new academic standards. *Review of Research in Education, 39*, 253–294.

Battey, D. (2013). "Good" mathematics teaching for students of color and those in poverty: The importance of relational interactions within instruction. *Educational Studies in Mathematics, 82*, 125–144.

Baugh, J. (2003). Linguistic profiling. In S. Makoni (Ed.), *Black linguistics: Language, society, and politics in Africa and the Americas* (pp. 155–168). London, England: Routledge.

Blanchard, S., Judy, J., Muller, C., Crawford, R. H., Petrosino, A. J., White, C. K., ... Wood, K. L. (2015). Beyond blackboards: Engaging underserved middle school students in engineering. *Journal of Pre-College Engineering Education Research, 5*(1), 1–14. doi.org/10.7771/2157-9288.1084

Bonner, E. P. (2014). Investigating practices of highly successful mathematics teachers of traditionally underserved students. *Educational Studies in Mathematics, 86*, 377–399.

Brooks, M. D. (2016). Notes and talk: An examination of a long-term English learner reading-to-learn in a high school biology classroom. *Language and Education, 30*, 235–251.

Brown, B., Boda, P., Lemmi, C., & Monroe, X. (2019). Moving culturally relevant pedagogy from theory to practice: Exploring teachers' application of culturally relevant education in science and mathematics. *Urban Education, 54*, 775–803. doi.org/10.1177/0042085918794802

Bybee, R. W. (1996). The contemporary reform of science education. In J. Rhoton & P. Bowers (Eds.), *Issues in science education* (pp. 1–14). Arlington, VA: National Science Education Leadership Association.

Bybee, R. W., Taylor, J. A., Gardner, A., Van Scotter, P., Powell, J. C., Westbrook, A., & Landes, N. (2006). *The BSCS 5E instructional model: Origins and effectiveness.* Colorado Springs, CO: BSCS.

Carey, S. (1986). Cognitive science and science education. *American Psychologist, 41*, 1123–1130.

Carter, P., & Darling-Hammond, L. (2016). Teaching diverse learners. In D. Gitomer & C. Bell (Eds.), *Handbook of research on teaching* (5th ed., pp. 593–638). Washington, DC: American Educational Research Association.

Casey, G. (2013). Interdisciplinary literacy through social media in the mathematics classroom: An action research study. *Journal of Adolescent & Adult Literacy, 57*, 60-71. doi:10.1002/jaal.216

Chen, L., Zhang, R., & Liu, C. (2014). Listening strategy use and influential factors in web-based computer assisted language learning. *Journal of Computer Assisted Learning, 30*, 207–219.

Cholewa, B., Amatea, E., West-Olatunji, C. A., & Wright, A. (2012). Examining the relational processes of a highly successful teacher of African American children. *Urban Education, 47*, 250–279.

Cook, C., Faulkner, S., & Howell, P. (2016). The developmentally responsive middle school: Meeting the needs of all students. *Middle School Journal, 47*(5), 3–13.

Crandall, J. (1993). Content-centered learning in the United States. *Annual Review of Applied Linguistics, 13*, 111–126.

de Schonewise, E. A., & Klingner, J. K. (2012). Linguistic and cultural issues in developing disciplinary literacy for adolescent English language learners. *Topics in Language Disorders, 32*, 51–68.

Faltis, C., & Valdés, G. (2016). Preparing teachers for teaching in and advocating for linguistically diverse classrooms: A vade mecum for teacher educators. In D. Gitomer & C. Bell (Eds.), *Handbook of research on teaching* (pp. 549–592). Washington, DC: American Educational Research Association.

Farrell, R., & Cirrincione, J. (1984). State certification requirements in reading for content area teachers. *Journal of Reading, 28*, 152–158.

Faulkner, S., Cook, C., Thompson, N., Howell, P., Rintamaa, M., & Miller, N. (2017). Mapping the varied terrain of specialized middle level teacher preparation and licensure. *Middle School Journal, 48*(2), 8–13.

Fisher, D., & Frey, N. (2004). *Improving adolescent literacy: Strategies that work.* Upper Saddle River, NJ: Pearson Merrill Prentice Hall.

Fisher, D., Frey, N., & Rothenberg, C. (2008). *Content-area conversations: How to plan discussion-based lessons for diverse language learners.* Alexandria, VA: Association for Supervision and Curriculum Development.

Garrett, N. (2009). Computer-assisted language learning trends and issues revisited: Integrating innovation. *The Modern Language Journal, 93*, 719–740.

Gay, G. (2002). Preparing for culturally responsive teaching. *Journal of Teacher Education, 53*, 106–116.

Gibson, S., & Terrell Shockley, E. (2018). Walking the tightrope between advocacy and knowledge: An appeal to SLPs regarding AAE. *Perspectives of the American Speech-Language-Hearing Association, 3*, 147–158. doi.org/10.1044/persp3. SIG1.147

González, N., Moll, L. C., & Amanti, C. (2005). *Funds of knowledge: Theorizing practice in households, communities, and classrooms.* Mahwah, NJ: Erlbaum.

Graham, A., Kerkhoff, S., & Spires, H. (2017). Disciplinary literacy in the middle school: Exploring pedagogical tensions. *Middle Grades Research Journal, 11*(1), 63–83.

Hartley, J. (2007). Reading, writing, speaking and listening: Perspectives in applied linguistics. *Applied Linguistics, 28*, 316–320.

Howard, T. C., & Rodriguez-Scheel, A. (2017). Culturally relevant pedagogy 20 years later: Progress or pontificating? What have we learned, and where do we go? *Teachers College Record, 119*, 1–32.

Hwang, W. Y., Shih, T. K., Ma, Z. H., Shadiev, R., & Chen, S. Y. (2016). Evaluating listening and speaking skills in a mobile game-based learning environment with situational contexts. *Computer Assisted Language Learning, 29*, 639–657.

International Literacy Association. (2015). *Collaborating for success: The vital role of content teachers in developing disciplinary literacy with students in grades 6–12* [Position statement]. Newark, DE: Author.

Jacobsen, D. (2019). Dropping out or dropping in? A connectivist approach to understanding participants' strategies in an e-learning MOOC pilot. *Technology, Knowledge and Learning, 24*, 1–21. doi.org/10.1007/s10758-017-9298-z

Kaywell, J. (2009). Helping struggling secondary students make connections to literature. In S. Parris, D. Fisher, & K. Headley (Eds.), *Adolescent literacy, field tested: Effective solutions for every classroom* (pp. 129–142). Newark, DE: International Reading Association.

Ladson-Billings, G. (1994). *The dreamkeepers: Successful teachers for African-American children.* San Francisco, CA: Jossey-Bass.

Ladson-Billings, G. (1995). But that's just good teaching! The case for culturally relevant pedagogy. *Theory Into Practice, 34*, 159–165.

Lara-Alecio, R., Tong, F., Irby, B., Guerrero, C., Huerta, M., & Fan, Y. (2012). The effect of an instructional intervention on middle school English learners' science and English reading achievement. *Journal of Research in Science Teaching, 49*, 987–1011.

Lee, O., Quinn, H., & Valdés, G. (2013). Science and language for English language learners in relation to the Next Generation Science Standards and with implications for Common Core State Standards for English language arts and mathematics. *Educational Researcher, 42*, 223–233.

Levy, M. (2009). Technologies in use for second language learning. *The Modern Language Journal, 93*, 769–782.

Liu, S. (2013). Pedagogical content knowledge: A case study of ESL teacher educator. *English Language Teaching, 6*(7), 128–138.

Marshall, C., & Rossman, G. B. (1995). *Designing qualitative research* (2nd ed.). Thousand Oaks, CA: SAGE.

Merriam, S. (1998). *Qualitative research and case study applications in education*. San Francisco, CA: Josey-Bass.

National Center for Education Statistics. (2015). *Fast facts*. Retrieved from https://nces.ed.gov/fastfacts/display.asp?id=96

Short, D. J., Vogt, M., & Echevarría, J. (2011). *The SIOP model for teaching science to English learners*. Boston, MA: Pearson.

Siemens, G. (2005). Connectivism: A learning theory for the digital age. *International Journal of Instructional Technology and Distance Learning, 2*(1). Retrieved from http://www.itdl.org/journal/jan_05/article01.htm

Solano-Flores, G. (2006). Language, dialect, and register: Sociolinguistics and the estimation of measurement error in the testing of English language learners. *Teachers College Record, 108*, 2354–2379.

Taliaferro, C., & Parris, S., (2009). Successful teachers share advice for motivating reluctant adolescents. In S. Parris, D. Fisher, & K. Headley (Eds.), *Adolescent literacy, field tested: Effective solutions for every classroom* (pp. 157–167). Newark, DE: International Reading Association.

Tan, L. H., Spinks, J. A., Eden, G. F., Perfetti, C. A., & Siok, W. T. (2005). Reading depends on writing, in Chinese. *Proceedings of the National Academy of Sciences of the United States of America, 102*, 8781–8785.

Taylor, E. V. (2013). The mathematics of tithing: A study of religious giving and mathematical development. *Mind, Culture, and Activity, 20*, 132–149.

Taylor, D., & Dorsey-Gaines, C. (1988). *Growing up literate: Learning from inner-city families*. Portsmouth, NH: Heinemann.

Terrell Shockley, E. (2017, April). Field notes: Strategies to encourage positive dispositions toward exceptional students. *ASCD Express, 12*(6). Retrieved from http://www.ascd.org/ascd-express/vol12/1216-shockley.aspx

Terrell Shockley, E., Orellana, C., & Chicas, A. G. (2018). Culturally relevant pedagogy in virtual classrooms. In B. Eisenbach and P. Greathouse (Eds.), *The online classroom: Resources for effective middle level virtual education*. Charlotte, NC: Information Age.

Thorne, T. (2016). Augmenting classroom practices with QR codes. *TESOL Journal, 7*, 746–754.

Tierney, R. J. (2009). Shaping new literacies research: Extrapolations from a review of the Handbook of Research on New Literacies. *Reading Research Quarterly, 44*, 322–339.

Ukpokodu, O. N. (2011). How do I teach mathematics in a culturally responsive way? Identifying empowering teaching practices. *Multicultural Education, 19*(3), 47–56.

U.S. Census Bureau. (2015). *Census Bureau reports at least 350 languages spoken in U.S. homes*. (Release number: CB15-185). Retrieved from https://www.census.gov/newsroom/press-releases/2015/cb15-185.html

Vygotsky, L. S. (1978). *Mind in society: The development of higher psychological processes* (A. R. Luria, M. Lopez-Morillas, & M. Cole [with J. V. Wertsch], Trans.) Cambridge, MA: Harvard University Press. (Original work [ca. 1930–1934]).

Wang, S., & Vásquez, C. (2012). Web 2.0 and second language learning: What does the research tell us? *Calico Journal, 29*, 412–430.

Wolfram, W., & Schilling-Estes, N. (1998). *American English: Dialects and variation*. Malden, MA: Blackwell.

Woodrich, M., & Fan, Y. (2017). Google docs as a tool for collaborative writing in the middle school classroom. *Journal of Information Technology Education: Research, 16*, 391–410.

Zhang, W. (2017). Quality matters: Content literacy for English language learners. *TESOL Journal, 8*, 166–189.

Zwiers, J. (2008). *Building academic language: Essential practices for content classrooms, grades 5-12*. Newark, DE: International Reading Association.

Zwiers, J., Dieckmann, J., Rutherford-Quach, S., Daro, V., Skarin, R., Weiss, S., & Malamut, J. (2017). *Principles for the design of mathematics curricula: Promoting language and content development*. Retrieved from Stanford University, Understanding Language/SCALE website: https://ell.stanford.edu/sites/default/files/u6232/ULSCALE_ToA_Principles_MLRs__Final_v2.0_030217.pdf

APPENDIX A

Interview Protocol

Time of interview: **Date:**

Interviewee: **Date consent form signed:**

Script: Thank you for meeting with me for this interview. I really appreciate your time. As a reminder, I will be audiotaping this interview. Please let me know if you need me to repeat or clarify any of the questions. If you do not feel comfortable answering the question that I ask, please respond by saying, "skip" and I will move on to the next question. If you need to take a break at any time, please let me know. Also, we can end the interview at any time at your request and you will not be penalized.

In our study, we define culturally and linguistically diverse learners as students of color, students enrolled in ESOL, and students who speak varieties of English that may be different from their school English. Please share how you engage your culturally and linguistically diverse learners in your classroom.

How do you define a culturally relevant pedagogy? Why do you choose to enact a culturally relevant pedagogy in your classroom? (Additional prompts: What do you hope to accomplish)?

What lessons are your most effective lessons for your culturally and linguistically diverse learners? What evidence are you using to make that claim? (Additional prompts: Can you describe 1 or 2 lessons that were effective lessons for your culturally and linguistically diverse learners, and share why? Can you describe how students learned the vocabulary in those lessons?)

What value (or affect), if any, do you believe enacting a culturally relevant lens has had on your culturally and linguistically diverse learners?

What resources have you used that had a positive impact on your students' performance? How did you capture that performance? (Additional prompts: Are technology and digital resources helpful in your classroom? Please explain.)

Do you think having a similar race/ethnicity or language pattern/language matters in connecting with culturally and linguistically diverse learners? Explain.

Have you faced any challenges or barriers while attempting to engage your students in a culturally relevant STEM experience? If so, please describe. Were you able to manage or overcome those challenges? If so, how?

CHAPTER 7

PEDAGOGICAL RESPONSES TO TECHNOLOGY IN THE MIDDLE LEVEL CLASSROOM

The Influence of Digital Tools on Instructional Methodologies and Learning Practices

Lorraine Radice
Hofstra University

ABSTRACT

The purpose of this ethnographic case study was to explore pedagogical responses to technology in the classroom, specifically how the one-to-one Chromebook initiative influenced the instructional methods that supported the development of digital literacy practices of middle level students. The participants of this study were three middle level teachers, two Grade 7 social studies teachers, and myself, a Grade 6 English teacher, in a diverse school district on Long Island. Data consisted of observations of teaching in classrooms, formal and informal interviews with the teachers, and instructional

Curriculum, Instruction, and Assessment:
Intersecting New Needs and New Approaches, pp. 155–183
Copyright © 2020 by Information Age Publishing

artifacts. The themes from data collection were teachers emerging as learners, the necessity to teach the technical skills of the Chromebook, student challenges with organization of materials, memorializing the multimodality of teaching, blending the digital and print platforms, collaboration, and logistical issues that stunted teachers in their progress in using new technology for learning. Future research needs to attend to the professional development middle-level teachers receive to implement a one-to-one technology initiative successfully and to study curriculum revisions school districts undergo to support the development of digital literacy competencies at the middle level.

The use of digital devices has become monumental in the ways that people communicate, socialize, gather information, learn, and establish connectivity. Outside of school, students live in an expanding mobile world of mobile lives and textual practices (Mills, 2016). Rideout (2015) reported that U.S. teenagers are spending an average of 9 hours a day media multitasking: watching television or movies, listening to music, communicating on social media, playing computer games, and at least some of the time reading. Similarly, in a related study, Rideout, Foehr, and Roberts (2010) shared that youth between the ages of 8 and 18 spend an average of 7 hours and 38 minutes daily (7 days a week) using popular media to portray meaning through images, sounds, icons, gestures, print texts, performances, and other multimodal forms of communication. However, when adding the time they spend using two or more media forms simultaneously (while multitasking throughout the day), the total number of hours of media exposure rises to 10 hours and 45 minutes per day. Adolescents spend time engaging with multimodal texts in the form of television content, music/audio, websites, video games, and movies (Alvermann & Hinchman, 2012). The well-documented literacies of adolescents reflect the shifting terrain of young people's communicative practices and the technologies that mediate them (Vasudevan, DeJaynes, & Schmier, 2010).

When considering the statistical data that shows adolescents' use of media and technology, not surprisingly, digital tools could invite the establishment of new routines and methods in the classroom. Adolescents' growing and consistent use of technology for entertainment, socialization, and communication has influenced the ways in which educators approach teaching and learning in the classroom. Teachers strive to build connections between the social behaviors of young people to methods of learning to promote students' engagement and to deepen understandings of content material. Middle level students' experiences in school reflect the shifts in their social practices with digital devices.

School district leaders and teachers are reaching a crossroad in the way they attend to these changes in technology. Many young people are now using digital platforms, like Google applications and Flipgrid (an online video discussion forum), to compose their work and share among teachers and peers, making earlier non-web-based platforms like Microsoft Word, PowerPoint, and Excel seem obsolete. School leaders and teachers need to be intentional in how they plan to support students in their connectivity to each other and a larger, and often unknown, audience and how their connectivity can influence their own academic work. School leaders and teachers are challenged with making a variety of complex decisions as to how students will engage with technology in ways that are supportive of learning, critical thinking, and the evolution of new literacy competencies.

In one school district, the assistant superintendent for curriculum and instruction notified teachers about the one-to-one Chromebook initiative through written communication. The middle school building principal distributed the Chromebooks to teachers in January 2016. Central office and building level administrators expected teachers to familiarize themselves with the device so that it could be an instructional tool for student learning. This research study addressed the particulars of pedagogy and instructional methods. The study attended to pedagogical shifts, meaning how teachers' conceptual understandings of their teaching practices changed due to teaching with technology. The study also investigated the instructional methods teachers employed in the classroom to support their pedagogical shifts and to engage students in learning content through digital literacy competencies, specifically relative to new media literacies at the middle level (Jenkins, 2009). New media literacies (Jenkins, 2009) include the traditional literacy that evolved with print culture as well as the newer forms of literacy within mass media and digital media. While there are many factors involved, the teacher is undoubtedly a critical factor in determining the success for any technology-based project. Similar to other initiatives, the teacher is the decision maker who has the greatest influence on classroom events (Groff & Mouza, 2008). The teacher needs to account intentionally for shifts in methods for learning and develop pedagogy in a purposeful way. Intentional plans of study and strong delivery of new instruction are necessary to set an appropriate precedent in the new age classroom. This research study examined instructional methodologies and pedagogical shifts as a result of using the Chromebook and the ways it was being used to influence teaching and learning at the middle level.

Statement of the Problem

District leaders acknowledged uncertainty about new instruction among teachers. For example, one of the first memos sent to all staff in my school district included, "You may be wondering how this will help you with your students or how you can utilize the technology in your class. We hope that over the next few months that we will all begin to explore these questions together" (K. Graham, personal communication, January 2016).

Middle school is a logical focal point for increasing integration of digital literacy in the curriculum. Teachers expect middle level school students to read independently and to find relevant textual information in specific-subject areas, and middle school is often where students acquire the foundation for future academic success in specialized subject areas (Colwell, Hunt-Barron, & Reinking, 2013). Access to a digital device, such as a Chromebook, for all students at all the time changes the basic premises for educational practices and implies challenges for schools, teachers, and students. The Internet is a powerful technological tool that has invited new perspective to literacy. No previous technology for literacy has provided access to so much information that is so useful, to so many people, in the history of the world (Coiro, Knobel, Lankshear, & Leu, 2008). While many school districts are adopting a "one-to-one" technology initiative where students are responsible for handling and using their own device for learning, teachers must understand how instruction supports the development of new literacy skills using these devices. In this research study, I investigated the instructional methods that invited students to develop digital literacy competencies to address the participatory and multimodal nature of learning. This research study addressed the following questions:

1. How are instructional methodologies supporting middle level students in developing digital literacy competencies?
2. How has teacher pedagogy been impacted by the invitation to use Chromebooks as an instructional tool for learning in middle school?

This study took place during a time in public schools where there was exploration, nuances in teaching and learning, and change. A larger audience of educators may be able to learn from the findings of this study and it may affect how teachers approach the cultivation of new literacy skills using Chromebooks or other devices.

THEORETICAL FRAMEWORK

This research study blended semiotic, multiliteracies, and sociocultural approaches to literacy as they related to pedagogy and instructional methodologies under the new literacy studies framework. Semiotic, multiliteracies, and sociocultural theories share the understanding that meaning-making resources are shaped by cultural and social contexts but remain distinctive in their methodological beginnings (Mills, 2016).

Semiotic theory acknowledges that all forms of representation—visual, gestural, spatial—have meaning (Mills, 2016). Literacy researchers use a semiotic perspective to explore alphabetic and nonalphabetic symbols to ask questions about how they are used to make and exchange meaning as well as how nonverbal meanings are captured, conveyed, and interpreted (Baker, Pearson, & Rozendal, 2010). Social semiotic theorists acknowledge the role of non-linguistic modes in human social meaning. Under the new literacies framework, the meaning of semiotics has expanded to include sign systems that are representative of technological contributions to meaning making. Image and text relations contribute to new literacies' typical representation of meaning in multiple modalities, which also include music, sound effects, and digital affordances such as windows and hyperlinks; this multimodal communication of meaning is one key dimension of the ongoing reconceptualization of literacy that led to the construct of multiliteracies (Unsworth, 2008).

New literacies from a sociocultural perspective signify that literacy changes as culture changes. Textual literacy remains a central skill in the 21st century—one that should not be abandoned because of the introduction of media literacy. New media literacies should be considered a social skill so students can contribute to and participate in larger communities (Baker et al., 2010; Jenkins, 2009). Students must be supported to develop both textual and media literacies simultaneously.

Lankshear and Knobel's (2007) mindsets under their new "ethos stuff" theory supported the theoretical framework of multimodal and social semiotic theories of literacy. Lankshear and Knobel described two mindsets. The first mindset assumes that the contemporary world is essential to the way it has been during the modern-industrial period, only now it has been technologized in a new and sophisticated way. The second mindset assumes that the contemporary world is different in important ways from how it was 30 years ago, much of which has been attributed to the growing internetworked technologies, new ways of doing things, and new ways that are enabled by technologies. It is arguable that the tools available are versions of traditional tools (e.g., pencils and markers) that predate technology, which supports the first mindset. The second mindset invites educators to explore the new possibilities that Chromebooks and other digital devices could offer to instructional methods and learning activities in the classroom.

LITERATURE REVIEW

Literacy is no longer a static construct from the standpoint of its defining technology for the past 500 years; it has come to mean a rapid and continuous process of change in the ways in which people read, write, view, listen, compose, and communicate information (Coiro et al., 2008). Literacy involves the ability to generate communications that others can comprehend and to comprehend communications that others generate (Mayer, 2008). It has become commonplace to observe that communication in the 21st century is no longer limited to print-based forms of literacy. To be effective participants in today's society, young people need to become capable and competent users of both print and other forms of meaning enabled by new technologies (Mills, 2016).

Just as literacy has adopted new dimensions overtime, middle level students will, as well. Teachers play an integral role in this process because do not assume that all students have the necessary skills for participation solely because they play video games for pleasure at home (Mills, 2016). Teachers need to consider the skills that students may enter with and revise and/or build upon those skills. Societal and technological changes require shifts in the way educators think about knowledge in literacy practices (Mills, 2016). These societal and technological changes (Mills, 2016) were part of the impetus for this study.

Shifts in discourse relative to technology in classrooms include rethinking the definition of literacy. Gee (2007) highlighted that the use of the word literacy is not traditional, as literacy usually references facets of language, like reading and writing. Educators need to consider literacy more broadly, as words and images are very often juxtaposed and integrated and because there is a multiplicity to print literacy. Literacy in any domain is actually not worth much if one knows nothing about the social practices of which that literacy is but a part of (Gee, 2007). In addition, teachers need to consider the inclusion of responsible processes of digital media design in schools. Students need textual knowledge, which includes both knowledge of the social and cultural context in which the text has been produced and used, and the multimodal elements within the text (Mills, 2016). Marcon (2016) illustrated the connections between multiliteracies (Gee, 2007; Mills, 2016), gaming (Gee, 2007), and capturing and sharing information and experiences (Giaccardi, 2012) in a study that was conducted in Year 7 of schooling over the course of 2 weeks. Marcon explored the use of the game *Minecraft* as a pedagogical tool to motivate girls' literacy practices in the secondary English classroom. *Minecraft* is a digital game that presents a virtual world, or space, or where users can create structures using the tools and objects of construction provided in the game to shape the geography and layout of the game space. There are expanded forms of literacy practices involved where players negotiate logic, knowledge, actions, and how to conduct themselves in what Gee referred to as affinity spaces (i.e., social semiotic spaces). Positioning, design of these spaces, and extensive knowledge of the multimodal environment is necessary (Gee, 2007). After a week of building structures within the game, students spent the second week playing and elaborating their level of play through forms of social media used by them in an out-of-school context. It was Marcon's intention to bridge formal and informal learning through this pedagogical and instructional planning.

Marcon's (2016) findings align with Kalantzis, Cope, and Cloonan's (2010) notions about the power of design when students engage in multiliteracies to authenticate meaning making. Marcon observed the girls' engagements in the design process, strategizing, and problem solving while playing *Minecraft*. The students collaborated while playing accessing real world and virtual-world contexts. There was oral interaction to discuss concepts throughout the digital game. Finally, the students created videos together by blending actions from the game and screen-shots to share on Instagram. Their online postings allowed them to share their constructed information (Giaccardi, 2012) and creative play. The students accessed many skills and modalities when publicly sharing their information.

> Outside the game, girls used language conventions with text structures and language features through their Instagram design. Students filmed each other on their phones as they played *Minecraft*, then, shared their game play action with an authentic audience—Instagram users—in a strongly multimodal way, using paratext for headings of their posts, the inclusion of the videos, and with written comments at the bottom of the posts. (Marcon, 2016, p. 67)

Students used their virtual world designs to stimulate the development of different multimodal literacy artifacts that blended traditional and digital literacies. The skills of creating content for Instagram posts were evident - composing, editing, and then publishing written and multimodal texts, all while considering audience and purpose (Marcon, 2016). Sound, music, and voice qualities also contributed to the meaning making of a multimodal text.

Marcon's (2016) study exemplifies the power gaming and social media as it relates to developing digital literacy competencies while preserving traditional skills. This research study served to examine if similar work occurred in current classrooms as schools adopt one-to-one initiatives and students had consistent access to technology. Marcon's work provided a framework for observing skills in this study and exploring how pedagogy and instruction that was inclusive of multiliteracies could inspire students to be creative and multifaceted in their production and meaning making processes.

Teachers need to incorporate multimodal texts into the literacy program because online environments challenge traditional notions of reading (Mills, 2016). Electronic texts have become nonlinear, which involves increasingly sophisticated navigational skills and search capabilities to support in meaning making and comprehension. Readers are encountering support options such as hyperlinks, interactive narratives, built-in dictionaries, and connected blogs (Al-Hazza & Lucking, 2012) and need to navigate texts differently from traditional readings because of these structural changes. Part of the meaning-making process has become to know when and where to stop your "search" and consider the multiplicity of resources available to influence thoughts, ideas, and understandings. The ability to bring a variety of modes together in the same text not only changes the way a text is conveyed, but also can open up new possibilities for what kinds of meaning can be transferred and solidified (Vasudevan et al., 2010). The multiplicity of literacy is reflective of the way that students will continue to learn and the way teachers need to develop their pedagogy. The shifts in learning and pedagogical development became apparent in the data from this research study.

Research relative to digital literacy development at the middle level suggests that there are obstacles to overcome. Colwell, Hunt-Barron, and Reinking (2013) conducted a study that investigated how the development of digital literacy could be realistically integrated into middle school instruction. The researchers (Colwell et al., 2013) argued that middle school is a logical place for there to be more of a focus on digital literacy skills due to the increasing independence that students acquire at the middle level in their studies. Even though the middle level students were invited to participate in an inquiry-based project using technology, the teacher still emerged as the first source of information for students and when they were not successful using the Internet, they resorted back to the teacher. The Internet was a failed fact-finder. In addition, students did not carry out the strategies taught independently. The findings invite teachers to think about how to better prepare students to use taught strategies in an academic setting when working independently, as well as how these strategies can serve students in their personal use of the Internet. These results also indicate how fixed middle level students can be in their own usage of the Internet and digital tools.

Research on middle level teachers' attitudes and perceptions on integrating technology to develop digital literacy skills in the classroom stresses the importance of training and support from school district officials (Al-Hazza & Lucking, 2012; Beriswill, Bracey, Sherman-Morris, Huang, & Lee, 2016; Sahin, Top, & Delen., 2016). Beriswill, Bracey, Sherman-Morris, Huang, and Lee (2016) studied the effect of Global Academic Essentials Teacher Institute (GAETI), a professional development program, on Grades 6–12 foreign language and social studies teachers' knowledge of content, pedagogy, and technology explorations centered on the teaching of the Common Core State Standards and 21st Century Skills. A key component of GAETI is building a firm foundation in media and technology skills; however, one of the obstacles that prevent teachers from promoting innovative use of technology is lack of training (Beriswill et al., 2016). After participating GAETI, teachers completed a survey to share feedback and insight on their new learning. The GAETI survey data and reflections indicated that participants significantly increased their confidence with Common Core State Standards, 21st Century Skills, and technology, as well as their actual technology, pedagogy, and content knowledge. These findings provide a positive precedent for school districts to consider. When teachers feel supported in new initiatives, pedagogy and instructional methodologies can improve to incorporate plans for digital literacies.

METHODOLOGY

Current research (Al-Hazza & Lucking, 2012; Beriswill et al., 2016; Colwell et al., 2013; Dooley, Ellison, & Welch, 2016; Sahin et al., 2016) demonstrated that many variables influence teachers' implementation of technology and how teachers develop pedagogy and instruction that is inclusive and supportive of digital literacy competencies. Teachers' implementation and pedagogical development becomes part of how teachers engage with curriculum design, planning, and instructional methods, which filters into a larger culture of how teachers collaborate and talk about their work to a larger audience of colleagues, parents, and administrators. This study explored this phenomenon.

Research Design

In this ethnographic case study, I served as a participant observer in my classroom along with two other middle level teachers. I used ethnographic methods (Glesne, 2011) to undertake a case study approach in one middle school to describe and explain how teachers develop pedagogy and design instruction to support the students' development of digital literacy competencies using the Chromebook. The ethnographic methods used to gather data were classroom observations (see Appendix A), interviews with teachers (see Appendix B), and collection of artifacts of material used for instruction and student work.

I visited each social studies class two times per week during the six months of the study. I arranged these times with the teachers based on when and how the teachers were using technology in the classroom. I collected data in my own classroom during three units of study—a narrative writing unit, a paragraph writing unit, and a response to literature unit. On the days when the use of the Chromebook was instrumental to the instructional time, I observed and recorded the teaching events and took pictures of artifacts during and after the class period.

I kept a digital journal to record my field notes during classroom observations and teacher responses during interviews. My observations focused on instructional methodologies practiced by the teacher for each 42-minute class period. I noted the tools teachers used for instruction, environmental print in the classroom that served as instructional material, classroom discourse that supported instruction, environmental print that supported instruction, and any other product that yielded learning.

I identified patterns among the three forms of data collection. The patterns exemplified the multiliteracies and sociocultural theories of literacy, highlighting what it means to be literate under the new literacies and what it means to teach and learn using digital tools. In this study, I also examined where there was a lack of new literacies competencies in instruction. In addition, I identified areas of instruction where there was not a shift in pedagogy, but rather use of technology to complete tasks that could be done with print tools. These data sources informed the implications for this study and areas for future work in schools

Context

This research study took place in a public middle school on Long Island that educates students in Grades 6, 7, and 8. There were 755 students in the middle school where the research study took place. Forty-nine percent of the students in the school were female and 51% of the students in the school were male. Multiple ethnicities were represented in this middle school: 63% of students were White, 20% of students were Hispanic or Latino, 12% of students were Black or African American, and 5% of students were Asian or Native Hawaiian/Other Pacific Islander. Thirty-seven percent of the students in the district were economically disadvantaged, 15% of the students were students with disabilities, and 4% of the students were English language learners. There were 257 students in Grade 6, 239 students in Grade 7, and 284 students in Grade 8. These data points were representative of information as of June 30, 2017 (New York State Department of Education, n.d.).

Schools across the United States have demonstrated a steady investment in computer technology to support student academic achievement (Maninger & Holden, 2009). A one-to-one initiative is one way in which school districts are embracing technology. School districts have chosen to adopt different devices, for example an iPad or a Chromebook. The teachers and students at the middle school where this study took place used the HP Chromebook 14 G4. This machine has a cloud-based infrastructure that allowed students and teachers to use the web to store files using 100

GB Google Drive. The device ran on a Chrome OS operating system and an Intel Celeron processor.

There were 85 teachers and 755 students who had their own device to use at home and at school. Prior to the first cohort of Grade 7 students receiving Chromebooks in April 2016, the teachers in the middle school received Chromebooks in January 2016. Teachers received professional development during the three months that they had Chromebooks in their possession before students received them. Teachers had opportunities to learn about how to use the Chromebook device, as well as how to use Google applications, through professional development sessions with in-house and out-of-district trainers that required half-day pull out learning sessions during the school day. The building level administrative team also used grade level meeting time once a week to support teachers in learning about the new tool. The roll out of the initiative was incremental. By September 2017, all students in Grades 6, 7, and 8 in the middle school where this study took place had Chromebooks.

Participants

Three teachers participated in this study—two teachers of Grade 7 social studies, Mr. Jones and Mr. Smith (pseudonyms), and myself, a teacher of Grade 6 English. Using a letter that described the study, I invited Mr. Jones and Mr. Smith to participate because of their extensive use of the Chromebook. Their consistent instructional practices using the Chromebook and comfortability with technology aligned with the research questions of this study, so I studied and observed their pedagogical responses and instructional methodologies. The observation of Mr. Jones' Grade 7 social studies class included 21 students, 11 males and 10 females. The observation of Mr. Smith's Grade 7 social studies class included 17 students, eight males and nine females. The teachers and I chose these classes because of scheduling convenience. I was the third participant in this study because I deliberately use a Chromebook and have background knowledge of theory that supports digital literacy development. I assumed the role of participant observer (Glesne, 2011) during my Grade 6 English class. The class included 19 students, 10 males and nine females.

Data Collection and Analysis

I collected the data using ethnographic methods (Glesne, 2011) as part of an ethnographic case study. I conducted observations for six months in each of the three classrooms during the 2017–18 school year. I scheduled interviews with the participating teachers were scheduled throughout the research study to discuss what was observed during instruction and student learning. The participating teachers gave me access to material used for instruction, like Google Slides presentations, organizers for student writing, informational sheets distributed to students, and project outlines. I also collected and took photographs of artifacts of student work, like print and digital writing pieces, print and digital projects, digital note-taking documents, and evidence of use of online platforms like Flipgrid, Noodle-Tools, and Quizlet. The teachers and I discussed the intentionality behind instructional methods and tools and what work the students produced relative to the use of technology for learning. As a participant observer in the study, I recorded my own reflections about my teaching methods and shifts in pedagogy relative to digital literacy. I also gathered instructional material and artifacts of student work for analysis.

I triangulated the data (Berg & Lune, 2012; Glesne, 2011) by providing multiple entry points into the classroom experience that would identify teachers' use of technology to engage students in digital literacy skills. Each data source offered an inherent perspective. The observations in classrooms targeted the perspective of the researcher, the interviews with teachers invited the viewpoint of the teacher, and the artifacts of material gave a concrete offering as to what was actually being produced and used in the classroom to support instruction.

The multiliteracies and sociocultural theories that explain the new literacies guided the analysis of the data collected from the study. I analyzed the data by coding the observations of instruction, interview responses, and artifacts of instruction and student work. Coding is not just a label, but also a link that leads you from the data to an idea (Saldaña, 2009). Helping to frame this study were the codes, or ideas, representative of the new literacies' theory and themes gathered from research studies, developed through multiple cycles of thematic analysis. Saldaña (2009) explained that coding is a cyclical act, which multiple cycles that filter the qualitative data by generating categories, themes, and concepts that grasp meaning and/or build upon theory. I categorized the coded data from this study and identified themes by theoretical representation. I used colors to represent the identified themes. As each color became more apparent in the analysis, it was a signal that a certain theme was evident. For example, if I highlighted multiple lines of dialogue from the observations and interviews, as well as highlighted several images from the artifacts with a similar idea in blue, I would narrow down that data group and name it by the overarching theme the data points shared. I filtered the data through four different cycles to uncover the strongest commonalities. The commonalities led to the following themes: teachers as learners and reflective practitioners, teaching the tool (Chromebook), organization (of digital space and of digital writing), memorializing teaching, a blended approach (where the digital and physical space meet), collaboration, and logistical issues that affected learning.

Limitations

Research to date provides informative snapshots regarding the presences and use of technology, yet it does not sufficiently answer questions about the specific ways that teams select a piece of technology to support instruction and learning (Staples & Edmister, 2014). This study was one of the informative "snapshots." While I collected data consistently for 6 months, the study could have been more informative if I collected data over a longer period. Another limitation was the number of participants in the study. Perhaps if there were more teachers in the study or if the teachers varied in grade level and discipline, the findings would have differed. Finally, I conducted this study in one middle school, with similar learning activities and expectations. Many school districts have adopted one-to-one initiatives, so the study could have been broader studying teaching and learning with the Chromebook in different schools or districts. I could have observed a wider range of teaching methodologies and instructional practices that supported the use of the Chromebook and development of digital literacy competencies.

FINDINGS

Researchers have been studying multimodality and sociocultural traditions in the 21st century (Mills, 2016). Many of their findings related to the multiplicity of literacy and the social nature of new literacy practices in digital spaces. Teachers experienced the roles of pioneers for the one-to-one initiative in the middle school setting.

Teachers Emerging as Learners

As Mr. Jones, Mr. Smith, and I shared about our new approaches, we emerged as reflective practitioners in this study, and our attitudes and perspectives about technology surfaced in discussions. Mr. Jones and Mr. Smith shared that they felt like new teachers beginning their careers and needed to dedicate hours to thinking about and planning instruction for the Chromebook. Mr. Jones expressed concern for his new beginnings as he reflected on his own journey as an educator. He shared, "[I find it challenging] to find time to do the planning. With digital tools, you have to find something for your lesson that you want. When we were doing NoodleTools [an online research platform], I had to learn it myself in order to teach it to my students" (interview, January 16, 2018).

There was uncertainty about teaching methods, as well as questions about whether teaching with the Chromebook impacted learning in a positive way. In a formal interview, Mr. Jones shared that there was not a natural spot to start using the Chromebook for instruction. He said, "I just jumped right in. I would find things that I could apply. Some things were easy, others less so.... Hit and misses happen when you're learning" (interview, January 16, 2018).

Mr. Jones and Mr. Smith shared that when their students first received Chromebooks, they digitally transformed their instruction and materials right way. Mr. Jones shared, "When I first started, one hundred percent was digital" (interview, January 16, 2018). Mr. Smith similarly stated, "We put homework, classwork, and assessments all on Google Classroom. We even turned to a digital textbook. The kids used Chromebooks for everything, and we were doing very little writing with pencil and paper" (interview, November 2, 2017). After a three-month pilot, Mr. Jones and Mr. Smith reflected on their instructional practices to plan for the 2016–17 school year. They noticed that students were not performing as well on assessments after becoming solely digital in their approach to teaching. Mr. Jones reflected:

> When I first started, one hundred percent was digital. But what we found was that retention wasn't happening. They weren't doing well on assessments. We started to pull back on the use of technology. This year [2017–2018], we are blended. (interview, January 16, 2018)

I took a different approach than Mr. Jones and Mr. Smith. I had more flexibility in my initial explorations that led me to adapt the curriculum to the new tool. To include use of the Chromebooks, I redesigned a literature unit of study that my students started around the time that they first received their Chromebooks. In a way, I was "starting over," because I had not designed unit engagements or a culminating project that were to be completed in school with the option for students to choose to work on their Chromebook. This invited me to think about how I was going to structure my approach to the literature unit and how the digital tool would support students in demonstrating their meaning making and understandings that they developed. I decided to create a choice project board where using the Chromebook was an option for students for some of the projects rather than a requirement. I thought that this would be an organic way to start using the technology as an instructional tool, while allowing students to develop a relationship with their new device. The focus of my mini-lessons slowly moved away from the novel we were reading and strategies to think about text and shifted more toward how to use digital tools for multimodal design and the features that are available to help show understanding and analysis in the culminating project. While the students were learning from each other, I was learning also. Some of my students were able to create in ways that I did not know how, so I practiced along with them. The culture in the classroom started to shift when we all realized that we were working together to use digital tools for learning. My less conventional way of approaching literacy instruction in my classroom was less "expert-dominated" (Lankshear & Knobel, 2007, p. 9) and more inclusive of collaboration to share knowledge and ideas.

Teaching Technical Skills

Teachers supported students as they learned to navigate online platforms and use keyboard functions while working with the Chromebook. One component of the process was teaching students how to navigate digital platforms and read across multiple spaces (or screens) to engage in classroom activities. Snyder and Bulfin (2008) explained that digital literacy practices are the abilities to use and understand information in multiple formats from a range of sources, when presented via the electronic screens of digital technologies. The technical skills that Mr. Jones and Mr. Smith taught their students during a research unit aligned with what Snyder and Bulfin (2008) defined as digital literacy practices. Mr. Jones reported:

> Kids had to learn to use the Chromebook to do what I wanted them to do. They don't have a lot of experience and they don't know the short cuts. I learned and played with it and taught them what I knew. (interview, January 16, 2018)

Mr. Smith shared a similar idea, "I was shocked at how much the kids need to learn in terms of technical skills" (interview, February 2, 2018).

As we began to use the Chromebook for teaching and students started to use it for learning and producing, we discovered what specific Chromebook skills need teaching, and it was through modeling that each of us approached this new aspect of our teaching. I asked Mr. Jones to reflect on the specific skills he found himself needing to teach with regard to technology and using the Chromebook effectively. Mr. Jones said, "I would focus on specific skills like copying and pasting so that they [the students] would get used to it, the specific keys on the machine and then also when copying and pasting is a useful tool" (interview, January 16, 2018). Mr. Jones also shared that he needed to teach his students that the Chromebook was a tool for learning and not solely a gaming platform (interview, January 18, 2018). I observed throughout the study that Mr. Jones and Mr. Smith used modeling on the SMART Board, modeling on individual Chromebooks, and verbal explanations to teach students explicitly the functions of the Chromebook. The students were engaged in a research project in social studies during the time of this study. Accessing, reading, and organizing information were important to the research project. During several formal and informal interviews, Mr. Jones and Mr. Smith shared that they made intentional decisions about the skills they introduced to students to work within their selected online spaces. As the teachers became more familiar with the online platforms, it became clear to them what they needed to teach explicitly to students so they could work productively in the online space.

In addition to teaching skills to navigate online platforms, Mr. Jones, Mr. Smith, and I taught students how to use certain functions of the Chromebook to aid in academic work. There are certain features that are unique to the Chromebook. We all taught our students skills such as how to save files automatically to Google Drive, key functions for screenshots, keyboard functions, how to navigate multiple windows and tabs simultaneously, how to organize files in digital space, and how to access information via the Internet.

Organization of Digital Material

Mr. Jones expressed concern for students' lack of ability to organize digital documents and work in multiple digital spaces. He realized that organizing documents was often challenging for middle level students, especially as they transition to middle school from elementary school, and that challenge was simply transferring over to the digital world. Mr. Jones said, "[I had to teach students how to] organize digital material.... We took a lot of time to show and model how to use Google Classroom folders and where documents were located within those folders" (interview, January 16, 2018). The need for online organization that surfaced led to another subtheme of using digital space as a tool to visualize progress for students with organizing and keeping track of assignments. Mr. Jones, Mr. Smith, and I explicitly taught skills and strategies for organization to our middle level students prior to working with technology, as these is a pivotal component to navigating middle school. We redefined organization for students as they began to learn and work with the Chromebook. Organizational skills took on different forms and responsibilities when using the new device.

Teachers and students became accustomed to using Google applications on the Chromebook. Although these applications offered a convenient approach to managing materials, the response from students was unforeseen. Mr. Jones and Mr. Smith used Google Classroom predominantly. Mr. Jones shared that he needed to teach students explicitly how to digitally access and organize materials constantly. Mr. Jones said, "The kids had no idea where to find digital material. I had to show them repeatedly where documents were on Google Classroom" (interview, January 16, 2018). When I asked Mr. Jones to discuss some of his goals for developing instructional approaches using technology and Chromebooks, he said:

> A lot of it comes down to figuring out the organization for the kids. If I give a paper worksheet, it will come back or the kids will use it. If I give a digital worksheet, it doesn't come in or the kids won't use it to help them with an assignment. Out of sight, out of mind we believe. (interview, January 16, 2018)

It was clear to me that digital organization was an entire new road to navigate. Grade 6 teachers needed to spend instructional time teaching students these new skills so that they could be better prepared for using the Chromebook in middle school. For the first two quarters of the school year, I decided not to use Google Classroom in my Grade 6 English class, knowing that my counterparts (teachers of math, science, and social studies) were using it. I wanted to teach my students how to use Google Drive, a more open digital space for organization that did not have the confines of Google Classroom. Students often expressed frustration about not being able to manage digital files in Google Drive because they became dependent on Google Classroom. I focused my instruction on initial skills: how to create folders for each subject, work within a folder, and have folders within folders. I used two strategies to teach these initial skills. First, I showed the students my own Google Drive on the SMART Board, and my organization of our English units of study with multiple folders. I demonstrated how to get in and out of folders and how the line of succession works on the toolbar on the screen. I also showed the concept of the organization with paper multicolored file folders. I had students put paper folders within paper folders using their hands. I felt that if I created a tactile experience first, the digital tools would not seem so abstract. I then invited my students to practice creating digital folders and moving digital files in and out of the folders. It continued to be a work in progress each time we used Google Drive to access and store materials in class.

Multimodality of Teaching and Learning

The one-to-one initiative inspired Mr. Jones and Mr. Smith to develop a new method to approach instruction, which was to capture teaching and make it last indefinitely through various modes. Mr. Jones and Mr. Smith began to make instructional videos of themselves teaching. They posted the videos on Google Classroom in folders with related content material. Through these videos, they were engaging their students in multimodality to support the learning of content material and captured images, sound, gestures, and live processes to make meaning of content material.

I observed Mr. Jones during his social studies class where he was teaching students how to make digital notecards on NoodleTools (n.d.), only online research platform. Before he taught this process in the classroom, he showed a video of the process. Mr. Jones used Obi, an open source audio book production tool. Mr. Jones shared with me, "Obi allows me to show my students the process of where to find and what to type in on the screen with my voice in the background explaining what to do as if I was teaching it to them right there" (interview, October 27, 2017). In another observation in Mr. Jones' classroom a few weeks later, the students were learning the process of writing a document-based question. Mr. Jones said:

> If you are working on your DBQ at home since it is due on Wednesday, there is a 10-minute video I made for you about writing a DBQ. It summarizes all of the class lessons in one place and will be especially helpful if you were absent at all. (observation, December 11, 2017)

A Blended Approach to Learning

As we began to use the Chromebook in various units of study, it became clear to Mr. Jones, Mr. Smith, and me that traditional skills were still necessary to teach students because the traditional skills independent of technology use support digital practices. Some of the traditional skills that were consistent in all of our classrooms were how to read for information, how to structure and organize writing, and how to use resources to gather information. We found that we were teaching traditional learning skills, but within a digital space. I refer to this as a blended approach. A blended approach is the inclusion of various digital and print approaches to teaching and learning.

Mr. Jones and Mr. Smith expressed that students were not accessing digital information that was available to them and were not performing as well on class assignments and assessments when they transformed their instructional approach completely into digital space. Mr. Jones reflected, "I want to have an even blend of traditional approaches as well as using the computers" (interview, January 16, 2017). Mr. Smith said, "We've discovered that the balance of methods before technology and now with the Chromebooks is extremely important" (interview, February 2, 2018). This idea of blended instruction surfaced in several areas such as environmental print in the classroom and negotiating material in digital space.

Environmental print. Mr. Jones, Mr. Smith, and I expected students to manage both types of materials when preparing to learn in school and be able to communicate across a range of modalities. For example, during an observation in Mr. Jones classroom, I noticed he wrote on the board, "Research Question: How does (topic) involve conflict and compromise? Open: (1) NoodleTools, (2) Thesis statement worksheet (Google Classroom), (3) Textbook" (personal communication, October 30, 3017). The students were expected to work across modes (Kress, 2003), to manage and work with two digital spaces (a research database and a Google Doc) and a print textbook.

Anchor charts were a common resource for my students and a staple in the types of environmental print available in my classroom. While the contents of the anchor charts usually reflected strategies for reading and writing, the charts began to include strategies and reminders for using digital tools as platforms to demonstrate learning. Using applications like Google Slides to create digital presentations became an area to explore for my students. The print displayed in my classroom began to shift when we started using the Chromebook. Students needed visible resources to support their learning process when working in the digital space, just as when they worked with print.

A new approach to writing. The students in my class engaged in a blended approach to the writing process for various genres and writing engagements. The students used traditional graphic organizers on paper during the brainstorming, planning, and drafting stages of the writing process, and then they used the Chromebook to continue drafting, edit, revise, and publish their writing. Students in Mr. Jones and Mr. Smith's classes engaged in a similar process for writing in social studies class when writing a traditional DBQ essay. Mini-lessons focused on how to transfer ideas from print outlines and thinking webs onto the digital platform, Google Docs. Mr. Jones, Mr. Smith, and I felt that students needed concrete tools to build conceptual understandings of writing. It was also a method to begin transitioning students to digital tools. Navigating the writing process across print and cyberspaces was the focus of much of the instruction that I observed in my own classroom.

Traditional skills approached through digital space. In Mr. Smith's class, students were learning how to access primary source documents through online databases. Mr. Smith shared with me, "They [the students] first had to learn what a primary document is before looking through the database. They are still learning what they are" (interview, November 20, 2017). The students in the class used NoodleTools (n.d.), an online platform for organizing research material. The program offered students scaffolded directions for approaching traditional skills. For example, students would paste in the primary source on the left side of the template. On the right of the primary source, there was a textbox titled, "In your own words." Under the title, the scaffolded directions said, "Explain it to yourself in words you understand; Look back at the quote ... got it all?" Summarizing and paraphrasing are two skills that students would learn whether working in physical or digital space. Mr. Smith shared:

> I had to teach the kids to summarize and write about primary sources in their own words before we started to use NoodleTools. I knew that the program would help them do this, but they still needed to know the skill before using the program. (interview, November 20, 2018)

When I interviewed Mr. Jones, we discussed the impact of the students' digital skill set on approaches to assessments. Traditionally, students prepared for assessments and completed assessments on paper, but Mr. Jones and Mr. Smith attempted to shift to digital assessments and study opportunities. Mr. Jones began to offer students multimodal study opportunities, as well as blended approaches to completing assessments. For example, at the beginning of a class period I observed, Mr. Jones reviewed the homework with the students that was written on the whiteboard and said, "There is a test on Friday. Half of the test is written, half of it is digital on the Chromebook. Please do not forget your Chromebook" (personal communication, December 11, 2017). Then, Mr. Jones displayed the Google Classroom page on the SMART Board that showed review material. It read, "Unit 2 Assessment Study Guide (paper); Unit 2 Assessment Review (Flashcards, Quizlets)" (personal communication, December 11, 2017). Mr. Jones provided paper and digital study material for the students to use. Mr. Jones shared that sometimes he and Mr. Smith used the Chromebook as an extension of paper for some of the assessments and that it did not invite students to demonstrate knowledge differently.

Mr. Jones and Mr. Smith also provided opportunities for students to demonstrate knowledge and understanding through multimodal assessments, grounded in Lankshear and Knobel's (2007) "second mindset" that assumes the contemporary world is different due to the introduction of technology. This theory, along with multimodal theories of literacy (Mills, 2016), were evident in Mr. Jones' explanation of choice assessments that students are sometimes invited to engage in, such as digital comic strips, digital posters, documentaries, websites, paper posters, and performances. The decision to invite students to use the Chromebook for assessment projects demonstrates a shift in pedagogy. Mr. Jones recognized the value of multimodal engagements and acknowledged that multimodality has a place in learning. While this pedagogical shift was evident in a choice assessment project, the shift was not always evident in instruction methods in the classroom. He invited students to use technology to complete a choice project, but he did not offer specific instruction in the classroom on how to use available tools for the completion of that project. Students needed to explore and learn independently.

Collaboration

The need for guidance in collaboration surfaced in several domains. Collaboration in digital space became apparent during the writing process and when reviewing content material for upcoming assessments. We, the three teachers in the study, also noticed that students need us to teach them a new set of social norms when working together in digital space. A new social emotional component to digital work became important to address with students.

Writing. During this study, collaboration with digital tools was significant to teaching and learning during writing instruction and review of content material for assessments. While students were digitally working together, teachers began to realize they needed to teach students how to be appropriate and kind citizens of the digital world while engaging in certain semiotic domains (Gee, 2007). Teachers needed to teach students explicitly manners and social protocols for participating in shared digital space.

When my students were finished drafting their personal narratives, they participated in digital peer writing conferences to give and receive feedback. Before engaging in the digital conferences, I prepared a series of mini-lessons that targeted how to conduct the conference. Some of my teaching points were applicable to peer conferencing on paper, but many of the teaching points referred specifically to digital etiquette because my students would be working in semiotic spaces (Gee, 2007) that required a skill set and discourse to navigate and make meaning. I explained to my students that we needed to honor and respect each other's digital space just as we do in our physical space to promote productivity and meaning making. This conversation with my students paralleled Jenkins's (2009) notion when he explained how meaning emerges collectively and collaboratively in the new media environment and how creativity operates differently in an open-source culture. Young people need the social skill set to facilitate these practices in online learning communities. I viewed the collaborative nature of a Google Doc as a preliminary, controlled online learning community (Jenkins, 2009) for my students to participate in where I could address the social skill set (Jenkins, 2009) they needed to develop to participate in the digital writing conferences and eventually in larger, more globalized online communities. When I prompted my students to think about the social skills necessary for meaning making in online learning communities, some of their responses included:

- "Don't erase someone's writing if you are on their Doc;"
- "Follow the directions and examples given, don't write something mean in the comment box;"
- "Don't write something you don't want a teacher to see;"
- "Don't turn off someone's computer;" and
- "Write messages that will help to improve each other's writing."

One of the ways that my instruction stressed to students the importance of cultivating a respectful digital community was through direct teaching of constructive language to use when participating in digital peer writing conferences. We discussed that language used in digital spaces often stays in that space and many people can revisit that language. The process my students engaged in is similar to what Black (2005) referred to as "beta-reading." Beta-reading provided by online fan communities helps contributors grow as writers and pushes writers to be close readers of their own works. Participants in the beta-reading process learn by receiving feedback on their own work and giving feedback to others; they created an ideal peer-to-peer learning community (Jenkins, 2009). Although my students were not engaged in fanfiction writing, my instructional decision paralleled Black's and Jenkin's notions about beta-reading and peer feedback for writing in online writing communities. To guide my students in the peer conference through digital comments, I provided them with a language reference chart to use to offer feedback to their partner. Literacy was evolving in these classrooms, as students were participatory in what Jenkins refers to as the social production of meaning. Working in Google spaces facilitated this for teachers and students.

Content review. Games are tools to motivate youths to learn other kinds of content; however, there is a growing recognition that play, as a means of exploring and processing knowledge and of problem solving, may be a valuable skill that children should master (Jenkins, 2009). This was evident in the game experience I observed in Mr. Jones' class as students used a game on Quizlet Live (n.d.) to review content material on the Chromebook. Mr. Jones created a Quizlet Live review game where students had to work together in groups of four across four Chromebooks to "win" while reviewing content material. Mr. Jones explained to the class, "The secret to Quizlet is not to win the game. The secret is to talk to your group about what you think the answer is" (personal communication, December 11, 2017). In a follow-up interview, I asked Mr. Jones about how he designed the game. Mr. Jones explained, "I made this game, the questions, but I designed it where the kids have to talk to each other because that is the only way they are going to learn" (interview, December 11, 2017). Mr. Jones was purposeful in creating a collaborative experience using technology.

Logistical Issues

A backdrop to implementing the Chromebook in the classroom was the logistical challenges that we had to face before even using the tool for instructional purposes. We, the three teachers in this study, experienced challenges with WiFi connectivity, student unpreparedness, student management of the Chromebook, and the GoGuardian program (an online filtering and monitoring program for Google-powered schools). Planning for instruction became difficult due to lack of certainty that the Chromebooks and Internet would work during instructional time. In addition, we expected students to manage a new tool with a different set of responsibilities. Teachers had to be very cautious in their planning and had to anticipate problems in the classroom before they arose. Difficulty connecting to WiFi was apparent in many of the classroom observations I conducted. Students were unable to access online resources or assignments because they were unable to connect or stay connected to the Internet.

Students were establishing routines for managing a new tool. Administrators and teachers placed a new expectation upon students when they received the Chromebooks. Administrators and teachers made it clear that students need to come to school with their Chromebooks charged each day. When students did not follow this protocol, teachers needed to provide alternate procedures and materials so that students could still participate in the lesson. Their learning was somewhat disrupted because they were not using the Chromebook, the tool for which the lesson was intended.

DISCUSSION

This ethnographic case study shared three teachers' experiences in the beginning stage of the one-to-one initiative with Chromebooks in the middle school setting. Lankshear and Knobel's (2007) mindsets in their new "ethos stuff" theory support the theoretical frameworks of multimodal and social semiotic theories of literacy, under which this study was conducted. In this study, evidence aligned with Lankshear and Knobel's second "mindset" where the contemporary world has changed as a result of technology. During this study, I observed teachers and students using and creating videos and other media, engaging in digital collaborative writing in online spaces, collaborating in digital game play, designing multimodal presentations, coding games in response to literature, and developing social protocols for digital citizenship while participating in an online community. These are examples of instructional decisions that are grounded in multimodal and social semiotic theories of literacy that indicate shifts in pedagogy to engage students in developing new digital literacy competencies, which implies a shift in middle level instruction.

The literacy community has recognized that a primary factor that makes a difference in children's literacy acquisition and development is the teacher (Baker et al., 2010). The data from this research study suggest that teachers were at a crossroad in their own teaching practices and pedagogical development relative to supporting students in developing the skills associated with new media (Jenkins, 2009) and digital literacy competencies. Teachers were still honoring traditional methods, skills, and strategies while trying to incorporate and explore the use of the Chromebook through the development of digital literacy competencies.

IMPLICATIONS

Based on this research study, we provide clear implications for effective practices for middle level teaching and learning for school districts that are adopting a one-to-one initiative or are establishing policies around using technology in the classroom. An implication of this study is that teachers need time to participate in middle level professional learning communities to discuss instructional methodologies and to explore practices that lead to improved student achievement. Teachers can be reflective practitioners as they share resources, strategies, and experiences in the classroom with each other. In addition, student achievement may need redefinition if stakeholders in the educational system are going to capitalize on the opportunities that technological tools, such as the Chromebook, can offer to students. This may lead to discussions about what it means for middle level students to be literate and what literacy competencies may look like in the secondary classroom.

Another implication of this study is that teachers and administrators may consider engaging in middle level curriculum revisions to allow students to use technology in innovative ways that focus on design and creativity. Curriculum revisions could invite students to develop new competencies to demonstrate understanding of content material and to manipulate technological tools and programs in ways that cultivate a new dimension to their identities as learners. Curriculum revisions could potentially inspire teachers to think differently about the content they teach, the methods they use, and the ways students learn.

Additionally, the findings in this study imply that school districts need to be purposeful and intentional in their planning of a large-scale initiative, like the Chromebook one-to-one initiative at the middle level. School districts may benefit from a standardized approach to students developing technical skills along the K–12 continuum so that middle level use of technology can be similar across classrooms. This implies that school districts should have a vision for how they want to use technology for teaching and learning and the skills that are necessary to do so. For example, school districts could develop a technology learning progression for students. There can be sequenced expectations for students as they move through their education experience ensuring that they learn a certain technology skill set by the time they reach certain grade levels. For example, middle level teachers could design complex tasks that invite students to practice higher-level technological skills if students receive consistent, scaffolded instruction throughout their elementary years.

CONCLUSIONS

The timing of this study was crucial. It was beneficial to examine instructional practices and pedagogical development during the initial stages of a one-to-one initiative in a middle school. The data provided a "first look" at teachers' response to using the Chromebook in the classroom. These initial reactions and thoughts from teachers could serve a larger conversation about how to implement technology in the classroom and to create a new culture for expectations in teaching and learning in schools. As more school districts adopt technology initiatives, it is important for administrators and teachers to gather information about what has already happened in schools and in classrooms to build the most engaging and purposeful programs for students to experience. What better way is there to learn about implementing technology effectively than from the trials and tribulations of teachers who have experienced the early struggles and successes? While this study was a "blip" on the radar, it could potentially contribute to a more elaborate vision for organizations.

Practices in teaching and learning in schools are embarking on a new frontier and the influences of young peoples' social practices are infiltrating into their academic work through the uses of digital devices. While some may believe that technology is replacing the role of teachers, the research prior to this study and the findings of this study indicate differently. Perhaps the most influential idea from this study is that teachers are important. They are essential. Teachers are crucial to supporting students in their development of digital literacy competencies and contextualizing the skills they bring to the classroom from their social experiences. With time, planning, and support, teachers can maximize the opportunities that lay ahead for middle level students as they engage with technology for learning.

REFERENCES

Al-Hazza, T. C., & Lucking, R. (2012). An examination of preservice teachers' view of multiliteracies: Habits, perceptions, demographics and slippery slopes. *Reading Improvement, 49*(2), 59–72.

Alvermann, D. E., & Hinchman, K. A. (2012). *Reconceptualizing the literacies in adolescents' lives: Bridging the everyday/academic divide*. New York, NY: Routledge.

Baker, E. A., Pearson, P. D., & Rozendal, M. S. (2010). Theoretical perspectives and literacy studies: An exploration of roles and insights. In E. A. Baker (Ed.), *The new literacies: Multiple perspectives on research and practice* (pp. 1–22). New York, NY: Guilford Press.

Berg, B. L., & Lune, H. (2012). *Qualitative research methods for the social sciences* (8th ed.). New York, NY: Pearson.

Beriswill, J. E., Bracey, P. S., Sherman-Morris, K., Huang, K., & Lee, S. J. (2016). Professional development for promoting 21st century skills and common core state standards in foreign language and social studies classrooms. *TechTrends, 60,* 77–84.

Black, R. W. (2005). Access and affiliation: The literacy and composition practices of English Language Learners in an online fanfiction community. *Journal of Adolescent & Adult Literacy, 49,* 118–128.

Coiro, J., Knobel, M., Lankshear, C., & Leu, D. J. (2008). Central issues in new literacies and new literacies research. In J. Coiro, M. Knobel, C. Lankshear, & D. J. Leu (Eds.), *Handbook of research on new literacies* (pp. 1–21). New York, NY: Taylor & Francis.

Colwell, J., Hunt-Barron, S., & Reinking, D. (2013) Obstacles to developing digital literacy on the internet in middle school science instruction. *Journal of Literacy Research, 45,* 295–324.

Dooley, C., Ellison, T., & Welch, M. (2016). Digital participatory pedagogy: Digital participation as a method for technology integration in curriculum. *Journal of Digital Learning in Teacher Education, 32,* 52–62.

Gee, J. P. (2007). *What video games have to teach us about learning and literacy*. New York, NY: Palgrave Macmillan.

Giaccardi, E. (2012). *Heritage and social media: Understanding heritage in a participatory culture*. New York, NY: Routledge.

Glesne, C. (2011). *Becoming qualitative researchers: An introduction*. Boston, MA: Pearson.

Groff, J., & Mouza. C. (2008). A framework for addressing challenges to classroom technology use. *AACE Journal, 61,* 21–46.

Jenkins, H. (2009). *Confronting the challenges of participatory culture: Media education for the 21st century*. Cambridge, MA: The MIT Press.

Kalantzis, M., Cope, B., & Cloonan, A. (2010). A multiliteracies perspective on the new literacies. In E. A. Baker (Ed.), *The new literacies: Multiple perspectives on research and practice* (pp. 62–74). New York, NY: Guilford Press.

Kress, G. (2003). *Literacy in the new media age.* London, England: Routledge.

Lankshear, C., & Knobel, M. (2007). *A new literacies sampler.* New York, NY: Peter Lang.

Maninger, R. M., & Holden, M. E. (2009). Put the textbooks away: Preparation and support for a middle school one-to-one laptop initiative. *American Secondary Education, 38*(1), 5–33.

Marcon, N. (2016). Exploring Minecraft as a pedagogy to motivate girls' literacy practices in the secondary English classroom. *English in Australia, 51*(1), 63–69.

Mayer, R. E. (2008). Multimedia literacy. In J. Coiro, M. Knobel, C. Lankshear & D. J. Leu (Eds.), *Handbook of research on new literacies* (pp. 359–376). New York, NY: Taylor & Francis.

Mills, K. (2016). *Literacy theories for the digital age: Social, critical, multimodal, spatial, material and sensory lenses.* Bristol, England: Multilingual Matters.

New York State Education Department. (n.d.). *New York State enrollment data (2017–18).* Retrieved from https://data.nysed.gov/enrollment.php?year=2018&state=yes

NoodleTools. (n.d.). Retrieved from https://www.noodletools.com/

Quizlet Live. (n.d.). Retrieved from https://quizlet.com/features/live

Rideout, V. (2015). *The Common Sense census: Media use by tweens and teens.* San Francisco, CA: Common Sense Media. Retrieved from https://www.commonsensemedia.org/sites/default/files/uploads/research/census_researchreport.pdf

Rideout, V. J., Foehr, U. G., & Roberts, D. F. (2010). *Generation M2: Media in the lives of 8–18 year olds.* Menlo Park, CA: The Kaiser Family Foundation. Retrieved from https://www.kff.org/other/event/generation-m2-media-in-the-lives-of

Sahin, A., Top, N., & Delen, E. (2016). Teacher's first-year experience with Chromebook laptops and their attitudes towards technology integration. *Tech Know Learn, 21*, 361–378.

Saldaña, J. (2009). *The coding manual for qualitative researchers.* Thousand Oaks, CA: SAGE.

Snyder, I., & Bulfin, S. (2008). Using new media in the secondary English classroom. In J. Coiro, M. Knobel, C. Lankshear, & D. J. Leu (Eds.), *Handbook of research on new literacies* (pp. 805–837). New York, NY: Taylor & Francis.

Staples, A., & Edmister, E. (2014). The reintegration of technology as a function of curriculum reform: Cases of two teachers. *Research and Practice for Persons with Severe Disabilities, 39*, 136–153.

Unsworth, L. (2008). Multiliteracies and metalanguage: Describing image/text relations as a resource for negotiating multimodal texts. In J. Coiro, M. Knobel, C. Lankshear & D. J. Leu (Eds.), *Handbook of research on new literacies* (pp. 377–405). New York, NY: Taylor & Francis.

Vasudevan, L., DeJaynes, T., & Schmier, S. (2010). Multimodal pedagogies: Playing, teaching and learning with adolescents' digital literacies. In D. Alvermann (Ed.), *Adolescents' online literacies* (pp. 5–25). New York, NY: Peter Lang.

APPENDIX A

Observation Protocol

Notes were digitally documented. I observed for events within the theoretical framework of the study. Items noted in the left side of the chart were teaching points, dialogue between teacher and student(s), environmental print, tools students were learning and working with, and work that was produced by students. The right side of the chart was used for making connections to the theoretical framework, as well as noting thoughts and questions I had to follow up on after the lesson and in the analysis of data.

Date of Observation: Time of Observation: Setting:	• **Connections to Theoretical Framework From Observed Lesson** • **Thoughts and Questions from the Researcher to Follow Up On**

APPENDIX B

Interview Protocol

The following questions were used in formal interview sessions during the study. These questions were also used during informal interview sessions following class observations. If I observed a literacy event in the classroom that prompted immediate explanation or feedback from the teacher, I followed up about that event using one of these questions or a modified version of a question to suit the event that was observed.

1. What were some of the first initial shifts you made in your teaching methodologies when your students received Chromebooks? How did you decide on a place to start?
2. What do you find yourself needing to explicitly teach students in regard to using technology? What specific digital skills need to be taught? How did you decide on a place to start?
3. What has changed about your approach to instruction now that you have the Chromebooks as a tool for learning?
4. What do you find challenging about planning and delivering instruction when using the Chromebooks?
5. Provide some examples of how you blend traditional approaches to teaching (pre-technology) and teaching with Chromebooks.
6. Provide some examples of opportunities you provide for students to demonstrate their learning using multiple modalities (media, images, sound, etc.)
7. How have your beliefs about teaching and learning changed in response to teaching using Chromebooks?
8. What are your goals for developing your instructional approaches using technology and Chromebooks? Are you planning on trying any new approaches and/or what have you been doing that needs some revision moving forward?
9. How have the Chromebooks enhanced teaching and instruction in your classroom?

CHAPTER 8

SHIFTING TOWARD PRODUCTIVE BELIEFS FOR BLACK STUDENTS IN THE MATHEMATICS CLASSROOM

Christa Jackson and Ashley Delaney
Iowa State University

ABSTRACT

Teachers' beliefs about society, their students, learning, and themselves influence their instructional practice. More specifically, teachers' beliefs about Black students, systemic inequities, and their own practices influence their instruction in the classroom. Self-observation, critical conversations, and reflection are essential to recognizing unproductive beliefs and begin the process of shifting toward productive beliefs. In this qualitative study, we examine the beliefs a White, sixth grade mathematics teacher has about Black students, how those beliefs are reflected in classroom instruction, and how reflecting on instructional practices begins to foster productive beliefs about Black students in the mathematics classroom. The results of the study reveal that initially the teacher embodied a colorblind ideology and had some unproductive beliefs about Black students. However, after engaging in critical reflections and self-observations, the teacher's beliefs shifted more

Curriculum, Instruction, and Assessment:
Intersecting New Needs and New Approaches, pp. 185–222
Copyright © 2020 by Information Age Publishing

toward productive beliefs of Black students and manifested in the teacher's instructional practice. The process of acknowledging unproductive beliefs and inequities encountered by Black students and actively reflecting on and having critical conversations about those unproductive beliefs and practices enables teachers to be effective teachers to Black students.

The commitment to access and equity (National Council of Teachers of Mathematics, 2000, 2014) has not been fully realized, especially for Black students. Ogbu and Simons (1998) argued, "The treatment of the minorities in the wider society is reflected in their treatment in education" (p. 158). Based on the treatment of Blacks in the wider society, even to this day, this is problematic. Establishing an equitable classroom environment that results in student learning for Blacks requires productive beliefs and dispositions that oppose the reflection Ogbu and Simons described. Within today's educational system, teachers, too often, hold beliefs that do not facilitate the academic participation and learning of Black students. For example, some public school teachers hold the belief that Blacks are lazy and cannot learn (Martin, 2007), and about half of White Americans believe Blacks are unintelligent (Smith, 1990). These beliefs may be grounded in the longstanding belief that Blacks were generations behind Whites with regard to skills and intelligence in an evolutionary sense (Anderson, 1988; Spring, 2005). These beliefs play a powerful role in the denied access to rigorous mathematics instruction and low expectations that result in the poor achievement of Black students.

Typically, students in U.S. classrooms are educated under a Eurocentric paradigm, in which teachers privilege White students and reprimand Black students, negatively affecting the educational experiences and resulting achievement of Black students (Parsons, 2005; White, 2010). Consequently, mathematics teachers must have high expectations and productive beliefs about Black students to support their learning of mathematics. More specifically, teachers need to act positively on those productive beliefs by implementing instructional strategies and practices that provide opportunities for Black students to engage in and learn rigorous, challenging mathematics. Mathematics teachers must challenge themselves to recognize and acknowledge the low expectations and unproductive beliefs they may have about Black students and shift their mindset and instructional practices towards an equity-centered paradigm. In this chapter, we investigate the beliefs of a sixth grade mathematics teacher who teaches in the Midwest region of the United States. More specifically, we examine the teacher's beliefs about Black students, how those beliefs are enacted in instruction, and how reflecting on instruction enables further development of productive beliefs about Black students in the mathematics classroom.

CONCEPTUAL FRAMEWORK

Teachers draw upon multiple knowledge bases to plan their mathematics instruction (Putnam & Borko, 2000). References to knowledge of the content, pedagogical content knowledge, and knowledge of pedagogical practices have been documented in mathematics education research (Borko & Livingston, 1989; Cess-Newsome, 1999; Hill, Ball, & Schilling, 2008; Loewenberg Ball, Thames, & Phelps, 2008). However, focusing only on pedagogical and content knowledge minimizes the humanity central to teaching and learning (Jackson, 2012). Teaching and learning are social processes that are influenced by the individuals and contexts in which they occur (Jackson, 2013).

Teachers' beliefs about society, their students, learning, and themselves influence their instructional practice (Barlow & Cates, 2006; Jackson, 2012; Thompson, 1992). Although researchers have described beliefs as a "messy construct" with multiple meanings and interpretations (Aguirre & Speer, 2000; Pajares, 1992; Philipp, 2007), Philipp (2007) asserted beliefs are "psychologically held understandings, premises, or propositions about the world that are thought to be true … beliefs might be thought of as lenses that affect one's view of some aspect of the world or as dispositions toward action" (p. 259). Figure 8.1 depicts how teachers' beliefs (both productive and unproductive) influence their instruction. As teachers critically reflect on their practice and beliefs, unproductive beliefs can be transformed to productive beliefs, which can have a positive influence on instruction. Teachers' beliefs about Black students, systemic inequities, and their own practices influence the instruction enacted in the classroom. It is important to note that not all of teachers' professed beliefs align with their enacted instruction (Polly et al., 2013). Teachers may have beliefs that are not reflected in their instructional practices. Similarly, teachers may hold conflicting beliefs about pedagogical practices, equity, and social influences on learning. For example, a teacher may believe Black students are as intelligent and capable as their White counterparts but may claim it is not problematic and justify why a disproportionate number of Black students are enrolled in remedial mathematics classes. In Figure 8.1, the potential disconnect between beliefs and enacted instruction is represented by the dashed border around teacher beliefs.

Transforming instructional practices to meet the needs of Black students requires teachers to shift beliefs and practices toward an equity-centered paradigm. To do so, teachers should undergo a multifaceted evolution that changes their mindset and approach in teaching and learning. Central to this evolution is engaging in critical exercises and professional development that requires teachers to examine their own unproductive beliefs. Self-observation, critical conversations, and reflection are essential to

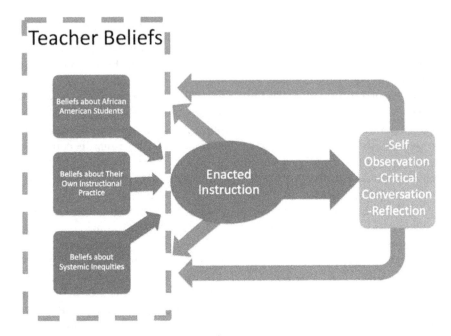

Figure 8.1.   Teacher beliefs framework.

recognizing unproductive beliefs and begin shifting toward productive beliefs. In previous frameworks (e.g., Pajares, 1992), enacted instruction and teaching practices stem from beliefs. However, in the framework in Figure 8.1, we contend a relationship exists between enacted instruction and beliefs. In our previous research (Jackson & Delaney, 2017), we discovered well-meaning White teachers were often willing to try research-based strategies to meet the needs of their Black students. Even when a strategy was outside of their comfort zone, the teachers were often willing to try equity-based instruction. The success or failure of enacting equitable instruction also proved to be a powerful force in shaping beliefs. Witnessing Black students engage and succeed helped transition teachers toward more productive beliefs.

LITERATURE REVIEW

Teachers need productive beliefs specifically related to Black students, how Black students learn, and teaching practices for Black students. Moreover, they need productive beliefs related to themselves as teachers and the roles they play as they teach mathematics through an equitable lens. There have been a relatively large number of studies related to teachers' beliefs and affect within the field of mathematics education (see Philipp, 2007, for an extensive review). Philipp's (2007) review of beliefs focused on four areas: students' mathematical thinking, technology, gender, and changes in beliefs due to the use of mathematics curricula. For this study, we focus the literature review on teachers' beliefs and expectations, instructional practice, and colorblind worldview.

Teachers' Beliefs and Expectations

Thompson (2010) argued a student's race is a determining factor to how a teacher will treat the student. Thompson (2009) administered a Mindset Questionnaire to 143 Texas educators and 94 preservice teachers in California and found that 94% of preservice and 90% of practicing teachers believed most teachers do not know how to work effectively with Black K–12 students, thereby hindering success. Furthermore, the questionnaire asked teachers (White and Black), preservice teachers, and administrators about educators' beliefs of Black students. Fifty to 75% of respondents indicated that the majority of teachers do not believe Black students are as intelligent as other ethnic groups. An overwhelming majority of respondents also believed that teachers do not treat or view Black students the same as other ethnic groups. The following beliefs about Black students are embedded in American society:

- White students are smarter than Black students;
- Black students do not have the aptitude to do outstanding work; and
- White teachers know what is best for Black students (Thompson & Louque, 2005).

These negative beliefs affect teachers' perceptions of Black students, and ultimately their instruction. According to Thompson (2007), many educators and policymakers believe that Black students are lazy, incapable, and inferior. No matter what type of reform is mandated or implemented, these individuals believe Black students will never get it. Thompson (2004) found that in-service teachers believe Black students do not want to learn. Thompson (2007) further indicated that the following two beliefs are interwoven in the framework of American society: (a) Whites are superior to all ethnic groups, specifically Blacks, and (b) Whites deserve to be leaders because they are more intelligent and are hard workers. These beliefs lead to low expectations of Black students, particularly in the mathematics classroom.

Thompson (2009) analyzed preservice and in-service teachers' responses on why Black students do not do as well as they could in school and found that the participants blamed school factors more than non-school factors. The participants reported the following were to blame for the low performance of Black students: (a) low teacher expectations (60%), (b) poor teaching methods dependent on nonculturally relevant curriculum (50%), (c) racist school practices (27%), (d) lack of parental involvement (27%), (e) teacher unfairness toward Black students (22%), (f) students' home life (19%), and (g) peer pressure (19%). Results of this study indicated that these school factors inhibiting the success of Black students must be challenged and changed if teachers want Black students to be successful.

In another study, Love and Kruger (2005) examined the beliefs of teachers using a survey adapted from a study of highly effective teachers of Black students conducted by Ladson-Billings (1994). The participants in the study were selected from a convenience sample from six urban schools that were primarily attended by Black students. The researchers designed 25 survey statements to capture the culturally relevant beliefs and practices of teachers, including: (a) student cooperation and interaction, (b) commitment to urban education, (c) high respect for students, (d) importance of students' race, ethnicity, and culture in teaching, and (e) community connections. The other 23 items were characterized as "assimilationist" beliefs—beliefs that reflect "a teaching style that operates without regard to the students' particular cultural characteristics" (Ladson-Billings, 1994, p. 24). According to Ladson-Billings (1994), "The teacher's role is to ensure that students fit into society" (p. 24). The researchers organized the survey statements into six categories: (a) students' race, ethnicity, and culture; (b) knowledge; (c) social relations in and beyond the classroom; (d) teaching as a profession; (e) teaching practice; and (f) students' needs and strengths. The response metric was based on a 5-point Likert scale ranging from 0 (*strongly disagree*) to 4 (*strongly agree*). The researchers found that 95% of the teachers believed learning from students is just as important as teaching them; however, 78% of the teachers believed it was their job to disseminate knowledge. Participants also believed students' race, culture, and ethnicity were important to teaching but responded they did not associate students with any particular race or culture—they only saw children. This statement affirmed the notion of colorblindness described by Rousseau and Tate (2003).

Researchers have shown teacher expectations and beliefs act as a self-fulfilling prophecy in the classroom (Rosenthal & Jacobson, 1968). Jamar and Pitts (2005) examined the high expectations of Mr. Lee, a White middle school mathematics teacher in an urban school district with over 20 years of experience. Mr. Lee believed his students were able to learn meaningful mathematics and respond in positive ways. He used his students' prior knowledge as stepping-stones to new knowledge and communicated to his students they already had the foundation needed to learn. In addition, he (a) expected his students to be active participants in their own learning, (b) provided opportunities for students to understand concepts prior to learning rules, and (c) made it clear that he knew they could understand the content and that it was understandable (Jamar & Pitts, 2005). In light of these high expectations, Mr. Lee's students not only responded favorably to him as the teacher but also to learning mathematics.

Instructional Practice

Black students are cognizant of racism that occurs in the classroom. For example, a student in an advanced placement high school class in St. Paul, Minnesota reported his teacher always asked challenging questions to White students and asked all the easy, less challenging questions to Black and Latino students (Landsman, 2004). When brought to the teachers' attention, the teacher acknowledged her actions and stated she assumed Black students did not know the answers. Therefore, to avoid any type of embarrassment, she only asked them questions she thought they could answer correctly. Perez (2000) also found that mathematics teachers posed more challenging questions to White students, interacted more with White students, and provided White students with more analytical feedback, thus privileging White students.

Malloy (2009) used both qualitative (e.g., interviews and classroom observations) and quantitative (e.g., survey) approaches to determine what instructional strategies and teachers' dispositions helped middle grade Black students gain conceptual understanding in mathematics. Malloy argued Black students must be visible in the mathematics classroom. This is accomplished by grounding instructional strategies in the learning preferences of Black students and connecting cultural experiences and social justice in Black communities with opportunities to learn.

Evertson, Anderson, Anderson, and Brophy (1980) concluded gains in urban students' achievement and attitudes toward mathematics were positively correlated with the time their junior high mathematics teachers spent lecturing, demonstrating, having class discussions, assigning a limited amount of seatwork, and asking both fact-related questions (mostly fact) and higher cognitive questions that created opportunities for students to respond. However, Ladson-Billings (1994) has argued that effective teaching of Black students involves more than just the instructional practices articulated by Evertson et al. Successful teachers of Black students need to promote academic excellence and recognize students' cultural heritages.

Landsman (2004) described a Black male student who was disruptive and difficult to handle in the classroom. One day the student threatened his teacher, and then he angrily left the classroom. The teacher immediately called the principal to schedule a meeting with him and the student. During the meeting, the student could not look the teacher in the eye. The principal inquired what steps needed to be taken so the student could return to class. The teacher looked directly into the Black student's eyes and said he wanted him to start coming to his gifted class. "[You are] too smart for the class [you have] been assigned to" (p. 30). After hearing the positive remark from his teacher, the student switched to the advanced class and started taking school more seriously. The teacher recognized the student's ability and capitalized on it.

> Good teaching, then, required them to see each child as an individual and to count the successful engagement of each child in learning as part of the larger ongoing task of contributing to their race and to the human race. Good teachers could help launch a child into a life that would otherwise not have been possible. (Walker, 1996, p. 150)

In Landsman's (2004) multicultural college education class, a student majoring in education, wrote "It is good I took this class from you, because before I took it, I thought all Black people were stupid because they let themselves be slaves" (p. 29) on a final paper. This student has gone through most of her education career believing that Blacks are inherently inferior beings. Landsman, an advocate to eliminate racism in classrooms, argued, "If educators read and reflect, engage in ongoing dialogue, immerse ourselves in other cultures, create safe classrooms, and challenge racist definitions of intelligence, then schools will stop using racist assumptions to determine a child's potential" (p. 32). If teachers are not willing to discuss openly and challenge racist viewpoints toward Black students in their classroom and school institutions, Blacks will continually be degraded and looked upon as inferior beings.

Colorblind Worldview

Many educators refuse to acknowledge racial inequities faced by Black students as one source of decline in mathematics achievement. They contend we live in a colorblind society and even argue that if teachers are good teachers, they are good teachers to anybody, anywhere; and from this, good teaching equitable outcomes automatically happen (Gay, 2000; Martin, 2007).

This colorblind belief facilitates ignorance about the impact of racism in the mathematics classroom. For example, Rousseau and Tate (2003) observed seven high school mathematics teachers who taught low-track mathematics courses that were overrepresented by students of color and found that when the teachers were asked about the failure rates of White and Black students in their classes, they did not acknowledge any differences existed.

> I would like say in my accelerated class they [Black students] were all like, they were probably fine, like ... my other races. In my, see in my pre-algebra, now like Samantha and Kammie, they were Black and they were my A students. But then we had like Mark who was also Black but he never did anything, never brought anything to class, so I didn't really have. There is no pattern with that.... Had my [accelerated algebra] students not done well, too, then maybe I would see something. But I have had those that did well and those that didn't ... *I don't see any race* [italics added]. (p. 213)

Furthermore, the researchers noticed particular patterns occurring in the mathematics classroom. In one low-track pre-algebra class containing four students (three Black and one White) the teacher used a "hands-off" approach as the method of instruction (i.e., the teacher did not provide any help to the students until the students took the initiative to ask for it). Two Black students, the individuals who needed help the most, sat for full 50-minute class periods without any instruction from or interaction with the teacher. Not surprisingly, the students were unsuccessful. This pattern of allowing students to fail was evident among Black students, particularly Black males. The teachers in this study did not see this pattern as problematic or how it disproportionately affected Black students.

As seen in Rousseau and Tate's (2003) research, possessing a colorblind ideology is detrimental to the learning of many Black students. Why do teachers and society continue to profess and adopt a colorblind ideology? In essence, the "enchantment of color-blind racism" provides teachers a politically correct escape that denies race is a central factor in determining life choices and success in America (Bonilla-Silva & Dietrich, 2011). Moreover, adopting the colorblind ideology enables teachers not to recognize the inequities Black students face without acknowledging how their own beliefs and practices may contribute to the perpetuation of systemic inequities embedded in education (Bonilla-Silva, 2018). Milner and Laughter (2015) argued the colorblind mentality is most often adopted by White teachers with good intentions; however, good intentions are not enough. Sleeter (1993) found White teachers responded in patterned ways regarding race that allowed them to avoid facing the paradox of being nurturing teachers who also participated in the systematic subordination of people of color. "Whites do not see much of the realities of the lives of people of color nor encounter their viewpoints in any depth. Nor do they really want to, since those viewpoints would challenge practices and beliefs that benefit white people" (p. 253). Sleeter's findings indicated that White teachers may adopt new strategies, but these do not necessarily translate into activism. Choi (2008) found colorblindness manifests in five different ways with teachers: (a) an apprenticeship focused on neutral knowledge and instructional strategies, (b) assimilationist, (c) deficit perspective, (d) meritocratic beliefs, and (e) neoliberal postmodern framework. Although not all of these approaches to colorblindness avoid discussing race, all five are products of socialization that "others" people of color through the explicit and hidden curriculum (Kincheloe, 2004). Critical discussion and personal reflection are two mechanisms for understanding race and becoming color conscious (Choi, 2008). Moreover, Ullucci and Battey (2011) examined how the colorblind ideology manifests in multiple ways with classroom teachers. Countering preservice teachers' colorblind perspectives is a critical process that has the potential to lead to confronting personal beliefs and shifting toward color-consciousness. Personal reflection, education, and critical conversations are essential in changing teachers' beliefs and mindsets about Black students (Jackson & Delaney, 2017). The shift in beliefs is central to adopting effective teaching practices for Black students (Matias, 2013).

METHODOLOGY

In this qualitative case study, we examined the following research questions: (a) What beliefs does a middle level mathematics teacher have about Black students? (b) How are those beliefs enacted in instruction? and (c) How does examining and reflecting on one's instruction help teachers develop productive beliefs about Black students in the mathematics classroom?

Participants

The lead author collaborated with the secondary mathematics curriculum coordinator to identify a pool of middle school mathematics teachers who had positive gains in Black students' achievement on district and state tests over a 3-year period. In addition, the teachers had to have a minimum of 5 years teaching experience. From the pool of teachers, the lead author spoke with building administrators about the rapport the teachers had with Black students. Ms. Chrisley (pseudonym), a White, sixth grade middle school mathematics teacher, met the criteria and agreed to participate in the study. Ms. Chrisley taught mathematics for 13 years in a large urban district in the Midwest region of the United States. She taught sixth grade mathematics, advanced sixth grade mathematics, seventh grade mathematics, eighth grade mathematics, and sixth grade science. For the purpose of this study, we focused on both her advanced and regular sixth grade mathematics classes, which each contained 28 and 27 students, respectively. The demographics of the advanced sixth grade mathematics class were 57% female and 18% Black, 78% White, 4% Asian, while her regular mathematics class was 52% female and 33% Black, 48% White, and 18% Hispanic. Her mathematics classes met every day for 65 minutes.

Data Collection

The first and second authors collected the data. The first author is a Black female who taught middle level students in the Midwest region of the United States for 12 years. The second author is a White female, classroom teacher who taught for 11 years in multiple districts throughout the Midwest.

We collected data for this study over a 2-year period, the 2016–17 and 2017–18 academic years. Data included both semi-structured interviews (see Appendix A) and classroom observations. During the 2016–17 academic year, Ms. Chrisley's mathematics instruction was videotaped three consecutive days at three different periods of time (i.e., beginning, middle, and end of the school year). Two stationary video cameras (one in the front and one in the back of the classroom) were used during each classroom observation to capture the teacher's instructional practices and student interaction and engagement. The teacher also wore a pair of camera eyeglasses during each observation. The eyeglass cameras allowed us to observe where and what the teacher focused on during instruction. In addition, each day two students wore a pair of camera eyeglasses to capture further what the students focused on during instruction. We intentionally selected one Black student each day to wear the camera eyeglasses. The other student was randomly selected. Each day a different pair of students wore the camera eyeglasses. For each observation, we collected Ms. Chrisley's lesson plans, handouts, and copies of student work.

Ms. Chrisley participated in three semi-structured interviews and three stimulated-recall interviews that each lasted about an hour. The first interview (i.e., Initial Interview) occurred at the beginning of the study and an interview occurred at the end of the 2016–17 academic year. The stimulated-recall interview occurred after each three-day observation period. During the stimulated-recall interview, Ms. Chrisley was shown video clips from the 3-day observation and was asked questions about her instructional decisions and student interaction. At the end of the 2016–17 academic year, Ms. Chrisley voluntarily signed up for an 18-month professional development course, led by the lead author, on effectively supporting all students to be successful in algebra. The goals of the professional development were to (a) increase sixth, seventh, and eighth grade teachers' specialized content knowledge (i.e., prerequisite algebraic content knowledge and pedagogical content knowledge); (b) increase teachers' understanding and use of research-based instructional practices to teach mathematics in culturally responsive ways, particularly to Black students and emergent bilinguals; and (c) increase middle level students' pre-requisite algebraic mathematics achievement. During this period (2017–18), we observed Ms. Chrisley's instruction three times and conducted a follow-up interview in 2018.

Data Analysis

We used an inductive approach to analyze the data that incorporated systematic methods of managing data through reduction, organization, and connection (Dey, 1993; LeCompte, 2000). We used initial coding to develop an early code list (Saldaña, 2016) based on the conceptual framework. The initial coding primarily employed descriptive coding, "summarizing in a word or short phrase … the basic topic of a passage of qualitative data" (Saldaña, 2016, p. 102). During this first cycle coding process, the descriptions began to paint a picture of Ms. Chrisley's beliefs and instructional practices.

Then, we used the preliminary codes to establish additional codes that were used to code an initial set of interview transcripts and video data. We reviewed the list of codes, revised them, and coded the remaining data. After the data were coded, we conducted a second cycle of pattern coding to appropriately group and label similarly coded data as a way to attribute meaning (Saldaña, 2016). Pattern coding helped us to identify common themes and divergent cases, looking across categories to see if there were underlying patterns to the responses (Delamont, 1992). Once the initial themes were drafted, we reviewed the themes and supporting data to add clarity and content validity to the themes. During this review process, important questions were raised about the appropriateness of the themes and whether they were well supported. All discrepancies were resolved during the final development of the overall themes.

RESULTS

"I used to be one of the teachers that used to say they couldn't do it. I just didn't believe they had the skill set. I've moved more into the belief that all students can rather than they can't." (Ms. Chrisley, Follow-up Interview, 2018)

Using the conceptual framework as a lens, we examined Ms. Chrisley's beliefs about Black students, systemic inequities, and instructional practice. Then, we engaged Ms. Chrisley in reflection and critical conversations via stimulated recall interviews, which allowed us to investigate Ms. Chrisley's professed beliefs with her enacted instruction. Through this iterative process, we noticed shifts in Ms. Chrisley's beliefs.

Beliefs About Black Students

Ms. Chrisley was initially hesitant and uncomfortable when discussing race and racial inequities faced by Black students. She generally prefaced her response with trepidation and nervous giggles, "I don't want to be offensive," or "It might be offensive," or "I hope it's not offensive" (Initial Interview, 2016). Consequently, she eased her initial discomfort by incorporating a colorblind ideology. She stated, "Everyone is the same" (Initial Interview, 2016) and "teaching a kid is teaching a kid, whether it be they're African American or purple with yellow stripes" (Stimulated-Recall Interview 3, May 2017). Ms. Chrisley commented she does not pay attention to the students' race—"it's more about their academic level and skill level than their background or cultures" (Final Interview, 2017). Instead of focusing on race and racial inequities in society and in the mathematics classroom, Ms. Chrisley deferred to discussing a child's socioeconomic background, student's prior knowledge, or family environment.

When Ms. Chrisley began to open up about and discuss her perceptions of Black students, she focused on the struggle Black students have with their identity, especially when they are enrolled in an advanced mathematics class in middle school. "Assuming that they're kind of struggling for who they are. They're kind of alone in, you know, racially in this atmosphere. I've had students talk to me about it. There's just no other Black kids in my class" (Final Interview, 2017). She noticed her Black students really trying to "fit in" with the White students. For example, Ms. Chrisley stated:

> My African American students in my accelerated classes typically, I have found, are trying to really excel academically and worked really hard and want to have those gains. But they're immersed in a group of Caucasians and Latinos that are also doing the same thing. (Final Interview, 2017)

Although this statement appears to be positive, it is an unproductive belief of equating that Blacks want to be like the White students in the class.

Ms. Chrisley stated she had conversations with her Black students to validate their right to be in the advanced mathematics class. Ms. Chrisley did not realize this made a difference to her students until they brought it up and discussed it with her. She admitted she never had to consider or think about what it was like to be the "only" minority student in the classroom. She recalls as a young girl she attended an "all Black" school, and she was in the minority, but she was never stigmatized or scrutinized for who she was—a White female—or for what she did. Ms. Chrisley was beginning to recognize and understand the racial make-up of a class can have an effect on students. However, she neglected to consider how her race provided privilege even in an environment where she was the minority.

We observed Ms. Chrisley interacting with her Black students in several contexts. While moving through the hallways, many children high-fived Ms. Chrisley and greeted her with hugs and smiles. On multiple occasions, a group of Black female students stopped by her classroom to share about their day and discuss concerns they were experiencing. We overheard one Black girl remark about how unfairly a seventh grade teacher was treating her. Ms. Chrisley listened intently and encouraged the student to talk to the teacher, but "don't smack your lips, roll your eyes, or huff like that! You have to respect [your teacher] when talking about stuff like this" (Field notes, November 2016). This student clearly trusted Ms. Chrisley and sought her input. They had established a positive relationship. Building authentic relationships with students and sharing of herself was something Ms. Chrisley prioritized. While we witnessed the longevity of her efforts, Ms. Chrisley also shared how important it was to be real with her students and make sure they know she cares (Initial Interview, 2016).

Ms. Chrisley had some dissonance with her beliefs about relationships with Black students and how females, in particular, engaged in her class. She argued that many of her Black females in the mathematics classroom like to take charge, naturally assuming a leadership role. Not only do her Black females like to take charge, they also require positive affirmation from Ms. Chrisley to verify they are working the mathematics problem correctly. While this is true for many of her other students, Ms. Chrisley attested that it is especially true for her Black female students due to their life experiences (e.g., not being allowed to visit biological mother). Moreover, Ms. Chrisley commented her Black students have a lot of attitude. "A lot of attitude. But like, which can go both ways, positive or negative, but confidence. A lot of my African-American students are confident, very proud. Also, very caring and understanding other people" (Final Interview, 2017). She further added:

> Honestly, most of my African American students have been louder than my Caucasian students. And I think that very cultural that you just speak, you're proud, and you're loud … and then when I meet their parents, Yep. Okay. Here we go. You talk pretty loud too. (Final Interview, 2017)

Ms. Chrisley stated it is important that she does not make this an issue in her classroom even though many teachers make it an issue and reprimand their Black students for talking loudly. "In so, just accepting some of those little things that really don't have to be an issue. But it's like that's who they are and so, accepting everything that they are" (Final Interview, 2017).

As Ms. Chrisley reflected on her practice and some of the questions we asked in the initial interview, she acknowledged it is uncomfortable for many White teachers to talk about Blacks and the negative stereotypes attributed to Blacks. She stated her school district required the teachers to attend professional development on stereotypes. She commented that during the professional development:

> They had us discuss what stereotypes we think about minority groups, which was intimidating and uncomfortable for a mostly White staff.... So we were all kind of like (groans) ... it kind of felt like a trap. Do you know what I mean? And I don't think that was the purpose, but it just felt like ugh! Just because those things [racial stereotypes] are said doesn't mean we feel comfortable talking about them, you know what I mean? (Stimulated-Recall Interview 3, May 2017)

Yet, Ms. Chrisley realized the importance of having professional development focused on teaching Black students because she taught in a building with White teachers who "don't really have a good understanding of what some of their [students] culture is like, and [they] are going to assume things and make your own thought processes around what they do" (Final Interview, 2017). This was a turning point for Ms. Chrisley in recognizing there was a lot more for her to learn, and she began to seek out ways to improve her own professional growth as an educator who taught Black students.

Systemic Inequities

Ms. Chrisley argued racism is "hatred for or dislike of people based on their race, and typically is founded in ignorance and not understanding someone that is different from yourself" (Final Interview, 2017). She elaborated:

> Some people are scared of what they don't understand. And so, if there is a culture or sometimes it is based around race or sometimes it's based around the other things, but that they don't understand or they can't relate to, and sometimes it becomes just a negative view of that. (Final Interview, 2017)

Ms. Chrisley acknowledged everyone, including herself, have biases and stereotypes. She noted that those biases are developed and can be developed from "seeing a pattern amongst students of a particular race for a particular culture, and then assuming that's how all people in that culture are" (Final Interview, 2017). She said within her school district, biases and stereotypes are reflected in where schools are located and who attends those schools. For example, the schools on the south side of town—the more affluent schools—have fewer Black students, and the students tend to have higher mathematical achievement because their parents care and are more involved in schools. She remarked that when grades are posted, parents immediately respond and say, "I noticed the grade was a little bit low, what can I work on at home?" (Stimulated-Recall Interview 2, February 2017). She added, "Those kids typically tend to be the students that I see with that deeper understanding of the math" (Stimulated-Recall Interview 2, February 2017). Ms. Chrisley identified the schools on the northeast side of town as having a large population of Black students, and the students live in "housing projects or trailer parks" (Final Interview, 2017).

Ms. Chrisley noticed accelerated mathematics classes were offered at her current south side school, but none were offered when she taught in the northeast school. She ascertained that her accelerated mathematics students had many "life experiences" that she could incorporate in her mathematics lessons and ultimately a stronger foundation because "their parents talk to them about a lot of things and help them with their homework. I don't feel like I have to scaffold as much. Instead of trying to get them up to grade level, I'm trying to challenge beyond that" (Initial Interview, 2016). However, she noted her students at the northeast school academically struggled. She said she spent the majority of her instructional time scaffolding the lesson because the "majority of my students were working below grade level" (Initial Interview, 2016).

The classroom instruction we observed fed into the systemic inequities common between grade-level and accelerated classes. Ms. Chrisley's accelerated classes experienced real-world applications of mathematics through projects such as creating a monthly budget and determine where they could afford to live based on the mean salary of their preferred career. Ms. Chrisley encouraged students in her accelerated classes to consider professions in the medical field, education, and law. The class also discussed college loans, luxuries available to them, and mortgages to purchase a home. In contrast, her grade-level classes were working through changes in percent and ratios using online textbook materials and classroom practice. These sections were noticeably more racially diverse than the accelerated section. Ms. Chrisley did not recognize her instruction was perpetuating systemic inequities.

At the beginning of this study, Ms. Chrisley did not think students' mathematical achievement had anything to do with race. Instead, she attributed the low academic performance to socioeconomic status but then realized many of the individuals who come from low socioeconomic backgrounds are Black. "But, unfortunately, many of those African American students are in both of those categories" (Initial Interview, 2016). Ms. Chrisley defaulted to blaming the parents for Black students' low mathematical performance. She is concerned Black parents "don't value education" (Final Interview, 2017), but quickly interjected that this was not true for all Black parents. Then, she immediately returned to a negative mindset she had of Black parents. "It seems to me, if parents were more involved, and if the parents were showing that that's the real value, then African American scores would go up and their academic progress would be different" (Final Interview, 2017).

Ms. Chrisley reflected why very few Black students were in the advanced mathematics classes, and concluded it was due to the structural inequities that exist in the United States, which had a domino effect on education. Ms. Chrisley now takes the liberty to have open conversations with her Black students on these structural inequities. She stated, "I feel like I can talk to them pretty openly about it. And they need to understand the overarching situation with minority groups and test scores. I'm pretty open with them about it" (Final Interview, 2017). She noted, in general, "More Caucasian people have had a positive experience with school. And, from my experience, a lot of African American students did not necessarily have a positive experience with school or a positive view toward it for whatever reason it may be" (Final Interview, 2017). To begin to take action against the negative experiences many Black people had in school, Ms. Chrisley continued to impress on her Black students that it was "cool to be smart" (Final Interview, 2017). Ms. Chrisley commented, "I've been blessed to be around some really motivated, amazing African American children that are in the accelerated program and have their sights set and goals set for some really big things in the world" (Final Interview, 2017). In addition, Ms. Chrisley intentionally makes positive phone calls home to parents. The phone calls surprise the parents because they are used to hearing negative feedback from their child's teachers. Ms. Chrisley shared, "I just start calling. And they be like, oh gosh! What'd he do? And I be like, oh no! We had an awesome day and I just wanted to call and say [I'm] so excited your son's in my class!" (Final Interview, 2017). She stated this practice had a tremendous impact not only with how the child was performing in class, but it established trust with the parents because the parents began to view her as an "ally [who] was supporting their child" (Final Interview, 2017).

Beliefs about Instruction and Instructional Practice

Ms. Chrisley claimed all students (i.e., all races) learn mathematics effectively when it relates to their life. "That's always my goal is to find things we have in common. Then, it doesn't matter what color you are or any of those things because you've gained their trust. And then, they want to work hard for you" (Final Interview, 2017). Ms. Chrisley noticed her Black students needed to feel like they could trust and relate to her before they could learn mathematics. It was more than teaching mathematics that was relevant; it centered on whether Ms. Chrisley could be trusted and if she could relate to them as individuals. She stated, "I have felt like my African American students needed that even more from me. So, they could trust me almost. But they needed [to] somehow relate to me and trust me before they really would give me their all" (Initial Interview, 2016). Furthermore, Ms. Chrisley realized that genuineness was important when teaching her Black students. She commented:

> Being honest and being genuine is a really big deal. The bigger front that you put on the less interest most of my African American students would have. I mean, honestly, I think you're dismissed if you're not honest and just who you are. (Final Interview, 2017)

Not only did Ms. Chrisley attest to the importance of being honest with her students, but also she stated teachers have to take the time to get to know their students. Having students complete a simple interest inventory would allow teachers to make connections with their students, especially their Black students. She insisted that the teachers need to find things that both the student and teacher can relate to and use it in their instruction because ...

> We've been so separate for so long, you know, Caucasians and African Americans. But, we're all human. An interest inventory, just a couple questions, just those little things can make such a huge difference. And you can bridge that whole racial situation. It doesn't even have to be an issue. (Final Interview, 2017)

Ms. Chrisley realized the importance of establishing a positive rapport with her Black students to instruct them effectively. She attributes her ability to relate to Black students to her personal background and experiences. Ms. Chrisley grew up in a predominately Black neighborhood where she was the ...

> Only White child in like a two-block radius. I also was really blessed to have my best friend was African American and her family kind of took me in, and we went back and forth to each other's homes. And so, I did get a chance to experience.... And there were times where I was like, Oh! This is different than what is going on, you know, at my house. But I got to learn that people are different. (Final Interview, 2017)

She believed this experience provided her with the knowledge on ways to relate to Black people.

Ms. Chrisley shared that her teaching philosophy when teaching mathematics centers on the "I do, we do, then you do" (Stimulated-Recall Interview 2, February 2017) approach. She contends this approach allows her to build her students' confidence because they have the opportunity to see how to solve the problem before working on it independently. She claimed the advantages of the "I do, we do, you do" approach is "students really gaining confidence when they see me do it. I'm modeling it, you know, the expert is telling them how it works, and then being able to work it through with somebody else and discuss it" (Stimulated-Recall Interview 2, February 2017). Ms. Chrisley further described her teaching approach as one that establishes a positive, open classroom community where students can trust her and others in the class. She believes it is important to connect her mathematics lessons to the real world and to make apparent why her students are learning the mathematical concepts. She also thinks it is important that she is "very clear about expectations and boundaries" (Initial Interview, 2016).

Ms. Chrisley noted that when she learned mathematics, she never really understood the mathematical concepts—everything was procedural. She commented, "I don't think I really truly understood fractions, percents, and decimals and the similarities and differences and all of those things until I taught it for a few years" (Initial Interview, 2016). But now Ms. Chrisley said she focuses on conceptual understanding. She contended that providing students with a conceptual understanding helps them become flexible thinkers, which gives them the ability to reason and think through the mathematics. Moreover, Ms. Chrisley found herself instructing her students to do a mathematics problem "the way I am telling you to do it" (Initial Interview, 2016). Then she realized:

> There are so many different ways of thinking about [and] solving a math problem. It's better to allow their strategy and actually have them share it. So, I had to open up my understanding about how people think and learn. (Initial Interview, 2016).

Ms. Chrisley further described a typical day of her classroom instruction would be one in which she "sit[s] back and watch[es] what [students] are doing" (Initial Interview, 2016). Her classroom would be "full of activity and talking" (Initial Interview, 2016). She stated that talking is necessary for students to understand the mathematical concept.

> That is how they are going to have a deeper understanding if they can communicate it with each other. So, there's a lot of "talk to your group." Especially when I feel like they are all looking at me like "I'm not sure." And

so, then I said, talk to everyone around you. Come to a consensus. Talk to your table about, you know, whatever it is we're discussing at that time. So, a lot of talking. (Initial Interview, 2016)

Ms. Chrisley contended her students' confidence level is high when they have the opportunity to talk to each other.

I think that getting the chance to talk to each other all of the time and have that opportunity to communicate about math has been really helpful for them to get more confidence. I noticed … they're always looking to me like, "Is that right?" and so I'm trying to build their own, you know, I want them to be more independently confident rather than always having to hear me say that it's good enough. (Stimulated-Recall Interview 2, February 2017)

Yet this philosophy is contrary to Ms. Chrisley's "I do, we do, you do" approach where the students view her as the "expert." In essence, the students are looking to the expert for validation of their work.

In addition to lots of talking, Ms. Chrisley shared it is imperative for teachers to "listen" to their students, particularly their Black students, and use what they learned as feedback to inform their instruction. "I ask them to tell me what they're not understanding...sometimes that helps them to better understand. But listening to that and making sure I understand what they do need" (Stimulated-Recall Interview 1, November 2016). Ms. Chrisley stated she incorporated a lot of movement and hands-on, small group activities within her instruction. Ms. Chrisley stipulated that incorporating movement is important within her instruction. She claimed, "If they're sitting for the hour and thirty minutes, I'm going to lose them within the first fifteen minutes, and so that talking and that movement really helps" (Stimulated-Recall Interview 2, February 2017).

Ms. Chrisley contended some of her sixth graders in her accelerated math class actually struggle with mathematical concepts. She claimed they were:

good at following direction[s] and show[ing] the steps [when solving a problem]. Probably about 20% of my students don't necessarily have a good grasp of the concepts. They can follow the steps, but they don't necessarily have a strong mathematical sense. (Stimulated-Recall Interview 2, February 2017)

Moreover, Ms. Chrisley articulated that some of the mathematical concepts she teaches are too abstract for her students to understand. For example, she commented:

I personally think that this topic [percent proportion] is a little too abstract for my students at their age. I personally believe that brain research, all the brain research from back in the day that made a lot of sense to me, and it shows in my classroom that 11- to 12-year-olds aren't quite ready for that very abstract type of problem solving situation. So, I keep trying to make it more concrete for them. (Stimulated-Recall Interview 3, May 2017)

Although Ms. Chrisley contended some of the mathematical concepts are too abstract for her students, she claims her sixth graders need to develop and deepen their understanding of fractions, decimals, and percentages. Consequently, she said she uses variations of number lines, "Trying to make sure students understand where those values belong" (Initial Interview, 206).

Ms. Chrisley purposefully selected mathematical problems she believes would be above her students' grade level. She claimed that if the students were successful at working the problems that are above their grade level, they would not have any difficulty doing well on the district assessment. She confirmed:

My philosophy has always been if you can do a little bit higher level work, then you should be able to do the, you know, the easier, not easier, but the little bit more concrete work. Our district assessments are actually very basic, and so I like to step it up because I think any student can rise to a challenge as long as you give them all the tools to do it, so that's what I try to do. (Stimulated-Recall Interview 2, February 2017)

She elaborated learning mathematics is about "bringing it to life, making it hands on, and, you know, being a kid but learning about the real world through all the topics we do" (Initial Interview, 2016).

Enacted Instruction

Ms. Chrisley noticed many of her students were relying on her too much to affirm their mathematical thinking. To reduce their overreliance on her as the sole authority of mathematical "correctness," she developed activities that supported and developed students' mathematical sense making. However, during classroom instruction, one of her Black females was working on a mathematics problem, and Ms. Chrisley decided to intervene because:

I find that she needs more specific directions. I knew that it was time to give her that part-whole, tell me which one is which, and so it was a little more explicit. The way that I kind of needed to get her to where she needed to be. (Stimulated-Recall Interview 1, November 2016)

Instead of allowing her Black student to struggle productively and make sense of the mathematics in the problem, Ms. Chrisley provided step-by-step directions on how to solve the problem. In essence, she took away the mathematical thinking and sense making from the student. Ms. Chrisley provided students who are struggling with "a push in the right direction" (Stimulated-Recall Interview 2, February 2017). However, she believed students, particularly her Black female students, are struggling because they lack confidence. She remarked, "It's more a confidence thing with math than it is the ability. So, I was trying to step them through because they needed to backtrack and kind of think about each figure and how to really find the area" (Stimulated-Recall Interview 2, February 2017).

During instruction, Ms. Chrisley incorporated movement and had her students work together. In one activity, she designed a scavenger hunt in which students had to go around and calculate the area of various states. Ms. Chrisley noted:

They can talk about it with a partner and they aren't sitting in a desk doing a worksheet. And so, I kind of trick them into doing the same thing that maybe another teacher would do by giving them a sheet to work on at their desk, but that movement and that chance to discuss it and communicate about it, I think helps solidify it for them. It's like, if you teach something, you know it better. A lot of times they'll have little debates about what they think and why and that is going to be huge in, you know, the deeper understanding of the concept. (Stimulated-Recall Interview 2, February 2017)

Although Ms. Chrisley claimed, she wanted her students to talk and communicate mathematically, she "struggles with giving them the freedom to talk" (Stimulated-Recall Interview 2, February 2017).

Ms. Chrisley stated one of her Black female students makes it a habit to "shush" the class. She believed the student does this because "she doesn't want the class [to get] in trouble" (Stimulated-Recall Interview 3, May 2017). Ms. Chrisley informed the student that it is "more distracting when there's like this big huge shush!" (Stimulated-Recall Interview 3, May 2017). She further explained:

Her shushing almost seems angry. And so, I kind of feel bad for her. Like, it really is a struggle for her to focus when people are talking, and so she really just does want them to stop. But, on the other side of that coin, sometimes it will be her that's talking. And she'll be talking really loud and she'll shush everybody else. (Stimulated-Recall Interview 3, May 2017)

However, what Ms. Chrisley failed to realize was that this student was doing exactly what Ms. Chrisley did on a consistent basis during instruction. During all of the classroom observations, Ms. Chrisley would "shush" the class a minimum of 20 times. In fact, during this particular class period where the Black female shushed the class, Ms. Chrisley reprimanded her for talking and shushed her a couple of times.

During one lesson we observed, a Black female raised her hand for over 10 minutes. Although she lowered it several times to rest or attempt to solve the problem, her hand was raised the majority of the time without any response from Ms. Chrisley. The student was quiet and respectful as she patiently waited for assistance that never arrived. We decided to show the clip to Ms. Chrisley in a stimulated recall interview. Only after watching the clip did Ms. Chrisley realized she "ignored" one of her Black students whose hand was raised for an extended period of time. She commented:

> I did notice that poor [student's name] hand was up almost that entire time. And I think when she kept putting it down, then I missed it. And then she would be like wait. And then somebody else would jump and put their hand up, but she was waiting for a long time for me. So, I'm like, "Awww. Poor thing. I'm sorry." (Stimulated-Recall Interview 1, November 2016)

In the same lesson, the same Black female student again raised her hand to ask a question, but then put it back down. Ms. Chrisley commented, "I was watching her during that clip, and I thought it was interesting that it was almost like she didn't want to bother me. I think it's a confidence thing" (Stimulated-Recall Interview 1, November 2016).

Ms. Chrisley noticed when she asked her students questions, especially open-ended questions, her students wanted her to supply the answer. Instead of providing the students with the answers, she asked them more questions such as "Well, what do you know about that? What don't you know? What part of that doesn't make sense to you? (Stimulated-Recall Interview 1, November 2016). She wanted her students to understand what they do and do not know before coming to her. She thought it is "important to teeter right on that line of them having worthwhile struggle because they learn more" (Stimulated-Recall Interview 1, November 2016).

Color Aware and Systemic Inequities

Ms. Chrisley began the study professing, "I don't see color. All of my kids are the same" (Initial interview, 2016). After engaging in self-reflection of her own beliefs and instructional practices, she shifted this belief. Instead, she acknowledges when teachers say they do not see color, it is their "valiant effort in being equitable. But I think we have to see the differences to meet the needs of our students" (Follow-up Interview, 2018). She further elaborated that Black people have been treated unequally and unfairly by society, and she needs to be cognizant on how that unfair treatment as well as discrimination manifests in the classroom. She commented, "It is feeling like they don't matter as much because as a society, that is a truth. I mean, [Black Americans] have been and are not treated equally" (Follow-up Interview, 2018). In essence, she heard her students questioning, "Why should I do what you're asking me?" (Follow-up Interview, 2018). Consequently, Ms. Chrisley struggled with helping her Black students persevere. She noticed that strong motivators for her White and Hispanic students are grades and people pleasing behaviors. However, she was still seeking and trying different approaches to reach her Black students and ensure they were learning rigorous mathematics.

Ms. Chrisley realized to meet effectively the needs of and build relationships with her Black students she had to be *color aware*. She had to make them intentionally visible players in the mathematics classroom. She argued:

> Just believing in them. I mean the human resource of compassion and belief they are capable as everybody else. It's funny I say I am not biased, but I truly see all of my students as capable, contributors to my classroom. (Follow-up Interview, 2018)

Ms. Chrisley exclaimed she is "terrify[ied] that other teachers do not see [Black students as capable]" (Follow-up Interview, 2018). Initially, Ms. Chrisley was not cognizant about how the colorblind ideology negatively affected her Black students. Now she asserted, "My eyes are open more" (Follow-up Interview, 2018), and she is going to make sure her Black students are full contributors who engage in rigorous, challenging mathematics.

We observed Ms. Chrisley's classroom one year after our initial study. Her classroom was set up for the students to work in small groups instead of teacher-focused. The students quickly filed into her classroom selecting their seats as they entered. Ms. Chrisley did not flinch when students moved desks to be with their friends and form a larger group. When one student asked, "Can I sit on the ground?" Ms. Chrisley replied, "I don't care. Do what you gotta do. Just be productive" (Field notes, May 2018). This was significant because, during the 45-minute lesson, all but 10-minutes were spent on group work, discussion, and students sharing their strategies. The choices Ms. Chrisley gave to students led to a student-centered environment and flexible instruction, a stark contrast to previous observations. Some students chose to work independently, but the majority of students were content to work in small groups or pairs. The classroom was full of chatter creating a much louder environment compared to previous visits. However, Ms. Chrisley seemed to relish in the students' interactions and collaboration. She only "shushed" the class one time when they were not listening to a peer present an answer. Based on our observations, the shifts in her instruction were notable and directly correlated to her changing beliefs about Black students and mathematical instruction.

One superficial, but impactful step she took toward fighting systemic inequities was making sure students saw others who look like them as successful mathematicians and scientists. Ms. Chrisley found a website entitled *Not Just White Dude Mathematicians*. The website had a list of mathematicians and scientists from all different races, ethnicities, and nationalities. She made a collage on one of the walls in her classroom representing various Blacks, Hispanics, and other contributors to mathematics and science (see Figure 8.2). Ms. Chrisley exclaimed, "I want kids to feel like they are represented … I thought, why would they think they should do well in math and science if they are not represented in our normal showing of who is important in math" (Follow-up Interview, 2018). As Ms. Chrisley began to search for posters, she primarily found mostly old, White men. She said:

> That made me mad because I was like, why is there not a set of posters I can buy that shows diversity of contributions to math and science? I know it's just not White people that contribut[ed] to world of math and science. (Follow-up Interview, 2018)

She further elaborated, "We are so biased in the way we present material. I personally think it is disgusting and horrible. Why would we not include everyone's contributions? I was like, how sad. We are evil human beings" (Follow-up Interview, 2018).

She became more disgruntled when she found several posters of White mathematicians and scientists that sold for only $6, whereas, the posters of the Black inventors were $25. She personally went to one of the stores that specialized in posters for educational purposes and asked the clerk about posters of Black scientists, mathematicians, and inventors. She said the clerk responded, "I never heard anything like that. No idea. [What you want] does not exist. I just have never seen anything like that" (Follow-up Interview, 2018). Ms. Chrisley felt dismayed that the clerk "had no clue" (Follow-up Interview, 2018). Although they may be small, Ms. Chrisley was taking actionable steps to ensure that her students did not feel inconsequential in her classroom.

As Ms. Chrisley became more and more color aware, she was able to "see" systemic inequities her Black students and Blacks in general encounter in society. "Access to resources is definitely a major issue. Poverty. Access to

Figure 8.2. Major contributors to mathematics and science.

education. Even just people believing in [Black students]. Part of it is a part of this ugly self-fulfilling prophecy, but part of it is this inherent evil" (Follow-up Interview, 2018). Instead of adopting a deficit mentality or a "missionary" mentality of rescuing her students, she simply empathized, "I understand why [my Black students] may feel as they do and they may just be like, 'I don't care,' and they may act out" (Follow-up Interview, 2018). Ms. Chrisley also recognized her empathy was not enough. Even though she felt like she understands, she admitted she is currently struggling with how to help her Black students.

> I am still stuck in "how do I get them to buy in." I understood it before, and I feel like it's gotten so much more prevalent. I feel like that has made [Black] students like, "Why should I care?" I'm figuring out how to shift [my instruction] with [my understanding]. (Follow-up Interview, 2018)

Importantly, Ms. Chrisley is being proactive about her struggle in teaching Black students. She is researching, reading, and getting involved in professional development.

Shift in Instructional Practices

Ms. Chrisley shifted her practice to teach mathematics through a problem-based approach instead of the "I do, we do, you do" approach. She described her problem-based instructional method as one that connects math to the real world where "more kids [are] willing to persevere, open up, and share" (Follow-up Interview, 2018). She has been implementing more open-ended problems, which "pushes students to do the thinking on their own, rather than [me] rescuing [them]" (Follow-up interview, 2018). She confessed:

> It is so easy to rescue or dumb down [the task] because you feel like you are helping the student. But I want to maintain the level of rigor. I am ready to ask questions instead of just giving a procedure. (Follow-up Interview, 2018)

To make this a reality in her instruction, she said she started to "plan less." She intentionally ensured her instruction did not focus on getting through a set number of mathematics problems. Instead, she planned her instruction around one problem-based activity and focused her remaining efforts on planning good questions. As she planned her questions, she anticipated what her students might say and do. She said this process helped her not to "rescue" her students by telling them what to do or how to solve the problem. In essence, she did not want to take away the thinking from her students. Ms. Chrisley said this was not an easy task to accomplish as she implemented her lesson because she is not very good at wait time, which is a necessary component for students to think and reason through the mathematics. She commented, "I am really bad at wait time. Super, super terrible. I have been working really hard to give everyone a chance to think about it before I go" (Follow-up Interview, 2018).

Perhaps a major shift in Ms. Chrisley's instructional practice was how she perceived how students, especially Black students, learn mathematics. Ms. Chrisley regretted how much energy was wasted forcing her Black students to comply instead of learn. "[Black] students need to be talking all the time where I was always trying to get them to do what I want. Comply" (Follow-up Interview, 2018). Refocusing her instructional practice on problem solving instead of "I do, we do, you do" helped her realign her beliefs about what it means to do mathematics. Ms. Chrisley proudly admits, "[the professional development sessions] made me realize they are going to comply. They are going to do what I ask them to do. It just might look different. It might not look like, 'sit and quietly do the work'" (Follow-up Interview, 2018). Ms. Chrisley realized that when she works, she normally sits quietly and does the work, which is a similar pattern of behavior for her White students. When she shifted her beliefs from a traditional Eurocentric perspective of teaching, she noticed a drastic and positive change in her Black students.

> When I've given them a little bit more freedom, socially, then it allowed them to get more out of what we're doing because there's not an argument of "Be quiet!" Now it's like, "I can do what I need to do, just on my terms." When I was always trying to get them to conform to the way I was thinking, what I wanted [their work time] to look like, it ended up they were focused on why I was being a jerk or whatever rather than being focused on the work at hand. Now, when I allow them to socialize or when I make it more of a partner activity, they can totally talk about it. It's not going to hurt them. They're not focused on anything but what they're doing. (Follow-up Interview, 2018)

In other words, Ms. Chrisley experienced the growth and success that occurs when Black students are given the opportunity to learn in culturally relevant environments, and she is not turning back. "A lot of my [Black] students are more willing to ask questions. They are more willing to try" (Follow-up Interview, 2018).

Although Ms. Chrisley initially professed the importance of having students talk about and make sense of the mathematics, she realized she was not actively putting her beliefs into practice. She had to self-reflect and not say what sounded good or what she thought people wanted to hear, but she had to be truthful and honest with herself. Only then did she realize that is what makes a difference.

Student Voice and Agency

Ms. Chrisley stood out as a leader in her district for over five years because of her Black students' high scores on standardized tests. When previously asked why she thought this was the case, she was not certain. Instead, she shared how she was generally "down to earth" (Initial interview, 2016), while other teachers were strict. After engaging in an activity about student voice and agency during the 18-month professional development session, she realized it was her attempt at giving Black students voice that made the difference. "One connection I made is that I've always tried to give my [Black] students voice, and now that I've expanded that I'm hoping I will have even better results with kids" (Follow-up interview, 2018). To give voice and agency to her Black students, Ms. Chrisley acknowledged she had to develop a better understanding and appreciation of the social aspect her Black students engage in, learn from, and be "more lenient with some of the socializing." She realized this made a difference in ensuring that her Black students "feel accepted and comfortable" (Follow-up interview, 2018).

Ms. Chrisley remarked that her goal of giving students, especially Black students a voice in the mathematics classroom had been welcomed by all students. "The students have been very receptive to it. I feel like most of them seem to feel more comfortable because they can say what they think and not feel like they are going to be wrong or shamed" (Follow-up interview, 2018). She further elaborated how the change in practice provided agency to her students. "It opened some doors for me about being a little less in charge and letting the students take more of the responsibility" (Follow-up interview, 2018). When we observed her instruction, this instructional practice was evident. During one of the lessons in her regular mathematics classes, Mrs. Chrisley began with an open-ended number talk where over half of the class contributed solutions and instructed Ms. Chrisley what to write on the board. Later in the same class period, students shared how they approached a complex spatial reasoning task with peers and then discussed their solutions with the whole class. Ms. Chrisley believed as a White female, her students viewed her as the *possessor* of knowledge.

> I try to get away from that. But I think they see me as an educated Caucasian teacher, and I possess all this knowledge that they don't have. I think they see me as the knower. I am hoping the kids can see they can do any of the stuff I can do. (Follow-up interview, 2018)

Through changes in practices and shifts in beliefs, Ms. Chrisley concluded that giving students agency is the key to successful teaching. "I have really been pushing students to feel like they own the math and own the thinking rather than feel like I own the answers. So, I do a lot of I'm not sure, what do you think?" (Follow-up interview, 2018). Ms. Chrisley believed student-centered teaching practices empower students as doers of mathematics and holders of mathematical knowledge. Ms. Chrisley has witnessed significant growth among her Black students in not only mathematical achievement but in their confidence in mathematics as well.

DISCUSSION

At the beginning of the study, Ms. Chrisley notably crafted her responses to ensure political correctness when referencing race—embodying the color-blind ideology (Choi, 2008). Milner (2006) found that many White teachers are not comfortable talking about racial issues. Ms. Chrisley initially was very uncomfortable and trepidatious when discussing race; however, by the end of the study, she became more open in discussing race and systemic inequities evident in the mathematics classroom. She no longer embodied a colorblind ideology, which is contrary to Milner's findings. Through-out the study, Ms. Chrisley had many unproductive beliefs and teaching practices common among many well-meaning teachers (Ullucci & Battey, 2011). As unintentionally as they may be, these beliefs and practice can have adverse impacts on Black students.

We followed Ms. Chrisley for three years and witnessed her repeatedly reflecting and analyzing her instruction, beliefs, and practices. Through-out the study, Ms. Chrisley never gave in to being out of her comfort zone. Instead, she engaged in critical reflections and conversations to shift both her beliefs and practice. Although there was nothing directly stated during any of the interviews, we noticed a change in Ms. Chrisley's humility. During our final interview, Ms. Chrisley did not answer with the same authority and certainty as she did in the beginning. Her responses were noticeably more measured and reverential. Instead of highlighting her strengths and professing the rest as "it is what it is," she repositioned herself to use her understanding of systemic inequities to engage her Black students. In particular, Ms. Chrisley's attention to the systemic effects of racism and acceptance of cultural differences repositioned her students as powerful doers of mathematics.

Ms. Chrisley is no longer intimidated or uncomfortable acknowledg-ing and confronting her unproductive beliefs and practices. She realized the power in engaging in critical reflections and self-observations, and she intends to make it a part of her daily practice. The process of shifting beliefs is not necessarily a comfortable one because it requires teachers to be real with themselves. However, going through the process of acknowledging unproductive beliefs and inequities encountered by Black students and actively reflecting on and having critical conversations about those unproductive beliefs and practices enables teachers to truly be effective teachers to Black students. More importantly, Black students will have the opportunities to engage in mathematics classes that are rich in problem solving and critical thinking because teachers shifted to productive beliefs and instructional practices.

CONCLUSION

The case of Ms. Chrisley emphasizes the importance of starting with critical reflection and shifting toward productive beliefs of mathematics teachers in the effort to transform instruction for Black students. Ms. Chrisley prioritized building relationships with her Black students, which researchers (e.g., Ladson-Billings, 1994; Malloy 2002, 2009; Matthews, 2005) have found as a critical component when teaching students, especially Black students. Ms. Chrisley's relationships were central to her success with Black students even though she held many unproductive beliefs. At the beginning of the study, Black students' voices were often quieted and at times were seen as invisible in the mathematics classroom. However, this did not last. Similar to Malloy's (2009) study, Ms. Chrisley began to ensure Black students were visible in the classroom by giving them voice and agency. Asking Ms. Chrisley to watch videos of her instruction and reflect on her interactions with students sparked a process of introspection and reflection about her instructional practices and beliefs.

Shifting teachers' beliefs and practices toward an equity-centered paradigm is paramount for transforming instructional practices that meet the needs of Black students. As the case of Ms. Chrisley highlights, this evolution requires diligence, time, and support. The critical exercises and professional development required to shift from unproductive to productive beliefs happens over an extended time. The three years we studied Ms. Chrisley's instruction and discussed her beliefs deepened our understanding of the relationship between enacted instruction and teacher beliefs (Jackson & Delaney, 2017). Well-meaning White teachers need time and experience to reform their beliefs and practices to successfully integrate equitable instruction for Black students. High expectations and equity-based instructional practices are a result of productive beliefs providing Black students opportunities to engage in rigorous mathematics.

REFERENCES

Aguirre, J., & Speer, N. M. (2000). Examining the relationship between beliefs and goals in teacher practice. *Journal of Mathematical Behavior, 18*(3), 327–356.

Anderson, J. D. (1988). *The education of Blacks in the South, 1860–1935*. Chapel Hill, NC: The University of North Carolina Press.

Barlow, A. T., & Cates, J. M. (2006). The impact of problem posing on elementary teachers' beliefs about mathematics and mathematics teaching. *School Science and Mathematics, 106*(2), 64–73.

Bonilla-Silva, E. (2018). *Racism without racists: Color-blind racism and the persistence of racial inequality in America* (5th ed.). Lantham, MD: Rowman & Littlefield.

Bonilla-Silva, E., & Dietrich, D. (2011). The sweet enchantment of color-blind racism in Obamerica. *The ANNALS of the American Academy of Political and Social Science, 634*(1), 190–206.

Borko, H., & Livingston, C. (1989). Cognition and improvisation: Differences in mathematics instruction by expert and novice teachers. *American Educational Research Journal, 26*(4), 473–498.

Cess-Newsome, J. (1999). Secondary teachers' knowledge and beliefs about subject matter and their impact on instruction. In J. Gess-Newsome & G. Norman (Eds.), *Examining pedagogical content knowledge* (pp. 51–94). Dordrecht, The Netherlands: Kluwer.

Choi, J. A. (2008). Unlearning colorblind ideologies in education class. *Educational Foundations, 22*, 53–71.

Delamont, S. (1992). *Fieldwork in educational settings: Methods, pitfalls, and perspectives.* London, England: Falmer.

Dey, I. (1993). *Qualitative data analysis: A user-friendly guide for social scientists.* New York, NY: Routledge.

Evertson, C. M., Anderson, C. W., Anderson, L. M., & Brophy, J. E. (1980). Relationships between classroom behaviors and student outcomes in junior high mathematics and English classes. *American Educational Research Journal, 17*(1), 43–60.

Gay, G. (2000). *Culturally responsive teaching: Theory, research, & practice.* New York, NY: Teachers College Press.

Hill, H. C., Ball, D. L., & Schilling, S. G. (2008). Unpacking pedagogical content knowledge: Conceptualizing and measuring teachers' topic-specific knowledge of students. *Journal for Research in Mathematics Education, 39*(4), 372–400.

Jackson, C. (2012). Elementary teachers' beliefs of African Americans in the mathematics classroom. *Journal of Mathematics Education at Teachers College, 3*(2), 90–96.

Jackson, C. (2013). Elementary mathematics teachers' knowledge of equity pedagogy. *Current Issues in Education, 16*(1), 1–13.

Jackson, C., & Delaney, A. (2017). Mindsets and practices: Shifting to an equity-centered paradigm. In A. Fernandes, S. Crespo, & M. Civil (Eds.), *Access and equity: Promoting high quality mathematics in grades 6–8* (pp. 143–155). Reston, VA: National Council of Teachers of Mathematics.

Jamar, I., & Pitts, V. R. (2005). High expectations: A "how" of achieving equitable mathematics classrooms. *The Negro Educational Review, 56*(2 & 3), 127–134.

Kincheloe, J. (2004). The knowledges of teacher education: Developing a critical complex epistemology. *Teacher Education Quarterly 31*(1), 49–66. Retrieved from https://files.eric.ed.gov/fulltext/EJ795234.pdf

Ladson-Billings, G. (1994). *The dreamkeepers: Successful teachers of African American children.* San Francisco, CA: Jossey-Bass.

Landsman, J. (2004). Confronting the racism of low expectations. *Educational Leadership 62*(3), 28–32.

LeCompte, M. (2000). Analyzing qualitative data. *Theory Into Practice, 39*, 146–154.

Loewenberg Ball, D., Thames, M. H., & Phelps, G. (2008). Content knowledge for teaching: What makes it special? *Journal of Teacher Education, 59*, 389–407.

Love, A., & Kruger, A. C. (2005). Teacher beliefs and student achievement in urban schools serving African American students. *The Journal of Educational Research, 99*(2), 87–98.

Malloy, C. E. (2002). Democratic access to mathematics through democratic education: An introduction. In L. D. English (Ed.), *Handbook of international research in mathematics education* (pp. 17–25). Mahwah, NJ: Erlbaum.

Malloy, C. E. (2009). Instructional strategies and dispositions of teachers who help African American students gain conceptual understanding. In D. Martin (Ed.), *Mathematics teaching, learning, and liberation in the lives of Black children* (pp. 88–122). New York, NY: Routledge.

Martin, D. B. (2007). Beyond missionaries or cannibals: Who should teach mathematics to African American children? *The High School Journal, 91*(1), 6–28. dx.doi.org/10.1353/hsj.2007.0023

Matias, C. E. (2013). Check yo'self before You wreck yo'self and our dids: Counter-stories from culturally responsive White teachers? ... to culturally responsive White teachers! *Interdisciplinary Journal of Teaching and Learning, 3*(2), 68–81.

Matthews, L. E. (2005). Towards design of clarifying equity messages in mathematics reform. *The High School Journal, 88*(4), 46–58.

Milner, H. R. (2006). Preservice teachers' learning about cultural and racial diversity: Implications for urban education. *Urban Education, 41*, 343–375.

Milner, H. R., & Laughter, J. C. (2015). But good intentions are not enough: Preparing teachers to center race and poverty. *The Urban Review, 47*, 341–363.

National Council of Teachers of Mathematics. (2000). *Principles and standards for school mathematics.* Reston, VA: Author.

National Council of Teachers of Mathematics. (2014). *Principles to actions: Ensuring mathematical success for all.* Reston, VA: Author.

Ogbu, J. U., & Simons, H. D. (1998). Voluntary and involuntary minorities: A cultural-ecological theory of school performance with some implications for education. *Anthropology and Education Quarterly, 29*(2), 155–188.

Pajares, F. M. (1992). Teachers' beliefs and educational research: Cleaning up a messy construct. *Review of Educational Research, 62*, 307–332.

Parsons, E. C. (2005). From caring as a relation to culturally relevant caring: A White teacher's bridge to Black students. *Equity & Excellence in Education, 38*, 25–34.

Perez, C. (2000). Equity in standards-based elementary mathematics classrooms: Weaving gender equity into math reform. *ENC Focus: A Magazine for Classroom*

Innovators, 1–6. Cambridge, MA: TERC. Retrieved from https://files.eric. ed.gov/fulltext/ED465503.pdf

Philipp, R. A. (2007). Mathematics teachers' beliefs and affect. In F. K. Lester (Ed.), *Second handbook of research on mathematics teaching and learning* (pp. 257–315). Charlotte, NC: Information Age.

Polly, D., McGee, J. R., Wang, C., Lambert, R. G., Pugalee, D. K., & Johnson, S. (2013). The association between teachers' beliefs, enacted practices, and student learning in mathematics. *Mathematics Educator, 22*(2), 11–30.

Putnam, R. T., & Borko, H. (2000). What do new views of knowledge and thinking have to say about research on teacher learning? *Educational Researcher, 29*(1), 4–15.

Rosenthal, R., & Jacobson, L. (1968). *Pygmalion in the classroom: Teacher expectation and pupils' intellectual development.* New York, NY: Holt, Rinehart and Winston.

Rousseau, C., & Tate, W. F. (2003). No time like the present: Reflecting on equity in school mathematics. *Theory Into Practice, 42*, 210–216.

Saldaña, J. (2016). *Ethnotheatre: Research from page to stage.* New York, NY: Routledge.

Sleeter, C. E. (1993). How White teachers construct race. In C. McCarthy & W. Crichlow (Eds.), *Race, identity and representation in education* (pp. 157–171). New York, NY: Routledge.

Smith, T. W. (1990). *Ethnic images* (GSS Topical Report No. 19). University of Chicago, National Opinion Research Center. Retrieved from https://gssdataexplorer. norc.org/documents/852/download

Spring, J. (2005). *The American school: 1642–2004* (6th ed.). New York, NY: McGraw Hill.

Thompson, A. (1992). Teachers' beliefs and conceptions: A synthesis of the research. In D. Grouws (Ed.), *Handbook of research in mathematics teaching and learning* (pp. 127–146). New York, NY: Macmillan.

Thompson, G. L. (2004). *Through ebony eyes: What teachers need to know but are afraid to ask about African American students.* San Francisco, CA: Jossey Bass.

Thompson, G. L. (2007). *Up where we belong: Helping African American and Latino students rise in school and in life.* San Francisco, CA: Jossey-Bass.

Thompson, G. L. (2009, April). *A "cry" for help: What pre-service teachers and educators believe about African American student underachievement.* Paper presented at the annual meeting of the American Educational Research Association, San Diego, CA.

Thompson, G. L. (2010). *The power of one: How you can help or harm African American students.* Thousand Oaks, CA: Corwin.

Thompson, G., & Louque, A. (2005). *Exposing the culture of arrogance in the academy: A blueprint for increasing Black faculty satisfaction.* Sterling, VA: Stylus.

Ullucci, K., & Battey, D. (2011). Exposing color blindness/grounding color consciousness: Challenges for teacher education. *Urban Education, 46*, 1195–1225.

Walker, V. S. (1996). *Their highest potential: An African American school community in the segregated south.* Chapel Hill, NC: University of North Carolina Press.

White, D. (2010, March). *Teacher education and professional development: A reaction.* Paper presented at the Practitioners and Researchers Learning Together: A National Conference on the Mathematics Teaching and Learning of Latinos/as, Tucson, AZ.

APPENDIX

Interview Protocols

Initial Interview Questions

1. Tell me a little about your teaching career. For example, when and where did you begin teaching? Have you taught in different types of schools? How long have you taught at your current school? Describe the student population of the schools you have taught.
2. Describe your teaching style.
3. How would you characterize the kinds of relationships you've had with parents? Particularly the parents of your African American students?
4. Tell me a story about a time when a student had a racial conflict. How would you handle that situation?
5. How do you think the schooling experience of the students you teach differ from students in other districts or schools within your district?
6. How do you think the background of your students influence their work with you as their teacher?
7. Throughout your career what have you learned about teaching mathematics to African American students? Where did you learn it?
8. When you are teaching mathematics, how does your race influence your work as a teacher of students of color?
9. How do you think students learn mathematics best? How do you think African American students learn mathematics best? What strategies do teachers use to accommodate how African American students learn mathematics?
10. What knowledge and experiences do your African American students bring to the mathematics classroom?
11. I would like you to reflect on your first couple of years of teaching mathematics and reflect on your last couple of years of teaching mathematics. How has your teaching changed? In relation to teaching mathematics to African American students, how has your teaching changed? What influenced those changes?
12. What advice would you give Ms. Maben in the following situation:
13. Eric, an African American third grader is extremely disruptive and often displays his anger during mathematics class. Ms. Maben, his teacher, is frustrated. First, what questions would you ask her, and then what advice would you offer?

14. What advice would you offer novice teachers on how to facilitate the participation of African American students in the mathematics classroom?

15. How would you explain the low mathematical achievement of African American students?

16. You are teaching a mathematics lesson, and you notice an African American child is off task and another African American student is gazing out of the window. How would you handle this situation? What would you do?

17. You are teaching your students ratios, and you notice one of your students is struggling with this concept, what strategies would you use to intervene? How would these strategies differ if notice one of your African American students who was off task and is now experiencing difficulty?

18. How would you describe an effective mathematics teacher of African American students? (Follow up prompts: What is the role of the teacher? What is the students' role?' Explain why you believe the students will experience success/excellence in this type of mathematics class.)

19. Describe a typical mathematics lesson. How do you engage all of your students, specifically your African American students, in the mathematics lesson?

20. What advice would you give Mrs. Skee, a novice teacher who teaches a racially mixed class, in the following situation: Mrs. Skee is a sixth grade mathematics teacher who has prepared a dynamic lesson, or at least she thought it was a dynamic lesson on dividing fractions. She organized her lesson by following the guidelines outlined in her textbook. Her White students are following along, and doing exactly what they are supposed to be doing in a "traditional" classroom; however, her Black students are not with her. They are busy doing their own things, and ultimately not learning. What advice would you offer her?

21. If you could design the way mathematics teacher education programs prepare teachers to be more effective with African American students, what would you include? What advice would you offer to preservice teachers?

End of Year Interview Questions

1. How would you define racism?

2. In our last video interview, you discussed a professional development session you had a Goodrell focused on race. You remarked it

was an uncomfortable and ultimately unproductive session. I am going to ask you to step outside of your comfort zone and repeat a little of that session. Do you think we all have racial biases? What are some racial biases you and/or your colleagues might hold?

3. I am going to give you a series of words. I want you to say the first word or phrase that comes to mind. (This may be a little uncomfortable, but I want to assure you this is completely confidential and will not be linked back to you.)

> Female –
> Doctor –
> Poverty –
> Scientist –
> African American –
> Teacher –
> Male –
> Good Student –
> Latino –
> Math Major –
> Criminal –

4. What professional development do you believe would better prepare you for teaching African American students?
5. African American students score significantly lower on standardized assessments currently and over time. What do you think is the cause of this?
6. What positive characteristics do your African American students bring to your classroom?
7. What concerns or fears do you have about African American students? Their parents?
8. How do you define equity?
9. How do you ensure you are treating all of your students equitably?
10. In your opinion, are race relations in the United States better or worse than when you were growing up? Explain.
11. Do you think racism exists in the schooling experience of students of color? If so, how? If not, why not?
12. Do you believe you could teach a classroom full of African American students? Why or why not? What changes would you have to make to your current teaching practices to meet their needs?
13. Many scholars say equal inputs do not equate to equity. What would you say to them?
14. When you think of African American students, what are your thoughts on African American male students?

15. If a teacher confided in you that he or she was fearful of being rejected by African American students because he or she was White, what would you tell him or her?
16. What do we need to do to provide students a variety of ways to demonstrate their learning?
17. What does a successful mathematics learner look and sound like?
18. When you were growing up, what did you learn about African Americans?

Follow-Up Interview Questions

1. Describe your classes and students you are teaching this year.
2. How have you incorporated student voice in your math lessons?
3. What challenges, if any, are you encountering as you give students voice in the classroom?
4. In what ways, if any, has your classroom instruction changed from when we first started working with you through the PD to now?
5. What connections did you make during the PD sessions in relation to our prior work together? What were your "ah ha" moments?
6. How do you believe African American students learn mathematics?
7. How do you make sure you African American students are engaged in and visible in your classroom instruction?
8. What systemic inequities have you noticed your African American students face?
9. When teaching mathematics, how does your race influence you work with students of color?
10. What are your priorities when planning instruction?
11. Based on the PD and previous project, what intentional changes have you made in your instruction?

CHAPTER 9

MIDDLE LEVEL TEACHERS' EDUCATIONAL TECHNOLOGY USE

Challenges, Barriers, and Successes

Thomas M. Brinthaupt and Scott B. Haupt
Middle Tennessee State University

Richard P. Lipka
St. Bonaventure University

Jill A. Robinson
Wellsville, NY, School District

ABSTRACT

In this chapter, we present the results of a comprehensive quantitative survey of (primarily public school) middle level educators ($N = 105$) from New York and Tennessee designed to examine middle level teachers' experiences with educational technology across various stakeholders they are likely to encoun-

Curriculum, Instruction, and Assessment:
Intersecting New Needs and New Approaches, pp. 223–245
Copyright © 2020 by Information Age Publishing
223

ter. Participant teachers completed survey measures of their experiences using educational and instructional technologies, including technology-related experiences with school administration, technology specialists/coaches, students, fellow teachers, and students' parents. After a discussion of the relevant research, we present the survey results as they reflect the challenges, barriers, and successes that teachers have had when using educational or instructional technologies in their classes and with their students. Teachers also rated a variety of barriers they have encountered in their efforts to use educational technologies. We conclude with an overall assessment of the relative importance of the different stakeholders and implications for future research with those groups.

Teachers frequently must find new and beneficial ways to incorporate educational technologies into their teaching. In this chapter, we highlight middle level teachers' perceptions and experiences with an extensive web of possible influences and support when using educational technologies. We designed this quantitative study to address middle level teachers' experiences with educational technology across the various stakeholders with whom they are most likely to come into contact. Particularly, we examined teacher experiences with technology with respect to school administration, technology specialists or coaches, students, fellow teachers, and students' parents.

We first review the relevant research literature associated with each stakeholder. Then, we describe the methodological procedures used in the study. Although space limitations prevented us from conducting comprehensive literature reviews for each group, we aimed to provide a brief, but representative sampling of recent work in educational technology to give the reader a feel for how teachers work with each group, along with the barriers that they frequently face. Then we report the results of the survey items pertinent to each group and describe how those results inform the literature with respect to helping or hindering teachers' uses of technology in their teaching. Throughout, we discuss the implications of the results for the integration of technology with curriculum and instruction.

Consideration of the use of educational technologies with young adolescents is valuable for several reasons. First, the ways that teachers incorporate technologies into their curriculum are likely to affect middle level students as they actively construct their emerging identities (e.g., Brinthaupt, Lipka, & Wallace, 2007). In addition, as Spector (2019) noted, the use of educational technologies can play an important role in the development of critical thinking, particularly among early adolescents. Similarly, Moreira, Cunha, Inman, and Oliveira (2019) argued that the proper use of educational technologies is one way to reduce student disengagement with school and facilitate healthy personality development.

LITERATURE REVIEW: TEACHING WITH TECHNOLOGY STAKEHOLDERS AND BARRIERS

Several different stakeholders or groups with whom teachers might interact are likely to affect and have implications for middle level teachers' incorporation of educational technologies. In addition to one's students, school and district administration, technology coaches or specialists, fellow teachers, and the parents all can have input and responses to the technologies that teachers decide to use. How teachers interact with these different groups and respond to their unique demands or questions can affect the ways that teachers work with educational technologies (e.g., Flanagan & Jacobsen, 2003; Lee, Cerreto, & Lee, 2010).

School Administration and Technology

Administrators play a potentially vital role in the acquisition and utilization of technologies in their schools. However, miscommunication and lack of trust can sometimes characterize and complicate administrator relationships with students and teachers (Gale & Bishop, 2014; Wilhelm, 2013). The existing literature suggests that administrators are not immune to the national economic climate that technology is the answer to everything. Some studies (e.g., Machado & Chung, 2015) indicate that many administrators are aware of the mixed results of technology and student achievement. However, little evidence suggests that administrators are fluent in the research findings of the influence of technology on students' cognitive, affective, and psychomotor development (McLeod, Bathon, & Richardson, 2011). While somewhat dated, none of the 10 tasks that Grady (2011) listed in the principal's role as technology leader detailed the impact of technology on student development in all domains of learning.

At the district level, some evidence reports that tech-savvy superintendents have been focusing less on technology initiatives and more on how educational technologies can be used to support effective teaching and learning (Richardson & Sterrett, 2018). In addition, good models exist of administrator-led technology integration at the school and district levels, even when there are resource and other kinds of challenges (e.g., Kotok & Kryst, 2017; McCombs, 2010). Hilton, Hilton, Dole, and Goos (2015) described a study in which teachers and school leaders collaborated in a professional development program. They found positive effects for both teachers and leaders with respect to implementing new technology-related knowledge and practices.

In their study of 42 principals, Machado and Chung (2015) examined the principal's role in technology integration in the schools. The principals perceived the top three challenges to technology integration to be (a) teacher willingness as exemplified by computer self-efficacy and computer anxiety, (b) adequate time and other resources to support professional development, and (c) district support for such resources as technology coaches. While these are reasonable concerns, educators must not lose sight of the role of technology as an assistive device. We argue that technology is not an end educational outcome for students. Rather, its role is to help students gain an education that addresses both their needs and interests. Therefore, teachers should view these challenges within the lens of both the assets and liabilities associated with the use of various technologies.

Technology Specialists/Coaches

Several types of technology-support individuals work in schools, separate from the technology support individuals who handle routine computer maintenance issues. Among the technology support roles teachers are likely to find are ed-tech coaches/mentors, technology (or tech) coaches, instructional technology specialists, instructional coaches, and technology resource teachers. For simplicity, we will use the term "technology coach" to encompass these various job titles. There is limited research literature specifically related to technology coaches and their impact on technology use in the educational setting.

One of the most effective ways to encourage the increased use of educational technologies in the classroom is to align staff development opportunities with school- and district-level goals. A designated technology coach can assume this function, as a practitioner with experience in both technology and curriculum, whose primary responsibility is providing teachers with the support and reassurance necessary for successful technology incorporation. Several researchers and reviewers (e.g., Blackwell, Lauricella, & Wartella, 2014; Keengwe & Onchwari, 2009; Kopcha, 2012) identify the benefits of having a technology coach whose focus is assisting teachers with weaving technology into the basic fabric of the school- and/or district-level curricula. Simply providing teachers with access to the technology is insufficient. School districts need to have the requisite technology practitioner(s) if their teachers are going to be encouraged to integrate technology properly and effectively in their classrooms.

While access to technology training and professional development opportunities has increased, teacher integration of technology in the classroom has not kept pace (Earle, 2002; Russell, Bebell, O'Dwyer, & O'Connor, 2003). Having a designated technology coach is especially beneficial for less experienced teachers and/or those individuals who are already open to incorporating various technologies into their teaching practices (Sugar,

2005; Wachira & Keengwe, 2011). Blackwell, Lauricella, and Wartella (2014) hypothesized that "teachers with higher perceived support from their schools have higher levels of confidence, more positive attitudes, and higher technology use compared to teachers with lower perceived support" (p. 84). Findings showed that support had a large direct effect on technology use among early childhood teacher respondents. Based on these results, we argue that it is reasonable to assume that increased confidence can be linked to two key components: the teachers' level of comfort/rapport with their respective technology coach and the technology coach's knowledge of the various technologies available as well as the best practices related to effectively implementing them in the classroom.

One of the main concerns reported by educators when it comes to incorporating technology into their lessons is finding the time to learn these new technologies in their already overflowing schedules (Bentley, 2017; Schrum, 1999). Whereas they will not be able to eliminate the time concern altogether, technology coaches can play a direct role in mitigating the impact of learning a new technology on teachers' time. Technology coaches can schedule professional development sessions during nonpeak demand times, teacher workdays, or during the school day. Some districts' instructional technology coaches have even gone as far as to provide job-embedded professional development. In these instances, the technology coach co-teaches a lesson with teachers in an attempt to model ways of incorporating technology that supports their learning goals and extends the curriculum as opposed to forcing them to build or re-create the curriculum to accommodate the use of technology (Lawless & Pellegrino, 2007).

Students and Technology

The middle-level teacher-student relationship is a complicated one that is characterized by challenges as well as opportunities (e.g., Brinthaupt, Lipka, & Wallace, 2007; Cornelius-White, 2007; Spilt, Koomen, & Thijs, 2011). With respect to educational technology, these relationships can offer several opportunities for teachers. The research literature illustrates that teachers can benefit from the technology knowledge and skills of their students. For example, in an assessment of a statewide wireless laptop initiative for middle level schools in Maine, Fairman (2004) found that teachers reported a variety of ways that they were able to partner with and learn from their students by tapping into student computer knowledge and fluency. Teachers also reported developing reciprocal relationships with their students, such as giving up some control and becoming more of a facilitator and collaborator in the classroom. Matteucci and Helker (2018) reported that at the middle level, students reported feeling that both they and their teachers share responsibility for the learning process. This suggests that an opportunity exists for teachers to benefit from the technology knowledge and experiences of their students to inform the teaching and learning process.

At least stereotypically, people see students as being more tech-savvy that their elders, including parents and teachers (Bennett, Maton, & Kervin, 2008; Clary, Kigotho, & Barros-Torning, 2013). If this stereotype holds some validity, then we would expect teachers to be open to learning from their students about new educational technologies or ways that other kinds of technologies might be adapted to meet their teaching and learning objectives. Research supports the need for teachers to be aware of their students' technological skills and access, so that technologically-enhanced teaching can be strengthened both in and out of school (e.g., Hughes, Read, Jones, & Mahometa, 2015; Martinez & Harper, 2008).

Preservice preparation programs also emphasize the need for teachers to increase their technology literacy to benefit and engage their tech-savvy students (e.g., Raulston & Alexiou-Ray, 2018). Innovative programs that train students as technology coaches or in other roles (Marcinek, 2015; Martinez & Harper, 2008) can help formalize the support that teachers can receive from their students. Such programs allow teachers to benefit from their students' technology knowledge and expertise, while also creating opportunities for students to apply their technology skills to the teaching and learning context. As Downes and Bishop (2012) noted, many teachers find integrating educational technology into the curriculum a difficult and challenging task. However, when teachers use engaging applications and involve students in the implementation of them, students appreciate the opportunities and are happy to collaborate with and provide feedback to the teachers about those technologies.

Fellow Teachers and Technology

The capacity for teachers to adapt to changing educational landscapes is especially important where the incorporation of educational technologies is concerned. However, we cannot and should not expect them to do it alone. Teachers pick up new educational ideas and strategies from a wide array of sources, ranging from structured professional development sessions to informal discussions with peers in the lunchroom. As many authors have noted, teachers need time to observe exemplars of integrated technology use, to reflect on and discuss these observations, and to collaborate with others (e.g., Ertmer, 1999; Glazer, Hannafin, & Song, 2005; Schrum, 1999). Through these activities, they can begin to incorporate newfound ideas into their previously held beliefs relating to teaching and learning with technology.

When teachers think about professional development or continuing education, they should not overlook the potential resource in the room next door. Access to conferences and classes is beneficial; unfortunately, attending these sessions is not always plausible for myriad reasons. Fellow teachers, however, are an ever-present source of encouragement and practical knowledge. The research literature points to using teachers with technology integration experience as mentors for their less experienced peers as an effective way to promote tech integration in the classroom (Earle, 2002; Kopcha, 2010; Zorfass & Rivero, 2005).

Using fellow teachers to help with technology integration can occur in various forms. The most common recommendations involve either (a) creating an informal or formal community of practice—a group of people who share a passion or concern for something they do and learn ways to do it better via regular interaction with one another (Kopcha, 2010; Zorfass & Rivero, 2005), or (b) establishing a collaborative apprenticeship—a teacher-to-teacher mentoring professional development model featuring reciprocal interactions between teacher-mentors and peer-teachers. According to Glazer, Hannafin, and Song (2005), "A strong collegial environment is needed to integrate technology effectively, where teachers share ideas, model best practices, ask difficult questions, and support one another where and when it is most needed" (p. 58). Teachers experienced in technology integration and utilization can serve as teacher-leaders in both instances. As the peer-teachers become more familiar with the concepts of designing and teaching technology-infused lessons, the teacher-leaders can begin to take a more hands-off approach. In the end, the peer-teachers begin autonomously developing their own lessons before finally transitioning into a teacher-mentor role of their own (Glazer & Hannafin, 2006).

Parents and Technology

Policymakers and researchers have long recognized the value of teacher-parent partnerships (Patrikakou, 2016; Reid, 2015). For example, the No Child Left Behind Act of 2001 (2002) required that schools promote partnerships with parents. Researchers have studied a variety of factors associated with general parental involvement in education. In a meta-analysis of the effects of parents' involvement with their children's school performance across all K–12 grade levels, Castro et al. (2015) identified several ways that parental involvement benefits students. Parents' general supervision of student learning activities is associated with higher academic achievement. Not surprisingly, students show greater achievement when their parents have high expectations for their academic performance and when parents frequently communicate with them about their school activities. Boonk, Gijselaers, Ritzen, and Brand-Gruwel's (2018) review found similar results.

In the extensive research literature on attributions of responsibility for student learning and performance, the three primary stakeholders are students, teachers, and parents. Teachers and parents tend to agree that they both share the responsibility for a child's education (e.g., Epstein, 2011). However, the perceived nature and direction of that responsibility can vary greatly. For example, Ramirez (1999) found that, whereas nearly all the high school teachers in his study reported valuing parental involvement, around half did not believe that they were personally responsible for fostering that involvement. Flynn (2007) argued that most schools do not have clearly articulated strategies for effectively involving parents. He also highlighted several obstacles to creating and maintaining successful teacher-parent relationships. These obstacles might be one reason why middle level teachers have reported not being strongly interested in parent involvement with curricular matters (Smith, 2002).

In a recent study of Italian middle and high schools, Matteucci and Helker (2018) found at the middle level that students, teachers, and parents largely agreed about the responsibility of students for their own learning outcomes. However, teachers believed that parents are more responsible for student learning than did the student and parent respondents. Conversely, students and parents believed that teachers are more responsible for student learning than what the teachers believed about themselves. Finally, the authors found that parents believed that middle school teachers were the ones most responsible for their students' learning. Results such as these suggest that there is potential for teacher-parent involvement with respect to the use of technology in and out of the classroom.

The research on parental involvement with educational technologies is very limited. As Downes and Bishop (2012) noted, schools can increase their effectiveness when they are intentional about engaging and informing parents about new technologies and programs, given that parents are sometimes uncomfortable about changes in the teaching and learning process. Blau and Hameiri (2017) reported that parents (especially mothers) appear to be willing to use mobile devices to access a school's digital educational database. However, their willingness is limited primarily to monitoring of assignments, grades, and other activities that are only marginally and indirectly related to the pedagogy of instructional technology use.

Other researchers have described web-based applications that provide access and monitoring capabilities for parents who want to follow their children's progress (e.g., Lysenko & Abrami, 2014). In an analysis of parent use of publicly available aggregated, grade-level student data, Mandinach and Miskell (2017) found that parents were more interested in safety, diversity, and demographic information than test scores and educator qualifications.

Barriers to the Use of Educational Technologies

The research literature is replete with studies focused on teacher beliefs about and barriers to technology integration in the classroom. Ertmer's (1999) seminal piece on first-order (incremental, institutional) and second-order (fundamental, personal) barriers that hamper the teachers' educational technology integration efforts laid the foundation for the majority of research efforts that followed. First-order or extrinsic barriers (e.g., computers, support, time, training) have been found to be easier to measure and eliminate than their less tangible second-order or intrinsic counterparts (e.g., attitudes, beliefs, perceptions) (Ertmer, Ottenbreit-Leftwich, Sadik, Sendurur, & Sendurur, 2012; Kopcha, 2012; Wachira & Keengwe, 2011). Belland (2009) identified these less tangible barriers as one's *habitus*, a set of dispositions to appreciate or do certain things, which represent what teachers unconsciously "know" about teaching from their years of experience as students and teachers.

Numerous large-scale studies (e.g., Barron, Kemker, Harmes, & Kalaydjian, 2003) have shown that technology integration increases once teachers address first- and second-order barriers. Unfortunately, the majority of increased usage has been the low-level variety, such as word processing and online research. Tsai and Chai (2012) proposed researching an additional barrier that could be impeding teachers' successful integration of technology, their design thinking skills. Once teachers sufficiently address first- and second-order barriers, they report still having issues successfully integrating technology with relative consistency. This third-order barrier addresses the dynamic nature of classroom contexts and the students themselves. As this is a somewhat new idea, however, there is a lack of research on the effectiveness of addressing teachers' lack of design thinking skills. Tsai and Chai argued that "[through] reducing the third-order barrier, teachers can undertake technology integration actively and fluently. By achieving this, teachers can use technology for instruction at the right time and right place" (p. 1059).

In summary, research suggests that it is interesting and important to examine the ways that middle level teachers rely on different stakeholders when teaching with technology. However, research has tended to look at teachers' use of instructional technologies with single stakeholders rather than with several relevant stakeholders simultaneously. In this exploratory study, we relied on teachers telling us about their experiences with these groups and the barriers and challenges that they experienced in their use of instructional technologies. Based on past research, we expected that teachers would report frequent input from and collaboration with their fellow teachers, with less feedback and influence from the other stakeholders. We also expected the teachers would report primarily positive working relationships with their technology coaches. Finally, we predicted that teachers would report more frequent first-order than second-order barriers to their technology integration.

METHODOLOGY

The research design was a nonexperimental questionnaire study that used a convenience sample of middle level teachers. Participants completed the survey through a commercial online survey application. For each of the relevant stakeholders, teachers rated a variety of ways in which their use of technology relied upon input and experiences with those groups.

Participants

Respondents included 105 middle level teachers (75% female, 22% male, three gender responses were "other" or missing) from New York and Tennessee. Although we did not record state information, roughly three-quarters of respondents came from the NY state network. We invited New York participants by sending the survey information and link to the directors from a statewide Teacher Center network. The directors then shared the invitation to participate with their teachers. Education professors who were familiar with middle level teacher rosters in school districts in the middle Tennessee area gathered participants from a convenience sampling.

The majority of participants (88%) reported holding a master's degree. They averaged 18.25 years teaching ($SD = 10.41$). Nearly all (97%) of the respondents reported working in a public school setting, with the average approximate size of the schools being 684.20 students ($SD = 385.69$). Participants came from four different school types, with 25% from Grades 5–8, 13% from Grades K–12, 31% from Grades K–8, and 31% from Grades 6–12. Most of the schools were either rural (57%) or urban (30%). We did not collect information about free or reduced-price lunch status. Teachers estimated an average of 51% of their students having limited access to the internet outside of school.

Measure and Procedure

We administered the author-developed survey during the 2015–16 school year. The first page of the survey included informed consent and institutional review board information. We described the purpose of the project as an effort to gain a better understanding of the challenges, barriers, and successes that teachers have had when using educational or instructional technologies in their classes and with their students. Approximately two weeks after the initial invitation to participants, we sent out a reminder with one additional week for teachers to complete the survey.

Participants rated a wide range of items pertaining to their experiences with using educational and instructional technologies. Survey sections included technology-related experiences with school administration, technology specialists/coaches, students, fellow teachers, and students' parents. Because the survey pertained to specific events, behaviors, or outcomes associated with each stakeholder group (as opposed to a single construct), it was not possible or feasible to address questions of the reliability or validity of the items. We generated these items based on our familiarity with the research literature, our experiences working with administration, technology coaches, and middle level students, and our expectations about the kinds of experiences teachers were most likely to have with each stakeholder. Teachers rated these items using a 6-point frequency scale (0 = *never*, 1 = *rarely*, 2 = *sometimes*, 3 = *frequently*, 4 = *very often*, 5 = *always*). See Table 9.1 for the list of these items.

For each stakeholder, teachers also provided open-ended responses to how they had been able to resolve, address, or work around any of the previously rated issues. We asked them to describe what they actually did or how they would recommend that teachers resolve, address, or work around those issues. These qualitative data are not the focus of the current chapter. We have published a middle-level teacher technology guidebook based on these open-ended teacher suggestions and recommendations (Brinthaupt, Lipka, & Robinson, 2019).

Teachers also rated a variety of barriers they had encountered in their efforts to use educational technologies (see Table 9.2), using a 5-point Likert scale (0 = *strongly disagree*, 1 = *disagree*, 2 = *neither disagree nor agree*, 3 = *agree*, 4 = *strongly agree*). We derived these items from our familiarity with the research literature on technology use and integration. Finally, teachers answered several demographic variables about their personal and educational background, years teaching, and characteristics of their school and students. With each stakeholder, we present the descriptive statistics and report basic statistical tests (i.e., comparison of means to the scale midpoints). This approach permitted us to make general conclusions about the roles of each stakeholder group in teachers' technology use.

Table 9.1.
Teachers' Use of Educational Technology Survey Items and Descriptive Statistics

Item	Mean (SD)	*t*-value
Teachers' Experiences With Administration		
System/district-level administrative policies block legitimate websites that I have wanted to use in my classes.	2.21 (0.94)	3.18**
I can get my school/principal to ease up on our online restrictions.	1.78 (1.33)	5.43***
I can get my system/district administration to ease up on its online restrictions.	1.70 (1.24)	6.47***
Equipment (software or hardware) purchases are made by my system/district administration without teacher input.	2.90 (1.36)	3.02**
Equipment (software or hardware) purchases are made by my school/principal without teacher input.	2.19 (1.33)	2.34*
I have input in my school's online technology policies and practices.	1.43 (1.38)	7.91***
My principal pressures me into using instructional technologies.	1.70 (1.36)	5.97***
I am required to use new software/technology with little or no training.	2.13 (1.35)	2.78**
Teachers' Experiences With Technology Specialists/Coaches		
The tech person at my school is available whenever I need help.	2.75 (1.46)	1.75
My tech person talks way over my head.	1.22 (0.91)	14.28***
Before using a new instructional technology, I first consult with my school's tech person about it.	2.00 (1.34)	3.79***
Teachers' Experiences With Their Students		
My students are using their devices in class when they shouldn't be.	1.82 (1.25)	5.56***
My students are blocked from accessing a legitimate website in class.	1.99 (0.99)	5.25***
My students would rather spend their school time using social media or playing games online.	3.24 (1.27)	5.97***
I get good educational technology ideas from my students.	1.68 (0.94)	9.02***
I get good feedback from my students about the educational technologies that I use in class.	2.10 (1.09)	3.71***
Teachers' Experiences With Their Fellow Teachers		
My fellow teachers pressure me into using instructional technologies.	0.66 (0.62)	30.58***
I introduce or recommend new instructional technologies to my fellow teachers.	1.92 (1.04)	5.65***
I rely on the opinions of my fellow teachers before deciding to use an instructional technology.	2.04 (0.97)	4.88***
I get good educational technology ideas from my fellow teachers.	2.47 (0.96)	0.36

(Table continues on next page)

Table 9.1.
Teachers' Use of Educational Technology Survey Items and Descriptive Statistics (Continued)

Item	Mean (SD)	t-value
Teachers' Experiences With Parents		
My students' parents complain about an online assignment that I've given their child.	0.78 (1.05)	16.70***
My students' parents request that I include more of my learning materials online.	0.57 (0.82)	23.99***
My students' parents introduce or recommend new instructional technologies to me.	0.31 (0.61)	36.75***
I rely on the opinions of my students' parents before deciding to use an instructional technology.	0.62 (0.82)	23.31***
I decide to stop using an instructional technology based on feedback from my students' parents.	0.63 (0.90)	21.13***

Note: $n = 105$; * $p < .05$, ** $p < .01$, *** $p < .001$; t-test represents the test of the mean against the midpoint of the response scale (2.5; 0 = *Never*, 5 = *Always*).

Table 9.2.
Teachers' General Barriers to Using Educational Technologies in Their Teaching

Item	Mean (SD)	t-value
A lack of support for publisher-provided resources is a barrier to my teaching with technology.	2.00 (1.02)	0.00
A lack of support and resources due to school policy is a barrier to my teaching with technology.	1.93 (1.02)	0.67
A lack of access to technology is a barrier to my teaching with technology.	2.13 (1.22)	1.12
A lack of strategies for integrating educational technology is a barrier to my teaching with technology.	2.32 (1.01)	3.21**
A lack of technology skills and knowledge is a barrier to my teaching with technology.	2.28 (1.18)	2.40*
A lack of time is a barrier to my teaching with technology.	2.92 (0.93)	10.21***

Note: $n = 105$; * $p < .05$, ** $p < .01$, *** $p < .001$; t-test represents the test of the mean against the midpoint of the response scale (2; 0 = *Strongly Disagree*, 4 = *Strongly Agree*).

RESULTS

In this section, we provide descriptive statistics that are pertinent to each stakeholder group. For each group, we also test the mean responses of the teachers against the scale midpoint to get a general sense of their levels of agreement or disagreement with the survey items.

School Administration and Technology

School administration survey items included teachers' experiences with being pressured to adopt specific technologies, system/district-level administrative policies that block legitimate websites, and their ability to work with administration regarding policies and practices and when encountering technology problems. Descriptive statistics for the administration survey items appear in the top portion of Table 9.1. The results indicate that, for the most part, teachers report infrequently experiencing pressure from administration to use educational technologies (50% of respondents chose the "never" or "rarely" option) or problems with access or training.

At the same time, teachers indicated having little input at the system and school level regarding equipment purchases and policies and procedures. The most frequent response for most of the items was "sometimes," including having legitimate websites blocked (51%) and getting the school/principal (43%) and system/district (43%) to ease up on online restrictions. In addition, 31% of respondents chose the "very often" or "always" option for the item about administrators making software or hardware purchases without their input. Finally, 58% of teachers reported "never" or "rarely" having input regarding their school's online technology policies and practices.

Technology Specialists/Coaches

Our survey included three items about teachers' assessments of availability and communication issues related to working with technology coaches. Table 9.1 provides descriptive statistics for the technology coach survey items. These data indicate that the teachers reported that their technology coach is generally available when needed (between the "sometimes" and "frequently" options), with 35% of respondents choosing the "very often" or "always" option.

Teachers also indicated that their technology coach usually speaks about technology at a level they understand or does not talk over their heads, with 66% of respondents choosing the "never" or "rarely" option. However, teachers reported that they do not often consult with their technology coach before using a new instructional technology, with 34% of respondents choosing the "never" or "rarely" option and 15% choosing the "very often" or "always" options.

Students and Technology

We included five survey items on technology-related issues, behaviors, and feedback from students. As the student section of Table 9.1 shows, teachers reported that their students tended to be infrequently using their devices when they should not. They also reported that being blocked from accessing legitimate websites was not a frequent occurrence for students. However, they noted that their students seemed less interested in using technology for learning purposes than for entertainment or non-school activities, as evidenced by the item about using social media and playing games online. For that item, 48% of teachers chose the "very often" or "always" option compared to 9% choosing the "never" or "rarely" option.

Teachers also reported that they did not often get good educational technology ideas from their students (41% reported "never" or "rarely" compared to 13% reporting "very often" or "always"). Similarly, teachers reported infrequently getting good feedback from their students about the technologies they use, with 21% choosing "never" or "rarely" compared to 9% choosing "very often" or "always."

Fellow Teachers and Technology

As part of our survey, teachers provided data on their experiences with fellow teachers when learning about and implementing educational technologies (see Table 9.1). As Table 9.1 shows, our respondents reported feeling very little pressure from their peers to use instructional technologies. No respondents reported frequently, very often, or always receiving such pressure from their fellow teachers.

Respondents also reported moderate levels of sharing technology ideas with their peers (49% indicating "sometimes") or receiving ideas from their fellow teachers (50% indicating "sometimes"). Finally, most teachers reported "sometimes" (45%) or "frequently" (30%) getting good educational technology ideas from their fellow teachers. Comparing the parallel item with the student group, we found that teachers reported being significantly more likely to get good educational technology ideas from their fellow teachers than from their students, $t(104) = 7.05, p < .001$.

Parents and Technology

The parental section of the survey (Table 9.1) included items about parental feedback and input regarding the use of instructional technologies. As the table shows, teachers reported very infrequent contact and feedback from parents with respect to educational technologies. In fact, 55% or more of the teachers chose the "never" option for all of these items. No teachers chose the "always" option for any item, with the exception of one teacher who would "always" stop the use of a technology based on parental feedback.

Barriers to the Use of Educational Technologies

Table 9.2 provides the descriptive statistics for the survey items pertaining to the general barriers that teachers might encounter in their efforts to use educational technologies in their teaching. As the table indicates, teachers tended to "agree" about time being a barrier, along with their lacking the skills, strategies, and knowledge for effectively integrating educational technologies. On the other hand, teachers tended to be neutral (neither disagreeing nor agreeing) about whether they lacked support from publisher-provided resources and whether school policies and lack of technology access were barriers to their teaching with technology.

DISCUSSION

In this study, we examined the experiences and perceptions of middle level teachers with a range of stakeholder groups as they use educational technologies. The results were consistent with our expectations. Particularly, fellow teachers proved to be the favored group when it came to ideas, support, and feedback regarding educational technologies. This pattern resembles the ways that teachers rely on their peers for other domains of their teaching practice and professional development (e.g., Burns, 2011; Gray, Kruse, & Tarter, 2016; Jeanpierre, 2007).

The school administration data are consistent with research on the challenges that teachers experience when balancing the tasks of acquiring and implementing new educational technologies while working within the constraints imposed by the system and school (e.g., Hilton et al., 2015). We found that this sample of middle level teachers reported little administrative pressure to use technologies but also little input with respect to policies and procedures for technology use. There are examples of successful educational technology collaborations between district and school administrators (Sterrett & Richardson, 2017); however, we found little evidence of such collaborations within our teacher responses. With this sample, collaborative relationships between teachers and administrators appear to be the exception rather than the norm when it comes to the use of educational technologies.

With respect to teachers' interactions with their technology coaches, we found that access and availability seem to be adequate for most teachers. The data also indicated that teachers' interactions with their technology coaches are generally productive, as we expected. However, teachers reported infrequently consulting with their technology coach prior to using a new technology. A likely explanation for this finding is that teachers may use technology coaches primarily for hardware and program set-up questions rather than for pedagogical applications or support.

Our results showed a lack of student input into teaching with technology. Teachers' knowledge and ability levels with technologies may be lower than that of their students, presenting a potential threat or challenge to the authority of the teacher. There may be other barriers to the successful integration of educational technologies. For example, even teachers who describe themselves as "tech-savvy" report difficulties in consistently incorporating technology into their classes (Bauer & Kenton, 2005).

Innovative ways exist for schools to partner with their students as technology coaches or in other roles (e.g., Marcinek, 2015; Martinez & Harper, 2008), and these programs can encourage productive relationships between teachers and students when integrating technology in the classroom. It would be interesting for future research to examine when and why middle level teachers do and do not rely on their students for technology help and whether their reliance on student technology knowledge enhances their instructional technology applications. Research might benefit especially from examining the characteristics of those teachers who report often getting good technology-related ideas and feedback from their students.

As we noted earlier, the fellow teacher results are somewhat encouraging, in the sense that there is at least some reported level of sharing and receiving of technology information or feedback. We did not ask specifically about formal programs, such as technology-related communities of practice or collaborative apprenticeships (Kopcha, 2010). However, the absence of more-frequent interaction with peers suggests that, with our sample, these approaches are likely not pervasive.

The bottom line with respect to teacher-parent communication regarding instructional technologies is that, at least with this sample, it is rarely if ever occurring. This is an important finding, given that some states and school districts are moving toward the inclusion of parent feedback as a metric for teacher evaluations (e.g., Fernández, LeChasseur, & Donaldson, 2018; Steinberg & Donaldson, 2016).

We believe that it would be helpful for all educators to build productive relationships with groups such as Parents Across America (n.d.). This group has undertaken a very powerful and thoughtful review of the literature detailing the liabilities of the overuse of various technologies. Their review ranges from popular literature sources (e.g., *Psychology Today* magazine) to refereed research journals such as *Archives of Pediatric and Adolescent Medicine*. Partnering with organizations like this one might help create a more-productive working relationship with the parents of one's students.

Finally, we expected that teachers would report more frequent first-order than second-order barriers to their technology integration. The barriers that teachers noted fell into the first- and third-order categories (Ertmer,

1999; Tsai & Chai, 2012). Access and resources (other first-order barriers) appeared to be less frequent obstacles to teaching with technology. As the literature on barriers to teaching with technology suggests, the pedagogical side continues to be a challenge for these teachers.

CONCLUSION

The main conclusion we draw from the present study is that, despite the various potential sources of educational technology information and support available to teachers, their utilization of those sources is limited, at best. Our specific results and interpretations need to be understood with respect to the limitations of our sample and methodology. In particular, most of our respondents came from public schools. The technology-related issues and challenges for middle level teachers working in public schools may not necessarily be the same as those encountered by private school teachers or by teachers who work in schools of smaller sizes.

Because we used a convenience sampling approach to recruit respondents, it is also possible that our participants might in some ways be biased. For example, those who agreed to complete the survey might be teachers who are already comfortable with implementing technology. Alternatively, we might have a disproportionate number of teachers who were dissatisfied with their educational technology experiences and support. A better, though more difficult to implement approach, would be a research design that randomly selected middle level teachers and surveyed their technology experiences with different stakeholders.

We did not ask our respondents about formal professional development activities; those opportunities might be the primary vehicle through which they learn about new technologies. Nonetheless, the picture painted by the present data suggests a situation in which middle level teachers struggle to integrate instructional technologies into their classes and curriculum and infrequently find support from the stakeholders that might help them in this struggle. Whether this situation is unique or exacerbated for middle level teachers compared to elementary or high school level teachers is also a worthy question for future research.

Future research might examine the ways that teachers can solicit and leverage input from the different stakeholder groups. Due to the exploratory nature of this study, we did not explicitly compare teachers' perceptions of the relative importance of each stakeholder group. It may be that the stakeholder profiles we found in this study will differ from teachers working at the elementary or high school levels.

Given the nature of and differing priorities of each stakeholder group, making direct comparisons of ideas or influence is difficult. That is, different stakeholders have different "stakes" when it comes to teachers' use of technologies in their classes. It would be interesting to explore how middle level teachers who are successful at integrating educational technologies balance the different concerns of these stakeholder groups.

Researchers have noted that teaching with technology has the potential to change middle level student identity (Brinthaupt et al., 2007), improve critical thinking (Spector, 2019), and foster personality development and engagement with learning (Moreira et al., 2019). We hope that by exploring how middle level teachers work with school administration, technology specialists/coaches, students, fellow teachers, and students' parents, readers will agree that additional and more thorough exploration of teachers' use of technology with young adolescents is warranted.

REFERENCES

Barron, A. E., Kemker, K., Harmes, C., & Kalaydjian, K. (2003). Large-scale research study on technology in K–12 schools: Technology integration as it relates to the National Technology Standards. *Journal of Research on Technology in Education, 35*, 489–507.

Bauer, J., & Kenton, J. (2005). Toward technology integration in the schools: Why it isn't happening. *Journal of Technology and Teacher Education, 13*, 519–546.

Belland, B. R. (2009). Using the theory of habitus to move beyond the study of barriers to technology integration. *Computers & Education, 52*, 353–364.

Bennett, S., Maton, K., & Kervin, L. (2008). The 'digital natives' debate: A critical review of the evidence. *British Journal of Educational Technology, 39*(5), 775–786.

Bentley, K. (2017, February 22). How school districts can adopt the technology coach model. Retrieved from http://www.govtech.com/education/news/technology-coaches.html

Blackwell, C. K., Lauricella, A. R., & Wartella, E. (2014). Factors influencing digital technology use in early childhood education. *Computers & Education, 77*, 82–90.

Blau, I., & Hameiri, M. (2017). Ubiquitous mobile educational data management by teachers, students and parents: Does technology change school-family communication and parental involvement? *Education and Information Technologies, 22*(3), 1231–1247.

Boonk, L., Gijselaers, H. J., Ritzen, H., & Brand-Gruwel, S. (2018). A review of the relationship between parental involvement indicators and academic achievement. *Educational Research Review, 24*, 10–30.

Brinthaupt, T. M., Lipka, R. P., & Robinson, J. (2019). *The middle-level teacher technology guidebook: 20 questions and 200+ answers.* Charlotte, NC: Information Age.

Brinthaupt, T. M., Lipka, R. P., & Wallace, M. A. (2007). Aligning student self and identity concerns with middle school practices. In S. B. Mertens, V. A. Anfara, Jr., & M. M. Caskey (Eds.), *The young adolescent and the middle school* (pp. 201–218). Charlotte, NC: Information Age.

Burns, M. (2011). Teacher collaboration gives schools better results. *Pacific Standard.* Retrieved from https://psmag.com/education/teacher-collaboration-gives-schools-better-results-34270

Castro, M., Expósito-Casas, E., López-Martín, E., Lizasoain, L., Nararro-Asencio, E., & Gaviria, J. L. (2015). Parental involvement on student academic achievement: A meta-analysis. *Educational Research Review, 14,* 33–46.

Clary, D., Kigotho, M., & Barros-Torning, M. (2013). Harnessing mobile technologies to enrich adolescents' multimodal literacy practices in middle years classrooms. *Literacy Learning: The Middle Years, 21*(3), 49–60.

Cornelius-White, J. (2007). Learner-centered teacher-student relationships are effective: A meta-analysis. *Review of Educational Research, 77*(1), 113–143.

Downes, J. M., & Bishop, P. (2012). Educators engage digital natives and learn from their experiences with technology. *Middle School Journal, 43*(5), 6–15.

Earle, R. S. (2002). The integration of instructional technology into public education: Promises and challenges. *Educational Technology, 42*(1), 5–13.

Epstein, J. L. (2011). *School, family, and community partnerships: Preparing educators and improving schools* (2nd ed.). Boulder, CO: Westview Press.

Ertmer, P. A. (1999). Addressing first- and second-order barriers to change: Strategies for technology implementation. *Educational Technology Research and Development, 47*(4), 47–61.

Ertmer, P. A., Ottenbreit-Leftwich, A. T., Sadik, O., Sendurur, E., & Sendurur, P. (2012). Teacher beliefs and technology integration practices: A critical relationship. *Computers & Education, 59,* 423–435.

Fairman, J. (2004, April). *Trading roles: Teachers and students learn with technology.* Paper presented at the Annual Conference of the New England Educational Research Organization, Portsmouth, NH.

Fernández, E., LeChasseur, K., & Donaldson, M. L. (2018). Responses to including parents in teacher evaluation policy: A critical policy analysis. *Journal of Education Policy, 33*(3), 398–413.

Flanagan, L., & Jacobsen, M. (2003). Technology leadership for the twenty-first century principal. *Journal of Educational Administration, 41*(2), 124-142.

Flynn, G. V. (2007). Increasing parental involvement in our schools: The need to overcome obstacles, promote critical behaviors, and provide teacher training. *Journal of College Teaching & Learning, 4*(2), 23–30.

Gale, J. J., & Bishop, P. A. (2014). The work of effective middle grades principals: Responsiveness and relationship. *Research in Middle Level Education Online, 37*(9), 1–23.

Glazer, E. M., & Hannafin, M. J. (2006). The collaborative apprenticeship model: Situated professional development within school settings. *Teaching and Teacher Education, 22,* 179–193.

Glazer, E., Hannafin, M. J., & Song, L. (2005). Promoting technology integration through collaborative apprenticeship. *Educational Technology Research and Development, 53*(4), 57–67.

Grady, M. L. (2011). *Leading the technology-powered school.* Thousand Oaks, CA: Corwin Press.

Gray, J., Kruse, S., & Tarter, C. J. (2016). Enabling school structures, collegial trust and academic emphasis: Antecedents of professional learning communities. *Educational Management Administration & Leadership*, 44(6), 875–891.

Hilton, A., Hilton, G., Dole, S., & Goos, M. (2015). School leaders as participants in teachers' professional development: The impact on teachers' and school leaders' professional growth. *Australian Journal of Teacher Education*, 40(12), 104–125.

Hughes, J. E., Read, M. F., Jones, S., & Mahometa, M. (2015). Predicting middle school students' use of web 2.0 technologies out of school using home and school technological variables. *Journal of Research on Technology in Education*, 47, 211–228.

Jeanpierre, B. (2007). Becoming an urban school middle-level science teacher. *Journal of Elementary Science Education*, 19(1), 45–55.

Keengwe, J., & Onchwari, G. (2009). Technology and early childhood education: A technology integration professional development model for practicing teachers. *Early Childhood Education Journal*, 37, 209–218. doi.org/10.1007/s10643-009-0341-0

Kopcha, T. J. (2010). A systems-based approach to technology integration using mentoring and communities of practice. *Educational Technology Research and Development*, 58, 175–190.

Kopcha, T. J. (2012). Teachers' perceptions of the barriers to technology integration and practices with technology under situated professional development. *Computers & Education*, 59, 1109–1121.

Kotok, S., & Kryst, E. L. (2017). Digital technology: A double-edged sword for a school principal in rural Pennsylvania. *Journal of Cases in Educational Leadership*, 20(4), 3–16.

Lawless, K. A., & Pellegrino, J. W. (2007). Professional development in integrating technology into teaching and learning: Knowns, unknowns, and ways to pursue better questions and answers. *Review of Educational Research*, 77(4), 575–614.

Lee, J., Cerreto, F. A., & Lee, J. (2010). Theory of planned behavior and teachers' decisions regarding use of educational technology. *Journal of Educational Technology & Society*, 13(1), 152–164.

Lysenko, L. V., & Abrami, P. C. (2014). Promoting reading comprehension with the use of technology. *Computers & Education*, 75, 162–172.

Machado, L. J., & Chung, C. (2015). Integrating technology: The principals' role and effect. *International Education Studies*, 8(5), 43–53.

Mandinach, E. B., & Miskell, R. C. (2017). *Focus groups to support the development and utility of EdWise for parental stakeholders: Findings from the parental focus groups.* San Francisco, CA: WestEd.org. Retrieved from https://files.eric.ed.gov/fulltext/ED582808.pdf

Marcinek, A. P. (2015). A class full of geniuses: For many districts, having students do tech support as part of their classwork has helped create a culture of trust and innovation. *THE (Technological Horizons in Education) Journal*, 42(2), 24–25.

Martinez, S., & Harper, D. (2008). Working with tech-savvy kids. *Educational Leadership*, 66(3), 64–69.

Matteucci, M. C., & Helker, K. (2018). Who is responsible for educational outcomes? Responsibility ascriptions for educational outcomes in a sample of Italian teachers, parents, and students. *Learning and Individual Differences, 61,* 239–249.

McCombs, B. (2010). Culture of collaboration. *Learning & Leading with Technology, 38*(3), 10–13.

McLeod, S., Bathon, J. M., & Richardson, J. W. (2011). Studies of technology tool usage are not enough: A response to the articles in this special issue. *Journal of Research on Leadership Education, 6*(5), 288–297.

Moreira, P. A., Cunha, D., Inman, R., & Oliveira, J. (2019). Integrating healthy personality development and educational practices: The case of student engagement with school. In D. Garci, T. Archer, & R. M. Kostrzewa (Eds.), *Personality and brain disorders: Associations and interventions* (pp. 227–250). Cham, Switzerland: Springer.

No Child Left Behind (NCLB) Act of 2001, Pub. L. No. 107-110, § 115, Stat. 1425 (2002).

Parents Across America. (n.d.). *Fact sheets.* Retrieved from http://parentsacrossamerica.org/parent-resources/

Patrikakou, E. N. (2016). Parent involvement, technology, and media: Now what? *School Community Journal, 26*(2), 9–24.

Ramirez, A. Y. F. (1999). Survey on teachers' attitudes regarding parents and parental involvement. *School Community Journal, 9*(2), 21–39.

Raulston, C. G., & Alexiou-Ray, J. (2018). Preparing more technology-literate pre-service teachers: A changing paradigm in higher education. *Delta Kappa Gamma Bulletin, 84*(5), 9–13.

Reid, K. S. (2015). Parent engagement on rise as priority for schools, districts. *Education Week, 34*(32), 9.

Richardson, J. W., & Sterrett, W. L. (2018). District technology leadership then and now: A comparative study of district technology leadership from 2001 to 2014. *Educational Administration Quarterly, 54*(4) 589–616.

Russell, M., Bebell, D., O'Dwyer, L., & O'Connor, K. (2003). Examining teacher technology use: Implications for preservice and inservice teacher preparation. *Journal of Teacher Education, 54*(4), 297–310. doi.org/10.1177/0022487103255985

Schrum, L. (1999). Technology professional development for teachers. *Educational Technology Research and Development. 47*(4), 83–90.

Smith, D. (2002). Teacher perceptions of parent involvement in middle school. *Journal of School Public Relations, 36,* 393–403.

Spector, J. M. (2019). Complexity, inquiry critical thinking, and technology: A holistic and developmental approach. In T. D. Parsons, L. Lin, & D. Cockerham (Eds.), *Mind, brain and technology: Learning in the age of emerging technologies* (pp. 17–25). Cham, Switzerland: Springer.

Spilt, J. L., Koomen, H. M., & Thijs, J. T. (2011). Teacher wellbeing: The importance of teacher–student relationships. *Educational Psychology Review, 23*(4), 457–477.

Steinberg, M. P., & Donaldson, M. L. (2016). The new educational accountability: Understanding the landscape of teacher evaluation in the post-NCLB era. *Education Finance and Policy*, *11*(3), 340–359.

Sterrett, W. L., & Richardson, J. W. (2017). Cultivating innovation in an age of accountability: Tech-savvy leadership. *Journal of Cases in Educational Leadership*, *20*(4), 27–41.

Sugar, W. (2005). Instructional technologist as a coach: Impact of a situated professional development program on teachers' technology use. *Journal of Technology and Teacher Education, 13*, 547–571.

Tsai, C., & Chai, C. S. (2012). The "third"-order barrier for technology-integration instruction: Implications for teacher education. *Australasian Journal of Educational Technology, 28*, 1057–1060.

Wachira, P., & Keengwe, J. (2011). Technology integration barriers: Urban school mathematics teachers' perspectives. *Journal of Science Education and Technology*, *20*(1), 17–25.

Wilhelm, T. (2013, February 26). *Teachers vs. administrators: Ending the adversarial relationship* [blog post]. Concordia University-Portland, OR. Retrieved from https://education.cu-portland.edu/blog/leaders-link/teachers-vs-administrators-ending-the-adversarial-relationship

Zorfass, J., & Rivero, H. K. (2005). Collaboration is key: How a community of practice promotes technology integration. *Journal of Special Education Technology, 20*(3), 51–67.

SECTION III

EXAMINING LEARNING THROUGH BROADER LENSES

CHAPTER 10

INSTRUCTIONAL STRATEGIES FOR ENGAGEMENT

Cultivating Emotional Awareness and a Challenge-Skill Imbalance

Chris Grodoski, Carrie Dabelow, Crystal Forbes, Margaret Hammer, Michelle Hoffmeyer, Jennifer Jim-Brundidge, and Kurt Makaryk
Franklin Middle School

ABSTRACT

In this collaborative, action research project, we sought to identify instructional strategies that supported middle level students in personalizing their own learning. Grounded in Csikszentmihalyi's (1996) theory about optimal experiences, *flow*, this study extends and refines the application of flow to middle level education. The Learning Experience Survey, developed for this project and derived from past flow measures, provided quantitative and qualitative information about the experiences of students in our arts and electives classes. Administered to nearly 300 middle level students in a pretest/posttest format, the survey found improved engagement in students. Because

Curriculum, Instruction, and Assessment:
Intersecting New Needs and New Approaches, pp. 249–277

the survey measures common features across different content areas, the findings reveal cross-disciplinary insights on instruction that foster student engagement. Qualitative findings also highlight the important role of a challenge-skill imbalance, where the challenges slightly exceed the skills. Additional findings suggest how social-emotional skills, explicitly taught and paired with content, facilitate the learning of middle level students. Conclusions emphasize a need to reconceptualize flow as dynamic and iterative when applied to education.

One tenet of middle level education is that students engage in active, purposeful learning (National Middle School Association, 2010). Yet lurking below the surface is a more challenging question: How can students *decide* to engage in active, *purposive* learning? The inclusion of "decide" and "purposive" is not semantic jujitsu; while the word purposeful denotes externally applied meaning it differs from purposive, which includes individual agency and personal meaning. While educators always have lessons and instructional strategies that engage students in meaningful learning, this question is challenging because it asks how students exercise personal agency to personalize their learning. This more nuanced aim is a fundamental, perennial question for teachers and animated the following research project.

During the 2017–18 academic year, district leaders challenged our team of middle level elective teachers to develop a common formative assessment and articulate our contributions to the district-wide social-emotional learning initiative. While we did not balk at the request, we collectively wondered: what data-producing practices did our different content areas have in common? No member of our team instructed a similar course. When collaboratively reflecting on our instructional practices, a collaborative eureka moment emerged. In considering how students might optimize their learning engagement, our discussion turned to *flow*, the notion of optimal experiences that Csikszentmihalyi (1997) articulated.

Flow describes a highly engaged cognitive and affective state that arises from an interplay of challenges and skills. This articulation of optimal experiences resonated with our middle level electives team, despite our different instructional content, and in terms of the learning experiences we hoped for our students. Enthusiastic discussions about the application of flow and the challenge-skill relationship in our classrooms followed, but this common interest raised a particular problem. We suspected that student engagement increased when they applied self-awareness and self-management to choose their approach when navigating the interplay of challenges and skills. Yet confirming this required uncovering instruction that facilitated the active, purposive learning of students. It also meant devising a way to capture the learning experiences of students.

This chapter documents a collaborative action research project that sought to assist students in purposively optimizing their learning experiences across different middle level content areas. It identifies instructional practices that benefit student efficacy in optimizing the relationship between their skill level and the degree of challenge as well as the role of social-emotional learning in facilitating the agency of middle level students.

THEORETICAL FRAMEWORK

Flow is a "hypothetical construct" that describes the peak performance experience (Jackson & Marsh, 1996, p. 21). Csikszentmihalyi (1997) developed the concept of flow from interviews with experts who shared their intrinsically rewarding and attention absorbing experiences. The concept of flow resonates deeply; literature on flow extends across all facets of human experiences from medicine to business, from athletics to education. Two categories emerge from decades of research: the necessary features for a flow experience and the relationship between challenges and skills.

The synthesis and verification of research has resulted in the identification of nine dimensions deemed necessary for a flow experience to occur (Jackson & Marsh, 1996):

- A challenging activity that requires skill;
- Linked action and awareness;
- Clear goals;
- Unambiguous feedback;
- Concentration on the task at hand;
- Control;
- Loss of self-consciousness;
- Transformation of time; and
- Autotelic experiences.

These dimensions readily overlap with the education context, and they are explored further in the literature review as they connect to studies and discussion of classroom environments and pedagogy. They provide a structure to understand the roles of teachers and their students in a way that encourages the personal agency of learners.

Flow theory also suggests a dynamic relationship between challenge and skill in the optimal experiences of peak performers. An x–y graph commonly depicts the interaction between skill and challenge, with x indicating the skill level and y indicating the level of challenge. The challenge-skill relationship includes a range of interactions that evoke different affective states. Subsequent research theorized that as the relationship between challenges and skills changes, an individual experiences emotions from anxious to relaxed, from disengaged to engaged (Csikszentmihalyi, 1997; Moneta, 2012). This affective framework is featured in Figure 10.1 with transformations from Csikszentmihalyi's 1997 version for the instruction of students in this study.

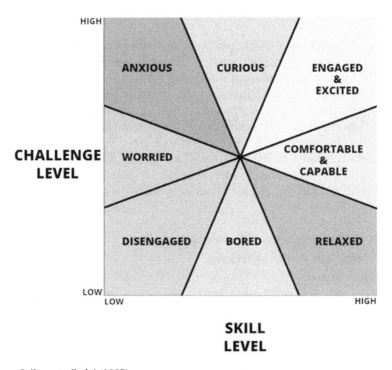

Source: Csikszentmihalyi (1997).

Figure 10.1.   Challenge and skills relationship graph with adapted affective language.

An ongoing debate exists about the necessity of a challenge-skill balance for a flow state. Some argue that an upper level of skill must be balanced with an upper level of challenge, while others argue that an imbalance, which enhances a feeling of risk, is necessary for an optimal experience (Abuhamdeh, Csikszentmihalyi, & Jalal, 2015; Engeser & Rheinberg, 2008; Jackson, Martin, & Eklund, 2008; Løvoll & Vittersø, 2014). The literature on flow related to education is highlighted in the next section and underscores its relevance to the education of middle level students.

LITERATURE REVIEW

Research on flow suggests it develops student attention, interest, and participation while advancing skills in complex ways (Baumann & Scheffer, 2010; Busch, Hofer, Chasiotis, & Campos, 2013; Gute & Gute, 2008). Flow in education represents a means to connect the affective and cognitive experiences of students while learning (Seligman, Ernst, Gillham, Reivich, & Linkins, 2009).

Dimensions of Flow in Education

The many ways of dissecting the flow experience create challenges for its practical application to classroom experiences (Beard, 2015). Yet many studies sought to identify the relationship of flow to education and the many ways in which the dimensions of flow have direct, unexplored applications for teaching and learning.

A challenging activity that requires skill. This relationship is fundamental to the flow experience; it has application in all education contexts, but particularly to the arts and electives contexts. However, as the instruction of basic skills is increasingly automated through ever-advancing technologies, all educators need to focus on how students apply knowledge in novel ways. The prominence of problem- and project-based learning, as well as calls for students to meet grand challenges, reflects the realization that teaching and learning require the advanced application of skills (Every Student Succeeds Act, 2015; Loyens, Magda, & Rikers, 2008; Savery, 2015). Teachers, students, or both working together can generate learning challenges that transcend basic skills.

Linked action and awareness. When self-awareness and learning are linked, it increases the ability of students to navigate their growth in healthy, less stressful ways. Student engagement in active, purposeful learning is not possible without linking actions to awareness (National Middle School Association, 2010). Of course, social-emotional learning not only promotes the affective skills necessary for navigating the learning process, but it also encourages overall well-being and supports students in becoming lifelong learners (Dahl et al., 2017). While self-awareness during a learning activity is primarily in the locus of control of the students themselves, teachers can explicitly assist students in developing such skills (Collaborative for Academic, Social, and Emotional Learning, 2015; Dent & Koenka, 2016; Marzano et al., 1992; Zepeda, Richey, Ronevich, & Nokes-Malach, 2015).

Clear goals. Clear goals can shape the optimal experience of learners. In education, goals emerge from curriculum plans and learning targets, and the educator delivers them through clear instruction (Moss & Brookhart,

2012; Schmoker, 2018; Walters, 2016). Students can articulate goals by either restating teacher-generated goals or when they structure their own challenges (Tomlinson & McTighe, 2006). Ultimately, a goal must be clear in the mind of the student, whether it is teacher-initiated, student-initiated, or a combination of both.

Unambiguous feedback. Both good teaching practice and the achievement of an optimal experience require unambiguous feedback. Teachers provide feedback, but when goals are clearly understood by learners, feedback can come from students in the form of peer- and self-assessments (Grant & Gareis, 2015). Relative to most arts and electives courses, feedback arises from the engagement of students with content. For example, a music student who is off rhythm or a mistyped line of code provides swift and obvious feedback. However, the ways knowledge is represented and communicated in arts and electives courses can differ from other content areas, requiring alternative considerations (Dorn, Sabol, Madeja, & Sabol, 2014; Efland, 2002; Hwang, Hung, & Chen, 2014; Savery, 2015). When students understand the intent of learning well enough to provide feedback, they become knowledge connoisseurs and are better able to engage with their own learning experiences.

Concentration on the task. Learner concentration emerges from a number of student-centered factors. That said, teachers can set the classroom climate, alter the physical space, and take steps to motivate the attention of students (Riva, Waterworth, Waterworth, & Mantovani, 2011; Tomlinson & McTighe, 2006). The notion of a shared role in student concentration reflects studies from neuroscience that have linked two theories about learning, the cognitive and the volitional (Pekrun, 2006). On one hand, cognitive studies consider how learners respond to their learning contexts, which reflects the role of the teacher. On the other hand, volitional studies highlight the agency of students that rises from their personal motives. Essentially, both teachers and students have a role in promoting student concentration.

Control. Control is the feeling of competency students have while applying skills. Both education and flow research suggest that teachers can support competency growth by fostering positive affect in students (Reyes, Brackett, Rivers, White, & Salovey, 2012; Schmuck & Schmuck, 1975; Shernoff, Csikszentmihalyi, Schneider, & Shernoff, 2014). A student's willingness to pursue control partially results from a classroom climate that promotes safety and relationships along with academic and emotional supports (Anderman & Patrick, 2012; Thapa, Cohen, Guffey, & Higgins-D'Alessandro, 2013). Of course, numerous student-level factors also drive a learner's pursuit of mastery (Heutte, Fenouillet, Kaplan, Martin-Krumm, & Bachelet, 2016; Malone & Lepper, 1987; Soni, 2003).

Loss of self-consciousness. The loss of self-consciousness, or a preoccupation with the self, is a difficult challenge for middle level learners. This likewise requires a feeling of safety in students, but at a time when they experience a heightened sense of self-consciousness. Therefore, while such an experience is internal to a student, the teacher can also support it.

Transformation of time. A feeling that time has transformed is an experience that is largely internal and student-centered. Importantly, and relevant to the young adolescent experience, many of these student-centered conditions vary from one day to another like mood and academic readiness. Teacher-initiated activities can support a context for students to experience such a moment. However, gauging that a student has experienced a transformation of time is difficult and not easily captured outside of self-reported data, similar to the autotelic experience.

Autotelic experiences. Like the transformation of time, students' autotelic experience is an internal one. Literally translated into "self-goal," autotelism in education occurs when students are intrinsically motivated to learn. Autotelic experiences represent a cultural hope for learners driven solely by their own curiosity. Viewed as a goal for a middle level student, it reflects a high-level of consistent self-awareness and self-efficacy (Brophy, 2013; Kang, 2012).

Some research suggests the autotelic experience is an outcome of teaching or technological interventions, while other research suggests it is an embedded personality trait (Busch et al., 2013; Heutte et al., 2016; Soni, 2003). It is reasonable to consider that, like the dimensions of concentration and control, teachers can contribute to and support autotelic experiences, but this experience remains difficult to measure. This fact is especially true in the dynamic environment of classrooms. Even when students report autotelic experiences in questionnaires, results risk an intentional fallacy limitation (Zollars, 2018).

Summarizing the Dimensions of Flow

The dimensions of flow have a clear overlap with the teaching and learning in schools. The application of flow for middle level education is crucial, as young adolescence represents a time when students are increasingly able to take ownership over their learning. Yet the dimensions are complex; flow arises from "a variety of contextual, instructional, and developmental and interpersonal factors" (Shernoff & Csikszentmihalyi, 2009, p. 143). The situational convergence of so many factors make it understandable that research is commonly structured to catch students in a flow state or to study flow in controlled environments; identifying individual antecedent factors is notably complex (Schmidt, Shernoff,

& Csikszentmihalyi, 2014). Yet while research acknowledges the role of instruction in addressing numerous factors, only a limited number of studies deeply explore the forms of instruction that address multiple dimensions simultaneously (Pekrun, 2006; Schmidt, 2010). Additionally, by supporting students through instruction, they may self-identify and independently address the dimensions that will enrich their learning experiences.

The number of factors within the dimensions also implies that flow, when applied to education, is best conceived as a dynamic range of experience rather than a static achievement (Kawabata & Mallett, 2011). In this way of thinking, teachers can support students in the process of continually moving towards optimal experiences. The success of students in optimizing their learning should be understood by degrees of achievement and not an absolute state. Corresponding with this dynamic view of flow is the dynamic relationship between challenges and skills.

Challenges and Skills in Education

The challenge-skill relationship is one that resonates deeply with learning in middle school arts and electives courses, as problem- and performance-based learning represents a continuous negotiation between challenges and skills. Some courses may be more challenge-based while others more skill-based. For example, students developing a logo design (i.e., the challenge) decide how to use and expand their compositional, color, and linear design skills. On the other hand, students solely focused on skill development have to set a challenge that fosters that skill. Students learning to read music (i.e., a skill) would have to find appropriately complex music (i.e., challenge) to improve their skill. Measuring the interaction between challenge and skill is a key feature of flow research across multiple contexts, including school environments (Custodero, 1998; Engeser & Rheinberg, 2008; Jackson & Marsh, 1996; Jackson et al., 2008; Shernoff & Csikszentmihalyi, 2009).

Summary of the Literature

The dimensions for a flow experience, the framework of challenges and skills, and the affective experiences that emerge from different challenge-skills balance all have direct application for the education context. The core attributes of flow are conditions to be supported and indicators of a students' learning experience; they are highly relevant as teaching tools to facilitate students in optimizing their own learning.

Like the dimensions of flow, the variety of possible challenge-skill relationships does not suggest that students will have consistent optimal experiences. It is unrealistic to expect all students to achieve flow at every moment of their school day. Learning is a dynamic process where both success and failure are beneficial. Students consistently experience inconsistent relationships between challenges and skills. Yet students' ability to move consistently themselves toward optimal states is a better way to conceptualize flow in the context of education.

As a result, teachers may want to encourage experiences in which the level of challenge does not align with the level of skill. In doing so, students must stretch themselves and face a personal risk. The literature implies that as students navigate the challenge-skill relationship through affective awareness, they may gain emotional regulation skills while they learn—linking awareness and action (Dent & Koenka, 2016; Heutte, Fenouillet, Kaplan, Martin-Krumm, & Bachelet, 2016; Pekrun, 2006; Shernoff, Csikszentmihalyi, Schneider, & Shernoff, 2014). Discrepancies between challenges and skills may motivate learning.

A peak learning performance, then, requires a student to use self-awareness to respond to the challenge and skill in a way that is personally relevant and growth centered. When viewed as an experiential and dynamic process, flow is even more applicable for the student experience. To understand how instruction promotes the flow experience, the instructional team developed the following research question: what forms of instruction encourage affective awareness and the navigation of the challenge and skill relationship for middle level students?

RESEARCH METHODOLOGY

To identify instructional practices that fostered student personalization of the challenge-skill relationship along with the role of social-emotional learning in facilitating student agency, the authors conceived of an action research project. The phenomenological framework that underpins action research enabled the teaching team to capture the experiences of students and our subjective role as teachers while conducting our inquiry (Caskey, 2005). Situating knowledge in this way enabled flexible migration across the boundaries of research and practice while aligning with multiple components of flow research literature. It also enabled thick descriptions from students about their lived experiences while acknowledging our involvement as their teachers. Ultimately, we sought actionable knowledge that could directly inform our instruction. For these reasons, our electives team employed the phenomenological and hermeneutic approaches of action research to explore our inquiry (Schmuck, 2006; Stringer, 2014).

Using a pretest/posttest design with an instructional intervention between each survey, this exploratory inquiry resulted in qualitative and quantitative data about the experiences of our students. Each of the seven teachers in the team targeted one of their semester-long courses for participation in this project. Early in the semester and following an instructional unit, students participated in the Learning Experience Survey as a pretest. The students were assembled in the auditorium for a presentation on flow. After reviewing results from the initial survey, teachers individually devised instructional methods that might best serve students in their unique courses. One team member interviewed the other teachers during this period; interview questions asked teachers to describe the before-pilot challenge and describe the instructional approaches they used following the first survey. Later, during the same semester and following another, different instructional unit, the survey was administered to students a second time.

Context and Sample

Our suburban middle school houses nearly 800 students in Grades 6, 7, and 8. Within a generally affluent community context, the school provides a diverse English learning program with over 40 different languages represented. Nearly a third of our students receive Title I support. Our instructional team of seven teachers each selected a single course within our schedules to participate in this project. As an electives team representing different content, no courses in the sample were similar. Courses included band, chorus, digital authorship, drama, navigating informational resources, orchestra, and visual arts. Courses were selected so that participating students were not engaged in multiple classes. For some of us, the survey was extended to two sections of a selected course; for example, two sections of visual arts completed the survey, a total of 65 student participants, representing nearly 20% of the sample.

Participants included 303 students in the initial survey and 297 of these same students participated in the post intervention survey, with a loss of six participants. While the sample reflects the school and surrounding community context, data on gender or student backgrounds was not collected, but the sample did include students from all grade levels. Of the students responding to the initial survey, 23.8% were in sixth grade, 25.1% in seventh grade, and 51.2% in eighth grade. For the follow-up survey, 22.8% of respondents were in sixth grade, 24.8% in seventh grade, and 52.3% in eighth grade. Students received nearly three months of targeted instruction, following the pretest and prior to the posttest.

Data Collection

The teaching team developed the central data collection instrument, the Learning Experience Survey (Appendix A), to capture the experiences of students following a learning activity. The Learning Experience Survey is derived from past flow measurement instruments, including the Experience Sampling Method, the Flow Short Scale, and the Dispositional Flow Scale (Custodero, 1998; Engeser & Rheinberg, 2008; Jackson & Marsh, 1996; Jackson et al., 2008). The wording of the survey questions was tailored for middle level students and the administration of the survey required between 10–15 minutes. The online survey organized responses by the grade level and/or by course. Laptops were distributed to each student and students completed the survey in the classroom of the course selected for participation in this project.

The survey features two interval level questions: "What was your skill level with this activity (1 beginner to 4 expert)?" and "How challenging was this task (1 super easy to 4 really hard)?" The survey utilized a 4-point response scale to avoid the neutral responses potentially generated from an odd numbered scale. In addition, the shortened 4-point scale provided greater alignment of responses across the full sample. A response metric with more items would allow for more varied responses and not capture the understanding that we sought in this exploratory project. Responses to these two questions were combined into a challenge-skills graph. Placement on the graph was assumed to align with the affective states indicated within flow theory (Csikszentmihalyi, 1997) (see Figure 10.1).

In the third survey question, a forced-choice response required students to identify a single phrase among eight that best described their affect while learning. Altered from the original survey to accommodate reading comprehension for middle level learners, these phrases served as common instructional language following the initial survey.

- I felt totally engaged and excited to learn this
- I felt comfortable and capable
- I felt increasingly curious
- I felt bored
- I felt anxious
- I felt disengaged
- I felt relaxed
- I felt worried

Finally, the survey included three open-ended response questions. These questions provided insights into how the students understood their responses. These questions also addressed the processes by which students navigated the challenge-skill relationship, providing insights into their agency as learners. This explicit inclusion of how students navigated the challenge-skill relationship diverged from past classroom measures.

1. Please describe your learning experience.
2. Please describe how you changed the challenge to improve your skill level?
3. Please describe how you stretched your skill level to meet the challenge?

Following the initial collection and review of data, each team member developed instructional strategies to support students in personalizing their learning. A designated team member documented these instructional practices in an interview with each member of our electives team.

Data Analysis

The Learning Experience Survey provided numeric and text-based qualitative data. Numeric data and forced choice responses were analyzed descriptively. The numeric data was graphed to analyze the relationship between the levels of challenge and skill. Numeric data was also analyzed for alignment to determine if students reported a level of challenge identical to their level of skill. Because the combined challenge-skill responses were theorized to align with an affective state, these responses were aligned with forced-choice responses to determine how affective states predicted by flow theory aligned with the challenge-skill reports of students (Csikszentmihalyi, 1997; Engeser & Rheinberg, 2008; Jackson et al., 2008). The team also conducted a comparison between the pre- and post-intervention surveys. Open-ended responses were categorized by course, which aligned with teachers and their specific instructional interventions.

Limitations

The design of this exploratory, action-research project honors the interactivity of teachers and their students but subject to a few notable limitations. This study is subject to a social desirability bias. Students gained, through our instruction, a clear understanding of flow and our intent for their learning processes. There is a risk that student self-reported data demonstrated the personalization of their learning even if personalization was minimal. To address this limitation, teachers informed students that we did not seek their highest scores, prior to administering the posttest, but only their honest reflections about their experiences. We also stated that the purpose of the survey was to help us improve the experiences we provided students in general; honest and thoughtful responses were the most beneficial. In this case, and whenever possible, our electives team aligned language among the participating students to address limitations.

Relatedly, following the pretest, all students gathered for a scripted presentation on flow, but applications of flow in our classrooms varied. As a result, this study lacks the aligned delivery of single intervention. However, as noted earlier, responses were sortable by course (teacher), which enabled reporting between instructional interventions and changes in student navigation of their learning experiences. The final limitation is a testing effect. By having students take an identical survey, changes in responses were readily identified. However, students may be likely to tailor their answers since the same survey was administered pre- and post-intervention.

FINDINGS

Three hundred and three students in Grades 6, 7, and 8 completed the pre-intervention survey. Students responded to the survey prior to explicit instruction about flow and the challenge-skills relationship. Responses to the two scalar questions (What is your skill level with this activity? and What is your level of challenge with this activity?) were combined and graphed as shown in Figure 10.2. The more densely colored bubbles indicate a higher frequency of student responses; Figure 10.2 shows that in general, students lean toward a higher perception of their skills and a lower perception of the challenge.

Figure 10.3 reports, in percentages, the student selection of preloaded affective statements to describe their emotional state during an activity. When comparing response data from the scalar questions and preloaded statements from Figure 10.2 and Figure 10.3, 60 total responses (20%) aligned relative to affective theories about different challenge-skill relationships. This suggests that for these 60 respondents, their reported level of challenge and skill aligned with their reported affect within current research on affect and flow. This also indicates that 80% of responses did not align, suggesting that theories about affect and the challenge-skill relationship may not be applicable to the experiences of students. However, if the affect and challenge-skill relationship is applicable, it suggests that 20% of respondents demonstrated self-awareness and accuracy in reporting their level of challenge, level of skill, and affect.

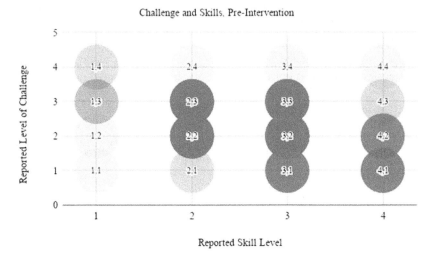

Figure 10.2. Student reported interaction between challenge and skill in their pre-intervention learning experiences.

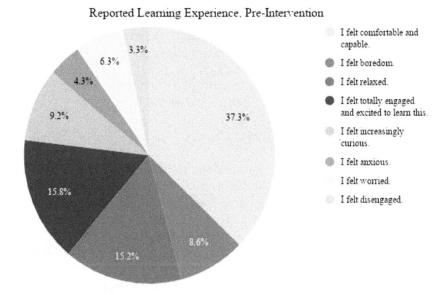

Figure 10.3. Student reports of their emotional state among different learning pre-intervention learning experiences.

Of the pre-intervention responses, 22% ($n = 61$) reported a level of challenge equaling the reported level of skill; this means challenge and skill values were reported as (1,1), (2,2), (3,3), or (4,4). Of these 79% ($n = 53$) aligned with generally positive statements like "I felt totally engaged and excited to learn this," "I felt comfortable and capable," "I felt increasingly curious," and "I felt relaxed." The positive responses may indicate that regardless of the level of a challenge or skill, equity between both creates a positive affective experience for students. As noted, all students who completed the pre-intervention survey had the flow framework shared with them. This included an overview of the challenge-skill relationship and the affect connected to challenge-skill interactions.

Instruction and the Challenge-Skill Relationship

Activities in our different content areas included both challenges and skills, simultaneously, but with different emphases. Some of our learning activities were challenge-centric and required students to apply their skills innovatively; some of us focused on skill development encouraging students to construct appropriate challenges. Students in the drama and technology courses faced activities that emphasized a challenge and provided flexibility in the application of skills. For example, the drama teacher challenged her eighth grade students to perform multiple and different characters from a familiar fairy tale. This meant that students had to apply their current physical and verbal skills to address the challenge. Similarly, the technology teacher challenged students to share an aspect of their life; students could choose a digital skill they deemed best suited for their work.

Analysis of the interview data revealed that both of these teachers utilized dual coding (the representation of ideas verbally and visually) and the generation effect (the development of one's own examples) to help students more deeply ground their skills in novel applications, a practice which reinforced skill development (McDaniel, Anderson, Derbish, & Morrisette, 2007; Moreno & Valdez, 2005). In these cases, the self-regulated application of knowledge can highlight for students various strengths and weaknesses in their skills set (Kruger & Dunning, 1999).

Other team members provided challenges intended to foster disequilibrium in the challenge-skill relationship to enhance a skill set (Løvoll & Vittersø, 2014). In the course, Navigating Informational Sources, the teacher taught a debate methodology. After learning this skill, students applied it to a debate topic; this was their challenge. However, students would prepare to use this method without knowing which side of the debate topic they would be arguing. Similarly, in music class, the teacher assigned one of five concert pitches and then challenged students to identify and play the related scale. Depending on the instrument they played, students had to transpose the note mentally, determine the key signature, and then play that scale up and down. Relative to instructional practices, both teachers provided desirable difficulties and cognitive flexibility (Meltzer, 2018; Metcalfe, 2011; Spiro, 1988).

In another variation of the challenge-skill relationship, the orchestra students developed their sight-reading skills by completing exercises of increasing complexity until they reached a challenge that exceeded their current skill level. The orchestra teacher asked students to identify and work within challenges that best suited their skill development. Students in the chorus classroom were also cultivating their sight-reading skills as they worked to determine their location on the scale and sight sing instantaneously. The teacher organized her students in collaborative groups that reflected a range of sight-singing capacity. In these groups, students labeled and then sang solfege measures to the level of complexity that they were able. Both of these teachers assisted students in finding their limits to identify an ideal level of tension between a challenge and skill, an instructional practice known as the Goldilocks Principle (Arredondo Rucinski, Beas Franco, Gomez Nocetti, Queirolo, & Daniel, 2009; Kruger & Dunning, 1999; Metcalfe & Kornell, 2005).

In the visual arts course, students applied five forms of compositions in five unique ways. The skill of spatially organizing a visual work could be met through a variety of pre-taught skills, art, and design skills. In allowing for skill selection, the teacher anticipated that the challenge would be greater than skill, enabling a focus on the application of composition. This approach utilizes perceptual motor grounding, the visualization of composition fundamentals with opportunities to manipulate applications, and the generation effect (the development of one's own examples) as an instructional strategy (Barsalou, 2010; Metcalfe & Kornell, 2007; Moreno & Valdez, 2005).

Each of these teachers provided challenges that culminated in a production or performance, encouraging students to assemble knowledge flexibly and apply their skills to meet the needs of a context (Efland, 2002). In most of these cases, students determined the specific degrees of the challenge-skill relationship employed. All cases provide students with immediate feedback through direct application of the skill in service to the challenge (Jackson & Marsh, 1996; Metcalfe & Kornell, 2007). However, in addition to instructing for content, teachers guided their students in navigating affective experiences of their learning within the flow framework.

Emotional Maps and Border Names

The emotional states associated with each challenge-skill relationship served as a guide for scaffolding students toward increased engagement. For the teacher of the Navigating Informational Sources course, the affective states, explicitly stated, guided students toward learning experiences as they conducted research for a debate. Relative to instructional strategies, students used metacognitive skills to be aware of their emotional state to guide their learning engagement, connecting awareness and action (Kuhn & Dean, 2004).

In orchestra, applying the affective framework to instruction required providing emotional supports for students. The teacher realized that students needed to feel safe to take active control over their process, a tension for learners. Where she encouraged student ownership, students initially wanted direct instruction at each step of the sight-reading process. She found it necessary to give explicit permission to students for them to navigate their affective state and the level of challenge they chose.

Similarly, the drama teacher noted the role of safety to enable students the ability to link their awareness and action. Similar to the other teachers, the drama teacher found that reinforcing a sense of collective safety and naming the affective needs of learners were necessary to enable students to activate personal agency as they performed different characters. Students in her classes revealed themselves as hovering between anxious and curious. To aid a confident transition into curious, she and her class named the border between anxious to curious "trust." Similarly, they named the transition between comfortable and capable and relaxed as "involved." For her students, naming these borders encouraged the risk-taking of students and a sense of shared support for one another. Providing concrete language gave students guides to increase their self-awareness and support one another to overcome the risk of public performance. The teacher noted that they "put themselves on display for an audience, which can make or break their whole day."

Other members of our team created spaces for student collaboration and teacher support that moved students toward increased self-awareness in service to their learning. These interactions functioned as a means to assist students in correctly evaluating a needed challenge and skill balance. After learning about the affective features of the challenge-skill framework, students in chorus were interested in how they could differentiate between challenges where they required external help and challenges they could meet independently. Thus, while the students felt willing to take control, they required direction to focus their goals. As a result, peer collaborations became an important way to clarify learning goals. As students engaged in more cooperative learning, it was crucial for the teacher to develop capacity in the students to give and receive increased amounts of feedback. To address this, she included a series of social-emotional learning goals to imbue collaborative work with a growth mindset.

The explicit sharing of flow helped the band students become more vocal about asking for help. Similar to the chorus teacher, the band teacher seized this opportunity by providing spaces for students to share their concerns. Within the spaces where students vocalized their perceptions, he helped students to separate and dispel notions of themselves as either a good or bad. Students gained a crucial realization: their affective states were malleable, not a judgment of worth. By enhancing their comfort and feeling less ashamed about their struggles, students fostered a more accurate awareness of their actions and increased their focus on skill development.

The affective language arising from the challenge-skill relationships guided continuous student reflection in the technology and visual arts course. In these classrooms, instruction before, during, and after learning activities featured the language of challenges, skills, and affect. For example, when students in visual arts constructed ceramic vessels, they initially under or overestimated the challenges they gave for themselves. Reflection on their affective states and the relationship between their skill level and the challenge encouraged students to adjust meaningfully the scope of their work, increasing personalized engagement while elevating the quality of their work.

Overall, our middle school electives team both applied the flow framework and restructured instruction for optimized student engagement. This included teaching the challenge-skill relationship in content specific ways as well as helping students understand their affective states as indicators of their challenge-skill balance. It also included utilizing instructional methods that would support student personalization of their learning process. Tightly connecting social-emotional learning with learning activities required continually helping middle level learners adjust their self-perceptions relative to their learning experiences.

Personalizing the Challenge

A total of 297 students in Grades 6, 7, and 8 participated in the post-intervention survey. Students responded to the survey following explicit instruction about flow and the challenge-skills relationship. They had also completed classroom activities as described in the previous sections. Figure 10.4 shows responses to the two scalar questions; the more densely colored bubbles indicate a higher frequency of student responses. Figure 10.4 shows that, in general, student perception of their skills remained consistent, but the perception of the challenges they faced increased, moving them closer to the flow experience.

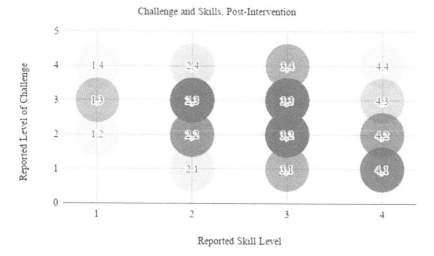

Figure 10.4.   Student reported interaction between challenge and skill in their post-intervention learning experiences.

Figure 10.5 demonstrates how students selected preloaded statements describing their emotional states during a learning activity. Figure 10.6 depicts a comparison between pre- and post-intervention responses to that same question. Notably, fewer students experienced boredom or disengagement. In general, students reported an increase in positive affect. However, more students reported being anxious in the post-intervention, possibly reflecting a greater awareness of the challenges, as noted in responses to the scalar questions.

Similar to the pre-intervention responses, 18.9% ($n = 56$) responses reported challenge-skill relationships that aligned with affective theories about flow. The repetition of nearly 20% of students aligning in this way is notable. It raises interesting questions. For example, are these students innately self-aware or perhaps more autotelic?

Agency and the Student Learning Experience

Across all courses, the open-ended responses from students indicated a shift in how they approached their learning. Responses in the pre-intervention survey indicated a nonspecific approach to improving their engagement, predominantly indicated by statements such as "I worked hard," "I tried my best," and "I thought harder."

Following the various interventions over the course of three months, students indicated a more focused approach to challenge and skill development. For example, an orchestra student noted changing "the challenge to

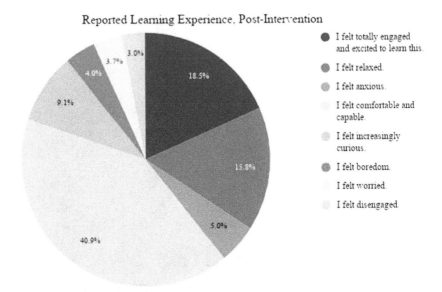

Figure 10.5. Student reports of their emotional state among different post-intervention learning experiences.

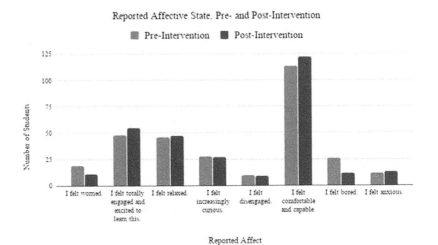

Figure 10.6. Comparison of student reported emotional states during learning experiences from pre-intervention to post-intervention.

improve my skill level by practicing dynamics and notes," while a drama student changed the level of challenge by "adding more character and depth to my lines." These responses also indicated ways that self-awareness linked with the challenges that students set. A visual arts student wrote, "At first, my vase was going to be very large, very intricate and wide, but because I had to restart a couple times, I now realize that dialing it down a bit and simplifying it can make it look better and make my experience better."

In addition, responses were more specific on how skills were stretched to meet a challenge. Often students described situations in which they knew what they hoped to achieve but needed to increase their knowledge and skills to complete a challenge. One student wrote:

> In a lot of instances, I had to stretch my skill level to meet the challenge asked. One was that I had no idea how to make the sound louder or softer and I had to stretch my thinking and find a way around that problem. Also, I had to find a way to make the instruments move like they do in real life and I had to think hard to solve that problem as well. Lastly, I had to make the music blend well together and sound good. I had to mess a lot with the timing to get the sound I wanted.

Another respondent who captured this type of increased ownership wrote that he "stretched my skill level to meet the challenge by trying to get the notes perfect and doing all the sharps and flats." As with responses on challenge setting, students reported benefits of a challenge-skill imbalance. For example, one respondent noted that "by picking things a little above my skill level … I could learn new skills and improve old ones by practicing." Similarly, another commented on having …

> Stretched my skill level by making sure I listen and pay attention to what the teacher has to say so I could get the most out of everything. I also challenged myself to do harder things each project, which built up my skill level.

Another student noted personal motivation to increase her level of concentration: "I had to manage my time quickly and focus on the main task."

Participating teachers reviewed open-ended responses for their participating course and noted an increase in the reflection, awareness, and ownership of their participating students. These responses shaped the conversations in a generative way: they created a shared understanding of how students experienced their learning, they prompted driving questions for each team member about how to refine their professional practice, and the responses increased reflection on our collective impact as a team. Finally, the positive changes across each course raised questions about the relationship between instructional approaches and content, which led to team members utilizing one another's approach to instructional interventions in ongoing pursuit of student personalization and self-awareness.

CONCLUSIONS

This chapter documented the application of the flow research to education and resulted in three major conclusions, suggesting directions for middle level practice and continued research. One key conclusion suggests that a challenge-skill imbalance promotes students' ownership of their learning. The findings suggest that the explicit teaching of flow, integrated with the three instructional strategies of desirable difficulties, cognitive flexibility, and the generation effect, fostered a beneficial challenge-skill imbalance for students. These instructional strategies addressed a number of the situational convergences outlined in the nine dimensions for flow. Additionally, the explicit instruction of flow served as a metacognitive instructional strategy, providing signposts that guided students in the personalization of learning. Importantly, however, these strategies, when paired with affective goals and with social-emotional skills, assisted students in addressing the tension of a challenge-skill imbalance. Through increased self-awareness, students recognized the affective experiences that emerge from their work as information that should inform changes to their challenge-skill relationship.

A second key finding of this study is that applying flow theory to learning requires conceptualization as an ever-fluctuating process. Instead of expecting students to achieve, and then remain in, a flow state, flow is a dynamic process of continuous renegotiation of a student's engagement. In this way, the dimensions of flow are not a checklist, but a tool for periodic evaluation by which to continuously reevaluate, and elevate, the teaching and learning process.

The third and final key finding arose from integrating flow research and education practice. At the level of professional practice, flow served as generative framework that facilitated a cross-disciplinary conversation about the integrated academic and affective experiences of students. Through the collection of shared data, the student online survey enhanced and informed this conversation. Thus, on the level of applied research, resources like the Learning Experience Survey provided valuable insights into the linked affective and academic experiences of learners. Subsequently, resources such as this, when centered on a core question, link teachers in a shared focusing on fundamental similarities across different content areas. Indeed, this professional endeavor elevated a shared focus that honors and encouraged the agency of middle level learners. As a result, students gained a consistent message that the content of school and the act of learning are a means to cultivate their self-awareness and decision- making abilities.

Explicitly supporting and contributing to the ability of students to personalize their learning is a central role for middle level educators. It has particular relevance as education increasingly moves towards applied knowledge through problem- and project-based learning. To this end, arts and electives teacher teams have much to contribute to the conversation, including how students come to personalize their learning experiences. The instruction and guidance that we provide as teachers and that helps students activate their agencies as learners may be our greatest contribution to their lives. When professional learning communities focus on the quality of the holistic experiences of students, illuminated by meaningful data, they support the increased engagement of middle level students with the skills necessary for a lifetime of relevant and meaningful learning.

REFERENCES

Abuhamdeh, S., Csikszentmihalyi, M., & Jalal, B. (2015). Enjoying the possibility of defeat: Outcome uncertainty, suspense, and intrinsic motivation. *Motivation and Emotion, 39*(1), 1–10.

Anderman, E. M., & Patrick, H. (2012). Achievement goal theory, conceptualization of ability/intelligence, and classroom climate. In S. L. Christenson, A. L. Reschly, & C. Wylie (Eds.), *Handbook of research on student engagement* (pp. 173–191). New York, NY: Springer.

Arredondo Rucinski, D., Beas Franco, J., Gomez Nocetti, V., Queirolo, P. T., & Daniel, G. C. (2009). Conceptual change among teachers involved in educational reform. *International Journal of Leadership in Education, 12*(2), 155–169.

Barsalou, L. W. (2010). Grounded cognition: Past, present, and future. *Topics in Cognitive Science, 2*, 716–724.

Baumann, N., & Scheffer, D. (2010). Seeing and mastering difficulty: The role of affective change in achievement flow. *Cognition and Emotion, 24*, 1304–1328.

Beard, K. S. (2015). Theoretically speaking: An interview with Mihaly Csikszentmihalyi on flow theory development and its usefulness in addressing contemporary challenges in education. *Educational Psychology Review, 27*, 353–364.

Brophy, J. (2013). *Motivating students to learn*. London, England: Routledge.

Busch, H., Hofer, J., Chasiotis, A., & Campos, D. (2013). The achievement flow motive as an element of the autotelic personality: Predicting educational attainment in three cultures. *European Journal of Psychology of Education, 28*, 239–254.

Caskey, M. M. (Ed.). (2005). *Making a difference: Action research in middle level education*. Greenwich, CT: Information Age.

Collaborative for Academic, Social, and Emotional Learning. (2015). *Effective social and emotional learning programs: Middle school and high school edition*. Chicago,

IL: Author. Retrieved from http://secondaryguide.casel.org/casel-secondary-guide.pdf

Csikszentmihalyi, M. (1996). *Creativity: Flow and the psychology of discovery and invention*. New York, NY: Harper Perennial.

Csikszentmihalyi, M. (1997). *Finding flow: The psychology of engagement with everyday life* New York, NY: Basic Books.

Custodero, L. A. (1998). Observing flow in young children's music learning. *General Music Today*, *12*(1), 21–27.

Dahl, R., Suleiman, A., Luna, B., Choudhury, S., Noble, K., Lupien, S., … Uncapher, M. R. (2017). *The adolescent brain: A second window to opportunity*. Florence, Italy: UNICEF Office of Research.

Dent, A., & Koenka, A. (2016). The relation between self-regulated learning and academic achievement across childhood and adolescence: A meta-analysis. *Education Psychology Review*, *28*, 425–474.

Dorn, C. M., Sabol, R., Madeja, S. S., & Sabol, F. R. (2014). *Assessing expressive learning: A practical guide for teacher-directed authentic assessment in K–12 visual arts education*. London, England: Routledge.

Efland, A. (2002). *Art and cognition: Integrating the visual art in the curriculum*. New York, NY: Teachers College Press.

Engeser, S., & Rheinberg, F. (2008). Flow, performance and moderators of challenge-skill balance. *Motivation and Emotion*, *32*(3), 158-172.

Every Student Succeeds Act (ESSA) of 2015, Pub. L. No. 114-95 § 114 Stat. 1177 (2015-2016).

Grant, L., & Gareis, C. (2015). *Teacher-made assessments: How to connect curriculum, instruction, and student learning*. London, England: Routledge.

Gute, D., & Gute, G. (2008). Flow writing in the liberal arts core and across the disciplines: A vehicle for confronting and transforming academic disengagement. *The Journal of General Education*, *57*, 191–222.

Heutte, J., Fenouillet, F., Kaplan, J., Martin-Krumm, C., & Bachelet, R. (2016). The EduFlow model: A contribution toward the study of optimal learning environments. In L.Harmat, F, Ø. Andersen, F. Ullén, J. Wright, & G. Sadlo (Eds.), *Flow experience: Empirical research and applications* (pp. 127–143). New York, NY: Springer. doi.org/10.1007/978-3-319-28634-1_9

Hwang, G. J., Hung, C. M., & Chen, N. S. (2014). Improving learning achievements, motivations and problem-solving skills through a peer assessment-based game development approach. *Educational Technology Research and Development*, *62*(2), 129–145.

Jackson, S. A., & Marsh, H. W. (1996). Development and validation of a scale to measure optimal experience: The flow state scale. *Journal of Sport and Exercise Psychology*, *18*(1), 17–35.

Jackson, S. A., Martin, A. J., & Eklund, R. C. (2008). Long and short measures of flow: The construct validity of the FSS-2, DFS-2, and new brief counterparts. *Journal of Sport and Exercise Psychology*, *30*, 561–587.

Kang, S. H. (2012). Structural relationship among the self-efficacy, self-directed learning ability, school adjustment, and learning flow in middle school students. *Journal of Fisheries and Marine Sciences Education*, *24*, 935–949.

Kawabata, M., & Mallett, C. J. (2011). Flow experience in physical activity: Examination of the internal structure of flow from a process-related perspective. *Motivation and Emotion, 35*, 393–402.

Kruger, J., & Dunning, D. (1999). Unskilled and unaware of it: How difficulties in recognizing one's own incompetence lead to inflated self-assessments. *Journal of Personality and Social Psychology, 77*(6), 1121–1134.

Kuhn, D., & Dean, D., Jr. (2004). Metacognition: A bridge between cognitive psychology and educational practice. *Theory Into Practice, 43*, 268–273.

Løvoll, H. S., & Vittersø, J. (2014). Can balance be boring? A critique of the "challenges should match skills" hypotheses in flow theory. *Social Indicators Research, 115*(1), 117–136.

Loyens, S. M., Magda, J., & Rikers, R. M. (2008). Self-directed learning in problem-based learning and its relationships with self-regulated learning. *Educational Psychology Review, 20*, 411–427.

Malone, T. W., & Lepper, M. R. (1987). Making learning fun: A taxonomy of intrinsic motivations for learning. In R. Snow & M. Farr (Eds.), *Aptitude, learning, and instruction volume 3: Cognitive and affective process analyses* (pp. 223–253). Hillsdale, NJ: Erlbaum.

Marzano, R. J., Pickering, D., Arredondo, D. E., Blackburn, G. J., Brandt, R. S., & Moffett, C. A. (1992). *Dimensions of learning*. Alexandria, VA: Association for Supervision and Curriculum Development.

McDaniel, M. A., Anderson, J. L., Derbish, M. H., & Morrisette, N. (2007). Testing the testing effect in the classroom. *European Journal of Cognitive Psychology, 19*, 494–513.

Meltzer, L. (Ed.). (2018). *Executive function in education: From theory to practice*. New York, NY: Guilford Press.

Metcalfe, J. (2011). Desirable difficulties and studying in the region of proximal learning. In A. S. Benjamin (Ed.), *Successful remembering and successful forgetting: A festschrift in honor of Robert A. Bjork* (pp. 259–276). New York, NY: Psychology Press.

Metcalfe, J., & Kornell, N. (2005). A region of proximal learning model of study time allocation. *Journal of Memory and Language, 52*(4), 463–477.

Metcalfe, J., & Kornell, N. (2007). Principles of cognitive science in education: The effects of generation, errors, and feedback. *Psychonomic Bulletin & Review, 14*(2), 225–229.

Moneta, G. B. (2012). On the measurement and conceptualization of flow. In S. Engeser (Ed.), *Advances in flow research* (pp. 23–50). New York, NY: Springer.

Moreno, R., & Valdez, A. (2005). Cognitive load and learning effects of having students organize pictures and words in multimedia environments: The role of student interactivity and feedback. *Educational Technology Research and Development, 53*(3), 35–45.

Moss, C. M., & Brookhart, S. M. (2012). *Learning targets: Helping students aim for understanding in today's lesson*. Alexandria, VA: Association for Supervision and Curriculum Development.

National Middle School Association. (2010). *This we believe: Keys to educating young adolescents*: Westerville, OH: Author.

Pekrun, R. (2006). The control-value theory of achievement emotions: Assumptions, corollaries, and implications for educational research and practice. *Educational Psychology Review, 18*, 315–341.

Reyes, M. R., Brackett, M. A., Rivers, S. E., White, M., & Salovey, P. (2012). Classroom emotional climate, student engagement, and academic achievement. *Journal of Educational Psychology, 104*, 700–712.

Riva, G., Waterworth, J. A., Waterworth, E. L., & Mantovani, F. (2011). From intention to action: The role of presence. *New Ideas in Psychology, 29*(1), 24–37.

Savery, J. R. (2015). Overview of problem-based learning: Definitions and distinctions. In A. Walker, H. Leary, C. Hmelo-Silver, & P. Ertmer (Eds.), *Essential readings in problem-based learning: Exploring and extending the legacy of Howard S. Barrows* (pp. 7–15). West Lafayette, IN: Purdue University Press.

Schmidt, J. A. (2010). Flow in education. In P. Peterson, E. L. Baker, & B. McGaw (Eds.), *International Encyclopedia of Education* (3rd ed., pp. 605–611). Oxford, England: Elsevier.

Schmidt, J. A., Shernoff, D. J., & Csikszentmihalyi, M. (2014). Individual and situational factors related to the experience of flow in adolescence. In M. Csikszentmihalyi (Ed.), *Applications of flow in human development and education* (pp. 379–405). Dordrecht, The Netherlands: Springer.

Schmoker, M. (2018). *Focus: Elevating the essentials to radically improve student learning.* Alexandria, VA: Association for Supervision and Curriculum Development.

Schmuck, R. A. (2006). *Practical action research for change.* Thousand Oaks, CA: Corwin Press.

Schmuck, R. A., & Schmuck, P. A. (1975). *Group processes in the classroom.* New York, NY: McGraw-Hill.

Seligman, M., Ernst, R., Gilham, J., Reivich, K., & Linkins, M. (2009). Positive education: Positive psychology and classroom interventions. *Oxford Review of Education, 35*(3), 293–311.

Shernoff, D. J., & Csikszentmihalyi, M. (2009). Flow in school revisited: Cultivating engaged learners and optimal learning environments. In R. Gilman, E. S. Huebner, & M. J. Furlong (Eds.), *Handbook of positive psychology in schools* (pp. 211–226). London, England: Routledge.

Shernoff, D. J., Csikszentmihalyi, M., Schneider, B., & Shernoff, E. S. (2014). Student engagement in high school classrooms from the perspective of flow theory. In M. Csikszentmihalyi (Ed.), *Applications of flow in human development and education* (pp. 475–494). Dordrecht, The Netherlands: Springer.

Soni, R. B. L. (2003). *Autotelic learning: A new learning approach for students of elementary classes.* New Delhi, India: Mittal Publications.

Spiro, R. J. (1988). *Cognitive flexibility theory: Advanced knowledge acquisition in ill-structured domains.* (Technical Report No. 441). Champaign, IL: Center for the Study of Reading, University of Illinois at Urbana-Champaign.

Stringer, E. T. (2014). *Action research* (4th ed.). Thousand Oaks, CA: SAGE.

Thapa, A., Cohen, J., Guffey, S., & Higgins-D'Alessandro, A. (2013). A review of school climate research. *Review of Educational Research, 83*, 357–385.

Tomlinson, C. A., & McTighe, J. (2006). *Integrating differentiated instruction & understanding by design: Connecting content and kids.* Alexandria, VA: Association for Supervision and Curriculum Development.

Walters, C. M. (2016). Choral singers "in the zone" toward flow through score study and analysis. *The Choral Journal, 57*(5), 8–19.

Zepeda, C. D., Richey, J. E., Ronevich, P., & Nokes-Malach, T. J. (2015). Direct instruction of metacognition benefits, adolescent science learning, transfer, and motivation: An in vivo study. *Journal of Educational Psychology, 107*(4), 954.

Zollars, J. (2018). *Flow theory and engagement: Observing engagement through the lens of flow in a middle school integrated maker space* (Doctoral dissertation). University of Pittsburgh. Retrieved from ProQuest Dissertations & Theses Global. (Order No. 10831894).

APPENDIX A

The Learning Experience Survey

1. What is your grade level?

   - 6th Grade
   - 7th Grade
   - 8th Grade

2. For which course are you filling out this form? *(students are presented this question only if they selected "6th Grade" on question 1).*

   - IRA Music
   - IRA Drama
   - IRA Visual Art
   - Chorus
   - Collaboration and Leadership
   - Woodwinds
   - Prelude Orchestra
   - Brass/Percussion

3. For which course are you filling out this form? *(students are presented this question only if they selected "7th Grade" on question 1).*

   - Digital Literacy
   - Design and Modeling
   - Speech Communication
   - Visual Arts and Media
   - Chorus (Vocal Ensemble)
   - Chorus (Lyric Singers)
   - Band
   - Navigating Informational Sources
   - Sinfonia Orchestra
   - Con Brio Orchestra

4. For which course are you filling out this form? *(students are presented this question only if they selected "8th Grade" on question 1).*

   - Chorus (Vocal Ensemble)
   - Chorus (Lyric Singers)

- Performance Seminar
- Entrepreneurship
- Automation and Robotics
- Visual Arts
- Digital Authorship
- Band
- Sinfonia Orchestra
- Con Brio Orchestra

5. What was your skill level with this activity?

- 1 (Beginner)
- 2
- 3
- 4 (Expert)

6. How challenging was this task?

- 1 (Super easy)
- 2
- 3
- 4 (Really hard)

7. Which of the following groups of words best describes your learning experience with this task?

- I felt totally engaged and excited to learn this.
- I felt comfortable and capable.
- I felt increasingly curious.
- I felt boredom.
- I felt anxious.
- I felt disengaged.
- I felt relaxed.
- I felt worried.

8. Please describe your learning experience.

9. Please describe how you changed the challenge to improve your skill level?

10. Please describe how you stretched your skill level to meet the challenge?

CHAPTER 11

"HOW WE ARE US"

Using Authentic Assessment in a History Classroom

Colleen Fitzpatrick
Wake Forest University

Stephanie van Hover
University of Virginia

ABSTRACT

In this case study, we explored how one history teacher, Mr. Crane, at a progressive middle school, integrated his instruction and assessment practices and how the students described their learning experiences from the classroom. We employed qualitative research methods to examine how and why Mr. Crane made instructional decisions based on the school context within which he worked. Using authentic intellectual work as a framework, analysis of the data indicated that Mr. Crane created a classroom where his eighth grade students became active participants and leaders in a yearlong project, a hand-drawn tapestry of U.S. history. In this chapter, we explore one unit of study, the Great Depression. Mr. Crane wove the tapestry into daily instruction, and the tapestry became the sole summative assessment.

Curriculum, Instruction, and Assessment:
Intersecting New Needs and New Approaches, pp. 279–303
Copyright © 2020 by Information Age Publishing
All rights of reproduction in any form reserved.

Students reported a high level of enjoyment of Mr. Crane's classroom and the tapestry. In addition to their engagement with the material, students also demonstrated a mastery of the historical content.

History courses in the middle grades have the potential to engage students in school because the nature of the content can "challenge young adolescents intellectually, help them develop informed opinions, and spur them to take action in their communities" (Conklin, 2008, p. 36). During this time of rapid developmental growth, middle schoolers "increasingly desire opportunities for voice and control" (Conklin, 2014, p. 456), which history classrooms can deliver, provided teachers offer authentic and challenging instruction and assessment that reflects history best practice. Effective teachers who engage in research-based best practice in history classrooms ask students to engage in "understanding and evaluating change and continuity over time and making appropriate use of historical evidence in answering questions and developing arguments about the past" (National Council for the Social Studies, 2013, p. 45). This vision of history education has students engage with historical content while also learning how to *do* history.

Yet the reality is that in most history classes, middle school students face a misalignment between their needs and the instruction and assessment they receive. As Brooks (2014) argued, middle schoolers "demonstrate an increased capacity for complex thought and desire to connect what they are learning to real-life situations," yet they experience history classrooms where instruction is "characterized by the transmission of isolated factual material and the absence of higher-order thinking" (p. 66). While the field of history education envisions history classrooms where students are active participants engaging in historical inquiry, assessments in history classrooms typically are in a multiple-choice format (Cuban, 2016). Additionally, as Smith (2018) argued, "Instruction tends to mirror the form and content of the tests that are used to assess students" (p. 2). Multiple-choice assessments, particularly in standards-based, high-stakes settings, drive instruction and compel teachers to rely on teacher-centric activities including lecture and worksheets (Au, 2007; Grant & Salinas, 2008; McEwin & Greene, 2010; Musoleno & White, 2010; Vogler & Virtue, 2007). Yet, reformers are calling for change in assessment practices in history classrooms, urging "new directions" in assessing history (Ercikan & Seixas, 2015; Reich, 2018) and greater use of authentic assessments, specifically performance assessments (Breakstone, 2014; Hernandez-Ramos & De La Paz, 2009; VanSledright, 2018). In this study, we explored how one teacher, pseudonym Mr. Crane, utilized a yearlong performance assessment that provided students with freedom, choice, and opportunities to engage in authentic work.

THEORETICAL FRAMEWORK

We draw on the framework for authentic intellectual work (AIW), research-based standards that Fred Newmann and his colleagues (Newmann, King, & Carmichael, 2007; Newmann, Marks, & Gamoran, 1996) developed. When engaging in AIW, students are required to "interpret, analyze, synthesize, or evaluate information rather than merely reproduce it" (DeWitt et al., 2013, pp. 385–386) and engage in "original application of knowledge and skills, rather than just routine use of facts and procedures" (King, Newmann, & Carmichael, 2009, p. 44). AIW uses three criteria (construction of knowledge, disciplined inquiry, and value beyond school) to guide teachers' instruction and assessment in the classroom. When students are engaging in "interpretation, analysis, synthesis, or evaluation," they are actively constructing knowledge "rather than merely retrieving or restating social studies facts, concepts, and definitions" (Newmann, King, & Carmichael, 2009, p. 58). This requires teachers to provide students with opportunities to engage in active work in the classroom and not rely on traditional forms of pedagogy in history classrooms, such as lecture. King, Newmann, and Carmichael (2009) argued that students need to do more than construct knowledge. Students need to be engaged in a disciplined inquiry that relies on their previous knowledge that seeks to promote a deep, complex understanding of a concept (Swan & Hofer, 2013). Finally, AIW goes beyond the classroom and attempts to influence the understanding or knowledge of a wider audience, requiring students to publicly present their work or have an intended audience outside the classroom teacher. This differs greatly from traditional multiple-choice tests, which typically only assesses the factual knowledge of the student, whether for the district, state, or classroom teacher. Thus, when engaging in AIW, students engage in "original application of knowledge and skills, rather than just routine use of facts and procedures" (King et al., 2009, p. 44). We use the criteria of AIW, grounded in the constructivist belief that knowledge is created between all participants in a classroom (van Hover & Hicks, 2017), to frame our study of Mr. Crane and his eighth grade U.S. history class.

LITERATURE REVIEW

We situate our study within research that explores student learning in history classrooms and draw from the authentic intellectual work (AIW) framework. Most of the research that examines student thinking in history centers around four main topics: (a) student understanding of history and historical narratives, (b) student interpretation and reading of sources,

(c) where students' ideas of history come from, and (d) what it means to think historically (Grant, 2001). Much of this research occurs outside the context of the classroom and involves interviews with students on topics disconnected from what they are experiencing in their history course (see Barton & Levstik, 1996; Barton & McCully, 2012; van Boxtel & van Drie, 2012). This work is significant and provides insight into student thinking about history. Yet many argue that an important, and understudied, focus is student learning *in context*—that is, the experiences of students in history classrooms versus students talking about history in settings outside a school or classroom setting (Barton & Avery, 2016; Monte-Sano, 2011; Reisman, 2012; van Hover & Hicks, 2017). Researchers have done little work in this area and almost none in middle school settings.

New Zealand researchers Graham Nuthall and Adrienne Alton-Lee (see Alton-Lee & Nuthall, 1990; Nuthall, 1996, 1999; Nuthall & Alton-Lee, 1993, 1995) conducted the substantive research on student learning in elementary classroom settings. Nuthall and Alton-Lee (1993) explored the relationship between teaching and learning to create an educational learning theory founded in classroom practice. To achieve this aim, they worked with classroom teachers to create assessments that aligned with the teachers' goals for the unit. Before the unit, students took a pretest. The researchers then conducted observations during the unit. At the end of the unit, the students took a posttest and participated in a think aloud of the posttest. During the unit, the researchers placed audio recorders near focal students to capture any conversations they engaged in during the unit. To collect evidence about whether or not students had retained substantive knowledge, or the factual content of history (Lee, 2005), the researchers had the focal students participate in a second think aloud one year after the conclusion of the unit. Then, Nuthall and Alton-Lee created "concept files" for each student and the concept they were supposed to learn. Based on the individual concept file, Nuthall and Alton-Lee could predict with relative accuracy (80–85%) whether students would answer test questions correctly (Brophy, 2006).

Nuthall (1999) found that student learning "results from the connections students make between newly evolving knowledge constructs and their background knowledge" (p. 335). Learning was not always based on what the teacher explicitly taught, but instead based on the "participation in those classroom activities in which students [were] required to recall and use their previous knowledge and experiences" (Nuthall, 2000, p. 248). Nuthall (1996) recognized that "every aspect of classroom life is complex, multilayered, and context dependent" (p. 209). Ultimately, student learning of substantive knowledge is a "dynamic interactive system" (p. 210) where "students' access to and participation in the learning activities of the classroom are structured by their negotiation of social status" (p. 211).

However, little research in history education has examined how contextual factors influence student learning of history, particularly in middle schools. The question is important as the field calls for a shift from history teaching as a didactic presentation of facts to a focus on historical thinking and inquiry. To assess this type of learning, such as historical writing (Monte-Sano, 2010) and source analysis (Smith, 2017), researchers are, as noted earlier, calling for performance assessments; that is, assessments *other* than multiple-choice tests that emphasize factual recall (Ercikan & Seixas, 2015; Smith, 2018). Performance assessments should be, by their very nature, an authentic form of measuring student learning.

Performance assessment is, as Darling-Hammond (2014) noted, "most easily defined by what it is not: specifically, it is not multiple-choice testing" (p. 15). Performance assessments can include projects, writing assignments, and other authentic activities that ask students to "construct an answer, produce a product, or perform an activity" for assessing "students' cognitive thinking and reasoning skills and their ability to apply knowledge to solve realistic, meaningful problems" (p. 15). This approach to assessment reflects the principles outlined by the 2010 position statement of the National Middle School Association (NMSA), *This We Believe*, which emphasized the importance of meaningful hands-on activities for middle school students that allow them to participate actively in and take control over their own learning. Educators continue to raise questions, however, of whether students learn 'as much' in classrooms promoting active learning and performance assessments as they do in teacher-centered classrooms. Some research suggests that performance assessment positively influences student learning in middle school history classrooms. In Hernandez-Ramos and De La Paz's (2009) study of two middle school history classrooms, they found that middle school students who participated in project-based learning, where they had greater control and freedom in the classroom, outperformed students who received traditional, teacher-centric instruction on an assessment of historical content knowledge. However, performance assessments are an understudied area in history education, particularly given the overwhelming dominance of multiple-choice testing in most school contexts.

In this study, we were interested in how students experienced learning in a context that promoted the use of performance assessment. Through a panel presentation to future teachers, we learned of a teacher, Mr. Crane (pseudonym), who was implementing a yearlong performance assessment in his middle school United States history class. His performance assessment, what he called a "tapestry," or a visual representation of a sequence of events, encouraged students to synthesize and apply what they had learned in each unit of study. Mr. Crane taught in a very particular context—an independent school with what we characterized as a 'progressive education' mission (Dewey, 1938) that seemed to reflect the principles outlined in *This We Believe* (NMSA, 2010) and promoted a vision of student-centered education with the teacher serving as facilitator. This unique context seemed like the perfect place to explore how middle school students experienced history teaching and learning in a student-centered setting that employed performance assessment. In this chapter, we describe the results of a study in which we purposefully sampled a teacher working in a school that embraced a progressive approach to education and did not require multiple-choice assessments but instead encouraged teachers to find new and non-traditional ways to assess student learning. We wondered what role the school context and teacher's particular approach to assessment would play in student learning of history as we focused on the Great Depression unit of the tapestry creation.

METHODOLOGY

We employed qualitative case study methodology to explore how a teacher, Mr. Crane, used a student led project (a tapestry) as both instruction and assessment in his classroom. We conducted observations in an eighth grade U.S. history course during an eight-day unit on the Great Depression. We were interested in the teacher's goals for the unit, what the students learned about the Great Depression, and how the teacher assessed his goals. Our research questions were as follows:

1. How does a teacher implement a student led project (the tapestry) that acts as both instruction and assessment?

   a. How does a teacher assess students' learning during a student led project?

2. What are students' experiences during the student led project?

   b. How does their experience relate to their learning of new knowledge and skills?

Context and Participants

The study took place in an eighth grade U.S. history class at Welsh School, a progressive PK–8 school, located in a small city in a mid-Atlantic state. At the time of the study, approximately 200 students, ranging from preschool to eighth grade, were enrolled at Welsh. The school consisted of four different buildings (a preschool, lower school (Grades K–5), a middle school (Grades 6– 8), and a gym). The school's philosophy centers on students and teachers acting as partners in the learning process. According to their mission statement, Welsh School wants to ensure that students have ownership over their own learning and emphasizes learning in authentic ways to give the students a sense of purpose of the content. Following this philosophy, the teacher becomes a facilitator in the classroom rather than the sole source of information. In an interview prior to implementing the Great Depression unit, the teacher Mr. Crane, a Caucasian male, described the school as a place where you could "teach your passion" and "fine tune your art of teaching." He believed that the school had "organically" created a sense of family where faculty worked to ensure that students became "the best they can be."

Mr. Crane had been teaching U.S. history for two and a half years, all at Welsh. Before entering teaching, Mr. Crane worked for 15 years as a financial analyst. He decided he wanted a career change and earned his master's degree in teaching and his social studies certification. While Mr. Crane taught history courses, he hoped to infuse his knowledge and background of economics into the classroom. He hoped of one day being able to "teach a personal finance class so [students] can make their own personal financial decisions and not have to be victims to the predatory lenders" that caused the recession in the 2000s. Mr. Crane taught all middle school social studies courses at Welsh including sixth grade world history, seventh grade U.S. history, and eighth grade U.S. history. Mr. Crane's goal was for all of his students to learn "how to be purposeful and analytical when they are viewing mass media …in such a way that they can make their own decisions."

The students. The eighth grade class at Welsh consisted of 10 students, six female and four male (see Table 11.1), who consented to be part of the study. Mr. Crane described the class as covering "the full spectrum… quiet ones, loud ones, talkers, analytical ones." He believed the class was "very artistic, musical, creative" and "really good examples of what we're trying to cultivate here … really caring, supportive of each other." When asked about his or her racial identity, every student in the classroom identified as White. Mr. Crane noted that this was representative of the larger Welsh community. According to Mr. Crane, there are very few minority students enrolled at Welsh as he described the school yearbook being "99.9% White."

Table 11.1.
Student Participants

Name	Gender	Racial Identity	Years at Welsh
Adam	Male	White	4 years
Chris	Male	White	4 years
George	Male	White	4 years
Michael	Male	White	3 years
Alicia	Female	White	4 years
Anne	Female	White	11 years
Michelle	Female	White	11 years
Nicole	Female	White	4 years
Rachel	Female	White	4.5 years
Selina	Female	White	12 years

Data Collection

To explore how students experienced learning in this context, we adapted Nuthall and Alton-Lee's (1995) protocol, described earlier in this chapter. While Nuthall and Alton-Lee's work focused on the moment-to-moment interactions students had with the specific instructional content, we focused our data collection and analysis on the teacher's larger instructional purposes, assessment practices, and the students' experiences in the classroom. Data collection included two, hour long interviews with the teacher (the first interview approximately one week before the unit began and the second interview approximately one week after the conclusion of student interviews), eight classroom observations each lasting 60–75 minutes (the entirety of the Great Depression unit), 10 semistructured interviews with the individual students, and collection of all student work (e.g., notes, worksheets) and teacher documents (e.g., rubrics, lesson plans) (Huberman & Miles, 2002). During the pre-unit interview, Mr. Crane explained his goals for the unit as well as how he planned to assess student learning through both summative and formative assessments (see Appendix A for interview protocols). We, along with Mr. Crane, developed a short-answer, pre-assessment for the unit based on his goals for the unit that mirrored the format of reflection questions Mr. Crane had used previously in the course. During the post-unit interview, Mr. Crane reflected on the unit, explained student performance on the assessments, and participated in a think aloud of the pre/post-assessment. (see Appendix A for interview protocols).

The day before the Great Depression unit began, the students completed the pre-assessment. These questions were intentionally general to allow students to draw on a wide breadth of knowledge. For example, the researchers asked students what the causes of the Great Depression were. During the eight instructional days, two video recorders were set up throughout the classroom in addition to one of the researchers taking detailed field notes. The researchers placed five audio recorders throughout the classroom to capture any student to student or student to teacher talk that would not have been captured by the video cameras or the observer. During the students' work on the assessment for the unit (the tapestry), each partner group was given a recorder to capture their group's discussions. After the unit's completion, students participated in a semistructured interview in which they reflected on what they learned in the unit, what classroom experiences they associated with their learning, and the process of designing the tapestry as well as the substantive knowledge they learned from it. Follow-up questions probed student misconceptions and clarified their thought process on the assessment (see Appendix A for interview protocols).

Data Analysis

Data analysis included many rounds of coding. The first round of data analysis included a holistic reading of the data corpus, making notes of any emergent themes (Gall, Gall, & Borg, 2015). The second round of data analysis focused on the classroom observations and used Mr. Crane's goals (causes, impacts, solutions) for the unit that he articulated during the pre-unit interview. We coded each classroom observation for how often (length and frequency) Mr. Crane or the students addressed one of the specific goals. The third round of coding focused on the instructional strategies and resources (e.g., video, graphic organizer) Mr. Crane used during the unit. The second and third rounds of data coding became the basis for what we called "item files" which allowed us to trace the instructional interactions a student had with the content (Nuthall & Alton-Lee, 1995). Because the assessment for the unit (the tapestry) was part of the instruction for the unit, we then coded the classroom moments related to the assessment for logistics (i.e. due date, partner work), historical content, design of the tapestry, teacher or student talk, and the audience of the conversation. The final round of analysis was the students' tapestries. The researchers analyzed the tapestries for the accuracy of the historical content as well as their alignment with Mr. Crane's goals for the unit.

FINDINGS

The Great Depression unit was the last unit of the year for Mr. Crane's class and lasted eight instructional days, approximately three calendar weeks. The class met three times a week, unless administration cancelled class for school assemblies or field trips. Mr. Crane had three main goals for the unit that he wanted the students to understand: the causes, impacts, and solutions of the Great Depression. When describing the causes of the Great Depression, Mr. Crane focused on the economic causes of the Great Depression, specifically the stock market crash. He wanted to ensure that students understood that the Great Depression was caused by "a systematic failure of a number of things" and that it "wasn't just one catastrophic thing that broke. It was all these bits and pieces." He told students during class that he wanted them to understand how the causes of the Great Depression led to "massive unemployment" and to see different "perspectives on how it impacted people's lives." Mr. Crane recognized there were "a million ways that people recovered" from the Great Depression, but the class was going to focus on "how the government stepped in and made changes." For the students to make sense of the causes, impacts, and solutions, Mr. Crane used a graphic representation to demonstrate how the goals connected to each other (see Figure 11.1).

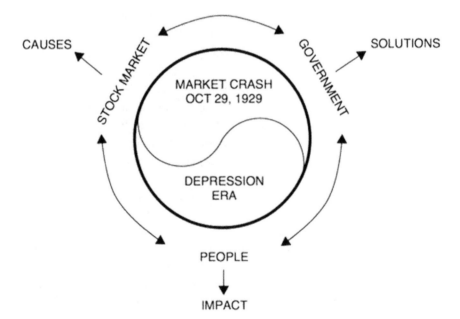

Figure 11.1.   Mr. Crane's diagram for the unit.

In addition to these goals, Mr. Crane also wanted to ensure that students understood the relevance of the Great Depression to modern times. He was particularly concerned about the students at Welsh because many of their parents were small business owners and "pretty wealthy." Mr. Crane was worried that "within the next 10 years, these kids will experience … going through a recession and possibly their lives being completely transformed." In the pre-unit interview, Mr. Crane frequently discussed the difficulties his contemporaries from college had experienced during the 2008 recession and how he wanted the students to avoid those same mistakes. Mr. Crane provided examples of how his friends suffered financially because they had fundamental misunderstandings of credit. He recalled how many of his classmates were put into debt because they used credit cards to buy "scooters and jackets and shoes and stuff and didn't realize that they had to pay it all back." Using the Great Depression as a historical backdrop, Mr. Crane wanted students to learn the basics of what credit is and how to use it wisely. To do this, Mr. Crane wanted students to understand the cyclical nature of the economy and how recessions and mini-depressions "happened over and over and over again."

Mr. Crane's Great Depression unit lasted eight instructional days and one day for student presentations of their tapestry. The unit began with an overview of the stock market before moving to learning about life during the Great Depression, and finally the class covered the New Deal. Interspersed throughout the instructional days were entire class periods dedicated to the assessment for the unit (see Table 11.2).

Mr. Crane's Assessments: The Tapestry

Mr. Crane described his approach to assessment as "not really focus[ed] on the dates or the names"; instead he "focus[ed] on the whys and the hows." Mr. Crane would occasionally use a multiple-choice test when there was a lot of factual information that he wanted students to learn, but more frequently he assigned the students papers or performance assessments to assess their knowledge and understanding of the topic. He discussed how this approach to assessment allowed the students to "do the work" rather "than me do the work." Mr. Crane explained that he wanted his instruction and assessment to be intertwined to bring out "the explorer and the creative part" of students and to "feed their need for exploration and curiosity."

As part of his approach to assessment and instruction, Mr. Crane wanted the students to engage in a yearlong project. Based on his previous experience and conversations with parents, Mr. Crane was particularly concerned about students' understanding of chronology of U.S. history. Mr. Crane

Table 11.2.
Unit Outline

Day	Content Focus	Instructional Approaches
Day 1	Unit Introduction Stock Market	Lecture
Day 2	---	Tapestry
Day 3	Stock Market Crash Economic Concepts/Terms	Personal Finance Reflection Video Lecture Journal Writing
Day 4	Life in the Great Depression	NPR Article Lecture
Day 5	Dust Bowl Life in the Great Depression	Visual Discovery Video Article: Hoover and Roosevelt's Inauguration
Day 6	New Deal	Website Jigsaw
Day 7	---	Tapestry
Day 8	---	Tapestry
Day 9	---	Student Presentations

first came up with the idea of having the students create a tapestry during a social studies methods course that he took during his master's program a few years prior. While he did not remember if the professor had outlined the project during the class, he remembered thinking of ways to include a tapestry project in his class. At the beginning of the school year, Mr. Crane and the students began creating a tapestry that represented the whole of the course content. At the beginning of the year, the students had examined the Bayeux Tapestry, an 11th century tapestry that depicts the early history of Great Britain through the Battle of Hastings and the ascension of William the Conqueror to the throne. Mr. Crane created the tapestry project based on the Bayeux Tapestry and wanted the students to depict the history of the United States in a continuous story. The students designed the panel using a variety of hand-drawn images and brief written statements. For example, during their unit on Reconstruction, the students drew images depicting the Supreme Court case *Plessy v. Ferguson*, the Supreme Court case establishing the precedence of separate but equal, with the specter of Abraham Lincoln in the background with speech bubbles stating why he was disappointed in what was happening in

America. One of the students, Michael, described a particular panel that he specifically remembered. For their panel on industrialization, they drew a "train coming towards you and on the train tracks in front of you … were words." The class created the tapestry entirely during class time and each student was responsible for a certain aspect of each panel (e.g., planning, drawing, coloring, writing). Each panel was approximately three feet by two feet and made of white butcher paper. The entire tapestry consisted of nineteen individual panels, including the ones from the Great Depression unit. The class created most of the panels as a whole, but some panels were done in smaller groups to cover all the content. In some units, Mr. Crane assigned additional summative assessments, such as a research project on an artist during the Harlem Renaissance unit. However, in the Great Depression unit, the tapestry was the only summative assessment.

Weaving a Tapestry

The tapestry was an ever-present topic in Mr. Crane's classroom as students and Mr. Crane would mention previous units or referenced tapestry panels the students had already created. Students understood clearly what Mr. Crane expected from the tapestry and what they were supposed to do, both behaviorally and academically, when working on the tapestry. When discussing with the students about the tapestry for the Great Depression for the first time, Mr. Crane spent less than two minutes outlining his expectations for the assignment. He then assigned partners and told students when they needed to have their tapestry completed. The students had very few questions for Mr. Crane about the logistics of what they were supposed to do. Anne was the only student who asked a clarifying question to Mr. Crane, inquiring whether the tapestry needed to cover "just the Depression or the Depression and the New Deal." Mr. Crane responded that the students needed to "turn back to [their] first page of notes" and he expected the tapestry to "explain the initial image I drew for you guys … the yin and yang" from the first day of the Great Depression unit. Various students vocally responded with yeses and pulled out their notebook to find the image. After this clarification, the students began to work with their partner, and Mr. Crane did not address the whole class until he was reminding them to wrap up for the day.

The students then began to plan the physical layout of their tapestry as well as to determine what historical content they wanted to include on their tapestry. Most of the groups began discussing what the images on the tapestry would be before thinking about the content they needed or what writing they would add to the tapestry. George and Michael were the only pair who reviewed the content before discussing what they could actually draw. While they had a vague plan of doing "some cool Cuphead thing," where they compared the New Deal to the video game Cuphead, most of their initial conversation centered on reviewing the historical information they wanted to include on their tapestry. The other four pairs of students discussed the images they could include on the tapestry and how they could organize the entire panel.

Three pairs (Chris/Rachel, Anne/Selina, Adam/Michelle) decided to plan their sheet around three separate images that depicted change over time. Anne and Selina planned to depict change over time by drawing images of New York City and its appearance before, during, and after the Great Depression. Anne and Selina worked collaboratively to draw their sketch of the tapestry. They frequently would shout out ideas and grab the pencil from the other person to sketch out their ideas. The two girls appeared to work well together and did not get frustrated or have outbursts when the other student grabbed the pencil. Similar to Anne and Selina, the other partners appeared to work collaboratively and engaged in a free exchange of ideas. For example, Nicole and Alicia went through three plans for their tapestry before they settled on their final idea. Each time either Nicole or Alicia made a suggestion, the other student acknowledged her idea before they mutually made a decision about whether to continue with that idea. One of the ideas that they dismissed included an image of a building with multiple columns that covered the entire tapestry sheet. Nicole suggested that the "building has different pillars and each pillar is one of the four pillars [of the New Deal]." Alicia stated, "We could try that" and they began to sketch out what the image might look like. After just a few minutes drawing, Nicole dismissed the idea saying, "forget everything I just said." Alicia encouraged Nicole to keep thinking of ideas and eventually the two decided to create a tapestry piece with a large dollar bill as the focal piece. Observations and audio-recordings of student conversations indicated that the students remained collegial and encouraging of the other students. Whether how to work as partners had been an emphasis of Mr. Crane's throughout the year or not is unclear, but the students understood how to work as partners and to treat their group mates with respect.

Data analysis of the student conversations revealed that students spent a high majority of the time on task, either discussing the visual layout of the poster or what historical content to include on the tapestry. While students spent the majority of time on task, they would frequently slide in and out of social conversation or relate their tapestry with other interests. The students would monitor themselves and return the conversation to the Great Depression and the tapestry without Mr. Crane having to remind the class to stay on task.

The Tapestries

Each partner group submitted a tapestry that they presented to the class on the last day of the unit. The students pinned up the tapestries around the classroom and participated in a gallery walk where they observed the other groups' tapestries. During the gallery walk, students asked each other questions about their design of the tapestry and discussed the tapestries in a very informal way. When the gallery walk was finished, Mr. Crane attached all five of the Great Depression pieces to the tapestry the students had created throughout the year.

While the student tapestries were very different in the images that they included, data analysis revealed many similarities. Four groups (Anne/Selina, Michelle/Adam, George/Michael, Chris/Rachel) divided their tapestry into three sections to represent Mr. Crane's three goals (causes, impacts, solutions) for the unit. Each panel or section included one image and a paragraph of writing near the image to explain the causes, examples, or solutions. For example, in their section on the impacts of the Great Depression, Michelle and Adam drew a group of people who had empty wallets and were carrying job applications. They wrote:

> Unemployment skyrocketed like never before. People never knew when they would have a job. They might get hired one morning and fired the next. Some effects included [:] more than 6,000 people selling apples for 5¢ or less, zippers gaining insane popularity, 2.5 million people were moving to the Great Plains, the top 1% of people owned 33% of things in the U.S. Even the people who moved west still got wiped out. The Dust Bowl wiped out hundreds of farms, houses, and families in the Great Plains.

Michelle and Adam took the facts for their write-up from the notes they had taken during the second day of the Great Depression Unit. On this day, Mr. Crane told the students a series of "fun facts" about the Great Depression. While not required to, Adam had written down each of the "fun facts" in his notebook, which he told us he relied on for all of the tapestry creations. Michelle and Adam's tapestry, both its images and writing, reflects the tapestries that Anne/Selina, George/Michael, and Chris/Rachel created. The students focused on the larger idea of how the lives of Americans changed over time due to the Great Depression.

Alicia and Nicole created a vastly different tapestry, both in images and writing, than their classmates. They created a singular image that covered the entire tapestry and had writing throughout. Alicia and Nicole turned the tapestry page into a large dollar bill that featured an image of Franklin Roosevelt in the center. In each of the four corners, where the monetary value is typically located, they described each of four pillars of the New Deal (civic uplift, job creation, improvement in public works, and economic recovery) that Mr. Crane had addressed during the sixth day of the unit. Each section provided a brief overview of what the pillar was and how it helped solve some of the issues from the Great Depression. In their section on economic recovery, Alicia and Nicole wrote, "The New Deal stabilized banks and prices for industry and agriculture. It helped bankrupt state and local governments." In the center of the bill, Alicia and Nicole wrote a longer, three-paragraph narrative of the Great Depression. Each of the paragraphs was dedicated to the causes, impacts, or solutions of the Great Depression. More than the other four groups, Alicia and Nicole focused on the New Deal and the solutions of the Great Depression. While they wrote briefly on the causes and impacts, the majority of the image and writing focused on how the New Deal solved the problems of the Great Depression. While Alicia and Nicole did mention the causes and impacts in writing, unlike the other groups, they did not depict them in images, nor did they take the approach of depicting change over time. During the gallery walk on the last day of the unit, Alicia and Nicole's tapestry caused the most discussion amongst the students. When Mr. Crane asked the class if they had to choose one tapestry to add to the full tapestry, the class almost unanimously choose Alicia and Nicole's tapestry. Alicia and Nicole did not vote for themselves; instead, they split their votes between two other tapestries.

Assessing the Tapestries

When Mr. Crane was reflecting on the unit in his post-unit interview, he was pleased with what the students had created. He discussed how the students created "superior" tapestry pieces which was based on "all the scaffolding early on" in the year that he provided. Mr. Crane wanted to give the students flexibility in their tapestry pieces and stated that the tapestry was:

> Not intended to be a burden. It's not intended to be high pressure because
> I found that once you start having 32 points that you need to check off,
> then the creativity really goes down, and I think that the connection that
> they make in their brain is weaker.

Mr. Crane reflected that by not giving the students as much structure or requirements for the tapestry, the students had greater "ownership" over the project and were self-motivated to produce a quality product.

While Mr. Crane was pleased with the quality of the tapestries the students created, the assessment of the tapestries focused on the process of creating the product. For the tapestry and other student-created projects, Mr. Crane used a rubric that the teachers and administrators developed at Welsh in conjunction with a professor at a local university. The rubric had three options, which Mr. Crane described in general as "they can't do it on their own, they can do it with help, or they can do it on their own." Teachers at Welsh school use this rubric across all disciplines in the middle school. The teachers check which level students are at for the specific assignment and then provide a written description as to why they chose the level and how students can improve. This philosophy of assessment aligned with Mr. Crane's personal philosophy toward assessment. He believed he was "not asking too much from [the students], but what I am asking for is a solid effort and focus and dedication to it."

For this particular tapestry assignment, all of the students scored on the top level "can do it on their own." While Mr. Crane stated that all students "took it to the next level and wanted to do their own thing" on the tapestry, he was particularly impressed with Michelle and Adam's tapestry. He thought it was very creative of them to use "the graph of the stock market … as a timeline to explain the other components." He was not surprised that the class voted to add Alicia and Nicole's tapestry to the larger tapestry. Mr. Crane considered Alicia as the "artist" of the class and created the tapestry piece that "looked the best," but her tapestry did not cover all the information that Michelle and Adam's did. Despite the class voting to include Alicia and Nicole's tapestry piece, Mr. Crane attached all five. He felt that the students had worked hard on their pieces and wanted their work represented on the larger tapestry.

Student Reflections on the Unit

Data analysis of the pre-assessment and post-assessment questions indicated that students clearly learned some historical information during the unit (see Table 11.3). The students also entered the unit with prior knowledge about the Great Depression. Specifically, Adam and Michelle both correctly answered four questions on the pre-assessment. However, not surprisingly, their answers on the post-assessment provided a greater level of detail and specificity.

On the post-assessment, all 10 students correctly answered the three questions (questions 1, 3, and 4) associated with what they were supposed to include on the tapestry. Despite the fact that they all answered these questions correctly, when asked how they learned the information to answer the question or when they remembered the content of the question coming up in class, only two students (Nicole and Alicia) mentioned the tapestry (see Table 11.4). Most students relied on classroom activities other than the tapestry as to how they remembered information. While most students did not associate their learning with the tapestry on the post-assessment, the students appeared to have much clearer understandings of the causes, impacts, and solutions of the Great Depression than they did other assessment questions.

Table 11.3.
Student Learning on Pre/Post-Assessment

Question	Number of students who answered correctly on the pre-assessment	Number of students who answered correctly on the post-assessment
1. What were the causes of the Great Depression?	4	10
2. What does it mean to buy something on credit?	2	4
3. What ended the Great Depression?	2	10
4. How did the Great Depression change the lives of Americans?	6	10
5. How did the federal government respond to the Great Depression?	0	8

Table 11.4.
Classroom Activities Associated With Student Learning

Question	Mr. Crane	Video	Tapestry	Prior Knowledge	Website	Handout	Simulation	Talked	Unsure
1	3	4	2	1		1	1		
2	3							1	1
3	2				8				
4		1	1	1		7	1		
5	2				5	2		2	

Note: Some rows add to more than 10 because students discussed multiple classroom activities.

Students described their experiences with the tapestry in very positive terms. All 10 students reported enjoying working on the tapestry albeit for a variety of reasons. Seven students (Alicia, Nicole, George, Michael, Michelle, Selina, Rachel) enjoyed working on the tapestry because they believed it helped them to better learn and remember information. Selina discussed how the tapestry "helps us understand the topics more because even without researching, we're drawing about it and writing about it." She appreciated the opportunity to recode the information they learned during class on the tapestry. Rachel thought the "reason that we do [the tapestry] is because every time I make a tapestry; I kind of remember that image in my head more." Rachel was able to visualize the different tapestry panels, which she believed helped her retain the information more. Rachel provided a second reason as to why she enjoyed working on the tapestry. She liked to look back at the tapestry panels from previous units because it helped her understand "how we are us"—that is, the tapestry panels explained how America developed into the country it is today.

The three remaining students (Adam, Anne, Chris) all stated they enjoyed working on the tapestry, but they did not relate the tapestry to their learning or the content from the class. Adam enjoyed working on the tapestry because he felt accomplished by the amount of work that they had put into the tapestry. He found it "satisfying and it's kind of cool that we'll look back at when we were learning about Appomattox and the end of the Civil War and like whoa." Similar to Rachel, Adam enjoyed looking at the tapestry as a whole, but unlike Rachel, instead of looking at the historical content, he reflected on the amount of work the class had put into the tapestry. Anne enjoyed working on the tapestry because "it's kind of almost like a break kind of, but it's really fun because you get to switch positions because sometimes you draw, sometimes you do the writing part, sometimes you're on the planning part."

DISCUSSION AND CONCLUSION

Mr. Crane's classroom provides an example of what a middle school classroom could look like when students become active participants in the classroom to take control of their own learning. Mr. Crane afforded students in his classroom choice, freedom, and control over both the content and the form of the tapestry. Mr. Crane acted as a guide and facilitator of student learning rather than attempting to control every action of students in the classroom. While many teachers fear giving up control to students, Mr. Crane relished in it and believed that for students to learn, they *had* to have ownership of the classroom. Clearly, the students responded. Even though most students did not relate their learning to the tapestry on the post assessment, some correlation existed between their work on the tapestry and the fact that all 10 students were able to answer correctly the assessment questions related to the tapestry. This supports Grant's (2003) argument that it is impossible to establish "a direct and causal connection" (p. 58) between teaching and learning. However, relationships between teacher's instruction and what students learn can be understood (Nuthall & Alton-Lee, 1995). While Mr. Crane worked in a progressive context that allowed more freedom than teachers may experience when facing the pressures of standardized testing, he provides an example for what instruction and assessment could look like in middle school history classrooms.

Within the frame of AIW and principles of the NMSA (now Association for Middle Level Education), Mr. Crane had varying levels of success of implementing a performance assessment that required students to become active participants in their learning. Students engaged in the construction of knowledge for their tapestry by synthesizing information from a variety of sources, provided by Mr. Crane, to make a visual argument about the causes, impacts, and solutions of the New Deal. Mr. Crane asked the students to use evidence to create an argument and organize information, a developmentally appropriate task according to the National Council of the Social Studies (2013). Through disciplined inquiry, students displayed a deep understanding of the Great Depression that "capture[d] the essence, nuances, and analogs of a particular topic" (Scheurman & Newmann, 1998, p. 24). The complex imagery of the tapestry demonstrated students' ability to understand both factual and conceptual knowledge (VanSledright & Limon, 2006). Lastly, there was a clear value for the tapestry outside of the classroom. Students were actively engaged in the tapestry with the understanding that it would be displayed in the school for future classes. While there was no formal presentation of the tapestry to the school or parents, it was displayed in the school during the students' "Step-Up" ceremony where they celebrated their completion of eighth grade. The students saw their creation of the tapestry along the same lines as the artists of the Bayeux tapestry. They had created a piece of artwork that would last beyond their time in Mr. Crane's classroom. For the students and Mr. Crane, this project had clear value and translated easily into real world work. While most of the students did not consider themselves artists or have any desire to enter into an artistic career, they still took pride in what they had created.

As middle level educators continue to grapple with the realities of teaching adolescents in the 21st century, they must consider ways for students to become active participants in the classroom and to have an ownership over their learning. By using assessments outside of traditional multiple-choice tests, teachers have the ability to create assessments that assess students' understanding of the domain of history knowledge, as opposed to only substantive knowledge, and allow students to have more freedom to participate in hands on learning. These types of assessment have the ability to increase integration between the disciplines, which allows for students to "understand the world and to advance a democratic way of life" (Hinde, 2015, p. 28). Mr. Crane created a classroom, supported by his administration, where assessment and instruction could be interwoven, and his assessment emphasized the "process rather than the product."

REFERENCES

Alton-Lee, A., & Nuthall, G. (1990). Pupil experiences and pupil learning in the elementary classroom: An illustration of a generative methodology. *Teaching and Teacher Education, 6,* 27–45.

Au, W. (2007). High-stakes testing and curricular control: A qualitative metasynthesis. *Educational Researcher, 36,* 258–267. doi:10.3102/0013189x07306523

Barton, K. C., & Avery, P. G. (2016). Research on social studies education: Diverse students, settings, and methods. In C. A. Bell & G. Gitomer (Eds.), *Handbook of research on teaching* (5th ed., pp. 985–1038). Washington, DC: American Educational Research Association.

Barton, K. C., & Levstik, L. S. (1996). "Back when God was round and everything": Elementary children's understanding of historical time. *American Educational Research Journal, 33,* 419–454.

Barton, K. C., & McCully, A. W. (2012). Trying to "see things differently": Northern Ireland students' struggle to understand alternative historical perspectives. *Theory & Research in Social Education, 40,* 371–408. doi.org/10.1080/009331 04.2012.710928

Breakstone, J. (2014). Try, try, try again: The process of designing new history assessments. *Theory and Research in Social Education, 42,* 453–485.

Brooks, S. (2014). Connecting the past to the present in the middle-level classroom: A comparative case study. *Theory and Research in Social Education, 42,* 65–95.

Brophy, J. (2006). Graham Nuthall and social constructivist teaching: Research-based cautions and qualifications. *Teaching and Teacher Education, 22,* 529–537.

Conklin, H. G. (2008). Promise and problems in two divergent pathways: Preparing social studies teachers for the middle school level. *Theory and Research in Social Education, 36,* 36–65.

Conklin, H. G. (2014). Toward more joyful learning: integrating play into frameworks of middle grades teaching. *American Educational Research Journal, 51,* 1227–1255.

Cuban, L. (2016). *Teaching history then and now: A story of stability and change in schools.* Boston, MA: Harvard Education Press.

Darling-Hammond, L. (2014). *Next generation assessment: Moving beyond the bubble test to support 21st century learning.* San Francisco, CA: Jossey Bass.

Dewey, J. (1938). *Education and experience.* New York, NY: Macmillan.

DeWitt, S. W., Patterson, N., Blankenship, W., Blevins, B., DiCamillo, L., Gerwin, D., & Saye, J. (2013). The lower-order expectations of high-stakes tests: A four-state analysis of social studies standards and test alignment. *Theory & Research in Social Education, 41,* 382–427.

Ercikan, K., & Seixas, P. (Eds.). (2015). *New directions in assessing historical thinking.* New York, NY: Routledge. doi:10.4324/9781315779539

Gall, M. D., Gall, J. P., & Borg, W. R. (2015). *Applying educational research* (7th ed.). Boston, MA: Pearson.

Grant, S. G. (2001). It's just the facts, or is it? The relationship between teachers' practices and students' understandings of history. *Theory & Research in Social Education, 29,* 65–108. doi:10.1080/00933104.2001.10505930

Grant, S. G. (2003). *History lessons: Teaching, learning, and testing in U.S. high school classrooms.* Mahwah, NJ: Erlbaum.

Grant, S. G., & Salinas, C. (2008). Assessment and accountability in the social studies. In L. S. Levstik & C. A. Tyson (Eds.), *Handbook of research in social studies education* (pp. 219–238). New York, NY: Routledge.

Hernandez-Ramos, P., & De La Paz, S. (2009). Learning history in middle school by designing multimedia in a project-based learning experience. *Journal of Research on Technology in Education, 42*(2), 151–173.

Hinde, E. R. (2015). The theoretical foundations of curriculum integration and its application in social studies instruction. In L. Bennett & E. R. Hinde (Eds.), *Becoming integrated thinkers: Case studies in elementary social studies* (pp. 9–20). Silver Spring, MD: National Council for the Social Studies.

Huberman, M., & Miles, M. B. (2002). *The qualitative researcher's companion.* Thousand Oaks: SAGE.

King, M. B., Newmann, F. M., & Carmichael, D. L. (2009). Authentic intellectual work: Common standards for teaching social studies. *Social Education, 73,* 43–49.

Lee, P. (2005). Putting principles into practice: Understanding history. In M. S. Donovan & J. D. Bransford (Eds.), *How students learn: History in the classroom* (pp. 31–77). Washington, DC: The National Academies Press.

McEwin, C., & Greene, M. (2010). Results and recommendations from the 2009 national surveys of randomly selected and highly successful middle level schools. *Middle School Journal, 42*(1), 49–63.

Monte-Sano, C. (2010). Disciplinary literacy in history: An exploration of the historical nature of adolescents' writing. *The Journal of the Learning Sciences, 19,* 539–568.

Monte-Sano, C. (2011). Beyond reading comprehension and summary: Learning to read and write in history by focusing on evidence, perspective, and interpretation. *Curriculum Inquiry, 41,* 212–249. doi:10.1111/j.1467-873X.2011.00547.x

Musoleno, R., & White, G. (2010). Influences of high-stakes testing on middle school mission and practice. *Research in Middle Level Education Online, 34*(3), 1–10. Retrieved from https://files.eric.ed.gov/fulltext/EJ914055.pdf

National Council for the Social Studies. (2013). *College, career, and civic life framework for social studies state standards.* Silver Spring, MD: Author. Retrieved from https://www.socialstudies.org/sites/default/files/2017/Jun/c3-framework-for-social-studies-rev0617.pdf

National Middle School Association. (2010). *This we believe: Keys to educating young adolescents.* Westerville, OH: Author.

Newmann, F. M., King, M. B., & Carmichael, D. L. (2007). *Authentic instruction and assessment: Common standards for rigor and relevance in teaching academic subjects.* Des Moines, IA: Iowa Department of Education.

Newmann, F. M., King, M. B., & Carmichael, D. L. (2009). *Teaching for authentic intellectual work: Standards and scoring criteria for teachers' tasks, student performance and instruction.* Minneapolis, MN: Tasora.

Newmann, F. M., Marks, H. M., & Gamoran, A. (1996). Authentic pedagogy and student performance. *American Journal of Education, 104,* 280–312.

Nuthall, G. (1996). Commentary: Of learning and language and understanding the complexity of the classroom. *Educational Psychologist, 31*, 207–214.

Nuthall, G. (1999). The way students learn: Acquiring knowledge from an integrated science and social studies unit. *The Elementary School Journal, 99*, 303–341.

Nuthall, G. (2000). The anatomy of memory in the classroom: Understanding how students acquire memory processes from classroom activities in science and social studies units. *American Educational Research Journal, 37*, 247–304.

Nuthall, G., & Alton-Lee, A. (1993). Predicting learning from student experience of teaching: A theory of student knowledge construction in classrooms. *American Educational Research Journal*, 30, 799–840.

Nuthall, G., & Alton-Lee, A. (1995). Assessing classroom learning: How students use their knowledge and experience to answer classroom achievement test questions in science and social studies. *American Educational Research Journal, 32*, 185–223.

Reich, G. (2018). The center fails: Devolving assessment authority to educators. In K. W. Meuwissen & P. G. Fitchett (Eds.), *Social studies in the new education policy era: Introducing conversations on purposes, perspectives, and practices* (pp. 152–157). New York, NY: Routledge.

Reisman, A. (2012). The 'Document-Based Lesson': Bringing disciplinary inquiry into high school history classrooms with adolescent struggling readers. *Journal of Curriculum Studies, 44*, 233–264.

Scheurman, G., & Newmann, F. M. (1998). Authentic intellectual work in social studies: Putting performance before pedagogy. *Social Education, 62*, 23–26.

Smith, M. D. (2017). Cognitive validity: Can multiple-choice items tap historical thinking processes? *American Educational Research Journal, 54*, 1256–1287.

Smith, M. D. (2018). New multiple-choice measures of historical thinking: An investigation of cognitive validity. *Theory and Research in Social Education, 46*, 1–34.

Swan, K., & Hofer, M. (2013). Examining student-created documentaries as a mechanism for engaging students in authentic intellectual work. *Theory & Research in Social Education, 41*, 133-175.

Van Boxtel, C., & van Drie, J. (2012). "That's in the time of the Romans!" Knowledge and strategies students use to contextualize historical images and documents. *Cognition and Instruction, 30*, 113–145.

van Hover, S., & Hicks, D. (2017). Social constructivism and students learning in social studies. In M. Manfra & C. Bolick (Eds.), *The handbook of social studies research* (pp. 270–286). Malden, MA: Wiley Blackwell.

VanSledright, B. (2018). Reframing the narrative: Research on how students learn as the basis for assessment policy. In K. W. Meuwissen & P. G. Fitchett (Eds.), *Social studies in the new education policy era: Introducing conversations on purposes, perspectives, and practices* (pp. 145–151). New York, NY: Routledge.

VanSledright, B., & Limon, M. (2006). Learning and teaching social studies: A review of cognitive research in history and geography. In P. Alexander & P. Winne (Eds.), *Handbook of educational psychology* (pp. 545–570). Mahwah, NJ: Erlbaum.

Vogler, K. E., & Virtue, D. (2007). " Just the facts, ma'am": Teaching social studies in the era of standards and high-stakes testing. *The Social Studies, 98*(2), 54–58.

APPENDIX A

Interview Protocols

Teacher Protocol (Pre-Unit)

Background:

- How long have you been teaching? How long have you been teaching this particular course?
- What is your educational background?
- Why did you decide to work in this school?
- Would you ever teach in a public school?
- Describe the class—what are the students like?
- Why did you want to teach social studies?
- Why do you find it important?

Learning Targets & Assessment of Student Learning

- What do you hope to accomplish during this unit of study?
- How do you approach planning for this unit?
- In this unit, what are your objectives or learning targets?
- What is your approach to assessment?
- How would you describe your teaching style?
- At the end of the unit, what do you want students to know, understand and be able to do?

Teacher Protocol (Post-Unit)

- How did the unit go?
- Why these instructional approaches?
- Did you meet your learning targets? How do you know?
- How do you think the tapestry went? Do you agree with the students' selection?
- How do you assess the tapestry?
- Talk through the test (what's the right answer, why is it the right answer, point to when the students would have learned it)?
- Let's talk through the assessment data. What jumps out at you? How do you think students learned [identify topics]?

Student Interview Protocol

1. Name & Age & Grade
2. Describe yourself to someone who has never met you.
3. How long have you lived in [town name]?
4. What school are you going to next year? Excited? Why that school?
5. Play sports/extracurricular
6. Overall experiences with school
7. What do you do for fun? What next in life?
8. Experiences with [insert social studies class]
9. What history class did you take last year?
10. What is history? Why do we study history?

Show each student an unanswered copy of the test. For each item on the post-assessment, ask each student to describe the correct answer, to recall how he or she had learned that answer, and to recall any experiences or activities that were relevant to learning the answer.

Ask student: "Please say anything that comes to mind as you answered the questions, any mental pictures, feelings or thoughts. Think aloud, so that you can talk as you are thinking, so that I can understand."

Prompts for each item:

a. How did you learn (know) that?
b. Where did you learn that?
c. Do you remember that coming up in class?
d. Was there anything said or done about that in class?
e. Where would you have seen (heard about) that?
f. Did you know that before the unit?
g. Did you learn that during class?

Tapestry Questions:

*   Explain your poster.
*   Why did you do it that way? Would you change anything about it?
*   What is a tapestry?
*   Have you enjoyed the tapestry?
*   What have you learned from the tapestry?
*   What sites do you do for your paragraphs? How do you know what to write?

CHAPTER 12

MIDDLE SCHOOLERS' WRITING OUT OF SCHOOL

(Fear), Freedom, Fluency, and Fellowship in Place-Based Education

Tom Meyer
State University of New York, New Paltz

ABSTRACT

During a period when U.S. education policy encroached upon teachers' curricular agency and narrowed definitions for writing curriculum, in this study, the author showed how middle level students, and to a lesser extent, their teachers, perceived the merging of school-ish work—writing—in place-based, out of school, summer settings. The author, a director of a northeastern site of the National Writing Project, analyzed data from nine weeklong, immersive summer youth writing programs. Data included program surveys from adolescent participants ($n = 138$), with a focus on middle level student surveys ($n = 88$), informal interviews of middle level students ($n = 8$) and teachers ($n = 12$), and participant observation. The thirdspace analysis describes place-based writing programs and the freedoms that they afford teachers and students. Teachers and their students appreciated selectively exploring topics

Curriculum, Instruction, and Assessment:
Intersecting New Needs and New Approaches, pp. 305–338
Copyright © 2020 by Information Age Publishing
All rights of reproduction in any form reserved.

of interest, set in proximal places; they valued being outdoors in natural set-tings with opportunities to move and opportunities to be alone and think. This work adds to place-based education literature, suggesting that when middle level students experience process-oriented writing instruction in out-of-school settings, they may develop *fluency* as writers.

One Friday morning, a 12-year old student, Sergio, remarked, "Going outside and sitting and just writing, I felt so free."[1] Picture Sergio, 24 hours earlier, sitting on a rock next to a stream, just steps away from a winding forest trail. Then, picture 15 more young writers, 12–14 year-olds, each sitting in the dappled light on their own rocks or logs, five to 10 yards apart from each other. Two teachers and an intern, almost indistinguishable from the others, write with Sergio and his peers in a makeshift, natural classroom next to a stream.

Several young writers echoed the theme of freedom in informal interviews and in their program surveys, sparking this inquiry into how 11–16 year-old students experienced weeklong writing programs, that were located within 50–80 miles of a large, urban U.S. city. Accomplished K–12 teachers coplanned and cotaught these programs that took place at national and state historic parks, museums, universities, forests, farms, and public libraries. Students wrote in places that neither looked nor sounded like conventional school classrooms. Depending on the program, students wrote under trees and towering sculptures, at picnic tables, in gardens, in kayaks, on lawns and logs, next to reservoirs, rivers, and creeks. They talked at tables in rooms without lockers, cubbies, or homework reminders; in churches, community centers, paneled libraries, college classrooms, and various visitor centers. Far from concerns about progress reports or grades, students discussed their writing and confided goals for their writing. On the fifth day of each program, Friday, the students contributed writing to an anthology and read their pieces at "celebrations of writing" to an audience of friends, family, and educators.

As the author of this study, I am invested in enrichment writing programs because I believe that writing offers an amazing tool for expression and discovery of the self and world, something too often lacking in children's experience in school. I direct a National Writing Project site; I broker part-nerships with formal and informal place-based educators and stakeholders; I work with writing project staff to publicize the programs and to recruit and register youth writers; I colead orientations for teacher leaders. Each summer, I visit youth programs. During my site visits, teachers invite me to join them. When and wherever teachers and students write and share, I write, listen, and share as I see fit. I sit with students in response groups and offer feedback. On Fridays, I attend celebrations of writing and provide welcoming remarks, congratulating the writers, their families, the teachers, interns, and place-based colleagues.

During some site visits, I conduct informal interviews of co-teachers and interns; I also conduct informal interviews with students who have time to talk with me about their experience and observations. It was in this context, on a hot Friday morning in early July, when I spoke with Sergio, a young man who had just completed sixth grade a few weeks earlier. In addition to my participant observation, I conducted and studied informal interviews with seven other middle level students and 12 teachers; I also studied 138 program surveys completed by adolescents, including 88 by middle level students. Writing Project teachers and graduate students helped both in the data collection and analysis.

Sergio's comment about freedom—"here I felt so free"—made me scratch my head as I drove northward from his program to another situated at a historic state park on the banks of a river. Free? What did he mean by free? Was Sergio simply *one* writer who felt free? Or was Sergio one of *many* writers who felt free? If the latter, what could explain the freedom? Sergio's access to place—the forest and river? His access to the expressive writing instruction? Or, perhaps both?

After discussing a theoretical framework that suggests how thirdspace theory coupled with sociocultural theory animates students' experience writing in a place-based, enrichment writing program, what follows is a description of the data collection and analysis, and a discussion of what happens when middle level students engage in out-of-school, place-based writing and why it matters.

THEORETICAL FRAMEWORK

Sociocultural theory coupled with thirdspace theory helped in understanding Sergio as a writer among others, writing in a forest setting away from conventional school. Sergio dressed the part. He wore clothes familiar to those who have been with middle level students, maybe a faded Sponge Bob T-shirt and shorts with many pockets. He carried a canvas backpack with a water bottle, some bugspray, a tan writing journal, pens, and pencils, and so on. He packed with him, however, tacit ideas about writing based on his experience of middle level education and about visiting a forest setting. The ideas he carried met with a community of practice in an unusual, time-bound, place-based writing program.

Soja (1996) theorized that literal, mapped physical places (like the winding trail next to a creek) can be construed as *first* spaces; *second space* representations incorporate the expected culture enacted within first spaces [perhaps people hiking or stopping to take a photograph along a winding trail]; in *thirdspaces*, places become sets for action and interaction that transcend the limitations of invisible, normative boundaries and expected behaviors. In Sergio's case, rather than simply hiking, he sat among a group redefining the space for their purposes—writing (Bhabha, 1994). In this way, while the set [forest] is fixed, the culture is not. In thirdspaces, "places are not only a medium but also an outcome of action, producing and being produced through human practice" (Moles, 2008, para. 4.1).

While thirdspace theory can shine a light on the "interanimation" between places and the people dynamically living in them (Oehler-Marx, 2017, p. 21), sociocultural theories help us understand the culture that people make in the new space. Invisible "identity kits" offer participants "instructions on how to act and talk so as to take on a particular role that others will recognize" as appropriate to the given community (Gee, 1989, p. 7). Sociolcultural theorists explain a "community of practice" (Lave & Wegner, 1991) within which participants gain access to and share collective purposes, dispositions, ways of being, and communicating (Gee, 1996). In a process orientation to writing instruction, teachers like those in the programs studied, invite students to start many "pieces" of writing in a variety of "genres" for purposes that transcend "getting better" at writing (Hull & Schultz, 2001, p. 584). In such a writing community, rather than assigning writing, teachers may position themselves as writers who share their own writing during mini-lessons (Atwell, 1987).

A process writing "classroom," whether indoors or outdoors, whether in schools or out of schools, has a cultural underpinning. Each writer in the community, whether student or teacher, has the capacity to bring others toward more competence (Vygotsky, 1978) as they discuss how to plan, generate, compose, and revise their work (Whitney et al., 2008). Process writing instruction defies a one-size-fits all approach and implores teachers to tune their ears to the needs, learning goals, and incipient ideas that students express. By "centering on students and their writing experiences … [the teacher] views the student as important and agentic" (Whitney & Johnson, 2017, p. 82). Atwell advocated that novice, middle level writers gain practice making decisions about what they will write as teachers expose them to many genres of writing. Together, they read and analyze "mentor texts" (models), cultivating students' awareness of writers' craft, so that students can strategically talk, plan, compose, and revise their writing (Wood-Ray, 1999).

LITERATURE REVIEW

Studies emphasizing the attributes of writing process, place-based education, and thirdspace theory as contributors to the purposive writing of middle level students are explored in the next sections. These studies demonstrate the possibilities for writing beyond the more traditional classroom practices and established settings.

Writing Process

In their meta-analysis of 107 studies, Graham and Perin (2007a) asked, "What instructional practices improve the quality of adolescent students' writing?" (p. 446). Their analysis included studies of young writers spanning Grades 4–12 and allowed them to build on earlier studies asking similar questions (Hillocks, 1986). For inclusion into their analysis, all studies involved control groups and outcome measures in which researchers had established reliability. They identified 11 statistically significant, high-impact instructional practices (Graham & Perin, 2007b). With the exception of sentence combining and summarization, program teachers utilized all of the high impact strategies such as the following: the *Process Writing Approach*, "which interweaves a number of writing instructional activities in a workshop environment that stresses extended writing opportunities, writing for authentic audiences, personalized instruction, and cycles of writing"; the *Study of Models*, "which provides students with opportunities to read, analyze, and emulate models of good writing"; *writing strategies* "for planning, revising, and editing their compositions"; and *prewriting*, "designed to help them generate or organize ideas for their composition" (Graham & Perin, 2017b).[2] Because Graham and Perin's (2007a) meta-analysis reflected a sample of almost exclusively school-based studies (p. 469), determining the role of place or place-based curriculum as a mediating factor in middle-level writing is difficult.

Pointing to the Graham and Perin study and drawing from her own study, Robb (2010) suggested that middle-level writing curriculum must involve a "writing process approach" in which teachers engage in prewriting, study models to learn craft techniques, and make choices about writing. She also advocated extended writing time in which students learn about and expand their understanding and facility with writing in a variety of genres to counterbalance the more formulaic and test preparation writing that they normally encounter. In her own study of middle level students that involved the collection and analysis of 1,392 surveys, Robb found that more than 90% completed some writing out of school; only 8.7% of the students' teachers knew about the out of school writing. In a subsequent analysis of 300 fifth to eighth grade students' surveys, Robb found that 103 students had positive responses and 197 had negative responses when asked about their experience writing in school: the most common reactions being "boring" and "confusing." Robb urged middle level teachers to incorporate choice into their writing instruction as a way to counterbalance the overuse of prompted writing; she noted that students who wrote at "home," often used words such as "free, no grade, no stress, I choose, have time, can choose topics, write in any genre, etc." (p. 24).

While Robb's study inadvertently links out of school with home, this study positions writing out of school in "place-based" educational settings. In a case study, Magnifico (2013) compared how students' motivation for writing and experience compared in three environments: a school-sponsored creative writing class; an extracurricular immersive, summer creative writing program; and an online game community. Magnifico suggested that discourse communities and the norms that they embody, likely mediate students' motivation for writing. In the case of the extracurricular summer program, Magnifico reported, "Young writers could express their ideas freely, rather than within the constraints imposed by classroom environments" and that "participants" were intrinsically motivated by their creative writing teachers' feedback in ways that transcended what they experienced in school settings (p. 29). This study focused on middle level learners' experience writing in immersive, enrichment programs set out-of-school and away from home.

Place-Based Education

Place-based education (PBE) aligns well with curricular recommendations for middle level education from the commission report, *Turning Points: Preparing American Youth for the 21st Century* (Carnegie Council on Adolescent Development, 1989) that advocates for students' regular opportunities for "inquiry, discovery, and reasoning across subjects" (as cited by Gross, 2002, p. xvi). In PBE, teachers value students' natural and locally derived curiosities (Smith, 2002) by identifying and designing learning opportunities, using "the local community and environment as a starting point to teach concepts in language arts, mathematics, social studies, science and other subjects across the curriculum ... emphasizing hands-on, real-world learning experiences" (Sobel, 2004, p. 6). Proponents argue that in PBE, students practice inherently useful and authentic literacy and disciplinary skills (Power, 2004) as students read about where they are and eventually write about their learning (Brooke, 2003).

PBE aligns well with middle level learning because it invites students' inquiry (Robb, 2010) and regularly "widen[s] the learning space to include places outside the classroom" while allowing students to set individual and collective goals and to assess their own progress in learning (Caskey, 2002, p. 113). As they lauded the potential, PBE advocates either implied or directly pointed out shortcomings of regular school and its curriculum.

Sobel (2004) quoted from Bill Bigelow's (1996) reflection looking back at his childhood schooling, "actively learn[ing] to not-think about the earth [or] about that place where we were" (p. 5). PBE advocates rhetorically distinguished how PBE reframes students and teachers' regular school experience.

> Students don't sit quietly at their desks listening to teachers or completing worksheets. They instead work and converse in teams and frequently leave the school itself, to engage in activities in the field or community. And teachers do not concentrate on drilling students for high stakes tests, relying instead on forms of understanding and knowledge that arise more organically through real-life investigations and problem-solving. (Smith, 2007, p. 204)

Smith's (2007) characterizations of regular school suggest didactic instruction in which alienated students sit passively at desks laden with worksheets. In contrast, PBE allows for immersive, "multidisciplinary and experiential" curriculum (Woodhouse & Knapp, 2000, p. 4) that can challenge teachers working in disciplinary silos typical to schools that chop learning into nine, 42-minute periods. In PBE, authentic, local community-learning opportunities invite ongoing peer interaction and problem solving; PBE affords students an integrated, democratic, curricular experience prized within the middle level education literature (Caskey, 2002, p. 111). Project-based learning or forms of community service (Smith, 2007) engage students *and* their teachers in a deliberative learning process; for instance, when local boardwalks have fallen into disrepair, they determine how to design, price, and enact a repair (McInerney, Smyth, & Down, 2011); students hone vocational skills while working to resurrect a Main Street General Store and its failing online candy business (Sobel, 2004). In some cases, PBE links to rural education, community revival, sustainability education (Theobald & Nachtigal, 1995), and environmental justice (McInerney et al., 2011). For example, students monitor the quality of air (Smith, 2007) or learn about contested local, water rights (Brooke, 2003).

By overemphasizing or even idealizing the goodness of *local* places (Nespor, 2008), however, place-based educators may miss the opportunity to fuse critical pedagogy and PBE (Gruenewald, 2003). Pursuing a more critical version of PBE, a group of students would not only measure, track, and report on the local air quality but also study how local air quality links to declining labor rates and to national debates about environmental regulations. In this way, PBE allows students to recognize *intradependence* (Theobald, 1997), namely how their local communities may be impacted by larger "social, economic, and [global] factors that contribute to poverty, exploitation, oppression" (McInerney et al., 2011, p. 6). When students understand the interconnected relationship between local places, local activism, and global problems (Gruenewald, 2003), PBE may mitigate against "the alienation and isolation of modern globalized life" (Oehler-Marx, 2017, p. 8).

In the literature, even as advocates valorize PBE as an antidote to the *placeless* curriculum that can plague schools (Gruenwald, 2003, p. 8), the voices of students rarely animate the discussion. A challenge for PBE researchers is that all places—even schools—are simply places; we need to understand the cultural practices with which they are imbued. This is why thirdspace theory offers a means for understanding and imagining what happens when place, community, and culture merge.

Thirdspace Theory

Gutierrez, Rymes, and Larson (1995) used thirdspace theory to suggest a resolution to unproductive talk in high school classrooms. In their study, the researchers coded high school teachers posing questions for which they knew the answer—as a first script (Mehan, 1979); the researchers coded students' simultaneous performance of answers and peer-to-peer protest as "counterscripts." Gutierrez et al. asserted that in "unscripted" dialogic moments, thirdspaces, the students and teachers could break from their conventional speech patterns and meet in mutual learning while "relinquish[ing] traditional notions of power and the need for rigid and structured power relations as requisites for learning. These new power arrangements [would] begin to rupture the transcendent script invoked at the local school site" (p. 24). Their findings show that if teachers hold tight to power and are deaf to students' voices, they miss opportunities for democratic participation and dialogic learning (see, for instance, Johnston, 2012).

In another application of thirdspace theory, Moje et al. (2004) wrote about the challenge that middle level students have in navigating the formal curriculum and expectations for how to talk and write as they move from one academic class to another. The authors suggested that in a productive thirdspace, teachers would strategically leverage students' deep knowledge of "home" language and of popular culture (first space) as a linguistic and cultural bridge to developing disciplinary literacy skills necessary in traditional science curriculum (second space). In their study, they noticed that teachers regularly ignored students' linguistic experience. To build this learning bridge, teachers would need to redesign curriculum responsive to their students' *funds of knowledge* (see for example, Moll, Amanti, Neff, & Gonzalez, 1992). Such work requires adequate administrative support, professional development, motivation, and agency for building the pedagogical content knowledge necessary to enact such challenging work.

Schillinger (2007) described interdisciplinary, middle level humanities curriculum as a thirdspace alternative to artificially constructed walls separating one discipline from another. In her action research, Schillinger highlighted a student, Nory, who breaks from the norms of social studies writing by crafting a poem about the Battle at Gettysburg. Schillinger suggested that poetry transcends expectations for disciplinary writing while still allowing for students' deep, historical understanding and empathetic imagination. Almost parenthetically, Schillinger described how the interdisciplinary thirdspace permitted her the freedom to write about history while pleasing her own poetic invention; she strategically shared her poetry with her students as part of her instruction. In this study, students like Nory thrived as they took *responsibility* for learning, making *choices* in their writing as they pursued areas of personal *inquiry*. In these ways, Schillinger's work resonates with Robb's (2010) beliefs about middle level writers' needs.

Similar to Schillinger (2007), McKinney, Lasley, and Holmes-Gull (2008) drew upon Bhabha's (1994) work to suggest that in educational thirdspaces, teachers can

> redefine themselves and their identities in productive ways because they can explore more fluid notions of what it means to teach and interact in social networks as opposed to defining themselves in opposition to a dominant discourse or set of expectations." (p. 54)

In their study of family writing programs away from regular school, McKinney et al. suggested that teachers had freedom "to grow more comfortable in their skins, to experiment with pedagogical practices" and to develop enduring relationships with each other, students, and their students' parents (p. 53).

When educational theorists apply thirdspace theory to curricular and instructional reforms, they portray students and teachers inhabiting alternative ways of "being"—as in we can be, act, talk, and write differently here than we can there. The goal of this study was to understand students' experience writing in place-based education settings, away from their conventional middle and high school settings.

METHODOLOGY

Using an emergent research design as a way to understand students' experiences, I modified my plans for data collection when I recognized opportunities to gain a deeper understanding. I sharpened my questions as I learned more from students through my participant observation and interviewing process (Creswell & Poth, 2018, p. 44).

My deep knowledge of the Writing Project community of practice, and my regard for the teachers, some of whom I had known and worked with for more than a decade, certainly colored my observations. I had a stake in the research: I hoped that students' participation in our community of practice might lead them to enjoy writing and to *care* about our local community's historic and natural treasures. Prioritizing the writers' perceptions of experience reflected my beliefs that students can and should inform us about their experience and hopes for learning (Cook-Sather, 2002). Too often, as Burton (2000) suggested, "We have treated young people as the objects of education [and assessment] rather than as participants in a shared enterprise, involving exchanges between young and old, experienced and inexperienced" (p. 330).

Consistent with the literature on participant observation (Yin, 2003, p. 94), and given my status as site director who had worked closely with many of the teachers for years, I benefitted from easy access to each of the program sites and an intimate view of students in the midst of writing and place-based learning. I felt comfortable as a participant observer—writing, sitting in a group, and sharing writing, offering feedback, sharing an observation of a sculpture, and so on. Being so close to the learners, I rarely took the kind of field notes a more dispassionate observer might have for fear that my note taking would set me apart and possibly disrupt the learners and the learning process (Van Maanen, 1988). I straddled between being an insider and outsider. During informal interviews, as a way to establish rapport and position myself as a learner, I posed authentic questions about participants' observations as writers in place-based settings (Glesne, 1999, p. 83). Although I was intimately familiar with process writing and the sorts of things students *might* have experienced, I was also naïve inasmuch as I did not know the students; nor did I know how the teachers had crafted the curriculum; nor did I have a deep knowledge of the settings.

Among other questions, I always asked students if they would be willing to read me a piece of their writing from the week and to tell me about their processes and inspirations for writing it. One Friday, during one such interview, I had the pleasure of listening to Nora describe why she chose to write a piece from the point of view of an Arctic moose watching little girls play in the drawing room. Especially gratifying an hour after the interview, I got to visit the historic house where Nora and another young writer, working as docents, described the storied history of the living room where the moose, a travel trophy, stared out from the wall and offered endless amusement to the young girls who had lived there more than a hundred years earlier.

I went into the study asking how student writers experienced the place-based writing programs. What did they learn about writing? About the place(s)? Over time, given my belief that the writing programs represented "thirdspaces," I sought to understand the nature of freedom that students linked to the programs and the writing that they did within them.

Research Settings and Participants

The weeklong summer programs took place in different locations in one state: a world famous sculpture park, a historic site of the National Park Service, a pre-Revolutionary War mansion and a Hall of Honor (both state historic parks), a public library, a university, a forest setting for the study of natural science, and a local community enclave that included a farm, historic houses, and a nature preserve.

The coteachers in each program had completed an "invitational institute," a rigorous, 160+ hour professional development program, offered by the local site of the National Writing Project called the Green Forest Writing Project (GFWP).[3] The GFWP coteachers, as instructional leaders in their own schools and school communities, volunteered and were paid stipends; many had taught during prior summers. In most programs, future teachers, museum educators, community volunteers, and/or park rangers assisted the lead teachers. The 12–15 heterogeneously grouped students in each program either elected to participate or had parents who enrolled them; most programs included a range of participants that spanned at least two and often three grade levels. The students ranged in age from 11–16 years old and with few exceptions, attended public schools in rural, suburban, and urban settings. Although the program was not free, approximately 50% of the students received tuition assistance based on a sliding scale of need. Cohorts were heterogeneous and included English language learners and students identified with special needs.

Program Instruction

Instruction during each weeklong program took a similar shape: a team of writing project teachers worked to build a learning community, introduced students to different writing opportunities through various prompts and models, and concurrently immersed the students in "place." While much of the immersion involved walking and hiking, depending on the program, students engaged with a variety of adults with knowledge of the place: museum educators, Rangers, naturalists, and farmers. For instance, at one site, students visited the basement of a stone building where African American slaves cooked for early, local "settlers." Sometimes, the teachers guided students in reading or viewing texts and films that linked to the place: a letter that a child wrote in the 1800s; a ghost story linked to an old stone hidden in a forest; or a film featuring a metal smith making a sculpture. By the fourth day of each program, students submitted pieces of writing for publication in a group anthology. Students read their pieces on the fifth day at a public celebration of writing attended by family members, guardians, and staff members from the various places (e.g., park rangers, museum educators, program volunteers).

At a two-hour orientation for their 2014 Youth Writing Program work, guided by the Coordinating Director of the YWPs and the author, GFWP program teachers read aloud the program's learning principles and then wrote for 10 minutes about how the principles aligned with or challenged their teaching practices and beliefs.

Green Forest Youth Writing Project Learning Principles

1. GFWP teachers create opportunities for students to experience writing and reading in a safe community in which people talk through ideas, share writing, and express multiple perspectives.
2. GFWP teachers provide opportunities that invite writers to explore who they are while honoring and expressing their voices.
3. GFWP teachers share their own writing and select "mentor texts" so that writers can study and talk about features of others' writing in order to inspire their own writing.
4. GFWP teachers provide students with writing choices and opportunities to draft several pieces and then work toward various forms of publication while learning about and practicing relevant revision, editing, and presentation skills.

After composing their thoughts, teachers shared excerpts from their writing and, those who had worked in the program before, discussed how the principles informed their work. Teacher teams then worked in pairs and triads launching their preliminary curriculum plans while also examining artifacts produced in prior years including blogs, anthologies, and teachers' lesson plans. This process of sharing materials, looking back and looking forward, aligns with a longstanding tradition in which National Writing Project sites convene teacher leaders to inquire collectively to understand, improve, and refine programs continually (Lieberman & Wood, 2002).

Data Collection

For the purposes of this chapter, I focus my analysis most closely on students' responses to a simple program survey the GFWP had developed and used for several years; the survey questions stem from the GFWP's organizational philosophy of appreciative inquiry, an orientation towards action research that focuses on what is going well to sustain and improve outcomes (National School Reform Faculty, n.d.). Students completed the surveys on Friday morning before the culminating celebrations of writing during the week of their program participation.[4] The survey, designed to be easy to administer and complete, included four questions to help us understand students' perspectives and to inform future programmatic curricula:

- What I liked about the program ...
- What helped my writing the most ...
- What I learned about my writing process ...'
- What I would change about the program ...

Because there are limits to participants' self-reports and surveys, and as a way to corroborate the students' accounts and to develop a "convergence of evidence" (Yin, 2003, p. 100), I visited the sites at least one time during the week of instruction, often spending two to three hours at a time, shadowing the students and serving as a participant observer supporting the teachers as they saw fit (Patton, 2002). This could involve going on writing hikes with the students in a forest or by a reservoir, sitting with groups of three and four students on the floor of a makeshift museum classroom, helping to facilitate writing groups on Wednesdays, Thursdays, or Fridays, or attending parent and family writing celebrations during which student authors read from an anthology of writing that the group produced that week.

To complement the surveys and participation observation, I conducted informal interviews with students and teachers (see Appendices B and C for sample informal interview questions). When I arrived at program sites, I asked teachers if there were a few students that I could interview with the understanding that my interview would not interfere with the students' writing time or needs. The teachers pointed me to students who were not in the final throes of writing. I conducted the interviews with this convenience sample just on the edge of the classroom or group. For instance, some interviews took place in rooms of historic houses, while others took place out of doors. I attempted to diminish my power by offering participants opportunities to turn off the tape recorder or to clarify or strike ideas that they did not want included in my subsequent analysis. Generally, I started with the same set of questions for all participants and attempted to listen more than talk. I asked follow up questions requesting more explanation, clarification, and description when I had authentic reasons for doing so (Glesne, 1999).

Table 12.1.
Data Collection and Procedure

Methods	Sources	Procedure
Surveys	11-16 year old students ($n = 138$)	Surveys distributed by teachers on the final day of 5-day programs
	• Middle level students ($n = 88$) • Rising sixth graders: 13 • Rising seventh graders: 24 • Rising eighth graders: 33 • Rising ninth graders: 18	Read all materials—open coding
Interviews	Teachers ($n = 12$) Middle level students ($n=8$); Focal students ($n = 6$)	Conducted and tape recorded, semistructured, informal interviews on fourth or fifth day of programs; transcribed interviews
	• Sergio, rising seventh grader • Nate, rising seventh grader • Juanita, rising eighth grader • Nora, rising eighth grader • Kali, rising eighth grader • Sahara, rising ninth grader	
Participant Observation	15 instances of 2–3 hours • 2 Teacher Orientations • 3 Monday visits • 3 Thursday visits • 7 Friday visits	Field notes, photographs, and document collection

Note: A "rising sixth grader" is a student who would become a sixth grader when regular school resumed after the summer.

Interviews occurred on the fourth and fifth day of five-day programs with students; I often interviewed teachers in the hours just after the students left on Fridays. In these short 10–20-minute interviews, I asked open-ended questions such as: "Talk about the week. What did you do? How was writing/teaching writing for you? Did you write something that you liked? How is this program similar/different to writing/writing instruction in your regular school?" I asked students to read a piece of writing that they worked on during the week and to tell me about their process drafting it. In addition to questions ostensibly about writing, I also asked participants about their experience of "place": "What did you see here? Would you ever want to return here? If you were to bring someone back, what would you show them?" I hoped that these questions might help me understand whether notions in the literature about "stewardship" might be at play in our short programs. In addition to the interviews, and as part of our regular writing project practice, I had access to a collection of teachers' curricular materials, teaching logs, interns' digital journals, and student writing.

Analytical Process

I initially studied the data with the goal of answering the guiding question: how do students experience out of school, place-based writing instruction? During this months-long process, with a small team of graduate students, I began with an open coding process designed to describe and conceptualize chunks of data and individual phenomena (Strauss & Corbin, 1990). Initial coding was "unfocused" and "open" and involved "breaking down, analysing, comparing, labelling, and categorising data" (Moghaddam, 2006, p. 55). We clustered some of the initial descriptions into placeholders, first codes helping us see that many of the students expressed a sense of fun and discussed some writing skills that they learned about: for instance, "I learned how to use more punctuation." They also discussed content that they had learned, relevant to the place of their immersive studies. For instance, one student who attended a program at a revolutionary war site wrote, "The cantonment sparked my writing when we learned about surgeons and apothecaries."

During this phase of analysis, we looked at an analytical heuristic from a study of youth writing that offered more precise language characterizing what students drew, discussed, and wrote about writing experiences in and out of school (Meyer, 2013; VanGarderen, Meyer, & Jacobowitz, 2007). This heuristic helped sort through the range of responses related to students' dispositions, to their declarative and procedural knowledge about writing (Hillocks, 1995), and to their feelings of efficacy. For instance, one student wrote, "I improved by using commas better and capitalizing when I need to." We revised codes so that we could "cluster all the segments relating to the particular question, hypothesis, concept or theme" (Miles & Huberman, 1994, p. 56), developing axial codes so that we could put our data "back together in new ways ... by making connections between categories" (Strauss & Corbin, 1990, p. 96).

At the end of each coding session, we wrote short memos about the data that we read, noting data that fit and did not fit our developing categories or those offered by the heuristic. One such student interview comment, Sergio's, "Going outside and sitting and just writing, I felt so free" (Interview, 2014), inspired our team to understand whether freedom was salient in the data. If so, what was the nature of freedom that students disclosed? Discourse markers students used to preface comments such as "being able to," "allowed to," "get to," and "got to" helped us identify various freedoms students ascribed to the place-based writing programs.

While many of the freedom markers connected to process-writing instruction, we noticed many students describing, "getting to be" alone, or "loving" nature, or "being allowed" to run or walk, or participate in social situations. Our analysis of what students "liked about the program" led us to Gardner's (2011) discussion of multiple intelligences and learning preferences.[5] Given the emphasis on oral language and writing woven into each program, we were not surprised when certain students described satisfaction with writing and speaking (linguistic intelligence) and writing and sharing with others (interpersonal intelligence), core features of all programs; we were surprised, however, by students' appreciation for and precise descriptions of natural settings (naturalistic intelligence). Some students noted the aesthetic beauty they observed; some linked nature with satisfying an inclination for being quiet and alone (intrapersonal intelligence). Finally, many described an appreciation for being "allowed" to move, walk, and be out of doors (bodily/kinesthetic intelligence).

We took these themes back to the data "to see added evidence of the same pattern" (Miles & Huberman, 1994, p. 246). Then, we fine-tuned the definitions of the larger codes so that we could train a small group of peers to recode data reflecting Guba's (1978) recommendation that "second observer[s] ... ought to be able to verify that a) the categories make sense in view of the data which are available, and b) the data have been appropriately arranged in the category system" (pp. 56–57). We had greater than 90% interrater reliability.

A limitation of the study is that I did not analyze students' writing even though I had access to it. The students wrote in journals every day and submitted at least one piece of writing for publication in an anthology. I listened to students read their writing aloud in whole group sessions, small writing groups, during interviews, and at celebrations. Because I never wanted my data collection to interfere with students' learning or privacy, I kept my focus on students' observations of experience. Given the limited nature of this inquiry, future researchers could study *what* students write in place-based programs that offer process-based writing instruction. Researchers could study the relationship between students' short, immersive writing experiences and any enduring sense of care for or eventual advocacy for the particular places and their history, culture, and natural beauty (Power, 2004; Sobel, 2004). Researchers could more systematically compare middle level students' experience writing in place-based versus school settings; critics offer bleak description of middle level writing instruction that can be so restrictive that students only learn how to write "highly structured essays that repeat information given to them as if they were filling out worksheets" (Urbanski, 2016, p. 103).

FINDINGS

In taking this grounded theory approach to our analysis (Glaser & Strauss, 1967), what emerged were three themes: (a) students described learning freedoms; (b) students suggested their fluency as writers; and, (c) students appreciated their experience of fellowship. In some cases, especially during interviews, students volunteered or implied ways in which their summer experience contrasted with their regular school writing experience, something that teachers corroborated during interviews.

Writing Freedoms: *Here, We're Allowed to Write About What We Want*

Students linked freedom to writing and the authorial agency they experienced when "getting to make" choices in the summer. Nate, a rising seventh grader, explained the contrast he observed.

> [This week] was just nice, because [I] would have the freedom instead of having to write about one thing; [I] could pick anything, and then write about it and [I] could write about something very fun and then [I] wouldn't have to write about just something…. Like in school, you have to write about a certain thing, like a certain time or something, or a certain story or something.[6]

They could choose topics; one student wrote, "I liked being able to write about a lot of things." They could choose to write in a variety of genres; they wrote personal journals and poems, recreated historical dialogues, short plays, short stories, letters, and narratives. They could choose what to do with a piece of writing that they had started: to let it go, develop it further, and/or share it with an audience. In interviews, students suggested contrasts between their experiences writing in the summer program versus regular school.

While students appreciated the freedom to write about *what* they wanted, they regularly noted their appreciation for writing prompts and the freedom to reject any prompt. One student explained how "writing prompts [helped my writing the most] because they helped me figure out what to write" and another linked prompts to "inspiration." Sahara, a rising ninth grader, underscored her appreciation for the opportunity to pursue or reject writing prompts; she paraphrased her summer teachers: "Well if you don't want to write about that, you don't have to … which is like really the best thing." Sahara contrasts this invitation to make decisions as a writer with an instructional refrain from her regular school classroom.

"Well, you have to do this. To write this, this is what you have to do to be a good writer."

Like Sahara, Sergio, a rising seventh grader, disclosed that his summer teachers offered parameters for writing that differed from those his middle level schoolteachers provided.

> [This summer] I just enjoyed myself because it was like free writing; I didn't have to write about a certain topic; there's no—like you have to write in school—you normally have to write, "Ok, I want you to write about such and such a thing at such and such a place." Like you have to write about being a person in the 1900s or something.... Everyone is writing the same thing in school; yet out here, you can write about everything that you see around you; it's much more interesting.

Sergio described summer writing as "free" and more "interesting." Similarly, Sahara described summer teachers who encourage students to "Do what you will feel comfortable with." In regular school, her teachers are more didactic. "When you learn in school, they're telling you like, 'This is the right way to write.' They'll give you outlines and all this stuff like oh, you know, 'You have to use these types of words or write about these types of people.' "

In addition to determining the content for their writing, students appreciated having the freedom to decide what to do with a piece of writing beyond initial drafting. Would they read it aloud? Would they seek response? Would they elect to revise, edit, or publish? Nora, a rising eighth grader, linked this aspect of writing to freedom. "I liked the fact that we were allowed a lot of freedom and that we were able to make decisions whether or not to share." Nora also explained sharing writing as an act of courage in the face of possible bullying, underscoring her appreciation for the freedom to make that choice in the summer setting.

> Well, if you didn't want to share, you weren't forced to. And in school, you're forced to share. And there's a lot of bullies in school, so I usually get judged a lot—that my writing is *lame* [using air quotes for emphasis]. But here, no one judges; it's only positive comments and it's really cool.

Freedom: *Here We Got to Go Outside—I Love Going Outside—And We Still Get to Write*

Students expressed the freedom they felt from being outside, and, in some cases, how nature inspired their learning and comfort writing. Perhaps the freedom is not solely about being "in" nature but also linked to *moving* their bodies. Nate contrasted place-based writing with his experience writing in school. "This is much more fun. School is not fun at all, with the writing ... because you have to just be sitting down the whole time for like forty minutes to an hour; but this is more of you get to get up and move and then you can write." Kali, a rising eighth grade student explained, "I liked walking on the estate [at the Historic Park]. Walking inspired me to write." A rising seventh grader wrote, "I liked going outside to get ideas for the story. Most teachers [at school] would keep us in a classroom."

In my participant observations at two settings, I saw teachers and students intermittently stopping during hikes for observation and writing. At a sculpture park, students sat on a wooded hillside under oak trees, next to old boulders and "decomposing" art installations. One of the teachers encouraged the writers to find a "quiet place" to listen, look, draw, and write about their observations. As a participant observer, I wrote in my fieldnotes, "It's amazing how quickly students get silently absorbed here." At a different program, in a similar exercise, students hiked down a forested hillside and sat next to a creek, with the only audible sounds coming from the creek's movement. In their surveys, several students described the pleasure of being alone and quiet. For instance, one rising seventh grader wrote, "Quiet writing time [helped my writing the most]." Another young writer, a rising sixth grader, reflected, "I am good at writing when I am alone." In a possible comparison to regular school, another rising sixth grader explained, "It is easier to write without people talking."

In program surveys, several students volunteered naturalistic details with satisfaction and precision. One student, a rising seventh grader, "loved" the opportunity for solo exploration in the woods.

> The thing that stood out for me this week was when we could explore by ourselves in the woods. I loved this because ... I found a bright red newt with orange circles on its back. I also discovered a bunch of red mushrooms and a trail behind this huge rock. This is why I love this activity and why it stood out to me.

Just as in the preceding example, Sahara, commenting on a different program, linked the word "love" to a naturalistic observation about the undulating hillside on the banks of a river. "My favorite part of the week was probably looking at the river" because "it's so pretty." She further explained the riverfront is "not flat land; ... it's like valleys ... I love that".

Sergio described surprise at the depth of water in the river. "When we went from the docking area down [to the river], it was weird because ... there were trees that sunk in the water because of a hurricane in the past.... The tide was probably only a foot deep, not even." He went on to explain that he wrote in his journal while on a kayak, remembering that at first "it look[ed] like there were monsters almost coming out of the water." Because it was so "interesting," he said that he "might incorporate supernatural images he observed on the river in a poem" he intended to write.

Fluency: *I Wrote 999,999,999 Poems*

Many students alluded to the fluency they experienced when writing in the summer programs. We linked fluency to students' descriptions of ease, flow, speed, and volume of writing generated. One student described production of writing in terms of volume and variety; "I wrote poetry, a story, and two music pieces." Another student described motivation to produce writing extending beyond the program setting; "I even wrote at home, every afternoon after I got home."

Many students explained how the volume of time spent writing made writing easier. Sahara noted:

> We wrote every day; we wrote a lot … but it's spread out in a way where it seems like you're not writing as much as you really are 'cuz they give us these little notebooks and by the end, you're like filling up the notebook but it doesn't feel like you're writing that much.

One teacher observed, "When we wanted them to stop, [the students] were like, 'Can we write for another 5 minutes?' And that's something you just don't see in the classroom."

Although knowing why students were fluent is difficult to isolate, one obvious explanation was the fact that many students enrolled in the program for the very reason that writing was already pleasurable or easy for them. Juanita, a rising eighth grader, complicated this idea, explaining in an interview that any ease and pleasure derived from writing can be fleeting rather than fixed.

> I like writing, but lately I've been kind of on a writer's block, like, I won't know what to write. But when I was here, all of a sudden there were all of these ideas I could have used, and it was pretty overwhelming. I wrote a folktale piece where I made things that aren't tangible like morning, afternoon, and night like people almost, and they were going through people-like situations and it was fun writing it.

Working from plenty rather than scarcity (Moffett, 1989) and given the freedom to select her topic, unlocked some of the "writer's block" that accompanied Juanita's arrival into the program. Juanita credited the summer teachers for offering her opportunities for "freewriting" and for a variety of creative "prompts" that she could "take home" which "help a lot, with creative juices."

Fellowship: *The Best Part of This Week Is the Friends I Made*

Campers generally liked camp experiences and found it enjoyable to make friends. Writing camp was similar, even "fun." A fun atmosphere that incorporates a common creative process and regular sharing of writing may have explained any fellowship students linked to the experience. "I liked how we were surrounded by people all working toward a common goal, and the environment was open." The students noticed that their teachers' work *as writers* contributed to the common goal. In one case, the students formed a "group hug" as their parents waited to take them home after a Friday celebration of writing.

Students described their feelings of fellowship generally, as in, "The best part of this week was the friends I made" or "[What I liked most about the program was] meeting new people." In two interviews, writers contrasted their summer feelings with those they experienced in school. Kali reflected, "I was thinking to myself, I'm not going to make any new friends. I'm just going to be a loner in the back, like I usually am in class; I'm very quiet. I was wrong." Another student contrasted the summer program with regular school. Nora stated, "Our teachers [here] actually enjoy laughter. Most teachers shush it or just don't want it, but they actually encourage laughing."

Some students explained that feelings of fellowship were due to being among kindred spirits—writers. Juanita said, "I could relate to a lot of the people here 'cause a lot of the people here love to write, and I love to write too. So, I made friends pretty quickly here because they were, I don't know, my kind of people, you know?" Another student, a rising fifth grader confided, "It makes me like I fit in; it makes me feel like I have one place that I can actually write." Whether they self-identified as writers or not, students often found themselves among strangers on Monday; by Friday, it was not unusual to see groups huddled for selfies, exchanging Instagram, Snapchat, and e-mail addresses.

The students' comments and evaluations suggested that the various social processes involved with generating and sharing writing played a role in the *fellowship* that they experienced. In many cases, students discussed the daily writing processes of generating and sharing fun.

> We got chances [to write] every morning when we got there; we would have to sit around in a circle, and they would give us a [prompt] and we would write. Then we would all share. Then some[times] we … would play a game, like, if you had to write something down and then share it with someone else, and then they had to write another story down that had something to do with that. And it just kept going and it was really fun.

Some students appreciated the routine use of conferring processes with peers and/or their teachers, who also engaged in writing. "I appreciated the peer editing and the teachers sitting down to read the writing." Another writer pointed to a "revision circle" because the process let the writer "learn what to improve." And another student remembered how "passing stories in a circle" was not only "fun" but also the activity that helped the writer learn the most about writing. Listening and responding to peers' writing also set up new opportunities for writers to meet new people and learn surprising things about all members of the class, including the teachers, something Kali described:

> The [other students'] writing style—they each have this unique voice.
> This group in particular, their voices are so unique and strong that it was
> definitely something to enjoy.... Both Denise and Eric, [program teachers],
> have been so encouraging and they themselves seem to love writing. So it's
> kind of interesting how both you and the teacher get to share something in
> common.

DISCUSSION

The program stood in contrast to typical middle level writing instruction in which teachers often "assign" writing, offer scripted, and/or limited prompts (Robb, 2010, p. 40), and serve as the sole audience and graders who set and enforce the rules (see, e.g., Atwell, 1987). In this program, the teachers invited students to design more actively their own questions and follow their own intellectual pursuits. Moreover, the teachers were also free to create writing curriculum unbounded from state mandates. In the following section, I offer various explanations for the freedom that teachers and middle level students experienced in place-based, process-writing instruction.

Does Acknowledgment of Fear Lead to Freedom?

Students rarely commented in their surveys or interviews about one element of instruction that our observations suggested was of central importance: Fear. In many programs on the first day of instruction, the teachers invited students to write about and share fears that they brought to the program. In one program, teachers asked students to write individual responses on a small stack of Post-its; they wrote responses to something they "were good at, a favorite book or movie." They also wrote about a "fear that they had about writing this week." After writing, one at a time, students placed their post-it notes on a large piece of brown, butcher paper subdivided into sections labeled according to each prompt.

With this visible evidence, adorning the classroom wall, that they were not alone in their fears—perhaps the students were "freer" to launch themselves into a program where other strangers shared a variety of fears. Here are some of the fears that students generated in one program:

- People will put labels on my writing.
- I'll be blocked and will write nothing good.
- I won't complete one piece of writing.
- I am afraid of trying new things.
- I fear wasting my time.
- I will be embarrassed.

Teachers in all programs worked to build a safe learning community on the first day—whether discussing fears or not, they set "norms" for willing experimentation, voluntary sharing, and safety. For adolescents to build strategic understanding of reading or writing, they "must feel comfortable expressing points of confusion, disagreement, and even disengagement.... They need to feel safe enough to talk about where they got lost in a text, what was confusing" (Schoenbach, Greenleaf, & Murphy, 2012, p. 27). The teachers and students in this study were all writers, attempting simultaneous, creative acts. Sometimes the teachers not only wrote; they made their writing efforts visible, discussing when appropriate what writing was like for them. "When I tried that, I felt a little stuck" or "If no one else wants to share, I'd like to ..." By positioning themselves as colearners, *do as I do* teachers, they reflected the kind of mentoring needed for 21st century middle level students (Springer, 2009, p. 25).

Students and Teachers "Got To" Teach and Learn Differently

Thirdspace theory offers another way to understand how and why students, and to a lesser extent, teachers, perceived the merging of schoolish work—writing—in place-based, out-of-school settings as something important and distinguished from their "regular" experience. As they crossed real and imagined learning borders for short periods of time, they may have found new possibilities for being learners, writers, and teachers for the very reason that they were not bound by familiar first spaces (e.g., classrooms, schools) or confining second spaces suggesting how students and teachers should accomplish their writing (e.g., policy-driven writing instruction). They were free from high stakes observations, student testing, and grades. Students and their teachers had a say in what to study and how to celebrate their learning; having agency in teaching and learning is motivating and engaging (Toshalis & Nakkula, 2012, p. 32).

While the writers' freedom and fluency may have been due to the satisfaction and inspiration of writing in and about culturally important, historic, and natural places, it is important to consider the larger policy context. The programs occurred in a state that had just "won" federal funding from H.R. 1532: Race to the Top Act of 2011. As part of its winning application, the state agreed to hasten its implementation of the Common Core State Standards (National Governors Association Center for Best Practices & Council of Chief State School Officers, 2010) and new systems for teacher evaluation. To accomplish these goals, the state education department built a website that included scripted curricular materials and a series of videos about how to teach to the standards. Many districts mandated that teachers adhere to a scripted scope and sequence while also undergoing high stakes performance reviews comprising formal classroom observations and heightened scrutiny of students' test scores.

The culture of this writing project encouraged teachers to promote narrative and expressive writing in the summer program, a stance at odds with the blueprint suggested by the Common Core State Standards (CCSS) which emphasized "close reading" of texts and production of argumentative and informational writing to demonstrate understanding. David Coleman (2011), often credited as the architect of CCSS, publicly dismissed and devalued expressive writing. At one speech he gave not far from where this study occurred, Coleman suggested that the problem with "personal opinion or the presentation of a personal matter ... [is that] in this world you realize people don't really give a shit about what you feel or think." (For a video of the speech, see Furman, 2012). Under these conditions, many teachers felt angry and devalued by the narrowing curriculum that deemphasized expressive writing and limited teachers' agency to determine curriculum, its content, and pace. In one post-program interview, a teacher explained that coteaching during a summer program offered her "oxygen" after a "suffocating" year.

Being outside the bounds of the rushed implementation of the Common Core, teachers may have felt intellectual freedom. They collaboratively developed immersive, place-based curriculum while studying local history, art, and nature. By building curriculum rather than "delivering" scripted "modules," the teachers challenged the rush to teach "codified sanitized versions of history, politics, and culture that ... leav[e] out the voices and concerns of our students and communities" (Karp, 2013, p. 2). One veteran teacher described that she was "excited" by the experience, because she had time to be inventive.

> I was excited to explore things and I was excited to do things in a free way, but I didn't know how it would feed me and it totally fed me … because it had given me time to play with ideas just like the kids had time to play with their ideas before they went to the museum.

In thirdspaces, outside the bounds of school and encroaching state policies, students experienced distinct freedom. Students got to write in genres and to express themselves in ways that were underemphasized by the Common Core. Rather than arguments, they wrote personal narratives, poetry, inventive stories, and journalistic writing about what they observed and experienced in the various places. In fact, where the constant close reading and genre limitations may have hindered fluency, in the summer, the students were poised to develop further their fluency, confidence, and identities as writers. Maybe the summer experience served as a vaccination, helping teachers and students survive the Common Core.

Place-Based Writing Supports Writing Fluency

This work adds to place-based education literature, suggesting that when adolescents experience process-oriented writing instruction in out-of-school settings, they may develop *fluency*. Sahara confided that she did not want to come to the program but soon realized that writing was simply putting thoughts on paper.

> I don't like writing that much.… Now I like it a lot more than I did when I started because … once you make us do it so much … it's kind of like writing down your thoughts, … writing down your thoughts like you're thinking it; just put it down on paper and before I never really thought about it just being that, but that's exactly what it is.

Sahara's realization may help explain the link between the program's writing process orientation and fluency. When students write daily, are free to write what they want, to write how they want, and to share when they want, many students may develop fluency that can elude them in other settings.

In these diverse program settings, the place itself provides material from which to write; through access to historical artifacts, art, and nature, students can generate ideas, listen to local stories, and view nature's spectacles. One student described, "When we wrote on site, I didn't have to remember what the place was like; so writing was easy." When asked, "What did you learn about writing?" another student responded, "Visiting places helped my writing flow" and simply explained that writing was easier because "walking around an old town, put me in the place of what I was writing." Ideas here about fluency align well with the high impact practice Graham and Perin (2007a) described as "inquiry activities" that "engag[e] students in activities that help them develop ideas and content for a particular writing task by analyzing immediate and concrete data (e.g., comparing and contrasting cases or collecting and evaluating evidence)" (p. 449). This study suggests that teachers could help students become more fluent as writers by incorporating more opportunities to move their bodies and to write about what they observe and see out of the classroom whether at the school or at home.

Place-Based Writing and Stewardship

Although beyond the scope of this study, interview data suggested that some young writers and their instructors may begin to *care* about a place because they have written themselves 'into' that place. In her evaluation study of four PBE programs, Power (2004) claimed that it is not just students who can be positively impacted; teachers who had access to sustained PBE-professional development became more comfortable drawing on local resources and places within their curriculum, engaging in interdisciplinary and collaborative teaching, and planning stronger curriculum with a greater use of service-learning.

Being on a hike at a national historic site, after a Park Ranger pointed out a U.S. President's favorite childhood tree, one student wrote a short history of America from the point of view of that tree. Another student, Kali, after having heard an account of how croquet permitted women and men to play a game *together,* rather than separately, elected to write a poem from the perspective of a young woman playing croquet and flirting. Each of these students intended to show the exact places that they had written about—the tree and the croquet garden—to family and friends. Interestingly, some of the teachers organized field trips for their regular-school students to the exact places of their summer programs. However, returning to a place is not the same as stewardship.

Teachers also value place-based writing programs for a variety of reasons including opportunities to coplan, coteach, and write. The teachers in this study had opportunities to work for short, immersive periods designing interdisciplinary, place-based curriculum. Although they did not teach writing for six hours a day, they had the freedom to teach writing during six hours of the day, on five consecutive days. They coplanned for several hours before and during their weeks of instruction. Their experience and satisfaction reflect literature suggesting that interdisciplinary, teacher teaming "is associated [with] more positive and productive learning environment" and students' "self-reported outcome" improvement (see Mertens, Flowers, & Mulhall, 2001, p. 130).

CONCLUSION

Writing programs like these afford middle level students and their teachers a learning culture that may elude them in regular schools whether for the prevailing policy environment or for the fact that they regularly lack agency in codetermining curriculum. In many ways, place-based writing programs are freeing. They offer opportunities for teachers and students to explore selectively topics of interest, set in proximal places. Participants value being outdoors in natural settings with opportunities to move and opportunities to be alone and think. They want the freedom to select writing prompts to pursue and the freedom to abandon writing that they have begun. They want the freedom to determine how and when to share writing. In short, they want the freedom to say no or yes. One teacher, Ann, implied that in thirdspaces like these, she could always answer "yes," something that can be difficult in her regular school.

> [During the summer] I like to always stress, "We're going to give you some prompts, but if you have something you want to write about, write about that. Always. You can always write about what you want to write about." They're constantly asking, "Can I do this? Can I do that?" The answer is always, "yes." I'm always saying, "The answer is always yes." I think that's what works about it—you get [to give them] the freedom that they don't have in school.

NOTES

1. All names in the chapter are pseudonyms.
2. See Appendix A.
3. This is a pseudonym.
4. I worked closely with the writing project administrators and teachers in the routine collection of program materials for the ongoing purpose of site evaluation and improvement. After data collection, I trained graduate students in data analysis.
5. For a concise discussion of Gardner and other theories of learning, see Pritchard (2009).
6. Quotations attributed to students by name come directly from interviews. Quotations not attributed to particular students come from de-identified survey data.

REFERENCES

Atwell, N. (1987). *In the middle: Writing, reading, and learning with adolescents.* Portsmouth, NH: Boynton-Cook/Heinemann.
Bhabha, H.K. (1994). *The location of culture.* New York, NY: Routledge.

Bigelow, B. (1996). How my schooling taught me contempt for the earth. *Rethinking Schools, 11*(1), 14–17.

Brooke, R. (2003). *Rural voices: Place-conscious education and the teaching of writing.* New York, NY & Berkeley, CA: Teachers College Press & the National Writing Project.

Burton, J. M. (2000). The configuration of meaning: Learner-centered art education revisited. *Studies in Art Education, 41,* 330–345.

Carnegie Council on Adolescent Development. (1989). *Turning points: Preparing American youth for the 21st century.* New York, NY: Carnegie Corporation.

Caskey, M. M. (2002). Authentic curriculum: Strengthening middle level education. In V. A. Anfara, Jr., & S. L. Stacki (Eds.), *Middle school curriculum, instruction and assessment* (pp.103–119). Greenwich, CT: Information Age.

Coleman, D. (2011, April). Bringing the Common Core to life. [Webinar]. Retrieved from the New York State Education Department website: http://usny.nysed.gov/rttt/resources/bringing-the-common-core-to-life.html

Cook-Sather, A. (2002). Authorizing students' perspectives: Toward trust, dialogue and change in education. *Educational Researcher, 31*(4), 3–14.

Creswell, J. W., & Poth, C. N. (2018). *Qualitative inquiry & research design: Choosing among five approaches.* Thousand Oaks, CA: SAGE.

Furman, T. (2012, March). *David Coleman, "Bringing the Common Core to life"* [Video File]. Retrieved from https://www.youtube.com/watch?v=Pu6lin88YXU

Gardner, H. (2011). *Frames of mind: The theory of multiple intelligences.* New York, NY: Basic Books.

Glaser, B. G., & Strauss, A. L. (1967). *The discovery of grounded theory: Strategies for qualitative research.* New York, NY: Aldine De Gruyter.

Gee, J. P. (1989). Literacy, discourse, and linguistics: Introduction and what is literacy. *Journal of Education, 171*(1), 5–25.

Gee, J. P. (1996). *Social linguistics and literacies* (2nd ed.). Bristol, PA: Taylor & Francis.

Glesne, C. (1999). *Becoming qualitative researchers: An introduction* (2nd ed.). New York, NY: Longman.

Graham, S., & Perin, D. (2007a). A meta-analysis of writing instruction for adolescent students. *Journal of Educational Psychology, 99,* 445–476.

Graham, S., & Perin, D. (2007b). *Writing next: Effective strategies to improve writing of adolescents in middle and high schools—A report* to *Carnegie Corporation of New York.* Washington, DC: Alliance for Excellent Education.

Gross, S. J. (2002). Introduction: Middle-level curriculum, instruction, and assessment. In V. A. Anfara, Jr., & S. L. Stacki (Eds.), *Middle school curriculum, instruction, and assessment* (pp. ix–xxxii). Greenwich, CN: Information Age.

Gruenewald, D. A. (2003). The best of both worlds: A critical pedagogy of place. *Educational Researcher, 32*(4), 3–12.

Guba, E. G. (1978). *Toward a methodology of naturalistic inquiry in educational evaluation* (CSE Monograph 8). Los Angeles, CA: University of California, Los Angeles, Center for the Study of Evaluation. Retrieved from http://cresst.org/wp-content/uploads/cse_monograph08.pdf

Gutierrez, K., Rymes, B., & Larson, J. (1995). Script, counterscript, and underlife in the classroom: James Brown versus Brown v. Board of Education. *Harvard Educational Review, 65,* 445–472.

Hillocks, G. (1986). *Research on written composition: New directions for teaching*. Urbana, IL: National Council of Teachers of English.

Hillocks, G. (1995). *Teaching writing as reflective practice*. New York, NY: Teachers College Press.

Hull, G., & Schultz, K. (2001). Literacy and learning out of school: A review of theory and research. *Review of Educational Research, 71*, 575–611.

Johnston, P. H. (2012). *Opening minds: Using language to change lives*. Portland, ME: Stenhouse.

Karp, S. (2013). The problems with the Common Core. *Rethinking Schools, 28*(2), 10–17.

Lave, J., & Wegner, E. (1991). *Situated learning: Legitimate peripheral participation*. New York, NY: Cambridge University Press.

Lieberman, A., & Wood, D. (2002). *Inside the National Writing Project: Connecting network learning and classroom teaching*. New York, NY: Teachers College Press.

Magnifico, A. M. (2013). 'Well, I have to write that': A cross-case qualitative analysis of young writers' motivations to write. *International Journal of Educational Psychology, 2*(1), 19–55.

McKinney, M., Lasley, S., & Holmes-Gull, R. (2008). The family writing Project: Creating space for sustaining teacher identity. *English Journal, 97*(5), 52–57.

McInerney, P., Smyth, J., & Down, B. (2011). 'Coming to a place near you?' The politics and possibilities of a critical pedagogy of place-based education. *Asia-Pacific Journal of Teacher Education, 39*(1), 3–16.

Mehan, H. (1979). *Learning lessons: Social organizations in the classroom*. Cambridge, MA: Harvard University Press.

Mertens, S. B., Flowers, N., & Mulhall, P. (2002). The relationship between middle-grades teacher certification and teaching practices. In V. A. Anfara, Jr., & S. L. Stacki (Eds.), *Middle school curriculum, instruction, and assessment* (pp. 119–138). Greenwich, CT: Information Age.

Meyer, T. (2013). Drawing art into the discussion of writing assessment. *English Journal, 103*(1), 81–87.

Miles, M. B., & Huberman, A. M. (1994). *Qualitative data analysis* (2nd ed.). Thousand Oaks, CA: SAGE.

Moffett, J. (1989). *Bridges: From personal writing to the formal essay* (Occasional Paper No. 9). Retrieved from https://www.nwp.org/cs/public/download/nwp_file/62/OP09.pdf?x-r=pcfile_d

Moghaddam, A. (2006). Coding issues in grounded theory. *Issues in Educational Research, 16*(1), 52–66.

Moje, E., Ciechanowski, K., Kramer, K., Ellis, L., Carrillo, R., & Collazo, T. (2004). Working toward third space in content area literacy: An examination of everyday funds of knowledge and discourse. *Reading Research Quarterly, 39*(1), 38–70.

Moles, K. (2008). A walk in thirdspace: Place, methods and walking. *Sociological Research Online, 13*(4). Retrieved from http://www.socresonline.org.uk/13/4/2.html

Moll, L. C., Amanti, C., Neff, D., & Gonzalez, N. (1992). Funds of knowledge for teaching: Using a qualitative approach to connect homes and classrooms. *Theory Into Practice, 31*(2), 132–141.

National Governors Association Center for Best Practices & Council of Chief State School Officers. (2010). *Common Core State Standards*. Washington, DC: Authors. Retrieved from http://www.corestandards.org/

National School Reform Faculty (n.d.). *Appreciative inquiry: A protocol for professional visitation*. Harmony Education Center. Retrieved from https://www.nsrfharmony.org/wp-content/uploads/2017/10/appreciative_inquiry_0.pdf

Nespor, J. (2008). Education and place: A review essay. *Educational Theory, 58*, 475–489.

Oehler-Marx, L. M. (2017). *"This is a beautiful place and it is worth protecting": An exploratory study about teacher beliefs and sense of place using activity theory*. (Unpublished doctoral dissertation). The University at Albany, Albany, NY.

Patton, M. Q. (2002). *Qualitative research and evaluation methods* (3rd ed.). Thousand Oaks, CA: SAGE.

Power, A. (2004). An evaluation of four place-based education programs. *The Journal of Environmental Education, 35*(4), 17–32.

Pritchard, A. (2009). *Ways of learning: Learning theories and learning styles in the classroom* (2nd ed.). Abingdon, England: Routledge.

Robb, L. (2010). *Teaching middle school writers*. Portsmouth, NH: Heinemann.

Schillinger, T. (2007). Humanities and the social studies: Studying the civil war through the third space. *Social Education, 71*, 384–389.

Schoenbach, R., Greenleaf, C., & Murphy, L. (2012). Engaged academic literacy for all. In *Reading for understanding: How reading apprenticeship improves disciplinary learning in secondary and college classrooms* (2nd ed.). San Francisco, CA: Jossey-Bass.

Smith, G. A. (2002). Place-based education: Learning to be where we are. *Phi Delta Kappan, 83*, 584–594.

Smith, G. A. (2007). Place-based education: Breaking through the constraining regularities of public school. *Environmental Education Research, 13*(2), 189–207.

Sobel, D. (2004). Place-based education: Connecting classroom and community. *Nature and Listening, 4*, 1–7.

Soja, E. (1996). *Thirdspace: Journeys to Los Angeles and other real-and-imagined places*. Oxford, England: Basil Blackwell.

Springer, M. A. (2009). Seeing the future of middle level education requires a mirror rather than a crystal ball. *Middle School Journal, 40*(5), 22–26.

Strauss, A., & Corbin, J. (1990). *Basics of qualitative research: Grounded theory procedures and techniques*. Newbury Park, CA: SAGE.

Theobald, P. (1997). *Teaching the commons: Place, pride, and the renewal of community*. Boulder, CO: Westview Press.

Theobald, P., & Nachtigal, P. (1995). Culture, community, and the promise of rural education. *Phi Delta Kappan, 77*, 132–135.

Toshalis, E., & Nakkula, M. J. (2012, April). *Motivation, engagement, and student voice*. Retrieved from the Students at the Center website: https://studentsatthecenterhub.org/resource/motivation-engagement-and-student-voice/

Urbanski, C. D. (2016). *Untangling urban middle school reform: Clashing agendas for literacy standards and student success*. New York, NY: Teachers College Press.

VanGarderen, D., Meyer, T., & Jacobowitz, R. (2007, April). *Drawing on experience: How do drawings measure up?* Paper presented at the annual meeting of the American Educational Research Association, Chicago, IL.

Van Maanen, J. (1988). *Tales of the field: On writing ethnography.* Chicago, IL: University of Chicago Press.

Vygotsky, L. S. (1978). *Mind in society: The development of higher psychological processes.* M. Cole, V. John-Steiner, S. Scribner, & E. Souberman (Eds.). Cambridge, MA: Harvard University Press.

Whitney, A., Blau, S., Bright, A., Cabe, R., Dewar, T., Levin, J., & Rogers, P. (2008). Beyond strategies: Teacher practice, writing process, and the influence of inquiry. *English Education, 40,* 201–230.

Whitney, A., & Johnson, L. (2017). The persistent relevance of a writing process orientation. *English Journal, 106*(4), 82–85.

Woodhouse, J. L., & Knapp, C. E. (2000). *Place-based curriculum and instruction: Outdoor and environmental education approaches.* Charleston, WV: ERIC Clearinghouse on Rural Education and Small Schools. Retrieved from ERIC database. (ED 448012)

Wood-Ray, K. (1999). *Wondrous words: Writers and writing in the elementary classroom.* Urbana, IL: National Council of Teachers of English.

Yin, R. K. (2003). *Case study research: Design and methods.* Thousand Oaks, CA: SAGE.

APPENDIX A

Effective Strategies to Improve Writing of Adolescents in Middle and High schools (Graham & Perin, 2007b)

1. **Writing Strategies,** which involves teaching students strategies for planning, revising, and editing their compositions
2. **Summarization,** which involves explicitly and systematically teaching students how to summarize texts
3. **Collaborative Writing,** which uses instructional arrangements in which adolescents work together to plan, draft, revise, and edit their compositions
4. **Specific Product Goals,** which assigns students specific, reachable goals for the writing they are to complete
5. **Word Processing,** which uses computers and word processors as instructional supports for writing assignments
6. **Sentence Combining,** which involves teaching students to construct more complex, sophisticated sentences
7. **Prewriting,** which engages students in activities designed to help them generate or organize ideas for their composition
8. **Inquiry Activities,** which engages students in analyzing immediate, concrete data to help them develop ideas and content for a particular writing task
9. **Process Writing Approach,** which interweaves a number of writing instructional activities in a workshop environment that stresses extended writing opportunities, writing for authentic audiences, personalized instruction, and cycles of writing
10. **Study of Models,** which provides students with opportunities to read, analyze, and emulate models of good writing
11. **Writing for Content Learning,** which uses writing as a tool for learning content material

APPENDIX B

Sample, Informal Interview Protocol for Middle Level Student Writers

1. Tell me a little bit about your week.
2. So you wrote. What are some of the writing chances that you guys had?
3. Did you share [your writing]?
4. Tell me about some of the [writing that] you shared.

5. Would you like to read your piece from the anthology?
   a. If you don't mind read/tell me about your inspiration before you start.

6. What is something you were pleased about in the piece you just read?
   a. Is there something that I wouldn't have noticed that you worked hard on and you were pleased with?

7. When you think about the pieces other kids wrote, is there any writing that jumped out at you?

8. Have you been in a writing project program before?

9. What's something about yourself as a writer that you know now?

10. And what's something you can do with writing that you didn't know you could do?

11. Have you been to [NAME OF PLACE] before?

12. Would you come back?

13. And let's say you had a cousin in from out of town or something like that...what are some of the things you would want to show them? What's something about [NAME OF PLACE] you know [now]?
    a. I have only been here one time before; tell me about [NAME OF PLACE].

14. One thing I'm kind of curious about, you obviously do some writing in school — what's something about the way writing happened here, that you noticed?
    a. Was this similar to that, or not?

15. You were mentioning the teachers — you've been in school your whole life and watched a lot of teachers. What's something that either X or X or both of them do that's different?

APPENDIX C

Sample, Informal Interview Protocol for Program Teachers

1. Talk a little about the program this week.
   a. What's one surprise from the program?

2. What was it like being AT THE PLACE, doing the program?

3. You have led youth writing programs now during the school year, summers, several summers....

   a. What's something you know now about how they work, or what makes them work?

   b. What works for you within them?

4. What would encourage teachers to know/do who haven't done this – cotaught in a youth writing program?
5. Did you find something that worked with regard to [writing instruction]?
6. Anything from here that you take back to your own classroom?
7. Is there anything else you want to talk about?

CHAPTER 13

IN THE MIDDLE OF NEXT PRACTICES

Barbara J. Mallory and James V. Davis
Coastal Carolina University

ABSTRACT

Although much research has focused on best practices that work in middle schools, scholars and future-ready school leaders have called for schools to blend best (research-based) and next (highly innovative) practices. In consideration of this blend of best practices and next practices, the purpose of this qualitative case study was to explore how one year-round, Title I middle school worked to operationalize best and next practices in school organization, instructional practices, uses of technology, and student engagement. We report our findings regarding factors related to organizational structures that contributed to middle school success in terms of academic growth and levels of proficiency, as well as findings related to best and next practices with instructional practices, uses of technology, student engagement, and diversity. Specific practices can potentially be replicated by other schools regarding the academic calendar, the seamless, yet intentional use of instructional technology strategies, and much more.

Curriculum, Instruction, and Assessment:
Intersecting New Needs and New Approaches, pp. 339–363
Copyright © 2020 by Information Age Publishing

In the world of education, many schools focus on building best practices in the teaching and learning environment. McNulty (2011) identified 'best practice' as a practice that "largely encompasses standardized strategies that have been deemed successful" (p. 3). However, McNulty suggested that schools really should be focusing on "next practices," if the idea is to transform a school to help each student be successful. He stated, "In order for schools to truly be transformed into something different, educators have to think differently—and offer something creative and new" (p. 4). Next practices, according to McNulty, are practices that evolve within an environment that encourage the introduction of innovative ideas and "implementing something so new that it has not been proven to work" (p. 4). Next practices come from a mindset of creativity; by their inherent nature, they are not known to work. In contrast, best practices have a proven track record to work in schools. A next practice may include, but is not limited to, innovative strategies such as inquiry-based learning, the use of QR codes, and problem-based learning. Although there is little empirical evidence to make the claim that "next practices" are "best practices," a school focused on continuous improvement and innovation in its approach to education will use a blend of best and next practices to remain relevant and significant in serving students (McNulty, 2011). In this chapter, we focus on a middle school that integrates best practices *and* next practices in its evolution to stay relevant and distinctive as a public school in service to the community.

We designed this case study of Next Middle School (NMS) (a pseudonym) to describe how one year-round, Title I middle school operationalized best and next practices in school organization, instructional practices, uses of technology, and student engagement. How does the middle school account for its success with its diverse student population? The selection of NMS as the setting of this study was purposeful, in that the authors were aware of the school through the National Forum to Accelerate Middle Grades Reform's Schools to Watch program (National Forum to Accelerate Middle-Grades Reform, n.d.) as a successful, minority-majority middle school, with a diverse population of students. It was designated as a School to Watch in 2008, and redesignated again in 2011, 2014, and 2017.

In our desire to explore a middle school through the lens of best practice and next practice, we sought to investigate teaching and learning practices employed in the school and the uses of technology and student engagement as part of the holistic school climate. Knowing that context always matters in the study of a specific school, we were especially curious about the school climate and culture, and year-round calendar employed at NMS.

NMS has operated on a year-round calendar since 2000. According to the National Center for Education Statistic's Schools and Staffing Survey (U.S. Department of Education, 2018), a "year-round cycle is defined as a cycle of school days distributed across 12 months of the calendar year and all students attending on the same cycle" (footnote 1). The year-round calendar at NMS began as a result of the feeder elementary school having a year-round calendar; therefore, NMS established a year-round calendar in 2000 to allow families to continue on this calendar option. This method of organization for a school is considered a next practice, or an innovative practice, as little empirical evidence exists to justify the decision to change from a traditional calendar to a year-round calendar.

We organized this chapter into the following sections: (a) background of the study, (b) problem statement, (c) purpose statement, (d) theoretical framework, (d) review of literature, (e) methodology, (f) limitations, (g) findings from the study, (h) discussion, and (i) concluding comments. NMS offered us the opportunity to study school organization, teaching and learning practices, uses of technology, and student engagement as a phenomenon of interest in its natural, real-life context.

BACKGROUND OF THE STUDY

More than elementary and high schools, the middle school has been in the business of transforming for years. In a brief history of middle school reform, Manning (2000) described how middle schools evolved rather rapidly from junior highs to developmentally appropriate places of learning for young adolescents. This transformation occurred as a result of the middle school seeking to be better at meeting needs of young adolescents ages 10–15, which makes the concept of an effective middle school part of a journey of evolution. To remain relevant and distinctive in service to young adolescents, middle schools, typically configured with Grades 6, 7, and 8, implement practices known to work. However, middle schools also are not afraid to implement practices that may work, or "next practices," as we refer to them in this study (National Middle School Association [NMSA], 2010).

By their very nature of being in the middle, middle schools serve a transitional group of young adolescents who are evolving from childhood to young adults. Perhaps, for these reasons, middle schools are not afraid to try what may work, along with what they know does work, regarding keeping students authentically engaged and reaching new heights with academics. The young adolescents who attend middle schools are going through major developmental changes—physically, socially, emotionally, and psychologically—that require middle school educators to focus on the social and emotional development of these students, as well as academic achievement (Armstrong, 2006). According to McNulty (2011), if organizations want to remain on top of their game, they must continually change, just as the environment in which young adolescents live will change. No school can rest on its laurels of best practices, as school improvement also falls within the realm of next practices.

NMS, a public, urban middle school in the southeastern United States, serves approximately 619 students in Grades 6 through 8. While NMS retains many concepts of the middle school model, including the organization of grade-level teams of students and teachers, a strong core and encore curriculum, and an interdisciplinary approach to curriculum, it is also in the middle of trying new, innovative practices. It seeks to be academically excellent, developmentally responsive, socially equitable, and supportive with solid structures built for teacher, parent, and student success. The school operates on a year-round schedule, which divides the year into 9-week quarters separated by 3-week intersession breaks.

As a year-round magnet school in the district, student enrollment is decided through a lottery system. With a growing enrollment of Hispanic students, the school is intentional in designing professional learning and advocacy initiatives to support Hispanic/Latino students and all English language learners. The middle school has been successful in implementation of positive behavior interventions and supports (PBIS), a practice that provides behavioral supports and a school culture needed for student success in middle school.

PROBLEM STATEMENT

In an era of school choice, legislators and the public have questioned the quality of public schools. In North Carolina, the School Report Card reports student achievement scores, achievement growth scores, achievement gaps, graduation rates, and other data from its accountability system to designate the performance level of schools (North Carolina School Report Cards, n.d.). The public school district where NMS is located is a minority-majority district that has been criticized for having over 20% of its schools being designated *low performing* by state standards (North Carolina School Report Cards, 2017). The district has been losing enrollment to charter schools, home schools, and private schools; however, since becoming a year-round, magnet school in 2000, one school, NMS, has been successful at keeping students engaged and academically performing in a manner that leads to growth with student achievement and higher levels of proficiency. By sharing insight into why and how practices used in the middle school are working to serve students in an urban community, we seek to add to the literature that quality, public middle schools not only exist as successful schools, but also thrive as distinctive schools.

Sharing positive stories of schools in this era of criticism of public schools is important. As a past-president of the National School Public Relations Association explained, "Teachers and students are beating the odds and succeeding despite a host of well-publicized risk factors associated with urban education" (Carr, 2004, p. 1). We sought to explore the middle school in perspective of beating the odds at NMS, a Title I, urban school that is experiencing success, despite risk factors often cited in reference to urban schools.

Berliner (2002) studied empirical evidence to conclude there is little evidence that effective teaching strategies and learning practices will work for all students and teachers, all of the time, because of the variability among students, teachers, families, and schools. Hattie (2012) also suggested from his meta-analysis of many studies on what works in schools to impact positive student achievement that everything works, but it is the context that matters. Because there is more than one way to make a school successful for all students, all schools need to be in the business of sharing narratives about best and next practices in context of what works.

PURPOSE STATEMENT

The purpose of this study was to explore how one year-round, Title I middle school worked to operationalize best and next practices in school organization, instructional practices, uses of technology, and student engagement. By interviewing the principal, who had been at the school for 3 years, studying the school's data reports and website, and collecting data from walk-through observations, we explored the middle school's practices to share the school's distinction as a middle School to Watch. The National Forum, through its Schools to Watch program, has developed highly specific criteria for identifying high-performing middle-grades schools. The criteria include the following four domains: (a) academic excellence, (b) developmental responsiveness, (c) social equity, and (d) effective organization structures. This case study drew from existing middle school literature about effective best practices, especially the Association for Middle Level Education (AMLE)'s seminal publication, *This We Believe: Keys to Educating Young Adolescents* (NMSA, 2010), a position paper that delineates the association's vision for successful middle schools.

The literature described many effective practices in middle schools, but this case study enabled us to explore the middle school's best and next practices that help the school to continue its transformation to a higher-performing status. Several research questions guided the study:

1. What are the factors related to year-round schooling that contribute to middle school success?
2. What are the best and next practices implemented in the areas of instructional practices, uses of technology, and student engagement?
3. How does the middle school account for its success in regard to diversity and subgroups of students?

THEORETICAL FRAMEWORK

Institutional theory offers some insight into why organizations tend to remain similar, even as competition would suggest that they become more distinctive to sustain a relevant existence. DiMaggio and Powell (1983) explained in their view of institutional theory, that even as organizations try to change, they become more similar. They referred to this process of becoming more homogeneous as *isomorphism*, defined as a "constraining process that forces one unit in a population to resemble other units that face the same set of environmental conditions" (p. 149).

In terms of schools as learning organizations, many argue that research-based evidence provides a foundation for what schools can do to produce high achieving students (Marzano, Simms, & Warrick, 2014; Schmoker, 2006). By having a "set" of best practices, a collection of what works well instructionally and regards student engagement, schools may migrate to these best practices to implement their teaching and learning processes. However, the prototype of an effective school cannot ignore the need for creativity and innovation (McNulty, 2011). According to McNulty (2011), a school's adoption of just a best practices approach may lead to homogenization, or improvement of status quo, which disavows the capacity of the school to become distinctive and significant as an innovative learning space. Elmore (2004) advocated for schools to learn to implement new practices in their context and setting. Middle schools, by mission, embrace the concept of meeting needs of adolescents and look for opportunities to meet needs of a shifting demographic group of students (Brighton, 2007; Quest to Learn, 2019). Isomorphism, in other words, may be counterintuitive to innovation.

As middle schools have been evolving since the 1960s into learning organizations to meet needs of young adolescents, the field of education and our society as a whole needs middle schools that are brave and curious about what is next in the quest to make middle schools even more effective at serving needs of these students. It is our belief that the field of education cannot afford schools that become satisfied with status quo, as an era of accountability and innovation needs schools that are willing to rise out of the sea of mediocrity and sameness to try new approaches in meeting needs of students in a global marketplace. We posit that middle schools grounded in best practices, with some percentage of next practices, lead to the most effective kinds of schools, as ones that are renewing to meet the needs of all students in context of their community. It is a middle school always in the middle of evolution.

The concept of the dynamic middle school relates to having a culture of best practices and next practices, combined. Blending the culture of best and next practices within the middle school identity keeps the middle school relevant and significant to the current and next generation of students.

REVIEW OF RELEVANT LITERATURE

For this study, we focused on three broad areas for reviewing the literature. First, we reviewed the literature on year-round schooling to understand the benefits and pitfalls, especially as related to middle schools. The second broad area focused on best practices in middle schools to prepare young adolescents to be successful in a global society. The review focused specifically on teaching and learning approaches used in middle schools that address diversity and uses of technology. The third area addressed innovative practices to meet academic and social-emotional needs of middle-level students. We focused on new practices that middle schools designed through an empathetic approach to solving problems in practice and opportunities for growth to meet needs of current and future students.

Year-Round Schools

The National Education Association (2019) reported that year-round schools operate 180 days per year, similar to traditional calendars, but the 180 days cover 365 days over a year with weekly breaks, or intercessions, between each block of school attendance. According to the NEA, the "most popular form of year-round education is the 45–15 plan, where students attend school for 45 days and then get three weeks (15 days) off. The usual holiday breaks are still built into this calendar" (para. 3). Some year-round school calendars employ a 60–20 or 90–30 plan, but according to the NEA, studies are inconclusive as to whether any year-round calendar is beneficial to student achievement.

Research on effectiveness of a year-round calendar, often referred to as a school reform calendar, reports little to no support that year-round schooling is more effective than schools employing a more traditional calendar (McMillen, 2001; Pedersen, 2011; Penta, 2001). Schools across the country have implemented extended school days or extended academic-year calendars, but research examining the relationship of these reform approaches and its impact on student achievement indicate mixed findings (Patall, Cooper, & Allen, 2010). Patall, Cooper, and Allen (2010) conducted a meta-analysis of 15 empirical studies of extended day and extended year school programs that yielded some evidence that extending school time can be an effective way to support student learning, particularly (a) for students most at risk of school failure and (b) when considerations are made for how time is used. More specifically, they found that extending time, especially quality time, might positively impact student learning, particularly for at-risk students. However, many of the study designs were incapable of yielding strong evidence about effects of extended time (Patall et al., 2010). From an international perspective, in the era of international school comparisons, nations with more than 180 instructional days or that implement calendars that are year-round have outperformed U.S. schools (Farbman & Kaplan, 2005).

However, year-round schools have not yet been added to the best practices literature, due to the inconclusive nature of the research, which leads one to query why year-round schools continue to exist. According to DeNisco (2015), in the United States in 2015, more than 3,700 schools operated on a year-round calendar, which accounted for about four percent of all public schools. Many year-round schools are Title I, which opted to change to a year-round organization to reduce summer slide in student achievement. However, research generally indicates "no effect or a small positive effect on student performance" (p. 1).

Both teachers and students are often referred to as beneficiaries of a year-round calendar. In their case study of three Title I, year-round, elementary schools, Haser and Nasser (2005) found benefits for teachers in a year-round setting from the perspective of continuity in curriculum and pacing of instruction. The National Association for Year-Round Education, (NAYRE) an advocacy group for the year-round school calendar, also promoted the advantage that teachers have time for professional learning consistency across a year (NAYRE, 2015). However, as an advocacy group, NAYRE acknowledged the scant research that the extended year calendar has been beneficial to lower socioeconomic students in preventing summer learning loss.

Other arguments for year-round education include three additional factors. First, the efficient use of school facilities is an advantage, in that schools are used throughout the year. The second factor is that the year-round calendar can be a magnet choice in an era where parents seek school choice. The third factor is the opportunity for remediation and acceleration to occur within a year-round calendar.

Even though these common-sense advantages may keep year-round calendars viable as a reform option, there is still the inconclusive nature of research. In California schools, where overcrowding in school facilities led some districts to institute the year-round calendar, Graves (2011) used longitudinal data from standardized test scores to study the impact of year-round schools. The findings showcased that there was little difference in student performance between students in a traditional calendar and those in a year-round calendar.

The disadvantages that may give school leaders pause in implementing the year-round calendar fall within the category of weak benefits of such a calendar. The lack of solid empirical evidence that a year-round calendar impacts student achievement does not help overcome the changes that have to take place for middle schools on a 10-month traditional calendar. Parents may not want the intersessions, which can be perceived as disruptive breaks. The inconclusive academic benefits also may not warrant the extra costs associated with year-round transportation, facility use, and program expenditures. Furthermore, within a state, athletic associations generate rules about scheduling practices and participation in extracurricular sports. Schools using a year-round calendar may find obstacles to scheduling events or activities with schools employing a traditional calendar.

Best Practices in Middle School Education

Balfanz (2009) examined the impact of middle school education on student graduation rates and found a strong correlation exists between a positive middle school experience and high school graduation rates, which provides insight into how important school transitions are for young adolescents. Recognizing the importance of the middle school as a place where young adolescents "make it or break it," we found credibility in AMLE's position statement (NMSA, 2010), which provides a framework to describe best practices in educating students ages 10–15. One constant and overarching practice is the climate for high expectations, which means teachers engage in strategies related to communicating high expectations to all students and providing active, purposeful learning and relevant curriculum (Demink-Carthew, 2017).

Middle school climate. Best practices do not exist outside of a context of a school. Generally, school culture and school climate constitute the context of the school. With culture being viewed as the way we do things around here and climate being viewed as the way we feel about the way we do things here, both become very important in the context of best practices. As Bergren (2014) found in his study of student achievement in middle schools in Virginia, climate matters in middle school with regard to student achievement. Bergren noted specifically that as the school climate becomes more positive, student achievement scores rise. The National School Climate Center (2018) identified five broad categories of school climate that must be attended to if the school is to achieve its goals: (a) safety, (b) teaching and learning, (c) interpersonal relationships, (d) social media, and (e) institutional environment. For the purposes of this study, we used these aforementioned categories to begin the process of coding data collected from walk-throughs, principal interviews, and documents at NMS.

Teaching and learning best practices. *This We Believe* (NMSA, 2010) included a framework for best practices in middle schools that includes an overview of curriculum and instruction best practices. It described 16 characteristics of middle level education divided into three areas: curriculum, instruction, and assessment; leadership and organization; and culture and community. Within this framework, practices in teaching and learning include educators valuing young adolescents, students and teachers engaged in active learning, and curriculum that is challenging, exploratory, integrative, and relevant. A major characteristic of successful middle schools is that every student has a known advocate who can seek outside support for students if needed.

The practice of teaching is a human enterprise; it is difficult to separate the practice from the person implementing it. Hattie (2012) identified many characteristics of teachers who have an impact on students, one of which is that effective teachers form strong relationships with their students and use evidence-based teaching strategies. According to researchers at the Center for Technology in Education at Johns Hopkins University, effective urban educators create and extend additional time for instruction in reading and math, offer tutoring, and reduce disruptions to teaching (Center for Technology in Education, n.d.).

Best practices related to uses of technology. The integration of technology in teaching and learning has presented challenges and opportunities for middle level educators. In a study of middle grades teachers' perspectives in China and the United States in regard to emerging technologies, Spires, Morris, and Zhang (2012) observed, "Confronting the challenges of new literacies and emerging technologies not only in the United States, the most developed country in the world, but also in China, the largest developing country, is a daunting task for educators" (p. 3). However, middle school teachers in the study agreed that technology use was important in building skills. In their study, Spires et al. found that teachers in both countries strongly agreed that using computers promoted middle school student-centered learning and self-discovery and that students mastered problem solving more effectively by using computers. They also found that

U.S. teachers named tools, such as digital cameras, PowerPoint presentations, wikis, and computerized gaming as they integrated technology into teaching.

Best practices related to student engagement. Davis (2017) defined student engagement as the "degree of attention, curiosity, interest, optimism, and passion that students show when they are learning or being taught" (para. 1). Then, he described practices that lead to student engagement, including inquiry-based learning; the use of quick response codes to gather feedback, to poll students, and as a tool to link to Google maps; project-based learning; implementation of classroom technology; and jigsaws. These strategies are linked to active learning, which is the overarching theme in successful middle schools.

This We Believe (NMSA, 2010) described active learning as a feature of successful middle schools. Edwards (2015) described a framework that delves deeply into the concept of active learning that involves getting students intellectually, socially, and physically active in their learning. Acknowledging that middle school learners are naturally curious, Edwards advocated for instructional strategies that capitalize both on students' curiosity and existing knowledge. Intellectually active learning strategies are tactics such as using concept maps, designing inquiry and problem-solving activities, and synthesizing information for presentations. Examples of engaging middle school students in socially active learning involve employing whole and small group discussions and projects. Instructional strategies that engage students physically are participating in experiments, playing games, and using manipulatives.

Next Practices in Middle School Education

While most of the strategies described as best practices have a research-base to support that they are effective in some contexts, McNulty (2011) shared an overview of next practices intended to keep schools transforming, as the global world around schools is dynamic and changing. McNulty advocated that schools employ best practices but also try next practices, even as they are mixed with uncertainty, ambiguity, and disruptive thinking. He explained that next practices increase the school's capacity to do things not done before, which is critical in times when schools are experiencing shifts in student demographics, equity issues in low-resourced environments, teacher shortages, STEM (science, technology, engineering, and math) and STEAM (science, technology, engineering, art, and math), and expectations in accountability.

Most of the next practices involve technology, such as gaming and technologies that engage students or connect with others in a virtual way.

Kopcha (2012) identified several factors that interfere with next practices related to teachers and technology, including access, vision, professional development time, and personal beliefs. In the traditional school setting, Kopcha studied elementary teachers to identify barriers to next practices related to planning and implementing new strategies integrating technology. He reported:

> Months after transitioning from mentoring to teacher-led communities of practice, teachers continued to report positive perceptions of several barriers and were observed engaging in desirable instructional practices. Interviews suggested that the situated professional development activities helped create an environment that supported teachers' decisions to integrate technology. (p. 1109)

McCoy (2017) described how the middle school schedule could serve as a driver to encourage innovation. School leaders who want to encourage next practices in both academics and social emotional learning create time for middle school teachers to meet with students to engage in project-based learning by building a master schedule that may look different than it has in the past. Principals who want to create a risk-taking environment in meeting students' needs will build master schedules that place value on collaborative time.

Another area in middle school that is ripe for next practice is what happens in the extended day. How is the extended day connected to school goals and the intended day, as well as students' preparation for life? McCoy (2017) described a built-in flex period that the middle schools use for enrichment, student supports, and student passions. He explained:

> We can do so much more with our middle school schedule than just make sure students get math, reading, and PE. Our middle schoolers need opportunities to explore and develop passions. We help our teachers get better when we keep them current on strategies and implementations. A great vision helps set the school on a great course and the schedule is an important part of seeing it realized. (para. 9)

METHODOLOGY

The purpose of this qualitative study was to describe how one year-round, Title I middle school operationalized best and next practices in school organization, instructional practices, uses of technology, and student engagement. The researchers used a case study design to explore the middle school's best and next practices. This natural setting provided the opportunity for many observations to create understanding and application of best and next practices.

Research Design

This descriptive case study focused on the phenomenon of a year-round, Title I middle school that was experiencing success in serving the needs of a minority-majority school population in an urban setting. Using qualitative methods of collecting data from document analysis, observations, and an interview, we explained the middle school in this study in terms of best practices and next practices through an action research process. In the end, the goal was to complete research and provide a rich and highly descriptive explanation.

In practices borrowed from grounded research, we began our data analysis as we collected each data set. After collecting qualitative data from walk-throughs, we used predetermined codes to begin coding, prior to the principal's interview. "In grounded theory, the analysis begins as soon as the first bit of data is collected" (Corbin & Strauss, 1990, p. 6). We used this technique of simultaneous data collection and analysis until the case yielded no new information.

Context of the Study

Next Middle School (NMS) is a middle school in a large, urban school district in the Southeastern United States. As a year-round middle school, it operates on a calendar of 180-days of instruction with 3-week intersessions throughout the annual calendar. The purpose of this calendar was to help NMS students retain their learning with fewer consecutive vacation weeks in the summer. Four intersessions, or breaks in the academic year, occur during the year: one during the fall, winter, spring, and summer rather than one long, 12-week summer break.

The first year that NMS offered the year-round calendar as a magnet choice within the district was 2000–01. Previously, NMS had been a sixth grade center, but with the magnet choice, Grades 7 and 8 were added. The public school district promoted magnet school offerings and school choice options through a lottery system to prevent families from leaving the district. Parents seemed to enjoy the calendar flexibility of the elementary feeder school, and NMS, desiring to retain enrollment as a primary motivator, adopted the year-round elementary school calendar as a magnet. It is the highest performing middle school in the district, based upon growth and levels of proficiency.

All of the 42 teachers at NMS are fully licensed in middle-level education, and 25% of the teachers are certified to serve academically and intellectually gifted students. Nine of the teachers have National Board Certification, and 50% of the teachers have graduate degrees. One-third of the teachers have more than 10 years of experience. Compared to other schools in the district and state, NMS has more fully licensed teachers. In addition, this school has more teachers with advanced degrees, when compared to their district and the state and has more national board certified teachers, when compared to the district.

The 619 students at NMS represent culturally diverse families, with 51% African American, 22% Hispanic, 19% Caucasian, 4% Asian, and 4% multiracial. Seventy-six percent of the students are on the A/B honor roll. In addition to academic achievement, many students also participate in sports and arts programs, including chorus, band, strings orchestra, and studio art. Students are also encouraged to participate on athletic and academic teams, science Olympiads, science fairs, and other school clubs.

Participants of the Study

The NMS principal is a Black female, who is a mid-career professional who holds a doctorate in educational leadership. Most of her career has been in middle school. Her peers respect her, as evidenced by her election as an officer in the state's middle school association. We interviewed her and exchanged emails for clarifying information as data were coded and analyzed.

Data Collection

Much of this study involved collecting new and existing data from the school that served as the setting for this case study. As the middle school had been identified as a School to Watch in 2008, 2011, 2014, and 2017, much data existed from the Schools to Watch application process, which the principal made readily available to the researchers in a conference room at the school. Other documents reviewed in our analyses included school improvement plans, student achievement data, school report card data, benchmark indicators, school newsletters, and school lottery recruitment materials. The walk-through observation notes and transcripts of principal interviews also provided depth to the school's narrative found in the existing documents.

Both of the researchers reviewed documents and collected data from walk-throughs to add to the study's credibility and trustworthiness. Our intent was to have enough data from walk-throughs to validate what was occurring in the school. According to Creswell (2013), one of the factors that contributes to credibility and trustworthiness of data is triangulation. We collected data from walk-throughs using anecdotal note taking to denote "what the teacher is doing" and "what the students are doing" during 10-minute walk-throughs on five different days. One of us visited 27 classrooms and the other visited 25 classrooms in order to generate rich data from the sixth, seventh, and eighth grade classroom walk-throughs. According to David (2008), walk-throughs are different from classroom observations used to assess and evaluate teachers; walk-throughs "typically involve looking at how well teachers are implementing a particular program or set of practices that the district or school has adopted" (p. 81).

Data Analysis

After reviewing school documents including school improvement plans, student achievement data, school report cards, benchmark indicators, school newsletters, and school lottery recruitment materials, we reviewed, coded, and analyzed the documents. We also read, coded, and analyzed data from the walk-through observations and interview transcripts. Our methods of analysis began with organizing all of the data and then applying a predetermined set of codes to yield a broad view of school culture and practices.

Because of the abundance of data, we first approached the data to organize it, as suggested by Ary, Jacobs, and Sorenson (2010). They suggested the concept of data analysis spiral when qualitative researchers have prolific data, which involved several rounds of reading and organizing to familiarize and organize data. After that initial process, they advise to read the data in the organized groups in order to code and reduce the data, followed by interpreting and then representing data in themes. Once the documents were organized and initial readings conducted, we continued reading and adding codes iteratively, using the following codes: safety, teaching and learning, interpersonal relationships, technology/social media, and institutional environment. The same reading and coding process took place with the walk-through observation and interview data.

After initial coding, we took each category through an additional reading and coding process, using the following codes: next practice, best practice, technology, student engagement, diversity, and teaching and learning. To reduce the potential for bias in data interpretation, we confirmed data as authentic, by comparing similar evidence found across all documents. Creswell and Miller (2000) suggested that validity of qualitative data implies that there is accuracy in the way participants see the phenomenon being studied. Therefore, the principal participant also helped with confirming data interpretation that emerged from the iterative coding processes.

Study Limitations

As a case study, this research and its findings relate to one urban middle school, with interview data from one educator who works at the school. Both of us had previously served as principals and we were the data collectors and analysts for this project. Although we aimed to reduce bias through triangulation of data, we may have had minimal bias based on experiences from our former principalships.

STUDY FINDINGS

After several iterations of reading and coding the interview transcripts, data from walk-throughs, and documents provided by the school and those on the website, we had rich insight into the NMS organization, teaching and learning practices in the middle school, uses of technology, and student engagement related to students' subgroup successes. First, we report what we found regarding factors related to organizational structures that contributed to NMS success. Second, we report the findings related to best and next practices in instructional practices. In the next sections, we describe findings related to uses of technology and student engagement. Lastly, we report the findings related to engagement of various subgroups of students.

Organizational Factors Contributing to Middle School Success

The first finding relates to the year-round calendar. The principal described the 9-week sessions of classes as intense periods of learning involving a dynamic level of engagement, interactions, and collaboration. After each of the 9-week sessions and high expectations for learning, inside the classroom, students have a three-week intersession, with many activities offered to appeal to student interest.

As a major component of year-round education, NMS extended the school day with meaningful and relevant experiences, where all students are required to attend for a minimum of 30 minutes, that allow intersessions to be used for acceleration purposes, rather than remediation that some year-round schools deem necessary.

The next finding falls into the category of next practice, as the school is a master in using technology and data for organizational communication and connectivity for learning exchanges. The structure of the school day always includes some dynamic use of technology, such as connecting with students in other parts of the state, country, or world, or updating parents, using data management in a way to enhance specifics for each young adolescent.

Instructional Best and Next Practices

From the walk-through observational data, we found that most occurrences of best practices related to assessment *for* teaching and learning. Whether it was teachers using data to design student-centered instruction or using formative assessment data from instructional use of exit tickets, quizzes, e-journals, or quick response codes, teachers use formative assessment daily to guide instructional decisions.

Another best instructional practice was the use of differentiation and distributed summarizing during the day and extended day. In addition, we found that the school adopted a significant pedagogy of inquiry-based learning. A high level of intentionality concerning student questioning was evident. Students were not simply asked to recall details from various tasks, but instead, at all grade levels and in all content areas, through questioning and deep inquiry, students are constantly synthesizing information, sharing their thoughts, and then justifying positions and beliefs.

With regard to instructional next practices, we found that the integration of technology across all subject areas and the incorporation of service learning to be major new approaches that the school was building into the dynamic culture. Many schools use technology, but at NMS the use of technology in instruction involved major collaboration with the media specialist, technology facilitator, and peer teachers in the interdisciplinary approach to student-centered projects. In addition, young adolescents at NMS take part in service-learning activities, where they are assessing situations, creating plans, helping others, but also learning valuable lessons that they can incorporate and use both inside and outside of the classroom.

Lastly, movement was a way that NMS has showcased innovation when it comes to instructional practices. Teachers at NMS work to incorporate movement into their lessons every 12–15 minutes. The expectation is that students are regularly moving. Students are moving from center to center, moving to group themselves, moving as part of the lesson, and moving to clap, tap, or signal certain things throughout the class.

Technology Best and Next Practices

Findings related to best and next practices in using technology were closely aligned to learning. Students use technology in many traditional ways, such as tools in math and science, but students at NMS also use technology to communicate and collaborate with students across the city, state, and nation. NMS students actively engage in face-to-face and virtual dialogue, often using peer review and assessment as e-learning opportunities. As a next practice, not only are students taught to use a variety of tools, apps, and devices, but also holistically, the school focuses on the seamless integration of technology.

Student Engagement Best and Next Practices

The best practice in engaging students at NMS is the use of high functioning cooperative learning teams, known as collaborative learning teams. It is common practice to find students working in collaborative groups, in the truest sense of the word, reading, writing, speaking, listening, creating, and planning with one another, where if any member were to be removed, the group could not proceed in an effective manner.

Another finding related to student engagement was the next practice of blending high expectations of student engagement, instructional practices involving movement and inquiry, and technology integration, to empower diversity. All students participate in extended day activities, with the school finding the means to support financially and transport students to ensure involvement and access to clubs, teams, and activities.

Diversity

As an urban minority-majority school, NMS embraces diversity across its student population. On the school calendar, NMS includes all holidays, such as Diwali, a Hindu holiday. The website, handbooks, and all school documents are available in English and Spanish. Student surveys, assessing satisfaction inside and outside of the classroom, twice a year, reveal to school leaders that students love their school and attribute their success to personalized counseling, teacher support, choices, and enjoyment of learning. Findings that explain student success with NMS's diverse students involve two best practices and a best and next practice.

First, as a best practice, the school uses a tactical approach to improve achievement of Hispanic students through more frequent progress monitoring of student performance. When Hispanic student performance was not what NMS expected, the school team, with parents, created a specific, measurable, achievable, relevant and time-bound (SMART) goal in their school improvement plan to check their progress every 3 weeks to determine if they were performing at, above, or below student-teacher-parent designed goals. Teachers then use the progress monitoring data to make instructional decisions.

Another best practice involved participation in the Enlaces program, which is a program that provides a differentiated approach to support academic and social-emotional needs of Hispanic students and families. NMS launched initiatives that built on the work of the Enlaces program, operated by Duke University's Office of Durham Affairs. At NMS, five faculty and administrators from the Enlaces 2.0 core team participated. Through a tiered approach, they provided academic and social support to Hispanic students. The Enlaces 2.0 core team engaged students and parents through in-school and afterschool clubs, intersession camps, and special projects.

As both best and next practices to support diversity, all students and parents, regardless of ethnicity, have a voice in decisions made at NMS. The level of engagement at NMS involves choice, opportunity, and access. Students at NMS, whether they meet expectations of the district's definition of "academically and intellectually gifted," or not, have the choice to take honors-level math and English language arts classes. NMS also embraces student choice when it comes to instructional practices. Teachers provide students with choices of a variety of writing topics across the curriculum, as well as a choice in how they demonstrate learning.

Teachers offer many opportunities for acceleration, remediation, and parent engagement in setting learning goals. All students have one-to-one advisement in a distributed counseling approach, which allows teachers to get to know their students well. Students also have access to after-school clubs, academic teams, sports, and/or arts events, with 100% of the students involved in the extended day. The school's parent-teacher-student organization also manages and plans opportunities for intersessions. They coordinate all types of camps, including gymnastics, arts, crafts, technology, dance, theatre, wildlife, yoga, recreation, digital studios, design, economics, and STEM education. They partner with local universities to offer academic camps, and they partner with the local YMCA to have camps available for students based on needs and desires. All students have access to these opportunities because parent groups and the sponsoring agency manage transportation issues.

DISCUSSION

NMS is a year-round middle school that is also a Title I school, meaning that more than 40% of the student population receives free or reduced lunch. The fact that NMS operates on a year-round calendar is considered a "next practice," as research is inconclusive about the impact of student achievement in year-round schools, even as they have grown in popularity by 26% from 2007 to 2012 (DeNisco, 2015). This overarching next practice led us to want to explore in more depth the practices going on at NMS to explain best and next practices related to the success of this Title I middle school.

What works is a combination of best and next practices. Implementing the year-round calendar as a next practice, works at NMS, especially with expectations of high levels of engagement, interactions, and collaboration during nine-week class sessions, extended day activities, and well-designed intersessions that provide opportunities for active growth and development of young adolescents. The next practice of blending high expectations of student engagement, instructional practices involving movement and inquiry, and technology integration helps to value and empower diversity. The use of data, as a best practice, works because teachers collect meaningful data from formative assessments that allow them to personalize learning that leads to impactful relationships with students.

Voice, choice, and rejoice dominate the school's climate, as teachers aim for high levels of engagement and encourage collaboration across all ethnic groups within NMS and many experts, academic friends, and peers external to NMS. Cooperative learning, a practice common in many middle schools, is a next practice—collaborative learning. Teachers implement service learning across all disciplines, which is a next practice in development because the link to academic achievement is yet to be determined. Students find joy in choosing topics and learning resources, as well as designing projects for service learning. They find joy and creativity in expectations of movement and using technology to facilitate their learning and demonstration of learning. Through best and next practices to support diversity, teachers of all students, regardless of ethnicity, empower student-centered decision making and engagement.

The educators at NMS keep effective instruction and student learning success at the forefront of their work. Their cause is to serve all students (and their families) well. There was a strong sense of individual accountability for both one's own learning and the team or group performance. Students were engaged actively in their learning, as the teacher posed a question or a social problem, as opposed to simply lecturing and sharing information. Students took part in service-learning activities and e-learning activities, in which they assess situations, create plans, and help others.

For example, in one service learning project, several classes were observed as they engaged in a recycling service-learning activity. Students explained how they were highly engaged in planning efforts, creating action steps, and implementing initiatives. They expressed joy in writing about the impact they had made on their local community.

In addition, a major factor in high levels of engagement is that NMS embraces student choice when it comes to instructional practices. Teachers encourage students to choose between a variety of activities to complete, and then, also encourage them to choose a way to showcase the material that they have learned. For example, when teaching the skill of summarizing, students choose texts they wish to summarize, and then choose how they would summarize the information: in a paragraph, with a song, as a rap, with a visual representation, or as an interpretative dance. No student is restricted to one assignment and one prescribed outcome. Teachers incorporate student choice into virtually every lesson, every day.

The seamless integration of technology was also impressive. It was immediately clear that at NMS, apps, cameras, and iPads are not used in isolation, but instead, incorporated into lessons throughout many content areas; learning drove teaching, not technology. However, teachers and students plan learning goals with technology as a resource. Gone are the days at NMS when students pack up their materials and head to the computer lab to complete an assignment in isolation of what they are regularly working on inside their classrooms, as classrooms are rich in the tools of technology. Teachers allow and empower students to choose the technology that serves them best and will help them reach their desired learning outcomes. While students in various classrooms may be utilizing iPads and laptops or choosing from a multitude of apps and online tutorials, as they work on Google docs and complete quizzlets, they may also be engaged in Kahoots or digital storytelling with famous educators and celebrities. They video conference with international pen pals, or, as in one instance, students were videoconferencing with a real-life marine biologist, using inquiry to learn about marine life and even college requirements for becoming a marine biologist. The bottom line becomes, in terms of best practices and instructional technology, teachers at NMS relinquish control, equip their students with the technology needed to thrive in today's society, and then, monitor them to work, reflect, assess themselves, and complete daily tasks in a high-quality manner.

CONCLUSIONS

Next Middle School, as McNulty (2011) suggested, implements a blend of best practices and next practices. The findings from this study suggest that the dynamic middle school, with blended best and next practices, promotes high levels of student engagement, using inquiry-based instruction, technology, and high expectations of movement, along with high levels of student voice, choice, and reasons to rejoice. At a glance, the practices at NMS can appear to be overwhelmingly traditional, best practices. However, teachers have taken best practices and enhanced them to a level where they are innovative. This dynamic middle school, as a place where best and next practices converge, varies the process and the products needed as learning demonstrations, so that students and families have a voice, a choice, and can rejoice in a climate where they know all students matter.

At NMS, it was obvious to see why students and teachers alike were excited about the creative ways that they use technology and high levels of engagement. In the context of social equity, all students have opportunities to an extended day, with a multitude of choices that encourage high levels of participation. Teachers are excited about the social equity and development of students as citizens of the world—not just NMS citizens.

This study of NMS provides insight into the idea of teacher ownership in student learning that motivates them to collaborate to learn more about instructional practice, which, in many ways, is a next practice. In best practice environments, the focus is on instructional strategies. However, as Hattie (2012) suggested, when teachers own the role they assume in achievement and growth of students, they become influencers of learning, rather than influencers of teaching. We considered this paradigm shift a next practice in the evolution of middle schools.

REFERENCES

Armstrong, T. (2006). *Best schools*. Alexandria, VA: Association for Supervision and Curriculum Development.

Ary, D., Jacobs, L. C., & Sorenson, C. (2010). *Introduction to research in education* (8th ed.). New York, NY: Wadsworth.

Balfanz, R. (2009). *Putting middle grades students on the graduation path: A policy and practice brief*. Westerville, OH: National Middle School Association. Retrieved from https://www.amle.org/portals/0/pdf/articles/policy_brief_balfanz.pdf

Bergren, D. A. (2014). *The impact of school climate on student achievement in the middle schools of the Commonwealth of Virginia: A quantitative analysis of existing data* (Doctoral dissertation). Retrieved from ProQuest Full Text. (UMI Number 3615518)

Berliner, D. C. (2002). Educational research: The hardest science lesson of all. *Educational Researcher, 31*(8), 18–20.

Brighton, K. L. (2007). *Coming of age: The education and development of young adolescents*. Westerville, OH: National Middle School Association.

Carr, N. (2004). *Telling your story: A toolkit for marketing urban education.* Alexandria, VA: National School Boards Association, Council of Urban Boards of Education. Retrieved from http://www.nvasb.org/assets/telling_your_story2.pdf

Center for Technology in Education. (n.d.). *Urban education. Research on best practices: Instruction time.* Retrieved from http://cte.jhu.edu/urbaneducation/ses4_act1_pag1.shtml

Corbin, J., & Strauss, A. (1990). Grounded theory research: Procedures, canons, and evaluative criteria. *Qualitative Sociology, 13*(1), 1–21. Retrieved from https://med-fom-familymed-research.sites.olt.ubc.ca/files/2012/03/W10-Corbin-and-Strauss-grounded-theory.pdf

Creswell, J. W. (2013). *Qualitative inquiry and research design: Choosing among five approaches* (3rd ed.). Los Angeles, CA: SAGE.

Creswell, J. W., & Miller, D. (2000). Determining validity in qualitative inquiry. *Theory Into Practice, 39*, 124–130.

David, J. L. (2008). What research says about … classroom walk-throughs. *Educational Leadership, 65*(4), 81–82.

Davis, J. (2017). *Five teaching strategies designed to challenge and engage students.* Westerville, OH: Association for Middle Level Education. Retrieved from http://www.amle.org/BrowsebyTopic/WhatsNew/WNDet.aspx?ArtMID=888&ArticleID=876

DeMink-Carthew, J. (2017). Reform-oriented collaborative inquiry as a pedagogy for student teaching in middle school. *Middle Grades Research Journal, 11*(1), 13–27.

DeNisco, A. (2015, September). Year-round schooling gains popularity. *District Administration.* Retrieved from https://districtadministration.com/year-round-schooling-gains-popularity/

DiMaggio, P., & Powell, W. (1983). The iron cage revisited: Institutional isomorphism and collective rationality in organizational fields. *American Sociological Review, 48*(2), 147–160.

Edwards, S. (2015). Active learning in the middle grades. *Middle School Journal, 46*(5), 26–32. Retrieved from https://files.eric.ed.gov/fulltext/EJ1059827.pdf

Elmore, R. F. (2004). *School reform from the inside out: Policy, practice, and performance.* Cambridge, MA: Harvard University Press.

Farbman, D., & Kaplan, C. (2005). *Time for a change: The promise of extended-time schools for promoting achievement.* Boston, MA: Massachusetts 2020. Retrieved from https://files.eric.ed.gov/fulltext/ED534912.pdf

Graves, J. (2011). Effects of year-round schooling on disadvantaged students and the distribution of standardized test performance. *Economics of Education Review, 30*, 1281–1305. doi.org/10.1016/j.econedurev.2011.04.003

Haser, S. G., & Nasser, I. (2005). *Year-round education: Change and choice for schools and teachers.* Lantham, MD: Rowman & Littlefield Education.

Hattie, J. (2012). *Visible learning for teachers: Maximizing impact on learning.* New York, NY: Routledge.

Kopcha, T. J. (2012). Teachers' perceptions of the barriers to technology integration and practices with technology under situated professional development. *Computers & Education, 59*, 1109–1121.

Manning, M. (2000). A brief history of the middle school. *The Clearing House, 73*(4), 192.

Marzano, R., Simms, J., & Warrick, P. (2014). *High reliability schools: The next step in school reform.* Bloomington, IN: Marzano Research Laboratory.

McCoy, D. (2017). *Middle school schedule as a driver for innovation.* Westerville, OH: Association for Middle Level Education. Retrieved from https://www.amle.org/BrowsebyTopic/WhatsNew/WNDet/TabId/270/ArtMID/888/ArticleID/814/Middle-School-Schedule-as-a-Driver-for-Innovation.aspx

McMillen, B. J. (2001) A statewide evaluation of academic achievement in year-round schools, *The Journal of Educational Research, 95*(2), 67–74. doi.org/10.1080/00220670109596574

McNulty, R. J. (2011). *Best practices to next practices: A new way of "Doing Business" for school transformation* [White paper]. International Center for Leadership in Education. Retrieved from https://dropoutprevention.org/wp-content/uploads/2015/07/Solutions_Jan2013_13.1_next_practices_white_paper.pdf

National Association for Year-Round Education. (2015). *Research* [PowerPoint slides]. Retrieved from https://www.nayre.org/PDFs/Basics_of_YRE_Part_2.pdf

National Education Association. (2019). Research spotlight on year-round education: NEA reviews of the research on best practices in education [Web blog]. Retrieved from http://www.nea.org/tools/17057.htm

National Forum to Accelerate Middle-Grades Reform. (n.d.) *Schools to Watch.* Retrieved from https://www.middlegradesforum.org/schools-to-watch-apply

National Middle School Association. (2010). *This we believe: Keys to educating young adolescents.* Westerville, OH: Author.

National School Climate Center. (2018). *How is school climate measured?* Retrieved from https://www.schoolclimate.org/about/our-approach/how-is-school-climate-measured

North Carolina School Report Cards. (2017). *Durham public schools.* Retrieved from https://ncreportcards.ondemand.sas.com/src/district?district=320LEA&year=2017&lang=undefined

Patall, E. A., Cooper, H., & Allen, A. B. (2010). Extending the school day or school year: A systematic review of research (1985–2009). *Review of Educational Research, 80,* 401–436. doi.org/10.3102/0034654310377086

Pedersen, J. M. (2011). *Length of school calendars and student achievement in high schools in California, Illinois and Texas* (Doctoral dissertation). Seton Hall University, South Orange, NJ. Retrieved from http://scholarship.shu.edu/dissertations/1773

Penta, M. Q. (2001). *Comparing student performance at program magnet, year-round magnet, and non-magnet elementary schools.* Eye on Evaluation, Evaluation & Research Department, Report No. 01.27. Retrieved from https://webarchive.wcpss.net/results/reports/2001/0127_MSAG.pdf

Quest to Learn. (2019). *Welcome to the middle school.* Retrieved from https://www.q2l.org/middle-school/

Schmoker, M. (2006). *Results now: How we can achieve unprecedented improvements in teaching and learning.* Alexandria, VA: Association for Supervision and Curriculum Development.

Spires, H. A., Morris, G., & Zhang, J. (2012). New literacies and emerging technologies: Perspectives from U.S. and Chinese middle level teachers. *Research in Middle Level Education Online, 35*(10), 1–11. doi.org/:10.1080/19404476.2012.11462093

U. S. Department of Education, National Center for Education Statistics. (2018). *Schools and Staffing Survey. Total number of schools, percentage of schools that have all students attending a year-round calendar cycle and average number of days in the cycle, by selected school characteristics: 2007–08*. Retrieved from https://nces.ed.gov/surveys/sass/tables/sass0708_030_s1n.asp

ABOUT THE CONTRIBUTORS

ABOUT THE EDITORS

Sandra L. Stacki is professor and chair in the Department of Teaching, Learning and Technology and Middle Childhood Director at Hofstra University, NY, United States. Her research in both international and national contexts includes teacher development and empowerment; middle childhood curriculum, instruction, and assessment; and after school programs, young adolescent girls' education; and policy analysis using critical, feminist lenses. She teaches middle school courses for pre- and in-service teachers, courses that explore the interconnections of curriculum and teaching with broader foundational influences, and qualitative research. E-mail: sandra.l.stacki@hofstra.edu

Micki M. Caskey is professor in the College of Education at Portland State University. Her specializations include middle grades education and doctoral education. She is coseries editor of *The Handbook of Research in Middle Level Education* and *The Handbook of Resources in Middle Level Education*. She is former editor of *Research in Middle Level Education Online* and previous chair of the AERA's Middle Level Education Research SIG. Micki is author or coauthor of more than 75 publications and 175 presentations. E-mail: caskeym@pdx.edu

Steven B. Mertens is professor in the School of Teaching and Learning at Illinois State University. He has authored over 70 publications and has presented papers at nearly 100 national, state, and regional conferences addressing varying aspects of middle level education and reform and teacher preparation. Steve is a past Chair of AERA's Middle Level Education Research SIG, a member of the National Forum to Accelerate Middle Grade's Reform, and a former member of AMLE's Research Advisory Board. He is the series co-editor for *The Handbook of Research in Middle Level Education* and the *The Handbook of Resources in Middle Level Education*. Email: smertens@ilstu.edu

ABOUT THE AUTHORS

Nancy L. Akhavan is associate professor in the Department of Educational Leadership at Fresno State University. She teaches courses in educational leadership, action research, and curriculum and instruction. Nancy is an author of numerous books for teachers on literacy. Her research interests include reading instruction for students who need reading support. She is a former pubic school teacher and principal with more than 25 years working with students from kindergarten through high school. E-mail: nakhavan@csufresno.edu

Gerald Ardito is assistant professor of STEM Education at Pace University in New York City. At Pace, he teaches courses in adolescent and elementary STEM methods, educational psychology, action research, and learning environments. His research interests focus on the design and implementation of autonomy supportive learning environments. He is also a former public school teacher with a decade of experience working with young adolescents. E-mail: gardito@pace.edu

Thomas M. Brinthaupt is professor of psychology at Middle Tennessee State University. He also serves as Director of Faculty Development for the Learning, Teaching, and Innovative Technologies Center at MTSU. He teaches undergraduate and graduate courses in personality psychology and research methods. His psychology research focuses on self and identity. He also has published extensively on the scholarship of teaching and learning in K–12 and higher education contexts. E-mail: tom. brinthaupt@mtsu.edu

Eric B. Claravall is assistant professor in the College of Education at California State University, Sacramento. He teaches literacy and special education courses. His research interest falls within the intersection of text-based literacy development, digital literacies, and disciplinary literacy. He seeks to understand the teaching and learning processes involved when students with special needs apply literacy as a tool to access knowledge in literature, social studies, science, and mathematics in paper-based and digital environments. E-mail: eric.claravall@csus.edu

Carrie L. Dabelow is Drama, Speech, and Performance Seminar teacher at Franklin Middle School in Wheaton, Illinois. Additionally, she has run drama programs at high schools and theatres in the greater metropolitan Chicago area. Carrie is a member of the International Theatre Association and the National Council of Teachers of English. She received her BA from St. Olaf College and her MA in Theater Direction from Roosevelt University. E-mail: carrie.dabelow@cusd200.org

James Davis is associate professor and coordinator of programs in educational leadership at Coastal Carolina University. Prior to the professoriate, he served as a middle school principal and school transformation principal in several public school districts. Having 20 years of experience in education, he holds certification as a teacher, administrator, curriculum specialist, Exceptional Children's Director, and Superintendent. He also serves as Executive Director of the North Carolina Association for Middle Level Education. E-mail: jdavis9@coastal.edu

Ashley Delaney is a science and STEM curriculum consultant in Iowa. She teaches mathematics and science methods courses as well as courses focused on special populations. Ashley's research interests are focused on early childhood STEM education, girls in STEM, and equity. Ashley taught multiple subjects and grade levels in K–12 over a 12-year period before becoming a consultant. She received her PhD in curriculum and instruction from Iowa State University. E-mail: delaneya@iastate.edu

Colleen Fitzpatrick is a teacher-scholar postdoctoral fellow at Wake Forest University where she teaches courses in social studies methods and action research. She graduated from the University of Virginia with her PhD in curriculum and instruction. Her research explores the complex and interactional role the context of a classroom, school, district or state plays in how teachers and students experience teaching and learning history. Colleen taught middle and high school social studies for 6 years. E-mail: fitzpacm@wfu.edu

Andrea García is cofounder of Pädi in Querétaro, Mexico, a literacy center providing literature rich services for literacy development inside and outside of schools. Her international consulting work promotes literacy in multilingual and transnational communities. For 15 years, Andrea was associate professor in the Literacy Studies program at Hofstra University, serving as director of the Reading/Writing Learning Clinic. She holds a PhD in language, reading and culture from the University of Arizona. E-mail: angasierra@gmail.com

Crystal Forbes teaches interrelated arts and directs five choral ensembles at Franklin Middle School in Wheaton, Illinois. She has coordinated Franklin's Interrelated Arts Department since 1988 and serves as the fine arts instructional team leader. Frequently a collaborative pianist, she also serves as an accompanist and curriculum designer for the Spirito Singers, a Chicago-area based music theory program. E-mail: crystal.forbes@cusd200.org

Chris Grodoski is an art, design, and media educator at Franklin Middle School in Wheaton, Illinois. He is currently the vice-president of the Illinois Art Education Association and previously served on the National Art Education Association's Research Commission. Chris earned his PhD in art education from Northern Illinois University. His research interests include creativity, policy, and student engagement. E-mail: cgrodoski@gmail.com

Maggie Hammer is an instructional technology teacher at Franklin Middle School in Wheaton, Illinois. In her 23rd year of teaching, she has taught fifth grade, sixth grade math, prior to instructional technology for the past 4 years. Maggie holds dual master's degrees: one in curriculum and instruction from Benedictine University and another in instructional technology from Northern Illinois University. E-mail: margaret.hammer@cusd200.org

Scott B. Haupt is an instructional design specialist for the Lucinda Taylor Lea Learning, Teaching, and Innovative Technologies Center at Middle Tennessee State University. He received his Educational Specialist degree from MTSU. He consults with faculty on pedagogy and technology and curriculum design. Prior to his employment by MTSU, he taught high school English. E-mail: scott.haupt@mtsu.edu

Michelle Hoffmeyer is a STEM and entrepreneurship teacher at Franklin Middle School in Wheaton, Illinois. Michelle is in her 23rd year of teaching and coaching. She holds endorsements in math, science, language arts, and English learner education, along with a masters in multicategorical special education with a learning behavior specialist certification. E-mail: michelle.hoffmeyer@cusd200.org

Robin Irey is a doctoral candidate in the School of Education at the University of California, Berkeley where she serves as the manuscript coordinator and senior editor for the *Berkeley Review of Education* journal. Her research interests are informed by her previous experience as a special education classroom teacher and instructor of credential teacher candidates. She focuses on reading acquisition, cognitive processes of reading, morphological awareness, learning disabilities, intervention, historical thinking, and assessment. E-mail: rirey6@berkeley.edu

Kelly Ivy is a doctoral candidate in mathematics education at the University of Maryland College Park in the Department of Teaching and Learning, Policy and Leadership. In addition to teaching high school mathematics, Kelly has also taught courses in development mathematics and continues to teach a Methods of Teaching Mathematics for Elementary School Teachers course at the university. Kelly's research interests include culturally responsive mathematics pedagogy, mathematics identity, and urban mathematics teachers' self-efficacy. E-mail: kellyk.watson@gmail.com

Christa Jackson is associate professor in the School of Education at Iowa State University. At Iowa State, she prepares prospective K–12 teachers to teach mathematics. Christa writes STEM curriculum and provides professional development to middle school teachers. Her research focuses on the instructional strategies and teaching practices that teachers use to afford opportunities for students from diverse cultures, ethnicities, and socioeconomic backgrounds to learn mathematics and STEM while simultaneously fostering productive mathematical and STEM identities. E-mail: jacksonc@iastate.edu

Jennifer Jim-Brundidge is Director of Orchestras at Franklin Middle School in Wheaton, Illinois. In 2016, she was named Secondary Level District Teacher of the Year in Twin Rivers Unified School District in Sacramento, California. She received her undergraduate degree in Music Education and Ethnomusicology at the University of California, Los Angeles and a master's degree in violin performance at California State University, Sacramento. E-mail: jennifer.jim@cusd200.org

Richard P. Lipka is Distinguished Professor in the School of Education at St. Bonaventure University. He has a long career of research on teacher preparation, master teachers, program evaluation, self and identity, and the role of instructional technologies in the schools. He has published more than a dozen books and spent many years as professor in the Special Services and Leadership Studies Department at Pittsburg State (KS)

University. Prior to receiving his advanced degrees, he taught sixth grade. E-mail: rlipka@sbu.edu

Kurt Makaryk is Director of Bands at Franklin Middle School in Wheaton, Illinois. He teaches four ensembles of sixth through eighth graders. Additionally, Kurt teaches small-group string lessons along with extracurricular Jazz Band, Symphony Orchestra, and Marching Band. Before his time at Franklin, Kurt was the beginning band instructor for fifth graders districtwide. He received his Bachelor of Music in instrumental music education from Western Illinois University in 2011. E-mail: kurt.makaryk@cusd200.org

Barbara J. Mallory is associate professor of educational leadership at Coastal Carolina University (CCU). At CCU, she teaches courses in educational policy, the principalship, and leadership theory. Her research interests are focused on school leadership, preparation of school leaders, leadership dispositions, and global perspectives of school leadership. She is a former middle school and high school principal. She received her EdD in educational leadership from East Carolina University in Greenville, NC. E-mail: bmallory@coastal.edu

Theresa McGinnis is associate professor in the Literacy Studies program at Hofstra University. She teaches courses on adolescent literacies and digital literacies. Theresa taught middle school students in Los Angeles County and in Philadelphia for 12 years. Her research interests include sociocultural theories of literacy, and the schooling experiences of urban and immigrant young adolescents. She received her doctorate in reading, writing and literacy from the University of Pennsylvania. E-mail: theresa.a.mcginnis@hofstra.edu

Tom Meyer is associate professor in the Department of Teaching and Learning at the State University of New York at New Paltz where he directs a site of the National Writing Project. He teaches courses in teacher leadership, action research, curriculum studies, and composition. Before receiving a PhD in curriculum and teacher education from Stanford University, he taught English at a public high school, natural science for upper elementary students, and art at a prison. E-mail: meyert@newpaltz.edu

Maria R. Peters is a middle school science teacher in Washington, D.C. Her undergraduate degree is in both chemistry and African American history from the College of Notre Dame of Maryland. After a decade of experience teaching middle school, she earned her Master of Arts degree in middle school science at the University of the District of Columbia. Maria's thesis focused on the interest in STEM among African-American girls in the southeastern quadrant of Washington, D.C. E-mail: MariaPeters143@gmail.com

Lorraine M. Radice is adjunct assistant professor in the Department of Specialized Programs in Education at Hofstra University where she teaches courses in the Literacy Studies program. Lorraine is also the pre-K–12 Director of Literacy in Long Beach Public Schools in New York. She was a middle level teacher for 10 years where she worked to cultivate the literacy lives of her students. Lorraine earned her PhD in literacy studies from Hofstra University. E-mail: Lorraine.M.Radice@hofstra.edu

Jill A. Robinson is a high school business and career teacher in Wellsville (NY). As director of Cattaraugus-Allegany Teacher Center for 7 years, she provided curriculum and technology support and development. As adjunct instructor at St. Bonaventure University, she taught various educational courses including Dignity for All Students Act workshops for undergraduate and graduate students. Her dedication to technology and its positive use in classrooms is demonstrated through her research/inquiry and participation on the New York State Teacher Centers technology committee. E-mail: jrobinson@wlsv.org Education's

Ebony Terrell Shockley is the College of Education's Diversity Officer, an associate clinical professor, and Director of the Office of Teacher and Leader Education for the Department of Teaching and Learning, Policy and Leadership at the University of Maryland College Park. She also leads the Master's Certification (MCERT) Program for prospective educators. Ebony is a former middle school science teacher who researches underrepresented students and their teachers in STEM, literacy, and exceptional education contexts. E-mail: Eterrell@umd.edu

Stephanie van Hover is professor of social studies education. A former middle school teacher, she serves as Chair of the Department of Curriculum, Instruction and Special Education and as the faculty advisor for the secondary social studies teacher education program at the Curry School of Education and Human Development at the University of Virginia. Her research explores teaching and learning history in standards-based settings. E-mail: sdv2w@virginia.edu

CPSIA information can be obtained
at www.ICGtesting.com
Printed in the USA
JSHW010131150820
7266JS00004B/26

9 781648 020285